Social Welfare in Ontario, 1791-1893

A STUDY OF PUBLIC WELFARE ADMINISTRATION

TO MARION

SOCIAL WELFARE IN ONTARIO 1791-1893

A Study of
Public Welfare Administration

RICHARD B. SPLANE

UNIVERSITY OF TORONTO PRESS

©University of Toronto Press 1965
Reprinted 1971
ISBN 0-8020-5155-3
Printed in the United States of America

Preface

THE DECISION to undertake a study of some aspect of the development of social welfare in Ontario was made as a result of separate but related discussions in the early 1950's with the late Dr. Harry M. Cassidy, Professor Frank H. Underhill, and Professor John S. Morgan, from each of whom I received helpful advice.

The topic first considered was child welfare, but some exploration revealed that programmes for the protection of children emerged rather late in the total structure of welfare services in the province and could hardly be assessed until earlier developments in the broader field had been examined. It was thus decided to carry out a study of the whole field of social welfare, with particular reference to the rôle played by the provincial government.

The initial assumption was that the study would be concerned mainly with the post-Confederation period. As research proceeded, however, it became obvious that substantial progress had been made much earlier. On the advice of Professor J. M. S. Careless, who had kindly agreed to read a draft of the early chapters, the decision was made to consider pre-Confederation developments in greater depth than had been originally intended.

A considerable amount of the work for the book was done during the academic year 1957–58 when I was granted leave of absence from the Department of National Health and Welfare. I wish to express my appreciation to the department and in particular to Dr. Joseph W. Willard, then director of the Research and Statistics Division and now deputy minister of welfare. The study was undertaken as a dissertation for the degree of Doctor of Social Work at the University of Toronto. In its preparation, I received valuable guidance from my doctoral committee, especially from its chairman, Professor Albert Rose.

Material for the study was obtained largely in the Public Archives of Canada, and I am indebted to Mlle J. Bourque and the staff of the Archives Library, and to Mr. W. Ormsby and the staff of the Manuscript Division. Officials of the Ontario Archives and of the Department of the Provincial Secretary assisted in the location and use of material under their care. Valuable information concerning E. A. Meredith was generously made available by his son, Colonel C. P. Meredith of Ottawa.

It is a pleasure, as well, to refer to the invaluable services of Miss Alice Pirie in typing and indexing the manuscript, and to mention, if only in general terms, the assistance and encouragement of many other friends and associates. I am also most grateful to officers of the University of Toronto Press: to Miss Francess Halpenny for general guidance on the process of transforming a dissertation into a book; to Mrs. J. D. Wismer for page by page suggestions offered towards the achievement of that goal.

The work has been published with the help of a grant from the Social Science Research Council using funds provided by the Canada Council, and with assistance from the Publications Fund of the University of Toronto Press.

Contents

List of Tables

Introduction

THIS STUDY, which deals largely with the nineteenth century, employs the widely used but ill-defined twentieth-century term, social welfare. Recent attempts at definition refer to it as a broad field of human endeavour based on "values rooted in conviction about individual worth and dignity and social interdependence and responsibility."[1] This indication of the present ethic of the field does little to stake out its boundaries, either now or in the past. Social welfare, however, is known to be the direct descendant of the nineteenth-century fields of charities and corrections, and although they emerged from activities undertaken in the furtherance of different values and in response to different motivations it is appropriate to employ the term social welfare to the work in those fields undertaken in Ontario during the first century of the province's history.

For only a quarter of that century was the province known as Ontario. It began its corporate life in 1791 as Upper Canada, but in 1841 lost some of its separate identity when, along with the predominantly French-speaking province of Lower Canada, it was taken into a legislative union known as the United Province of Canada. With Confederation in 1867 it regained much of its earlier autonomy, a position of great influence in the new Canadian federation, and the name Ontario which, in this work, as in many others, is applied to the province over the whole course of its history.

The selection of 1893 rather than 1891 as the terminal year of the "century" allowed the study to extend to the establishment of the provincial child welfare programme in 1893, a landmark in Ontario's

[1]Irving Weisman, *Social Welfare Policy and Services in Social Work Education* (New York, 1959), p. 29.

social welfare development. Carrying the study to 1893 had the further value of making possible some assessment of the effect of the Royal Commission on the Prison and Reformatory System of Ontario which presented its report in 1891.

The period covered in the book was one of notable progress in the development of Ontario's resources and in the establishment of a flourishing society. The people who came to Ontario from Europe and the United States or who grew up in the province were generally able to realize their hope of gaining a fair measure of individual prosperity and of enjoying a satisfactory way of life. At the same time, many experienced acute and sometimes prolonged hardships—at first the privations of the frontier, later the concomitants of industrialization. Histories of Ontario, although showing some recognition of the adversities of pioneer life, have taken, as their great themes, the province's political, constitutional, and material progress. Little has been written about the privations of its people, or about the organized measures that were adopted to relieve suffering and want, illness, and dependency. It is with such measures, and especially those taken by government, that this study is concerned.

Social Welfare in Ontario, 1791-1893

A STUDY OF PUBLIC WELFARE ADMINISTRATION

1

A Century of Progress in Social Welfare: Background

THE SOCIAL WELFARE needs that emerged in Ontario and the measures that were adopted to deal with them ought, ideally, to be viewed against the whole background of the life of the province from the time the pioneers began to take possession of the shores and hinterland of the upper waterways of the St. Lawrence, through the century that followed in which new settlers and native sons created within the region a prosperous economy and a flourishing society. To mention this ideal is to declare it unattainable, and in default of it this introductory review attempts to sketch only those features of the Upper Canadian scene that tell something of how the society grew and those factors within it, or impinging upon it, that were of importance in the development of social welfare measures and programmes in the province.

The year of Confederation, 1867, provides a good initial vantage point in time from which to view the century considered in the study. To the Upper Canadians it was a year both of deliverance and of promise: deliverance from the legislative union with Lower Canada which, they were convinced, had impeded their progress and warped their development; promise that Confederation would launch a new era of national development from which they would benefit directly and bountifully; promise, as well, that Confederation would give them virtual autonomy in matters of provincial concern and a voice in the affairs of the nation proportionate to their predominant and expanding population.

The Upper Canadians' anticipation of a bright future within the new federation flowed from the sense of accomplishment with which they could look back over the province's brief history. They felt justified in regarding it as a period of solid development, much of it achieved under unfavourable circumstances. Politically, they had borne with half a century of government by an incompetent oligarchy, followed by a quarter century of enforced union with Lower Canada which, although solving many problems, created others hardly less vexatious. Within the Union they and their Lower Canadian compatriots had none the less forged responsible government and gained sufficient political experience and competence to become the prime movers in the achievement of Confederation. The Upper Canadians had meanwhile built a strong fabric of municipal government, and with it a capacity to use public means at the local level to accomplish a variety of developmental and social ends. Politically, too, Upper Canada had withstood strong pressures from the United States. The province had helped to repulse the American forces in the war of 1812 and in the decades that followed had periodically thrust back border raids organized from American soil. The province, moreover, had resisted the lure of annexation with the latter's tempting promise of a share of the greater American prosperity.

Upper Canada's own material advancement prior to Confederation, if less spectacular than that across the border, was none the less remarkable. The seemingly impenetrable forest wilderness which had faced the few thousand United Empire Loyalists and British soldiers who had entered the province following the American Revolution had given way to prosperous farms, embracing virtually all the arable land in the southern part of the province. Substantial villages and towns dotted the countryside, and there were a few centres that claimed the title of city. A vigorous forest industry, some mining, and the beginnings of manufacturing for more than a local market were also characteristic of the Upper Canadian economy on the eve of Confederation. The growth had been achieved in the face of formidable difficulties, many of them associated with the remoteness of markets and the related problems of transport and communication. The challenge of distance, however, had served as a spur to the opening of roads and to the acceptance of great risks and sacrifices in the building of canals and railways.

Upper Canadians at Confederation could reflect with some pride, as well, on their success in developing a distinctive and reasonably integrated social structure. To the original stock of Loyalists and the succeeding migration of Americans in search of land, thousands of immigrants, mostly British, had been received over the years and absorbed without undue strain. In spite of losses to the United States, the population had increased steadily, and at times dramatically, from some 70,000 in 1806 to 150,000 in 1824, 432,000 in 1840, 952,000 in 1850, and 1,525,000 at Confederation.[1]

Out of their struggle, first to survive and then to prosper, the Upper Canadians developed strong and distinctive loyalties. Early loyalties to their local communities did not bar loyalty to Upper Canada as a cherished political entity. Loyalties to Britain and the Crown, though sometimes strained in the struggle for responsible government, were always powerful. Less powerful were feelings of identification with British North America at large, although by the mid-1860's Upper Canadians came to sense compelling defensive values in a union with the Atlantic provinces, and to see merit in joining with the maritime region in a common area of trade. Increasingly too, they began to view the prospect of expansion across the western prairies and to see themselves as the manifest successors to the Hudson's Bay Company in possessing and developing the great Northwest. To succeed to that inheritance became, in fact, the central focus of their national aspirations.

These loyalties and aspirations nourished the Upper Canadian identity under the Union government which might have been expected to weaken it. They generated, moreover, the communal strength needed by the people of the province to reach enough agreement on contentious social, religious, and political issues to construct the social institutions essential to the development of a civilized society. The creation of a system of general education was one such issue, and the Upper Canadians succeeded after much bitterness and debate in reversing the early attempts to place education under the control of the Church of England. They succeeded, by stages, in developing elementary and secondary education within a public framework, locally administered but with strong central direction, and, although provision was made for separate schools under religious auspices where this was the local preference, the system was essentially secular.

The development of secular schools was a reflection not of religious indifference but of denominational diversity. The presence in many villages and most towns of two or more nonconformist churches in addition to Anglican and Roman Catholic churches strengthened the trend towards secular organization of institutions which, in communities less segmented denominationally, might have developed under religious auspices. As in the case of education, the existence

[1]Canada, *Census*, 1931, pp. 146–50; and D. G. Creighton, *British North America at Confederation* (Ottawa, 1939), p. 20.

of many denominations and the dominance of none was to influence the organization and support of voluntary social welfare institutions, a matter of central interest in this study.

Although Upper Canadians in the pre-Confederation period were primarily preoccupied with material advancement and much distracted by constitutional and political struggles, the period was remarkable for the degree of progress in the field of social welfare. Many developments in the period testify to a deep social concern and to a vigorous attack on the principal social problems of the times. The chapters that follow review, from their early beginnings, provisions for the poor, the physically and mentally ill, neglected and dependent children, and the criminal and delinquent. Although later generations have not been in the habit of crediting earlier generations of Upper Canadians with significant social advances, the historical record indicates that social welfare developments in post-Confederation Ontario flowed directly from measures that were in existence or were proposed during the Union period, and these in turn had substantial roots in the pre-Union era.

The pace of advance prior to Confederation had, moreover, been accelerating as the wealth of the province increased, as its people were enabled to turn from an intense preoccupation with material development, and as increasing population and the growth of towns and cities caused an intensification of the social problems that required action. Thus, in view of the problems requiring increased attention and on the basis of the progress already made, an observer standing at the threshold of Confederation would have been justified in predicting that the new province, while continuing to direct its principal efforts to material development, would devote substantial attention to social welfare.

The first few years after 1867 seemed to confirm the expectations of the citizens of Ontario that the post-Confederation period would bring both prosperity and substantial autonomy and thus give them the means and the scope for distinctive and untrammelled development. Year after year the Lieutenant-Governor appeared before the new provincial Legislature to deliver speeches brimming with optimism and satisfaction, and attributing much of the prosperity to the "boon of local self-government"[2] and the virtues of British institutions. The

---

[2]Ontario, *Journals*, 1870–71, p. 2. Note: the term *Journals* used here and throughout the study refers to the Journals of the Legislature; during the pre-Union and Union periods it refers to the Journals only of the lower house; no reference is made to the Journals of the Legislative Councils.

citizens of Ontario, he asserted, had no cause to envy their American neighbours or to take second place to them in material or social development.

References to abounding prosperity continued to appear in the viceregal addresses to the Legislature until 1875, but, in fact, the economic depression which affected most of the world from 1873 to 1896 had made itself felt in Ontario before its presence was acknowledged by the provincial government. Even before 1873, the rate of provincial growth had fallen well below the rates attained during the two decades preceding Confederation. The census of 1871, for example, showed a population of 1,621,000, representing a growth in ten years of only about 235,000, a figure lower than that produced by the province's natural increase and so much lower than had been anticipated that the Toronto *Globe* found it difficult to accept as accurate. Thus, while the province had appeared to attract scores of thousands of immigrants during the decade, it was actually losing through emigration more than it was gaining by immigration.

The principal cause of the slackened rate of growth was that Ontario no longer had a rich, unoccupied agricultural frontier. Although the province vigorously encouraged the building of branch railways and took other measures to help the development of those areas in southern Ontario which still had unoccupied lands, the remaining farm properties proved to be neither numerous nor productive enough to sustain the agricultural boom. It therefore became increasingly apparent that if rapid development, in terms of expanding population and wealth, was to continue in Ontario it would have to be based on something other than agriculture. The era of absolute agricultural dominance in Ontario was approaching its end, and the *Canadian Monthly*, in commenting on the shift in political power, was justified in remarking that "it may not be amiss to warn our agriculturalists that in any 'struggle for existence' politically speaking, they must inevitably go to the wall."[3]

This decline was much accelerated in the late 1870's by the adoption, in the federal field, of the interrelated policies of pressing forward with western development and of encouraging manufacturing through the "National Policy" of protective tariffs. These two policies struck hard at the low-cost economy on which agricultural prosperity in Ontario was dependent. In adopting them, the Dominion gambled on rapid western development to sustain the cost of such expensive projects as the transcontinental railway. But development was not

[3]*Canadian Monthly*, Feb. 1877, p. 213.

rapid, and in the long interval, almost to the end of the century, before a favourable economic tide began to flow, the farmers and other primary producers of Ontario paid a high price for the country's national aspirations.

For the manufacturing interest in the province, the story was much different. It may have hoped for even better things than it received, during the 1880's and early 1890's, but manufacturing none the less blossomed under the protection of the National Policy. Ontario was the chief region to benefit, and between 1871 and 1891 the number of employees in industrial establishments in Ontario increased from 87,000 to 166,000; the amount paid in wages went up from 21.4 to 49.7 million dollars, and the industrial output mounted from 114.7 to 239.7 million dollars.[4]

The story of industrial growth is also told in the shift of population from the countryside to the towns and cities, particularly between 1881 and 1891. While the population of the province in that period increased by less than 10 per cent, the population of those cities and towns which in the latter year had over 5,000 residents increased 23 per cent. Table I shows the cities and towns whose growth in the

TABLE I

POPULATION OF SELECTED CITIES AND TOWNS OF ONTARIO,
1881 AND 1891

City or town	1881	1891	Percentage increase
Toronto	96,196	181,220	88.4
Hamilton	35,960	48,980	36.2
Ottawa	31,307	44,154	41.0
Kingston	14,091	19,264	36.7
Windsor	6,561	10,322	57.3
Peterborough	6,812	9,717	42.6
Woodstock	5,373	8,612	60.4
Galt	5,187	7,535	45.2
Owen Sound	4,426	7,497	69.5
Berlin (Kitchener)	4,054	7,425	83.1
Cornwall	4,468	6,805	52.3
Sarnia	3,874	6,693	72.7

SOURCE: Canada, *Census*, 1891.

decade exceeded 35 per cent. Between Confederation and the early 1890's Toronto achieved a clear supremacy over all its provincial rivals and began to assume the characteristics of a metropolis.[5] It became the undisputed political, commercial, and financial centre,

4Canada, *Census*, 1871, 1891.
5D. C. Masters, *The Rise of Toronto, 1850–1890* (Toronto, 1947).

and it also exerted a strong social and cultural influence over the rest of the province.

Although there were few other changes during the quarter century following Confederation that were as dramatic as the growth of urban centres, there were significant economic, social, and political changes, many of which had to do with the favoured position the province enjoyed in relation to national development. The period saw the virtual completion of the network of railways throughout the southern part of the province, and with the completion of the Canadian Pacific Railway in 1885 exploitation of the mineral areas of the northern regions began. Strong banking, trust, and insurance companies were established within the province, and the Toronto Stock Exchange, founded in 1855, was playing an increasingly important rôle in mobilizing capital for developmental projects. The financial and commercial dominance of Montreal was progressively reduced and the province proceeded to build up the institutional resources with which to meet all competitors in the development of the north and northwest.

The industrial expansion in the cities and towns brought problems for labour which it sought to solve through trade union organization. Prior to the early 1870's trade unions had made little headway in the province, except in the printing trades, but by 1872 labour had given evidence of enough strength to bring about the passage of the Trade Union Act, a federal statute designed to remove from union activity the threat of indictment for conspiracy in restraint of trade.[6] This improved legal position and the extent of union organization by 1875 were insufficient, however, to withstand the onslaught of the depression, and between 1876 and 1880 every labour union except that of the printers ceased to function. There were signs of revival by the latter year when the movement known as the Knights of Labour crossed from the United States and organized assemblies in a number of centres throughout the province. By the middle of the 1880's a new organization, the Trades and Labour Congress of Canada, had come into being, its membership at the beginning drawn almost wholly from Ontario.[7] The recommendations of the congress for industrial legislation undoubtedly played a part in the labour legislation which began to appear on the provincial statute books: a Factories' Act was passed in 1884 and amended in 1887, and a Workmen's Compensation Act was passed in 1886 and amended in 1887 and 1892.

[6]H. A. Logan, *Trade Unions in Canada: Their Development and Functioning* (Toronto, 1948), p. 33.
[7]*Ibid.*, p. 59.

Education, proceeding on lines clearly marked out before Confederation, made steady progress, its importance recognized by the appointment of a minister of education in 1876. Mechanics institutes assisted by government grants continued to play an important rôle in adult education, and although the appearance of a few free libraries in the 1880's foreshadowed the institutes' ultimate decline, no less than 268 existed in 1892, four having been established in that year.[8] Primary schooling became free in the 1870's and compulsory in the 1880's, with effective enforcement dating from 1891 when provision was made for the appointment of truant officers. Attendance at high schools and collegiate institutes rose from under 6,000 in 1867 to nearly 23,000 in 1892. University enrolment increased steadily and women students began to be admitted in the 1880's. The establishment in 1878 of the School of Practical Science, later united with the University of Toronto, and of a technical high school in Toronto in 1891, indicated the expanding demand of the economy for technically qualified personnel. In looking back in 1893 over fifty years of educational advance, the Minister of Education could thus take pride in the province's accomplishments. Illiteracy in the whole of the adult population had been reduced to less than 10 per cent, and among persons between the ages of ten and twenty it stood at less than 6 per cent. The province expressed its pride and satisfaction by sending a large and much admired educational exhibit to the Chicago World Fair in 1893, where it was displayed under the motto "Education Our Glory."[9]

Political developments in the province after Confederation at first assumed a somewhat different complexion than might have been expected on the basis of trends in evidence prior to the federal union. In the years before 1867, the tide had been running strongly in favour of the Reform party[10] led by George Brown, the editor of the Toronto *Globe* and it would have seemed natural for the Reformers to have won political control at the first provincial election. Sir John A. Macdonald, as the prime minister of the new Dominion government, however, made good use of his constitutional prerogatives, and by astute political moves had the first government of Ontario established on a coalition basis headed by John Sandfield Macdonald who, though a Reformer, was a bitter antagonist of George Brown.

Sandfield Macdonald launched the province on its new political

[8]Ontario, *Sessional Papers*, 1894, no. 3, p. 220.
[9]*Ibid.*
[10]Although the term "Liberal" was used increasingly by the federal wing of the party, "Reform" continued throughout the period to be the preferred label for the provincial group.

course rather cautiously and found time from his responsibilities as premier to sit as a member in the Dominion Parliament. Although his administration was not distinguished for its record as a whole, its accomplishments in the field of social welfare were extensive and important. Following the first election in 1871, he was defeated in the Legislature, largely owing to the debating skill and deft political management displayed by Edward Blake, who was then called upon to form the province's second ministry. Blake retained the premiership for only one session, albeit an active and productive one, before deciding to make his career in the Dominion Parliament.

He was succeeded by Oliver Mowat who proved to be one of the most successful administrators and political strategists in the province's history. Undefeated throughout the remainder of the period under review here, Mowat continued as the head of the Reform ministries until 1896. His government was characterized by vigorous promotion of material development, careful administration, the determined assertion of provincial rights, relatively progressive policies in the fields of education and social welfare, and shrewd handling of vexatious political issues such as those involving nationality, religion, and the thorny question of temperance, or rather of liquor control. Mowat succeeded in retaining rural support for his government without adopting, to an extreme degree, the cheap government policies identified with agrarian parties generally and with the early Reform party in particular. And although, in terms of political philosophy, he thought of himself as a devoted follower of the Manchester School, many of the policies of his administration violated the doctrine of laissez-faire. His term of office, in fact, coincided in general with the period which has been described as witnessing the beginning of the social welfare state in Canada.[11]

A factor of the utmost importance to governmental policy during the period was the highly favourable fiscal position in which the province found itself. This felicitous condition was brought about principally by the fact that the Dominion had assumed the debt of the old province of Canada and had agreed to provide an annual grant to all provinces on a per capita basis. Because of the needs of some of the other provinces, the amount of the grant was increased in 1873 and again in 1884, with Ontario profiting more than needier provinces because of its large population. On the revenue side as well, the province found that its Crown lands and especially its timber areas

[11]Elisabeth Wallace, "The Origin of the Social Welfare State in Canada, 1867–1900," Canadian Journal of Economics and Political Science, Aug. 1950.

were unexpectedly productive. Its expenditures, on the other hand, were, on a per capita basis, less than those of other provinces because of Ontario's highly developed municipal system and the willingness of its citizens to tax themselves locally for the support of the matters which the province had delegated to the various units of municipal government.

The government of Sandfield Macdonald was literally embarrassed by the buoyancy of its revenues. The Premier's Grit background led him to place the highest emphasis on retaining a low-cost economy through keeping down the expenses of government, and his government initially lacked a political philosophy to guide it in programmes involving public expenditures for any but the most elementary administrative purposes. The government's relatively generous treatment of social welfare programmes, however, stands as an exception to its general approach, reflecting, among other pressures, the skilful advocacy and promotion of vigorous advance in this field by the public official responsible for prisons, asylums, and charitable institutions, J. W. Langmuir.

While the Sandfield Macdonald government was building up surpluses which totalled nearly $5 million by the end of four years in office, the Reform party on the opposition side of the Legislature was reaching the conclusion that when a government found itself in possession of a superabundance of revenue it ought to use it boldly, primarily for projects such as colonization roads, subsidies to narrow-gauge railways, and the encouragement of immigration, but also, though secondarily, for projects of a humanitarian nature such as the building of institutions for the blind, deaf, and mentally ill, the assistance of private charitable institutions, and the improvement of the penal system.

A more liberal use of revenues was, accordingly, instituted by Mowat. In a speech in 1879, he pointed out that only about one-fifth of the province's annual revenue of approximately $2.5 million was required to meet "the cost of the great governmental purposes of legislation, civil government, and the administration of justice . . . which alone are essential functions of Government."[12] What could be done with the balance? It should not, Mowat was certain be hoarded for later and richer generations, whose interests in any case would be better served by its current use in productive projects and in measures required for the well-being of the living. The correct policy, as Mowat

[12]Oliver Mowat, *Speeches on Reform Government in Ontario* (Toronto, 1879), p. 37.

saw it, and the one his government followed, he described in the following terms:

Having a balance of the former surplus, and having an annual surplus besides, what have we been doing with them? Besides the large sums granted to railways and municipalities, we have, with the sanction of the Legislature and the approval of the country, been using the money in part for building and enlarging our public institutions, giving increased accommodation for the deaf, the dumb, the blind, the insane, etc. These objects commend themselves to the humanity of our people. The existing institutions were not capable of receiving all who needed to have entrance to them and having the money, we made provision for as many as possible of these afflicted classes to receive the benefits which the institutions were intended to afford.[13]

Throughout the rest of the period, Mowat could repeat and substantiate this claim that his government was using the province's bountiful revenues to good purpose for a variety of developmental and social ends. He was fond of inviting comparisons with other provinces, states, and countries. Where else, he could ask, were great public projects financed wholly on a current basis? What other jurisdiction was developing its resources, erecting its public buildings, and establishing its charitable institutions without either taxation or borrowing? And where else could one find a record of annual surpluses in all but four years in twenty, surpluses which, by 1892, had produced a cumulative figure even higher than the sum amassed by Sandfield Macdonald?[14]

Prevailing Ideas and Their Influence on Social Welfare

The first hundred years of Ontario's corporate life was a period in which creative and conflicting ideas were competing for attention throughout the community of Western Europe and North America of which Ontario was an integral, though a somewhat remote part. The province was thrust into existence as a by-product of the American Revolution and early in its life felt the impact of the French Revolution, especially its Napoleonic phase. The post-Napoleonic revival of conservatism and the subsequent struggle and triumph, in Great Britain, of the reform movement directly and decisively affected Canadian political and constitutional developments which were also influenced, though less profoundly, by the competing ideas of American democracy and the principles expressed in Chartism.

[13]*Ibid.*, p. 40.
[14]Ontario Liberal Association, *Liberal Government 1872–1896* (Toronto, 1898), p. 168.

Although the first victory for the concepts of the Manchester School of free trade and laissez-faire—Britain's abandonment of mercantilism—had a convulsive, if short-lived, effect on the economic and political life of the province, the Manchester doctrine was to become the core of the philosophy of Canadian liberalism during the last half of the period covered by this study. At the same time, the competing ideas of nationalism and imperialism which were in ferment in nineteenth-century Europe found expression both in Canadian aspirations for nationhood and in Ontario's identification with Britain's revived interest in extending the Empire. Ontario was directly affected too, especially in the matter of education, by the Ultramontane movement within the Roman Catholic Church. Even Marxist thought and Bismarckian ideas on social insurance found echoes in public discussion in the province, though they made no practical impact during the period.

An important and pervasive consideration affecting the Upper Canadians' reaction to many new ideas had to do with the problem of reconciling their determination to be British with the fact that they were North American. Much of their difficulty in achieving this reconciliation was rooted in their uncertainty about what being British meant. Did it involve being true to the concept of society envisaged in the Constitutional Act of 1791 and the policies associated with it, which together provided for hereditary titles, an established church, and local government by a squirearchy of appointed justices? In the long run, and in the case of the provision of hereditary titles even in the short run, it did not. Yet a privileged class, endowed with power and claiming to express British values, developed and persisted well into the nineteenth century. Later, in a curious reversal, many Upper Canadians thought it un-British to be opposed to the tenets of Manchester liberalism.

The early plan of creating in Upper Canada a society modelled essentially on that of late eighteenth-century England foundered on the shoals of economics and of nineteenth-century religious, political, and social ideas. Economic organization in Upper Canada, consisting largely of family-based agriculture, gave no encouragement to the kind of social structure envisaged by the early colonial administrators and their supporters. The population was small relative both to the size of the country and to the frontiers of opportunity which kept expanding as settlement proceeded. Thus the essential conditions for the creation of a ruling class based on a large and exploitable supply of labour did not emerge. The social implications of the Upper Canadian economy, on the contrary, appeared to make for receptivity to democratic political thought, nonconformity in religion, and egalitarianism in social relationships.

Democratic social and political ideas were no novelty either to the Loyalists who had lived through the American Revolution or to the American settlers who followed them to the fertile lands of Upper Canada. But although many who made up both of these groups accepted the political and social ideas of the Revolution, the Loyalist tradition, in general, stood for opposition to the American political philosophy. It was not until the reform movement had triumphed in England that Upper Canada was able to begin to move from an oligarchy of political power and social privilege to the British type of responsible government with democratic control of the executive vested in a popularly elected legislature.

Nonconformist religious ideas and modes of organization found fertile soil in Upper Canada and again there were strong British and American influences. Vigorous nonconformist churches operating largely on the basis of congregational control gave expression to democratic ideas and developed leadership capable of effectively challenging the claims of any one church to special recognition by the state. Their struggle for the principle of "separation" and for the related principle that churches should be supported wholly by the voluntary giving of their adherents was rewarded by the secularization of the reserves of land which had been set aside for the support of the clergy of the Church of England.

Encouraged by the principal forms of economic organization in the province, egalitarianism in Upper Canada was also nurtured by influences from the northern states where it had been a distinguishing social phenomenon even in the colonial era. In Upper Canada, as well as in the nearby states, the existence of an expanding agricultural frontier allowed a young person to hope for a rise from poverty to comfortable independence by middle life. As the means of creating wealth increased, the rewards accruing to thrift, hard work, and ability multiplied and were widely distributed. Wealth brought status in a society which came to pay relatively little heed to birth and to place increasing value on material success.

Associated with egalitarianism was the dogma that success could be obtained by all who lived respectably and worked hard. It was frequently asserted that no able-bodied person who wanted work in the young undeveloped province of Upper Canada could fail to find it or to find with it a livelihood and opportunity for advancement. The other side of this widely circulated coin had a direct impact upon social welfare. On it was inscribed the proposition that those who failed to work and prosper failed because they were lazy or immoral. When persons in need sought assistance, the question posed was whether help should be given to them in the form of material aid or whether they should be subjected to some process designed to improve their moral life or strengthen their work habits. Should they not, that is, be refused assistance in their own homes and be committed instead to houses of industry or correction?

There was some support for an even more rigorous approach to the problem. Malthusian doctrines gained some acceptance[15] and were strengthened by what were held to be the implications for human society of the Darwinian theory of evolution. The argument was advanced that population was certain to expand beyond the resources to support it, and it was thus folly to interfere with the great corrective principle of nature which used the superabundance of births to winnow out the weak and leave the adaptable fit to carry on the race. The observable facts of the growth of population and the production of food in nineteenth-century North America, it is true, gave little support to the demographic theories of Malthus or the sociological theories of Spencer, but it continued to be intellectually respectable to maintain that human society, like nature, must be harsh to its weaklings or it would foster within itself cancerous and destructive social ills. With this approach it was possible to regard Upper Canada's failure to enact a poor law as a wise decision and to warn, as did the Toronto *Globe* on February 27, 1874, against voluntary alms giving: "Promiscuous alms giving is fatal . . . it is the patent process for the manufacture of paupers out of the worthless and improvident. A poor law is a legislative machine for the manufacture of pauperism. It is true mercy to say that it would be better that a few individuals should die of starvation than that a pauper class should be raised up with thousands devoted to crime and the victims of misery."

Although such views were rather widely held and had some influence on public policy and private philanthropy, the measures which were taken throughout the period by private groups and by governments testify to the existence and practical consequences of a different philosophy. The public conscience was not prepared to sanction a policy of deliberate starvation. Nor could it quite agree that those whose sloth and improvidence were placing a serious drain on

[15]For an account of the much greater impact that they had in Nova Scotia, see George E. Hart, "The Halifax Poor Man's Friend Society, 1820–27: An Early Social Experiment," *Canadian Historical Review*, June 1953.

the wealth of the community were entirely "worthless," beyond the pale of hope and undeserving of help. It would appear, indeed, that a kind of practical humanitarianism always found a significant degree of expression both in public and in private endeavours.

Perhaps the earliest force for humanitarian action was the shared experience of pioneer life. During the province's early years, few in the colony were far removed from want. All were able to observe directly the calamitous effects of illness, accidents, and crop failures. These hazards were perceived at close quarters and recognized as common risks. Almost the only source of security to the family in need was the bond of neighbourliness within the community. Later when wealth had accumulated to the point where this sentiment could be expressed in organized forms—in publicly supported relief, in the building of hospitals, refuges for the aged and infirm, and institutions for orphan children—such measures were regarded as a natural extension of the earlier neighbourly response to human needs.

The churches, which played a very important part in the life of Upper Canada in the nineteenth century, were also sources of the impetus for humanitarian action. The Roman Catholic church, in following its long tradition of developing health and welfare institutions in close connection with its religious missions, established its own institutions and programmes in the centres which served large Roman Catholic groups. More important, because of the predominance of Protestants in Ontario,[16] was the less direct contribution of the various Protestant denominations. These, with certain exceptions, did not undertake independently to establish social welfare institutions but rather collaborated informally in establishing and supporting institutions and programmes which were designed to serve the whole community or, where Roman Catholic institutions existed, to serve the non-Catholic population. In their origin and early development, many institutions were thus inter-denominational rather than non-sectarian.

Some of the voluntary institutions which developed under combined Protestant auspices were organized by women who were leaders in their own churches and who were, as well, often members of the principal families in the community. They displayed notable vigour and enterprise in establishing and maintaining institutions, especially for children, unmarried mothers, and widows. Perhaps because their

[16]Canada *Census*, 1871. This showed 274,162 persons classified as "Catholics," out of a total provincial population of 1,620,851. The non-Catholic majority comprised over forty separate denominations or recognizable sub-divisions of denominations.

work was chiefly with these groups, they appear to have been little affected by the prevailing ideas about the supposed dangers of excessive philanthropy. Their motivation, however, was not always a simple response to the obvious needs which presented themselves; the programmes they established usually expressed a strong moral and evangelical emphasis.

An evangelical purpose was also evident in many of the other endeavours for moral, religious, and social improvement throughout the province. Leading members of the various denominations, prompted by Christian conviction, collaborated in promoting movements for temperance, sabbatarianism, and measures within the field of social welfare. In his study, *The Rise of Toronto* (pp. 186–87), D. C. Masters has referred to the activities of a group of prominent citizens of Toronto, most of whom were associated with the evangelical movement within the Church of England. Professor Masters draws particular attention to William H. Howland, Samuel Blake, George Allan, and Casimir Gzowski. A broader representation could have been cited because similar contributions in the fields of religion, education, and philanthropy were made by such leaders in other denominations as William McMaster (Baptist), John Macdonald (Methodist), and J. W. Langmuir (Presbyterian). All these men were leaders in business and the professions and entered into a variety of endeavours from essentially religious motives. The direct contact they made with a broad range of human needs and the insight they gained of some of the causative factors proved effective antidotes both to the contention that philanthropic efforts were unnecessary and dangerous, and to over-simplified views of how to remedy the human problems that were making themselves felt with mounting insistence as industrialization advanced.

Throughout the period, the development of social welfare continued to be affected not only by the ideas that were current in the daily life of the community, but also by ideas expressed in the social theories and movements which came to prominence in Europe and America. Social welfare programmes were frequently made the testing ground for theories of social dynamics or ethics, such as Utilitarianism, although far less so in Ontario than in Great Britain and the United States. More influential was the growth of the belief that social problems could be approached scientifically and that the application of scientific methods would make possible their ultimate solution. This approach was formally embodied in social science associations which were formed in Great Britain in 1857 (National Association for the

Promotion of Social Science) and in the United States in 1865 (American Social Science Association). Even though no comparable organization emerged at the time in Canada, the influence of the British and American associations was felt here.[17]

As programmes developed in specific areas of social welfare such as corrections and as their administration became more specialized, other types of formal associations developed. Prison organizations were formed on both sides of the Atlantic, and, recognizing that their interests were not confined within national limits,[18] they were able to establish sufficiently close communications to make possible the holding of international prison congresses, the first of which met in London in 1872. The prison reform movement made itself felt in Ontario where a prison reform association was formed during the late 1870's and became influential during the following decade in securing reforms, not only in the area of corrections, but in other fields as well.

During the 1870's another development of importance to social welfare in Ontario was the establishment in the United States of the National Conference of Charities and Correction.[19] The nucleus of this organization was a group of administrators from the state boards of charities who first met as a section of the American Social Science Association but by 1878 had found that it was more useful to place the principal emphasis in their discussions upon problems of administration and methods of practice, "giving only secondary consideration to scientific procedures under the title of 'prevention'."[20] Through its annual conferences the new organization was to prove highly influential in the development of social welfare in North America. Ontario's early interest in the conference is indicated by the participation of the province's Inspector of Prisons, Asylums and Public Charities in the third conference held in Cleveland in 1880.

[17]At the American Social Science Association's second general meeting, held in Boston on December 27 and 28, 1865, E. A. Meredith, then secretary of the Board of Inspectors of Prisons, Asylums and Public Charities of the United Province of Canada, was elected an honorary member, and he continued to be in touch thereafter with leaders of the association—notably F. B. Sandborn. (Correspondence dated December 28, 1865, in the possession of Colonel C. P. Meredith, Ottawa.)

[18]The National Prison Association of the United States held its annual congress in 1887 at Toronto, led by its President, R. B. Hayes, former president of the United States. A few Canadians had previously attended the association's annual meetings in various cities in the United States.

[19]Frank J. Bruno, *Trends in Social Work as Reflected in the Proceedings of the National Conference of Social Work 1874–1946* (New York, 1948), pp. 3–9. In 1917 the conference became the National Conference of Social Work and more recently the National Conference on Social Welfare.   [20]*Ibid.*, p. 7.

Ontario was influenced by two other social welfare developments, both of which originated earlier than the Conference of Charities and Correction but took longer to make themselves felt within the province. They were the children's aid movement which began in New York City in the 1850's and the charity organization movement which started in England late in the 60's, took root some ten years later in the United States, and began to affect approaches to some welfare problems in Ontario at about the same time. These two movements represent the beginning of the era in which social welfare no longer took the form, almost invariable up to that time, of the establishment of institutions for the care, training, treatment, or custody of persons within their walls. Both approached social welfare problems in ways which placed more emphasis than had generally been true of the institutional programmes upon the methods that were being used to achieve their ends. In this they proved to have the seeds of a new discipline and a new profession because it was largely from these movements that the leaders emerged who identified and elaborated the methods, principles, and philosophy of social work and who later established schools of social work and professional associations of social workers. These were the achievements of a later era, but they had their roots in the period covered by this study, and they owe much to the pioneering endeavours with which the study is concerned.

2

The Development of the Administrative
Structure

THE CONSTITUTIONAL ACT of 1791, by which Upper Canada became a political entity, authorized the governor "by and with the advice and consent of the Legislative Council and Assembly . . . to make laws for the peace, welfare and good Government" of the province. The period in which this act was in force, however, was not distinguished for the attainment of these objectives, and the main source of the failure to achieve them was, ironically, constitutional.

The Legislature

The act gave the colony representative but not responsible government. The Legislative Assembly provided a forum for popularly elected representatives, but it was denied any effective control over the executive. This situation proved to be a source of mounting conflict, destined to carry the colony over the brink of armed rebellion. The history of the government of the province during the period is not, however, solely an account of legislative and executive conflict. There was division, too, between the Assembly and the appointed Legislative Council. There were also defects in the legislative process and the effect of these was compounded by an evident lack of capacity in the members of the Assembly to make the best use of the powers they did possess. In spite of these circumstances, a substantial amount of important legislation was enacted in the pre-Union period, some of it touching upon matters within the field of social welfare.

The Executive

The executive branch of government, upon which responsibility for the administration of legislation might have been expected to fall, was perhaps the weakest link in the provincial constitution. The Constitutional Act failed to define either the executive powers or the offices through which such powers should be exercised. The Executive Council, to which the governor was to look for advice and which was presumably created to carry out administrative policy, was mentioned only casually in three sections of the act. At no time during the pre-Union period did the Council assume the characteristics of a modern cabinet. It was not composed of ministers individually responsible for the administration of a provincial department; it did not perform as a team in its relations with either the Legislature or the Governor; and, as already noted, it acknowledged no responsibility to the Assembly.[1]

The governor had the authority to appoint to the Executive Council anyone he wished and also to make whatever appointments to the public service he thought fit, but in Upper Canada, as in other colonies, early appointees to the Executive and Legislative councils and to judicial offices, along with the Anglican clergy, bankers, and certain merchants, soon formed the powerful elite known to its detractors as the "Family Compact." Effective executive power, throughout much of the period, resided with this tight-knit oligarchy rather than with the governor, and the recurring differences between it and the Assembly were to form the central theme of the political history of the period. When, as a result of the disorder and rebellion produced by these constitutional and political struggles, Lord Durham was sent to the colony on a mission of investigation and reconstruction, he reported that "from the highest to the lowest offices of the executive government no important department is so organized as to act vigorously and completely throughout the Province and every duty which a government owes to its subjects is imperfectly discharged."[2]

A combination of the inefficiency of the executive and the distrust in which it was held by the Assembly may have contributed to the minor rôle assigned to it in carrying out many of the statutes passed by the Legislature. None the less, certain duties did of necessity fall on the officers of the provincial government. In the realm of social

[1]J. E. Hodgetts, *Pioneer Public Service: An Administrative History of the United Canadas, 1841–1867* (Toronto, 1955), p. 22.

[2]C. P. Lucas (ed.), *Lord Durham's Report on the Affairs of British North America*, vol. I (London, 1912), p. 98.

welfare, gaol statistics, for instance, had to be collected from the sheriff for forwarding to the Colonial Office.[3] The grants paid to charitable institutions and hospitals and, in the years of cholera epidemics, to boards of health, as well as money advanced for the construction of the penitentiary and the asylum, all had to be paid by the receiver-general with approval, by way of audit, of the inspector-general. Welfare responsibilities were also involved in the work of the "emigration agent" in Toronto and the part-time agents at other ports of entry who assisted immigrants who because of illness or indigency or a combination of the two necessitated care or relief before they could proceed to their destination.[4]

Although the total involvement of the provincial executive with social welfare measures in the pre-Union period remained small, there was, by 1840, a growing recognition that the promotion of the peace, welfare, and good government of the province required both more efficient and more active administration by the provincial government.[5] This emerged forcefully in the findings of a large royal commission made up of members of the Legislature who investigated the "business conduct and organization" of most of the government departments in 1839. The necessity of reforming and developing the executive branch of the government was also strongly emphasized in the Durham Report.

Local Government

Deficiencies in the administration of the central government might have been of less concern in Upper Canada if the province had been endowed with a good system of local government. British colonial policy, however, ordained that the new colonies should not be given the New England type of local government which had been characterized by a large measure of self-rule. The decision, rather, was in favour of the type developed in Virginia, which was government by magistrates or justices of the peace appointed by the governor.[6] Like

[3]The government of each of the colonies had to forward annually to the Colonial Office what were known as the Blue Books, containing statistical data under some twenty-two headings, of which "gaols and prisoners" was one.

[4]Immigration during the period was only partly under provincial control; not until well into the Union period did full control pass to the colonial administration. The term "emigration" is a clue to the imperial orientation of the office.

[5]Upper Canada, *Journals*, 1839–40, Report on the Public Departments of the Province.

[6]Adam Shortt, "Municipal History, 1791–1867," in Adam Shortt and Arthur G. Doughty (eds.), *Canada and Its Provinces*, vol. XVIII (Toronto, 1914), pp. 405–8. J. H. Aitchison, "The Development of Local Government in Upper Canada, 1783–

their contemporary counterparts in England, the justices exercised both judicial and administrative powers, and when summoned to meet as a body for a whole district in courts of quarter sessions they also had legislative authority. The justices were chosen from retired military officers, large landowners, lawyers, and merchants, and, as representatives of the central government and holders of all the real power in their communities, they were centres of a "network of little local family compacts"[7] throughout the province. In the opinion of Professor Aitchison, they were "the rulers of the District" to an even greater degree "than their English counterparts."[8]

At first the courts or meetings of quarter sessions had limited powers, but with the increase of population and in the absence of other local machinery their authority was extended to many local matters relating to the physical development of their areas and to the social well-being of their people. They were, for example, authorized to erect court houses and gaols and to frame rules and regulations (subject to the approval of a judge of the Supreme Court) for the administration of the gaols and to set the salary to be paid to the gaoler and his assistants.[9] Although given no authority by legislation to provide for the poor or to meet other residual welfare needs, they none the less voted expenditures from time to time to meet the pressing needs of the people in their districts.

Although the centrally appointed justices in the courts of quarter sessions initiated and carried out most local measures in the pre-Union period, the democratic inclinations of the Loyalist settlers and other early residents of the province could not wholly be held in check. In 1793 the Legislature passed an act[10] which provided for the holding of annual "town" meetings for the election of township officers. These included a clerk, two assessors, a collector, a number of poundkeepers, six overseers of roads and highways, and two town wardens (one of whom was, however, to be appointed by the clergyman whenever an Anglican church was built in the area). The town meeting which, except during a brief period in the 1830's, could be called only on the

---

1850" (unpublished Ph.D. dissertation, Dept. of Political Economy, University of Toronto, 1954), pp. 187–94, suggests, however, that the structure of local government adopted in Upper Canada was closer to the colonial pattern in New York state, from which most of the Loyalists to Upper Canada came, than it was to that of either New England or Virginia.

[7]D. G. Creighton, *Dominion of the North* (Boston, 1944), p. 234.

[8]Aitchison, "Local Government in Upper Canada," p. 28.

[9]Upper Canada, *Statutes*, 1792, c. 8.

[10]Upper Canada, *Statutes*, 1793, c. 2. The act was frequently amended during the pre-Union period.

issuance of a warrant signed by two justices of the peace had no powers beyond the election of these officials. Upon their election, the officers carried out duties described in legislation and were under the supervision of the justices of the peace. A few of the duties of the township officers were related to social welfare. The town wardens, for example, were charged with the education and support of orphan children[11] and the township assessors were required to collect statistics on certain characteristics of the population which were thought to be associated with dependency;[12] they were to enumerate the deaf and dumb and the insane, but, oddly, the blind were not included. No township officers were directed to act as overseers of the poor—a notable omission from the act of 1793 which was perpetuated throughout the whole of the pre-Union period.

Local administration by elected officials in this period was, however, not limited to the work of the township officers. In 1816 the Legislature, in passing an act for the establishment of common schools to be administered by locally elected trustees, laid the cornerstone of what was to become the great structure of public education in the province. Even more important in the development of local government was the beginning made during the 1830's in the granting of rights of local self-government to towns and cities. In 1832 Brockville was given the right to elect a council, called a board of police, to which most of the powers exercised by the courts of quarter sessions for the district were transferred.[13] By the end of the period eight other cities and towns were incorporated with elected councils. These communities were given broader welfare powers, particularly in relation to the poor, than had been extended to the districts.

Although this trend towards a large measure of local self-government and improved municipal machinery was strongly in evidence by the end of the period, the system fell far short of meeting the province's need for vigorous and efficient municipal administration. Reaching this conclusion, Lord Durham, in his report, recommended municipal reform no less than the reform of the central government.

Special Commissions and Boards

In a review of the development of machinery for administering social welfare programmes in the pre-Union period, the boards and commissions authorized or set up to carry out specific measures merit particular attention. Those established by legislation for the building

11*Ibid.*, 1799, c. 3.   12*Ibid.*, 1837–38, c. 21.   13*Ibid.*, 1831–32, c. 17.

and later for the operation of the penitentiary are important examples. An act passed in 1832 provided for the appointment of two commissioners whose duty it would be to secure information respecting the management of penitentiaries.[14] In the following year funds were voted to proceed with the erection of the penitentiary at Kingston, and the commissioners appointed were authorized to let contracts and supervise the construction of the institution.[15] In 1834, as the opening date of the penitentiary seemed to be approaching, legislation was passed providing for the appointment of a board of five inspectors who had full power to make the necessary disciplinary rules for the penitentiary,[16] and whose duty it was from time to time to examine and inquire into all matters connected with the government of the institution, including its financial management and the treatment of prisoners. In order that the work of inspection would not be impeded, the warden and other officers were required to admit the inspectors to the penitentiary at all times and to make available to them, at request, all records. The inspectors could inquire into charges against the warden or other officers and to this end could compel the attendance of witnesses and hear testimony under oath.

A policy-making and supervisory board of five inspectors was also proposed in permissive legislation for the establishment of houses of industry. The statute passed in 1837,[17] and destined never to be implemented, authorized the erection of a house of industry in any district where it was recommended by three successive grand juries. It was then the responsibility of the court of general quarter sessions to procure plans and estimates for the erection of suitable buildings, to obtain an appropriate site for them, and to let contracts for their construction. From that point, responsibility would be assumed by the inspectors appointed by the court. They would appoint the staff to run the institution, would make regulations and by-laws for its government, and would supervise its general operation.

A board of different composition was provided for in the act of 1838 "to regulate the future erection of Gaols in this Province."[18] The lieutenant-governor was authorized to appoint three persons who, with the chief justice of the province, the vice-chancellor, the judges of the Court of King's Bench, and the sheriffs of all districts, would form a board of gaol commissioners, the functions of which were to ensure the proper planning of future gaols and to frame rules and regulations

[14]Ibid., c. 30.
[15]Ibid., 1833, c. 44.
[16]Ibid., 1834, c. 37.　　　　[17]Ibid., 1836–37, c. 24.　　　　[18]Ibid., 1837–38, c. 5.

for the administration of all common gaols in the province. The board was to meet at the call of the chairman and was to report annually to both branches of the Legislature.[19]

Another approach was employed for the building and management of the provincial asylum. The legislation[20] in this instance provided for the appointment of three commissioners who were authorized to employ an architect and to take other measures necessary for erecting suitable buildings. The act also provided that, as soon as the building was ready for the reception of patients, a board of twelve directors should be appointed with powers similar to those of a board of inspectors of a house of industry and more extensive than those of the board of the penitentiary. The asylum board was authorized to make all staff appointments subject to the approval of the lieutenant-governor, to fix salaries within certain limits, to make rules and regulations for the management of the institution, and to make annual reports to the lieutenant-governor.

Thus, during the pre-Union period, the Legislature found it necessary to provide for the establishment of six special boards and commissions to carry out social welfare functions, the performance of which neither the central nor the local governments were considered capable.

UNION PERIOD, 1841–1867

The Constitutional and Political Setting

It has been noted that Lord Durham recommended broad changes in the organization of the executive branch of government and that he advocated the establishment of strong municipal institutions based on the principle of local self-government. He also accepted the view of the Upper Canadian, Robert Baldwin, that responsible government in all local matters could be granted to the more politically mature colonies, and for this principle, which was to become the key to the development of the British Commonwealth, he made an eloquent case in his report. These recommendations and a number of less sweeping ones dealing with such matters as land management, immigration, education, and public works were well calculated to advance the interests of Upper Canada.

[19]The work of the board in framing rules for the gaols is discussed in chapter 4.
[20]Upper Canada, *Statutes*, 1839, c. 11.

The value to the upper province of two other major recommendations, the interrelated ones of uniting Upper and Lower Canada and
of seeking to submerge the French-Canadian nationality, is more de-
batable. Legislative union, though useful for the economic development of the St. Lawrence region, became unworkable by the 1860's,
and French-Canadian nationality proved far more robust than Durham
had anticipated. Its strength reinforced the sense of identity of the two
parts of the United Province and produced political dualism, represented in its extreme by the principle of the double majority in the
Legislature (that is, the support of a majority of members from both
Upper and Lower Canada), and administrative dualism, represented
by the emergence in many parts of the executive branch of the Union
government of two staffs, one English and one French, serving Upper
Canada and Lower Canada respectively.[21] Thus, although the United
Province advanced materially at a good pace, and although it not
only won responsible government but showed an increasing capacity
to rise to its demands, its progress continued to be retarded by constitutional defects which ultimately produced political deadlock.

The developments during the Union period which bore principally
upon social welfare were the creation of a sound system of municipal
government, the delegation to the municipalities of social welfare
responsibilities, the continued growth of provincial institutions in the
functional areas of corrections and mental health, and, of the most
significance to this study, the emergence of a board of inspectors as
the government's main instrument in the administration of social
welfare programmes.

Municipal Government

Lord Durham's plan "of making the establishment of good municipal
institutions for the whole country a part of the colonial constitution"[22]
was not carried out in the drafting of the Act of Union, an omission
which filled Lord Sydenham, whose task it was to inaugurate the new
constitution, "with the deepest mortification."[23] Sydenham managed,
however, in what he regarded as one of the crowning achievements
of his governorship, to have a municipal ordinance for Lower Canada
adopted on the eve of the Union by the special council which had

[21]Hodgetts, Pioneer Public Service, pp. 55–60.
[22]W. P. M. Kennedy, Statutes, Treaties and Documents of the Canadian Constitution, 1713–1929 (London, 1930), p. 446.
[23]Ibid., p. 445.

governed the lower province since the rebellion, and to have a similar act passed for Upper Canada in the first session following the Union.

The legislation for Upper Canada, known as the District Councils Act,[24] provided for the transference of much of the power which had been exercised by the courts of quarter sessions to councils in each of the fourteen districts into which the province was then divided. Incorporated cities and towns and those with boards of police remained outside the act. The district councils consisted of a warden appointed by the governor, and councillors elected by the "inhabitant freeholders and householders" of each township within the district. Because the province exercised a considerable measure of control over the councils and also because the districts were excessive in size, the act was unable to provide a sound system of local government. The district councils were not given any powers in the field of social welfare beyond those held by the previous courts of quarter sessions. There was, in fact, no mention of welfare matters throughout the entire act. Responsibility for gaols was taken over by the councils but there is some uncertainty as to whether they had the power, which had been given earlier to the quarter sessions, to establish a house of refuge or industry.

The District Councils Act formed a useful bridge between the rudimentary local government prevailing in the pre-Union period and the more advanced Municipal Corporations Act adopted for Upper Canada in 1849.[25] This latter measure, introduced by Robert Baldwin, established a comprehensive system which made townships, incorporated towns, and villages the basic units of local government. Heads of the councils elected in these units formed the council of the second tier of government, the county. The counties, which had existed up to this time chiefly as judicial and electoral areas, now replaced the districts, and it was to the counties that the social welfare responsibilities which had been inherited by the districts were transferred. The three cities of Kingston, Toronto, and Hamilton were not included in the two-tier system, and they exercised, in general, the powers and responsibilities which in the rural areas were divided between the counties and their constituent units.

Among the powers granted to the counties were those of erecting and maintaining a gaol, house of correction, and house of industry.[26] Towns, though they were units within the county system, were also given the power to pass by-laws for "establishing and regulating one or more Alms-houses and Houses of Refuge for the relief of the Poor

[24]Canada, *Statutes*, 1841, c. 10.   [25]*Ibid.*, 1849, c. 81.   [26]*Ibid.*, s. 41.

and destitute; for erecting and establishing and also providing for the proper keeping of any Work-house or House of Correction that may hereafter be erected in and for such Town."[27] Cities, too, could pass by-laws "for erecting and establishing and also providing for the proper keeping of a City Hall, Court House, Gaol, House of Correction and House of Industry . . . and appointing the Inspectors of any such House of Industry."[28]

Although the Municipal Corporations Act created an enduring structure of municipal government for the province, it did not carry social welfare provisions beyond the point of institutional care established in previous legislation. On the other hand, the new municipal structure did make possible the first important steps away from institutional care, and by 1859 the towns, cities, and townships had been assigned the authority to extend non-institutional or outdoor relief to the resident poor, as well as to make grants to charitable institutions.[29] It will thus be apparent that Upper Canada, having devised a municipal system which seemed well suited to its needs, was prepared to delegate many important responsibilities to the municipalities, including those in the sphere of social welfare.

The Development of the Provincial Administration

One of the principal accomplishments of the Union period was the reform of the civil administration inherited from the pre-Union era and the forging of a public service through which the province could proceed with an orderly development. Responsible government could hardly have been won and sustained had it not been for the progressive improvement and expansion of a civil service rationally structured and with permanent officers capable not only of administering the laws enacted by the Legislature and carrying forward with some measure of efficiency the day-to-day business of government, but also of advising on the formulation of policy.

The obstacles to the development of the public service, however, were formidable in the extreme.[30] There were problems in the transfer of responsibility from the Imperial government in such matters as postal services, immigration, and customs. There were difficulties in merging the existing services of the two parts of the province following the Union—difficulties so formidable that they resulted, in some

[27]*Ibid.*, s. 81.
[28]*Ibid.*, s. 107.
[29]See pages 73–75 for details of developments between 1849 and 1859.
[30]Hodgetts, *Pioneer Public Service*, pp. 12–95.

departments, in a dual administration which reflected the continued separateness of the two regions. There was the related problem of the perambulating provincial capital, which shifted back and forth from Toronto to Quebec, with interludes at Montreal and Kingston, before it came at last to a more secure base in Ottawa. Finally, there were the difficulties inherent in administering a vast and rapidly developing region, much of it still being carved from the wilderness.

Because of these obstacles, and in spite of the excellent beginning made under the skilful direction of Lord Sydenham, the process of creating rationally organized departments capable of efficient administration was still incomplete at Confederation. In the area of social welfare, for example, although the progress made must, in the general context of the times be regarded as truly remarkable, throughout most of the period there was no co-ordination of provincial activities relating to the local gaols, the penitentiary, the mental hospitals, and the allocation of grants to private hospitals and charitable institutions. Problems of gaol standards, which had called for some provincial action before 1841, became increasingly insistent; the operation of the provincial penitentiary proved complex and politically explosive; reformatories for young offenders had to be established; institutions for the mentally ill had to be greatly expanded; attention had to be given to the apportioning of grants to charitable institutions under private auspices. The co-ordination of these and related activities within one department under a minister responsible for them might appear to have been the course dictated by administrative considerations. In some other fields, such as agriculture, this did occur, but for corrections and charities to have been given departmental status would have been to attain in mid-Victorian times what was not to be achieved in the Canadian provinces until the third, fourth, and fifth decades of the twentieth century.[31]

The step actually taken was, none the less, well in advance of its time, for in the appointment in 1859 of the Board of Inspectors of Prisons, Asylums and Public Charities,[32] endowed with extensive

[31]By the time departmental status was granted in Ontario, corrections in the province had gone its separate way; a Department of Public Welfare was established in 1930 and a Department of Reform Institutions in 1944.

[32]The proper designation of this board and of the inspector who carried on its work in Ontario after Confederation presents a problem because of the various terms used in the legislation, reports, and other sources. The short title of the act of 1859 is the Prison and Asylum Inspection Act, and the same title was used for the Ontario statute of 1868. The earlier act referred in its text to the role of the inspectors in respect to hospitals and "other benevolent institutions." The inspectors were often referred to collectively in public reports as "the Board of Inspectors of

administrative as well as supervisory and inspectional powers, the United Province of Canada anticipated by four years the comparable appointment of the first state board of public charities in the United States.[33] This early development in social welfare administration and the excellence of the work of the board during the seven and a half years of its operation, from its formation to its dissolution at Confederation, have unaccountably been overlooked by Canadian historians, political scientists, and social workers.[34]

The pressures that led to the formation of the board came principally from the problems of administering the social welfare institutions that existed at the beginning of the period or developed between 1841 and the late 1850's to meet the insistent needs of the time. In terms of intensity, the pressures came, in ascending order, from the health programme for immigrants and mariners, from the public and private institutions for the insane, and from the problems created by the gaols and penitentiary.

PROVINCIAL HOSPITALS

In the first of these categories were two hospitals, both located in Lower Canada and operated directly by the province. One was the Marine and Emigrant Hospital situated at Quebec and the other the Quarantine Hospital located a few miles away at Grosse Isle. Both were rather costly undertakings and both posed complex administrative problems. What establishment, for example, was required to maintain the Marine Hospital at a satisfactory level of efficiency when its services were needed principally during the summer navigation season? The same question was asked about the Quarantine Hospital. When it

Asylums, Prisons, etc., etc." During the early years after Confederation, the inspector was most frequently called "the Inspector of Asylums, Prisons and Public Charities." By the mid-1880's the word "prisons" was usually placed ahead of the word "asylums" and often the latter was dropped altogether and the office known as that of "Inspector of Prisons and Public Charities," the term "charities" having become more widely used than "benevolent institutions." The designation which seems best to describe the board and later the office of inspector, in the light of the foregoing, is that of "prisons, asylums and public charities." Accordingly that term is generally used throughout this work.

[33]Frank J. Bruno, Trends in Social Work (New York, 1948), pp. 1 and 31–44.

[34]The hasty canter through the period made by Margaret Kirkpatrick Strong in Public Welfare Administration in Canada (Chicago, 1930) prepares one for her deplorably inadequate treatment of inspection provisions (pp. 32, 33, 43). More surprising, perhaps, is that Professor Hodgetts, in Pioneer Public Service, did not make more of the fact that the board, to which he refers only in passing, offered ideal support for his thesis that the Union period was distinguished by many admirable and permanently significant developments in Canada's public service.

proved incapable of dealing effectively with the calamitous epidemic of 1847, an emergency programme to establish extensive additional facilities was proposed. Later, as the measures to improve the conditions under which immigrants were brought to Canada bore fruit, and the threat of epidemics had receded, there was some advocacy of the complete abolition of the quarantine station and the liquidation of its plant, which was estimated to have cost some $200,000. The question was further complicated by the heated public health controversy between the contagionists and the non-contagionists.[35] To arrive at and carry out sound decisions on issues stemming from the operation of these hospitals, the government needed an administrative unit competent to secure and analyze the relevant data, to advise the cabinet, and to see that the policies formulated by the government were implemented.

INSTITUTIONS FOR THE INSANE

A similar situation obtained in respect to the provision of care for the insane. The need for institutions for the mentally ill, which had become pressing in Upper Canada before 1841, continued to demand attention throughout the Union period. It was not until the early 1850's that a specially designed building was in operation under an able medical director. Although the cabinet was thus relieved of some of the problems raised in earlier years, it was now subjected to pressure for expanded and improved resources for the development of an effective programme.

The care of the insane in Lower Canada confronted the government with a different group of problems. The principal asylum there had developed under private auspices, and the government had to decide what responsibilities it had for the formulation and enforcement of the asylum's standards and for the financial support of its programme.

CORRECTIONAL INSTITUTIONS

The problems that placed the heaviest strain on the government and which led most directly to the creation of the Board of Inspectors were in the corrections field, many arising from the operation of the penitentiary at Kingston. The penitentiary had been operating as an Upper Canadian prison for over five years prior to the Union but

[35]Canada, *Sessional Papers*, 1861, no. 24, n.p. The special report of Dr. J. E. Taché contained a review of the history of the quarantine station and factors affecting decisions about the size of its establishment.

became the institution for long-term prisoners from both parts of the United Province after 1840. It continued to be administered by a warden, with policy-making and inspectional responsibilities being carried by the local, unpaid board of five inspectors. This arrangement appears not to have been very satisfactory at any time, and by 1846 it had largely broken down, perhaps because of its inherent weaknesses, although the performance and methods of the warden, Henry Smith, must have placed it under considerable strain.

Smith's administration became the subject of an inquiry by a royal commission[36] in 1848–49 on which George Brown was the dominant figure. The inquiry provided one of the first and most prolonged issues on which George Brown and John A. Macdonald, the archantagonists of the Union period, were to clash.[37] Smith was a constituent, supporter, and good friend of Macdonald, and Macdonald never ceased to contend that the commission, in its investigation of the administration of the penitentiary and the treatment of the prisoners, was prejudiced and vindictive. Whatever the merits of its decision to dismiss Smith, there can be no doubt that the Commission adopted a humane and enlightened view of the rôle of correctional institutions and that it succeeded in formulating a number of broad recommendations which over the next several years were to become public policy. Some were embodied in "An Act for the better Management of the Provincial Penitentiary" passed in 1851.[38] This statute provided that the unpaid board of five inspectors should be replaced by two inspectors who were to receive £400 a year and who would be directly responsible to the provincial government.

A further recommendation of the Royal Commission to make the

[36]Canada, *Journals*, 1849, Appendix B.B.B.B.B.

[37]Differing views on the merits of the positions taken by the two men continue to be held. Donald G. Creighton, *John A. Macdonald: The Young Politician* (Toronto, 1952), pp. 159–60, 166, 229, accepts Macdonald's view and states that the "injustice" to Smith "was patent and unquestionable." J. M. S. Careless, *Brown of the Globe*, vol. I (Toronto, 1959), pp. 78–87, 101, 121–22, 137, 218–23, 224–26, examines the question at greater length and with more attention to the weight of evidence of maladministration and gross brutality practised in the penitentiary during Smith's régime. Professor Careless notes that Brown, "feeling certain of the Warden's culpability, had worked to pile up overwhelming evidence against him" (p. 86), but suggests that Macdonald, "wholly ignoring the facts of Smith's disreputable regime," was on dubious ground in concentrating his prolonged attack on what he asserted were weaknesses of the Commission's inquiry grave enough to make its findings entirely invalid. When a parliamentary committee, politically weighted in favour of Macdonald, investigated the matter in 1856, it produced so little evidence to support Macdonald's charges as to make them appear irresponsible and malicious.

[38]Canada, *Statutes*, 1851, c. 2.

penitentiary inspectors also responsible for the formulation and enforcement of standards of the common gaols, although not acted upon immediately, was the germ of the idea which was to grow into the Board of Inspectors. Among those who kept the notion alive were the two inspectors of the penitentiary who were appointed in 1851 and whose annual reports were, as recommended by the commissioners, replete with statistics of crime and punishment, and enlivened by discussions of the principles of penal administration. They advocated co-ordination of all penal institutions and, more radically, the "uniform direction and management" of the common gaols.[39]

The idea of an integrated inspectorate with broad administrative powers reached full flower by 1857 and appeared about to be translated into action at that time. It was embodied in the Prison Inspection Act of 1857, a curiously conglomerate statute[40] which provided for the establishment of prisons for young offenders, authorized the erection of an asylum for criminal lunatics, and made provincial funds available for improvements in the county gaols. Interspersed with these provisions were others which, in recognition of the expediency of establishing "a uniform system for the government and inspection of Public Asylums, Hospitals and Prisons, and to provide for the better construction of the Common Gaols of this Province," empowered the governor to appoint five persons to form a board of inspectors. The inspectors, when appointed, were to assume the powers and duties of the inspectors of the provincial penitentiary, and those of the commissioners of the provincial lunatic asylum. They were also to inspect the asylum at Beauport in Quebec and all gaols, houses of correction, and prisons. In respect to the county gaols of Upper Canada, the inspectors were to have a number of specific responsibilities which were designed to secure the improvement of their buildings, their programme, and their management. These responsibilities were set out in considerable detail. It was also the duty of the inspectors, singly or together, "to visit, examine and report . . . upon the state and management of every Hospital or Benevolent Institution supported wholly by grant of public money, or by money levied under authority of Law." Whenever required to do so by the governor, the inspectors were to make similar inspections of institutions supported "in part by grant of public money." If the inspectors were refused admission to one of these institutions, they were to report the circumstances of such refusal to the governor.

[39]Canada, *Journals*, 1856, Appendix 10, n.p.
[40]Canada, *Statutes*, 1857, c. 28.

Although the act contained references which seemed to promise an early appointment of the board of inspectors, no action was taken to that end in 1857 or in 1858. In the consolidated statutes of the following year, however, there was a separate inspection act[41] containing all the provisions relating to inspection that had been included in the statute of 1857, although the 1859 provisions were presented in a more orderly way and at much greater length than their forerunners. This act also incorporated all that was appropriate from the separate acts relating to the inspection and management of the penitentiary, the asylum, and the gaols. It was this statute that was acted upon in the historic appointment on December 9, 1859, of the Board of Inspectors of Prisons, Asylums and Public Charities. The five inspectors held their initial meeting on December 27, and in their own words "on that day was formed, for the first time in Canada, an administrative body charged with the general direction of Public Institutions."[42]

The five inspectors initially appointed to the board and those later selected to fill vacancies were men of outstanding attainments and ability, especially the three who were successively to serve as the chairman of the board. The first was Dr. Wolfred Nelson, who had returned from exile following the rebellion of 1837 and resumed a distinguished career which included two terms in the Legislative Assembly before his appointment in 1851 as one of the two inspectors of the penitentiary. The inspector appointed to the chairmanship after Nelson's death in 1863 was Dr. J. C. Taché, who like his predecessor had a medical background and had served (though as a Conservative) in the Legislative Assembly. He also had literary, constitutional, and scientific interests, the last of which led, in 1864, to his selection as the first deputy minister of agriculture, a post he continued to hold in the federal civil service after Confederation. The third chairman was E. A. Meredith, LL.D., who, in addition, served as secretary of the board during its entire life and must therefore be considered the member of the board with whom its work can be most closely identified. Meredith, who had been president of McGill College before entering the public service, also held the position of assistant provincial secretary and after Confederation continued as under-secretary of state for the provinces.[43] The appointment of men

[41]Canada, *Consolidated Statutes*, 1859, c. 110.

[42]Canada, *Sessional Papers*, 1860, no. 32, p. 5.

[43]Meredith was one of three of the original five inspectors who served on the board in a part-time capacity, the other two being John Langton and D. A. Macdonell, both of whom served until mid-August 1861 when they were replaced

of this calibre to the board indicates the high importance the government attached to it.

In a preliminary review of their responsibilities, the inspectors found that they had "charge of sixty-one Public Institutions of various kinds; classified as follows: namely, Two Hospitals, Four Lunatic Asylums, One large Penitentiary, Two Reformatory Prisons and Fifty-two Common Gaols; scattered all in every direction over the vast territory of both Provinces."[44] To look after these far-flung institutions, the board divided the territory into five regions designated as the Quebec, Montreal, Kingston, Toronto, and London divisions. Each was placed under the immediate superintendence of one inspector, who was responsible for visiting all the establishments within his division twice a year. The act also required collective visits of the inspectors to the larger institutions and, as noted above, special visits at the direction of the governor. The board further divided its work into five committees, each composed of two or three inspectors, on accounts, correspondence and records, hospitals and asylums, penitentiaries and prisons, and recent information and statistics.

In their first annual report, the inspectors described their work as "susceptible of division into two categories: those of inspection, and those of administration."[45] By "inspection" they meant their work of finding out what was taking place in the institutions and the related activity of seeing that the board's regulations were being followed and its standards maintained. Inspection involved relationships not only with the executive officers of the institutions, but also with the municipal councils whose responsibility it was to build and operate the gaols and who had to be persuaded or goaded into the measures needed to raise the gaols' standards of accommodation, staffing, and programme. By "administration" the inspectors meant the formulation of regulations and standards, the determination of the need for new or expanded facilities, and the presentation to the government of recommendations for action in establishing the facilities and for the adoption of new or revised policies.

---

by full-time inspectors. MacDonell was the warden of the penitentiary and John Langton was the province's first auditor. Langton, described by Hodgetts as an "able, forthright and courageous" fiscal reformer, was, like Meredith and Taché, one of the senior officials who served with great distinction in the Canadian civil service both before and after Confederation.

[44]Canada, *Sessional Papers*, 1860, no. 32, p. 3. The reference to "both Provinces" provides an illustration of the failure of the Union to produce a unified political community.

[45]*Ibid.*, 1861, no. 24, n.p.

The inspectors regarded their administrative functions, thus defined, as the more important part of their work and felt that the numerous inspections they had to make across the wide expanse of the province left insufficient time for adequately discharging their administrative functions. They felt especially strongly on this matter in the years after 1864 when the government failed to fill a vacancy on the board. They pointed out that after completing the statutory inspections there was "no very large margin of leisure left for studying the many difficult and important questions connected with their functions as a Board, and for reporting upon the various matters of detail from time to time referred to them by the Government, or by the officers of the different institutions under their charge."[46]

The inspectors regarded study and reflection as integral and highly important parts of their administrative rôle. They saw it as essential that they first identify the principles on which the various classes of institutions under their charge should operate and that they then determine what measures were required to make the principles effective in the institutional programme. To these ends, they appear to have read widely in the social science literature of the day. Their reports abound in quotations from British, French, and American sources, to which they looked both for basic principles and for the specifics of institutional management.

The inspectors also placed a strong emphasis on reporting. A typical annual report began with a joint statement of thirty or forty closely printed pages signed by all the inspectors telling of their collective activities and expressing their common views. Next were the inspectors' individual reports which, as a group, were also thirty or forty pages long, and finally there were some seventy to ninety pages of appendices in the form of reports by the officials of the various institutions.

The record of the board as it emerges from these reports is one of solid accomplishment. The hospitals and asylums coming under the terms of the inspection legislation benefited materially from the work of the board. The Quarantine Hospital was placed in a state of efficiency and operated at about a third of the annual cost of maintaining it prior to the establishment of the board. The intake policy of the Marine and Emigrant Hospital at Quebec was changed to convert the institution into a general hospital serving local residents both as in-patients and out-patients. The mental health needs of the province were given the most zealous attention by the board with the conscious aim of determining the extent of the existing and

[46]*Ibid.*, 1865, no. 14, p. 2.

future need for institutional care, and a programme of expansion and diversification was formulated and set in motion.

In the corrections area, the board guided the penitentiary in its continued expansion and in the development, in association with it, of the Rockwood Asylum for the criminally insane. In assisting the two juvenile reformatories in their early years of operation, the board saw one of them through a crisis of leadership, a change of location, and a serious fire, and for both institutions secured a reversal of the initial plan of having them receive members of both sexes. Even in relation to the local gaols, which required so much effort and which proved so resistant to progressive change, the board achieved a substantial measure of success. Thirteen new gaols were constructed and ten old ones altered during the period, on plans approved by the inspectors. Uniform statistical reporting was introduced and enforced by the board, and a uniform dietary was instituted which, together with controlled accounting procedures, resulted in substantial economies in the purchase of food and other supplies. These and related improvements in the correctional institutions of Canada were described by the contemporary American penal authority, Enoch C. Wines, as "exceedingly gratifying results, not a tithe of which could have been secured, except through the existence and agency of this board."[47]

Many of the board's objectives, however, were not attained. In the penal area it repeatedly and unsuccessfully recommended to the government the establishment of central or district prisons intermediate between the gaols and the penitentiary. Its attempts to secure reforms in the county gaols were seldom wholly successful, and at Confederation there were half a dozen gaols upon which the board's efforts had wrought few visible results. In the mental health area, too, the board failed to obtain the necessary measure of governmental acceptance of its plans, and its last published report contains a lengthy statement on the seriousness of the shortage of adequate facilities and the necessity of accelerated action.

PRIVATE CHARITABLE INSTITUTIONS

Another direction in which the board failed to achieve its full potential was in respect to the private charitable institutions receiving provincial grants. Although the Inspection Act provided that such institutions could be inspected by the board at the governor-general's request, it would appear that this request was not made, and there is

[47]Enoch C. Wines, *Report on the Prisons and Reformatories of the United States and Canada* (New York, National Prison Association, 1867), p. 83.

no evidence that the inspectors sought the right to bring the voluntary institutions under their scrutiny. This failure to turn over to the board responsibility for developing a policy on grants to private institutions, and the related failure to have it assume other responsibilities in relation to them suggest that the government had come to accommodate itself to the difficulties presented by the makeshift grant structure which had grown up over the years.

Although there is little evidence of any approach towards rationalizing the grant system, there were some efforts to halt the increasing number of appeals from charitable institutions for public financial help.[48] Successive governments found it difficult to deny grants to new petitioners when other institutions offering similar programmes

TABLE II

PRIVATE CHARITABLE INSTITUTIONS IN UPPER CANADA RECEIVING
GRANTS FROM THE GOVERNMENT OF CANADA DURING THE
UNION PERIOD

Institution	First year grant paid	Amount paid in 1866 (in dollars)
General Hospital, Toronto	1841	11,200
House of Industry, Toronto	1841	2,400
Protestant Orphans' Home, Toronto	1855	640
Magdalen Asylum, Toronto	1860	480
Roman Catholic Orphan Asylum, Toronto	1854	640
Lying-in Hospital, Toronto	1857	480
Girls' Home and Public Nursery, Toronto	1859	320
House of Providence, Toronto	1859	320
Deaf and Dumb Institution, Toronto	1859	3,000
General Hospital, Kingston	1852	4,800
House of Industry, Kingston	1841	2,400
Hotel-Dieu Hospital, Kingston	1852	800
Orphans' Home, Kingston	1857	640
Hamilton Hospital, Hamilton	1852	4,800
Orphan Asylum, Hamilton	1853	640
Roman Catholic Asylum, Hamilton	1854	640
London Hospital, London	1860	2,400
Protestant Hospital, Ottawa	1852	1,200
Roman Catholic Hospital, Ottawa	1855	1,200

SOURCE: Canada, *Public Accounts*, 1841–67.

were receiving them. Thus, the number of Upper Canadian institutions receiving grants, though always greatly exceeded by that in Lower Canada (where the development of social welfare under private auspices largely reflected the Roman Catholic view that the Church, rather than the State, should play the dominant rôle in the organization of such programmes), increased from three in 1841 to nineteen

[48]Canada, *Executive Council Minutes*, State Book D, March 10, 1845.

in 1866, most of the growth occurring in the 1850's. However, a glance at Table II suggests that the amounts of these grants bore little relation to the extent of the services provided by the different institutions. It can also be assumed that the reform of the system, which was bound to work to the disadvantage of those institutions receiving generous grants through their success in bringing political influence to bear in the Legislature, would require considerable political courage—more, it proved, than could be mobilized on such an issue during the Union period.

The province, therefore, continued to give financial help to the growing numbers of private charitable institutions on a piecemeal and unsystematic basis. It showed an awareness, in the terms of the Inspection Act, that it had some responsibility for seeing that institutions receiving public money and engaged in activities deeply affecting the lives of the persons they served provided an adequate quality of service. But, just as it failed to develop a rational system of making grants to the institutions, the province also failed to extend to private institutions the system of inspection it was using for prisons, asylums, and its own hospitals. The extension of inspection to the private institutions and the rationalization of the grant system were two matters left over as a test of post-Confederation statesmanship in the new provinces.

CONFEDERATION

"Canadian" Influences

The federal constitution embodied in the British North America Act in 1867 reflected primarily the thinking of the political leaders of the United Province of Canada. One would expect, therefore, to find "Canadian" ideas on social welfare incorporated in the act and in the associated arrangements made following its proclamation, notably the act of the Dominion Parliament providing that persons sentenced to more than two years would be sent to a federal penitentiary. Perhaps it is less "Canadian" ideas than it is "Canadian" practices that are found in the act. No distinct philosophy about the appropriate rôles of the central and provincial governments in social welfare matters can be discovered either in the act or in the debates preceding it. Rather, one finds, in looking at how the act affected Ontario, that the social welfare responsibilities given to the new province were, with one exception, those which had been assumed by Upper Canada before the Union (albeit on a modest scale). Thus the province would again be responsible for "the Establishment, Maintenance, and Management of Public and Reformatory Prisons in and for the Province,"[49] and for "the Establishment, Maintenance, and Management of Hospitals, Asylums, Charities, and Eleemosynary Institutions in and for the Province . . . ."[50]

The provision in section 91 of the act that the central government would assume responsibility for "Quarantine and the Establishment and Maintenance of Marine Hospitals"[51] also would have seemed natural enough to Upper Canadians who had not had much to do with these matters at any time. Even the Dominion's responsibility for "the Establishment, Maintenance, and Management of Penitentiaries"[52] fitted into Upper Canadian notions of the appropriate; for although the penitentiary at Kingston had been initiated as a purely Upper Canadian institution, it had been a shared venture throughout the Union period. It is, however, not without significance that in the Quebec Resolutions the responsibility for penitentiaries had been assigned to the provinces. It was not until the draft resolutions adopted in London, England, on December 4, 1866, that penitentiaries appear as a responsibility of the Dominion.[53]

There was, then, nothing about the division of social welfare responsibilities between the Dominion and the province which would seem inappropriate in Upper Canadian eyes. In fact, the approach embodied in the British North America Act was to be expected in a constitution written largely by Upper Canadians. Had the principal authorship come from the Maritime provinces one might have found some reference to responsibility for the poor. Instead, the province's responsibility is described not in terms of persons in need, but rather in terms of institutions. Upper Canada, it is true, was dealing on an appreciable scale with need through non-institutional forms of assistance, but its initial renunciation of the poor law and its officially expressed preference for institutional programmes are clearly reflected in the terms of the constitution.

Financial Provisions

The contention that the constitution's social welfare provisions were "Upper Canadian" in design does not lose its validity in the face of

---

[49]Great Britain, *Statutes*, 1867, c. 3, s. 92, ss. 6.

[50]*Ibid.*, ss. 7.   [51]*Ibid.*, s. 91, ss. 11.   [52]*Ibid.*, ss. 28.

[53]Joseph Pope, *Confederation Documents Bearing on the British North America Act* (Toronto, 1895), p. 47.

the financial terms of the constitution—the extent to which social welfare costs were to be borne by the province, notwithstanding. Expenditures were to be based on those made in the last year of the Union period, with about 63 per cent to be borne by the provinces and 37 per cent by the Dominion.[54] This proportion, however, did not dismay the Upper Canadians, who indicated in the Confederation debates in 1865 that they were prepared to accept without question not only the items which were destined to be assigned to the provinces under the new constitution, but the additional burden of the penitentiary as well. In one estimate of what the expenditures would be in Ontario after Confederation, the item "hospitals and charities" was shown as $125,000 and "penitentiaries and reformatories" as $76,000.[55] The two together constituted 24 per cent of the total estimated expenditures of the province.

One of two principal reasons for the apparent readiness of Upper Canadians to accept this level of expenditure for social welfare was their desire to have control of matters that were of direct local concern to them. The second was the anticipated effect of the financial terms of Confederation worked out at the Quebec Conference. These were seen as giving Upper Canada an abundance of revenue to finance all the matters which were to fall within the provincial sphere. In the estimate quoted above, for example, it was predicted that the excess of provincial revenue over all foreseeable provincial expenditure would be some $270,000 annually.

When, in the final constitutional arrangements, the burden on the province was lightened by the transfer of penitentiaries to the federal sphere, there would have seemed to Upper Canadians little reason to fear the extent of expenditures on social welfare. If, however, they had examined the extent of the increase that had occurred between 1841 and 1866 and employed this as an indication of future growth, they might not have been so confident of the province's ability to assume indefinitely the major responsibility for social welfare services and the expenditures they involved.

POST-CONFEDERATION PERIOD, 1867–1893

Despite the eagerness of the Upper Canadians to have their own government and legislature, John Sandfield Macdonald proceeded

[54]On the basis of calculations made from Canada, *Public Accounts*, 1866–67.
[55]Canada, *Parliamentary Debates on Confederation*, 1865, p. 207.

rather deliberately. The first session of the Legislature was not called until December 27, 1867, and it was not until March 4, 1868, that legislation, much of it relating to the machinery of government, received royal assent.

The Inspection Legislation

Among the statutes coming into force on that date was the Prison and Asylum Inspection Act[56] which was to stand throughout the period as the basic definition of provincial responsibility for social welfare. This act was expressed in much the same terms as was the act of 1859, but it differed in two respects: the penitentiary of course, was not dealt with in the post-Confederation enactment, and the Board of Inspectors was replaced by a single inspector. About half of the act was concerned with corrections, defining in detail the responsibilities of the inspector to look into and report upon all correctional institutions. It was particularly explicit concerning all county and other common gaols for which the inspector was to frame and enforce detailed regulations. He was also given broad powers respecting all new gaols and the reconstruction of existing ones. In this provision the new legislation was stronger than the act of 1859.

The new statute gave less explicit directions to the inspector in respect to the mental institutions, but his powers relating to them were broad. At least three times a year, he was to examine thoroughly the provincial lunatic asylum at Toronto and the branch asylums at Orillia and Malden and report his findings to the lieutenant-governor. He was empowered to "frame such by-laws as may seem to him most conducive to the peace, welfare and good government of the said asylums," the by-laws to take effect when assented to by the lieutenant-governor.

The inspector's responsibilities for hospitals and other benevolent institutions that were supported either wholly or only in part by public money were the same in the new act as in that of 1859. In the case of private asylums "established under the provision of any act in force respecting private lunatic asylums" or of any asylum for idiots, or for the deaf, dumb, or blind erected at the public expense, the inspector was given the same powers as he had for the asylum at Toronto.

The new act was much more detailed than the old one in defining the inspector's responsibilities for reporting. It contained the same

[56]Ontario, *Statutes*, 1867–68, c. 21.

general statement requiring him to present "a full and accurate report of the state, condition and management of the several asylums, hospitals, gaols and other institutions under his inspection, and inspected by him during the preceding year, together with such suggestions for the improvement of the same as he may deem necessary and expedient." In addition, however, the report was to contain, either in its body or as appendices, fourteen specific items including statistical data on the inmates of the institutions inspected, information of a special nature such as the number of offenders who had the royal pardon extended to them during the year, and a substantial amount of data on the revenue, expenditure, assets, and liabilities of the institutions.

The reasons for the Sandfield Macdonald government's decision to introduce an act providing for a single inspector, rather than a board as in the Union period, probably had more to do with the Premier's commitment to the maintenance of cheap government than with a careful assessment of the relative merits of single administrators and administrative boards. In supporting its decision, the government could have argued that four inspectors, one of whom carried heavy additional responsibilities, had functioned adequately in the United Province in the two years just prior to Confederation but that the duties of the former board had included the penitentiary and the Quarantine and Marine hospitals—all of which were now responsibilities of the Dominion; that the success of the board in improving services and raising standards had reduced the work that would henceforth be required; that Ontario could abandon the "wasteful" practice of the Union period of doubling the number of essential civil service positions to satisfy the two national groups linked by the legislative union.

The suggestion that economy was a principal motivating factor in the decision to have a single inspector gains support from the salary provision made for the inspector. The arrangement of "two thousand dollars per annum, inclusive of travelling expenses,"[57] was much less favourable than that enjoyed by the full-time members of the former board. Their salaries were also $2,000 but over and above this they received travel expenses which in the last year of the board's operation averaged $1,050 for each of the three full-time inspectors.[58] Thus, the income offered for the new position was less by a third than that provided by the Union government, and less than a fifth of the

[57]*Ibid.*
[58]Canada, *Public Accounts*, 1866–67.

amount, some $10,782, expended on inspection by the United Province in 1866–67.

The Inspectorship, 1868–1882

The salary Ontario was offering would have seemed unattractive by comparison to members of the old board had any of these been available for the position. All, however, had received appointment with the Dominion government: Meredith as under-secretary for the provinces, and the other three as members of the Penitentiaries' Board.[59]

The person appointed to fill the position was John Woodburn Langmuir. Unlike most of the members (eight in all) who had served on the Board of Inspectors, he was not a member of a profession and he could make little claim to experience in the fields in which he would be working. In the fourteen years in which he was to serve as inspector, however, Langmuir was to prove to be a brilliant administrator, with strong convictions about the importance of the work of which he had charge and with an outstanding ability to win support and acceptance for the measures he regarded as necessary for the development of social welfare in the province. It would be difficult to conceive a more felicitous appointment at this crucial point, when the province, for the first time in its history, possessed both a workable democratic constitution and freedom from "outside" interference in the development of the policies and institutions needed to promote the material and social well-being of its people. If a primary responsibility of a government is to place its programmes under the direction of able administrators, the government of Sandfield Macdonald may be said to have discharged this responsibility in the field of social welfare with extraordinary success.

When Langmuir took up his appointment in June 1868, he was thirty-two years of age. He had received his education at Osborne's Academy in Kilmarnock, Scotland, before coming to Canada at the age of fifteen. He had been articled for five years in a mercantile firm with branches in Kingston and Picton, and within a few years had acquired the Picton branch and built up a considerable business as a grain merchant and ship builder.[60] At the age of twenty-four, he had been elected mayor of Picton. He thus brought to the position of inspector a rather brief Scottish education and experience in business and in municipal government. With the passage of the Prison and

[59]N. Omer Cote, *Political Appointments, Dominion of Canada, 1867 to 1895* (Ottawa, 1890), pp. 31, 132, and 137.

[60]Alexander Fraser, *A History of Ontario* (Toronto, 1907), pp. 554–55.

Asylum Inspection Act and the appointment of Langmuir, the province had taken the essential steps to provide a basic administrative structure. The effectiveness of the administration would depend, in large measure, upon the ability of the inspector to identify the social welfare problems upon which action was needed, and upon his success in recommending to the government suitable methods of dealing with them and in having the recommendations adopted as public policy.

The second and third of these requisites to the successful administration of the Prison and Asylum Inspection Act require some elaboration because the only references in the legislation to the relations of the inspector with the government were to the reports he must make to the lieutenant-governor-in-council respecting regulations for the institutions under his charge. However, the real key to an inspector's success depended upon his ability to enter into close and harmonious relationships with the minister designated by the government as having general responsibility for the matters dealt with by the act. Throughout the period reviewed here the inspector worked through the provincial secretary.[61]

In an address before the National Conference of Charities and Correction at Cleveland in 1880, Langmuir, after describing the duties that he carried out under the act, referred to the inspector's relationship to the government in the following terms:

It is hardly necessary to point out that such extensive powers, the chief of which have just been detailed, would not be conferred upon any official without a direct check and partial control being exercised over him by the Government conferring the authority, and this is very simply but most effectively furnished. One of the members of the Ontario Government is the executive head of the Inspector's department, and with him the Inspector is in constant communication, consulting with him and advising him respecting all matters pertaining to the institution service. The Cabinet Minister is of necessity a member of the Legislature of the Province. He is, therefore, both as a Cabinet Minister and as a member of the Legislature, together with his colleagues in the Government, directly responsible to the people for the proper administration of the affairs of the institutions referred to. He introduces and takes charge of all legislation required in connection with the public institution service, and obtains the requisite money appropriations for their maintenance.[62]

Langmuir's understanding of the constitutional and political framework in which he had to work and his ready acceptance of it appears

---

[61]There were some exceptions to this arrangement. On some matters the inspector communicated with the premier or with the president of the council. See, for example, Ontario, *Sessional Papers*, 1874 (vol. VI), no. 2, p. 56.

[62]*Ibid.*, 1881, no. 8, p. 8.

to have provided the foundation on which he based his fruitful relationships with the provincial secretaries under whom he served.

What were the social welfare problems that called for attention as the Inspector took up his new responsibilities? The most comprehensive answer to this question was given in Langmuir's tenth annual report and was thus marred somewhat by the distortion of time. Moreover, Langmuir drew an unduly dark picture of the social welfare scene as he had found it, so that he could make the progress achieved by the end of the ensuing decade seem the brighter by contrast. These defects notwithstanding, his account of the initial situation, as seen from 1877, together with his remarks on the political context in which it was to be viewed, are of interest.

Of all the benefits that have accrued to Ontario from the Act of Confederation, none should be more highly prized than the privilege of founding and organizing such institutions as are actually required, and just at the time required, for the care, treatment and relief, of her mental, physical and moral defectives, without having to consult the wishes, or wait the action of a neighbouring Province, or very likely having to determine the *quid pro quo* to be given to such Province before a grant could be obtained for any institution for Upper Canada, even though absolutely needed.

Perhaps in no branch of the various services bequeathed by Old Canada to the Province of Ontario, was there greater necessity for vigorous action and the introduction of progressive ideas, than in that having charge of the Asylums, Prisons and Public Charities; the proper organization and supervision of which so vitally affect the lives, health and morals of the community.

Previous to Confederation, the accommodation for the treatment of insanity and the care of the insane, was not only in some instances exceedingly bad, but it was entirely inadequate to the wants of that afflicted class, necessitating their detention in private families, or protracted confinement in gaols, until, through lack of proper treatment, their insanity, in a great many cases, became chronic and incurable. No provision whatever was made for idiots so that they had to remain in private houses, no matter how filthy or vicious their habits, or how dangerous their propensities. With the exception of an insignificant grant to a private school, which was struggling for an existence, the education and instruction of the deaf and dumb were entirely neglected by the Government, and the youth of that class were being allowed to grow up in ignorance and moral darkness. The blind were wholly uncared for by Government, both as to education and industrial instruction. While a good deal had been done to improve the condition and discipline of the common gaols, a large majority of them were faulty in construction, defective in arrangement, wanting in the means of classification, loose in discipline, and, worse than all, associated idleness with all its evils reigned supreme within their walls. The Hospitals and Benevolent Institutions were aided by the grant of an arbitrary sum to each without reference to the character or volume of work performed, and without any inspectorial supervision on the part of the Government either in respect to the management of the affairs of the institutions or their structural condition.

Such was the state of this branch of the Public Service prior to Confederation.[63]

During the fourteen years of Langmuir's inspectorship, efforts were made to meet these social welfare needs. Year after year in his annual reports Langmuir outlined problems which required public attention and made specific recommendations for solving them. Nearly every year he was able to point to important gains that had been made since his previous report. It was his custom in his preamble to express his appreciation for the measures the government had taken and then to outline the next steps which he believed were required in the further development of adequate institutions and programmes.

A brief review of the progress made from year to year during Langmuir's period of office is set out in Appendix A which provides a chronology of the major developments in the expansion and improvement of the province's social welfare facilities and resources. It indicates that there was hardly a year from 1868 to 1881 which did not witness major advances in one or more of the fields of corrections, the care of the mentally ill and mentally retarded, the education of the blind and the deaf, and the expansion and improvement, with provincial financial aid and supervision, of voluntary institutions for the care of the ill, the aged, homeless children, and unmarried mothers.

It is thus apparent that strong action was taken and substantial progress made in remedying all the initial deficiencies that Langmuir had outlined in his tenth report. When he addressed the National Conference of Charities and Correction in 1880, he was able to make the claim that the institutions which the province had established since Confederation, together with those which it had inherited from the previous era, formed "one of the most complete charitable and correctional systems on the continent."[64]

This remarkable progress was attributable, in the main, to the fact that the prevailing ideas in the province made for receptivity to programmes of social improvement.[65] The political leaders of the province were ready to give earnest consideration to meeting social welfare needs. They were prepared to use the experience of other jurisdictions as a guide and to weigh Ontario's progress critically against developments in the United States and Europe. Accordingly, when the governments of the period were presented with evidence of

[63]*Ibid.*, 1878, no. 4, pp. 1–2.
[64]*Ibid.*, 1881, no. 8, p. 15.   [65]See chapter 1, pages 13–20.

a social welfare need and with a clearly worked out proposal for meeting it, they were prepared to submit an appropriate measure for its implementation to the provincial Legislature. The Legislature proved willing to adopt, and the electors of Ontario to support, the rapid pace of social welfare advance that was set during the period.

In a political speech in 1879, Mowat commented on the support of social welfare programmes by politicians and the public: "The Asylums and Institutions established before Mr. Blake came into power, having become inadequate to afford accommodation for the afflicted classes for which these Institutions were designed, it was the public desire that a further part of the money should be employed on enlarging and extending the respective buildings so that there should be room for all. This was done. Was it wrong? Nobody said so at the time, and nobody ventures to say so now."[66]

Although the promotion, adoption, and support of these extensive social welfare measures did not occur in a period of continuous material prosperity (during about half of it "the state of trade was depressed"), it did take place at a time when the province's fiscal condition was consistently strong. This fact, together with the comparatively limited demands upon the treasury, provided an unusually favourable opportunity for vigorous leadership in the promotion of programmes of social welfare. The opportunity was seized upon by Langmuir, and his work as inspector provides a notable example of the effect of strong leadership from within the public service. He did not exceed the mandate of the Inspection Act requiring him to make recommendations for the improvement of the programme of which he had charge, but he used it to the full.

Langmuir's capacity for strong administrative leadership may thus be identified as the key to the vigorous pace of social welfare development in the early post-Confederation era. With great skill and consistency, he utilized the favourable fiscal and political factors in promoting the social welfare goals for which he was working.

Langmuir outlined his duties as inspector in a number of his annual reports, the best review appearing in the report for 1878. An excerpt from this report appears in Appendix B. It indicates the manifold duties involved in the office of inspector, emphasizing the operational aspects of the position rather than the function of developing policy. In view of the volume of work which, because of the paucity of the supporting staff, the inspector himself had to discharge, it seems

[66]Oliver Mowat, *Speeches on Reform Government in Ontario* (Toronto, 1879), p. 52.

remarkable that Langmuir was able to deal with it all and at the same time provide brilliant leadership in the realm of policy. His ability to do so gives the measure of his extraordinary qualities of intellect, his capacity for work, and his commitment to the task he had undertaken. These qualities and others which contributed to the effectiveness of his work are illustrated at many points in the following chapters where the programmes he was instrumental in developing are fully discussed.

Langmuir's career as a public servant ended in 1882 when, at the age of forty-six, he re-entered private business. He joined in founding Canada's first trust company, the Toronto General Trusts Limited, and, until his death in 1915, was its general manager. In his new work he utilized the knowledge he had gained as inspector when one of his duties was to administer the estates of inmates of the asylums who had property but who did not have any relatives or friends legally competent to administer it. Also, he carried his experience in directing the policies of institutions for the mentally ill into the establishment of the Homewood Asylum, Guelph, which proved to be both a well-run mental hospital and a profitable business venture. On various occasions—notably when he assumed the chairmanship of the Royal Commission on Prisons in 1890—he undertook important public assignments. Thus his contributions to social welfare by no means came to an end with his resignation in 1882.

The Inspectorship after Langmuir, 1882–1893

In Langmuir's last report he was able to announce that "owing to the great increase both in the clerical and in the inspectorial work of the department, and the necessity for at least one officer to be almost constantly engaged in the actual work of inspection . . . it became necessary to appoint an Assistant to the Inspector."[67] The person appointed was Dr. W. T. O'Reilly who had previously been inspector of insurance for Ontario. He was given responsibility for the hospitals and mental institutions, and from his appointment in April 1881 until his death in July 1890 his work was mainly with the institutions in the health field.[68] Following Langmuir's resignation a second inspector, Robert Christie, was appointed. From May 1882, until Dr. O'Reilly's

[67]Ontario, *Sessional Papers*, 1882, no. 8, p. 6.

[68]In reporting O'Reilly's death, which occurred during his official visit to the Kingston asylum, Christie paid tribute to his "zeal and earnestness" and remarked that "it was his principal aim to secure to the patients in the institutions under his care the utmost consideration and relief that it was possible to afford them." (*Ibid.*, 1891, no. 6, p. 1.)

death, Christie assumed the principal responsibility for the correctional institutions and for the inspection of the houses of refuge and the orphan and magdalen asylums. He then took over the health institutions, and his former duties were assumed by T. F. Chamberlain.

The dual inspectorship took legislative form in an amendment to the Prison and Asylum Inspection Act. Passed in 1883, this amendment provided that "the Lieutenant-Governor may appoint two fit and proper persons to be each an inspector of the public asylums, hospitals, common gaols and reformatories."[69] The inspector whose commission bore the earlier date was designated the senior inspector and the legal entity to whom various legal responsibilities of the office were attached. The senior inspector was also accountable for lunatic asylums and the custody of insane persons—a fact which would explain Christie's move from the correctional to the health institutions following the death of Dr. O'Reilly.

In adopting this new policy, the government appeared to be taking the view that the work of the office could be satisfactorily discharged by dividing it into two roughly equal parts, with asylum inspection forming the core of one part, and prison inspection the core of the other. Whatever gains there may have been in this seemingly logical division, there was an immediate and important loss. It became apparent at once that the many social welfare programmes which were combined in the office would no longer be viewed in their entirety, as they had been during Langmuir's administration. Although the fact that both inspectors reported to the provincial secretary might seem to have promoted an integrated approach, the actual result of the dual inspectorship was a cleavage which seriously impaired the value of the office and set the stage for further functional divisions in areas of work which, until 1882, had been viewed as a single field.

The reports of the inspectors reflected the change. Langmuir's report, though divided into different sections, had been presented as a unit, with an introduction reviewing the whole field. From 1883, this practice was abandoned and six quite separate reports were prepared dealing respectively with: the asylums for the insane and the asylum for idiots; the common gaols, prisons, and reformatories; the Ontario Institution for the Education and Instruction of the Deaf and Dumb, Belleville; the Ontario Institution for the Education and Instruction of the Blind, Brantford; the hospitals; the houses of refuge and orphan and magdalen asylums. In the *Sessional Papers* for 1883, and in those for one or two other years, these several reports were bound in a single

69Ontario, *Statutes*, 1882–83, c. 30.

volume, but more often they were dispersed through two or more volumes.

Near the end of the period a further division was made in the office of inspector, this time without any change in the legislation establishing the office, and without any outright definition of the rôle of the third inspector. Even though assistants had been used to carry out a number of the inspections of private institutions and local gaols, it appears that increased work necessitated an additional senior member of the inspectional staff. The appointment of a third inspector, named James Noxon, was made in 1892. Instead of taking the opportunity to re-assess the work of the office and re-define its functions through amended legislation, the government limited the Legislature's rôle in the matter to voting the new inspector's salary in the expenditures of 1893.[70]

Langmuir's successors appear to have produced work of a fairly good quality, but they failed to achieve Langmuir's mastery of the office. They inherited a well-developed structure of institutions and programmes and, in general, appeared content to work within it. They were unable to emulate Langmuir's success in recognizing new or growing areas of need and in identifying the policy decisions and formulating the plans required to meet them. They were also unable to arrest tendencies towards stagnation that became apparent both in the institutions wholly operated by the province and in those coming under its supervision.

Social Welfare Developments, 1882–1893

Developments in the field of social welfare during the period from Langmuir's resignation to 1893, though not strongly promoted from the office of the inspector, were none the less extensive and important. The period was one in which the National Policy, with its emphasis on the protection of manufacturing industries, was resulting in the rapid growth of cities in central Canada, chiefly in southern Ontario. Accordingly, the problems that called for attention were mainly urban problems and problems characteristic of rapid industrial development. The Factories' Act of 1884 and its subsequent amendments reflected the need for the protection of persons employed in manufacturing, and the Workmen's Compensation Act of 1887 and its further amendments recognized, however inadequately, the need to protect the victims of industrial accidents and their dependants. The creation of the first

[70]Ontario, *Sessional Papers*, 1894, no. 1, p. 42.

permanent provincial board of health was a response to the more acute public health needs of urban populations, although it was a product, as well, of the advancement of public health knowledge and of the protective techniques necessary for success in organized attacks on the threats to the health of the public.

The impact of industrialization on the family also found legislative expression in statutes which attempted, if not to strengthen the family, at least to offer some protection to those who suffered when the family proved unable to fill the rôles it had played in rural society. Thus there was a law in 1888 respecting the maintenance of wives deserted by their husbands; a law in 1890 to encourage the development, under municipal auspices, of homes for the aged; an act in 1893 respecting houses of refuge for females; and throughout the period a series of acts designed to help solve the problem of growing numbers of neglected and delinquent children.

Some of this legislation, such as that respecting deserted wives and injured workmen, did little more than offer the individual recourse to the courts when he had suffered some injury or wrong. Other acts went further and expressed the willingness of the province to intervene actively to prevent certain types of evil or misfortune in some instances and to attempt to ameliorate the effects of misfortune in others. Thus it undertook, through the appointment of factory inspectors, to see that safe conditions were maintained in factories and that limits were placed on the kinds and conditions of work performed by children, young girls, and women. Similarly, the government appointed a central board of health with a permanent paid secretary to administer the board's policy of promoting public health measures across the province. And in 1893 Ontario took the historic step of appointing an officer whose duty it was to superintend measures for the protection of abandoned, exploited, and neglected children.

The Royal Commission of 1890

The lack of strong social welfare leadership from the office of the inspector of prisons, asylums and public charities seems to have encouraged leadership to emerge from other quarters. In the late 1880's and during the early years of the 1890's movements for the more humane treatment of animals and children and movements for prison reform gained sufficient strength to command the attention of the provincial government, resulting, among other developments, in the appointment in 1890 of the Royal Commission on the Prison and Reformatory System of Ontario. This commission had as its chairman

J. W. Langmuir, who in the eight years following his resignation from the inspectorship had become a successful and respected leader in the business community. The other members of the commission were Hon. Charles Drury, Dr. A. M. Rosebrugh, A. F. Jury, and Hon. T. W. Anglin, the last mentioned serving as secretary.

The function of this commission was "to collect information regarding Prisons, Houses of Correction, Reformatories, Industrial Schools, etc., with a view to ascertaining any practical improvements which may be made in the methods of dealing with the criminal classes, so far as the subject is within the jurisdiction of the Provincial Legislature and Government."[71] These terms of reference, however, give an imperfect impression of the breadth of the area the commission's work was to encompass, for without losing its focus on practical improvements in the penal system, the commission was able to extend its inquiry into the causes of crime, especially those traceable to the childhood years, and to explore in some detail the problems of the vagrant and the alcoholic. In the area of correctional practice, it examined the value of the indeterminate sentence, probation, the classification of prisoners and their employment, the rôle of the industrial school, and the management of the county gaols.

The commission began its work by collecting and reviewing penal statistics and literature and by preparing schedules of questions to ask particular categories of witnesses. It then held hearings to take the testimony of witnesses at Toronto, Hamilton, Kingston, Ottawa, and London, and visited institutions in Massachusetts, New York, Michigan, and Ohio. The witnesses heard included the officials responsible for penal matters in Ontario, as well as Dr. T. J. Barnardo, founder of children's homes in England; John Edward Pell, secretary of the Associated Charities of Toronto; Miss Elizabeth C. Putnam, a child welfare reformer in Boston; W. H. Howland, mayor of Toronto, who was actively engaged in prisoner aid work; Goldwin Smith, eminent English author and educator and, from 1872, a devoted community leader in Toronto; and J. J. Kelso, newspaperman and president of the Toronto Humane Society. The commission also received a memorandum from E. A. Meredith, who in the years since he had been chairman of the Board of Inspectors of Prisons, Asylums and Public Charities had retained an active interest in social welfare matters.[72]

[71]*Ibid.*, 1891, no. 18, p. 3.
[72]Following Meredith's retirement in 1878 as federal deputy minister of the interior, he moved to Toronto and became one of the group who founded the Toronto General Trusts Company in which, as a vice-president, he carried some administrative responsibility. He also helped to found the Homewood Asylum. Thus Meredith and Langmuir, the two figures who made the greatest contribution to

The commission's report, which merits recognition as one of the outstanding documents in the literature of social welfare in Canada, consists of 569 pages of the testimony of the witnesses heard and 225 pages of discussion and recommendations for specific types of action which ought to be taken by public and private bodies. The commission also gave eloquent expression to a general philosophy of social responsibility. The problems which it had examined could not, it felt, be regarded solely as a product of the failure or weakness of the individual. The causative factors went deep into the structure of society and it was, accordingly, through broad social policies, formulated and carried out both by public and by voluntary organizations, that progress would be made in the prevention of crime and in the reformation of the criminal. A representative expression of this approach appears in the following passage from the report:

> The neglect of its duties by the State and by society in all its other forms of organization, is largely responsible for the prevalence of vice and crime. The State has not done its whole duty when it has enacted that those who commit crimes shall be punished, and has provided police by whom offenders and criminals may be arrested, tribunals before which they may be tried, and gaols in which the penalties imposed may be exacted. The public arrest of a child, his public appearance as a culprit in a police court, his imprisonment in a common gaol, where he must associate with criminals of all sorts, are usually so many stages in his progress from vice to crime. Such a mode of treatment not infrequently has a most injurious effect on children who have committed merely some law-made offence. All this system of dealing with criminals and offenders rests upon the exploded principle that crime can be prevented, and criminals kept in check only by deterrent agencies. Nor is it enough that the state provides in addition, a school system the benefits of which all who choose and who have the opportunities may share. Charitable associations make a great mistake if they suppose that when they provide food and clothing, and fuel and shelter for all who seem to be indigent, they do all that is necessary to supplement the work done by the State. The example of Great Britain proves, most conclusively, that much more can be done by the State and by associations to save those who are in danger, and to raise those who have fallen than has yet been attempted in this Province. What more can be done in this country where the work ought to be much easier should be done. How it can best be done is a question which demands the most serious consideration.[73]

Charity Aid Act

A final matter for general consideration in respect to the administration of public welfare, and one which requires attention prior to a

public administration in the field of social welfare, became closely linked in their private business ventures.

[73]Ontario, *Sessional Papers*, 1891, no. 18, p. 44.

more detailed review of the special programmes for the relief of the poor, the correction of the offender, the care of the ill, and the protection of dependent children, is the rôle of the province in assisting voluntary institutions and agencies. With the exception of grants extended to the Prisoners' Aid Association and the industrial schools—to which reference is made in later chapters—financial aid by the province to private endeavours in the welfare field was granted under the Charity Aid Act, a measure of great importance during the period under review and of continuing significance long thereafter. It represented the first legislative attempt to express and enforce the province's right to require privately operated social welfare institutions, or at least those institutions receiving provincial grants, to accept provincial inspection and to maintain standards deemed adequate for the performance of their functions.

The roots of the act go back to the second year of Langmuir's inspectorship at which time he was instructed to begin inspection of the private institutions receiving grants. His first reference to them appears in his third annual report when he presented detailed information about the eight general hospitals and the two houses of refuge being aided by the province, together with statistical data about fourteen other institutions. Although this first report on the private institutions was largely descriptive, Langmuir did make a number of critical comments on some of the institutions' buildings, programmes, and methods of financing. It was obvious that he would not be satisfied for long to carry out similar inspections under the weak provisions of the Prison and Asylum Inspection Act of 1868 or to condone indefinitely the inequities of the proportions in which the grants were distributed.

It must, therefore, have been a matter of satisfaction to him when he was asked by the government in 1872 "to examine fully into the method of granting Legislative aid to Hospitals and Benevolent Institutions," and to report his findings.[74] He presented this report to the Provincial Secretary on July 18 of that year and also included it in his annual report, noting in the latter that he had not hesitated to point out "certain defects and anomalies in the system; as well as irregularities in the administration of the affairs of some of the establishments in receipt of Government aid."[75]

He described the manner in which he attacked his assignment in the following terms:

Assuming that it is desirable and expedient to assist, with Provincial funds, certain benevolent Institutions, it becomes of the utmost importance to

[74]*Ibid.*, 1872–73, no. 2, p. 66.
[75]*Ibid.*

determine what class of Institutions are entitled to aid, and to what extent and upon what principle such aid shall be granted.

I think it will generally be admitted, that the best means of determining whether a charitable institution is entitled to aid is by an examination into its design and the character of the work it is endeavouring to accomplish. If the objects aimed at in its establishment and maintenance are calculated to benefit the Province at large, and if its affairs are conducted in such a manner as to accomplish the objects, it may very properly be assumed that such an institution has a good claim upon the Province for aid.

Applying this test to the institutions aided by Provincial funds for the year, 1871, we find:

1st. That there were ten Hospitals or Institutions of a curative character for the treatment of disease or bodily ailment,

2nd. Two Houses of Industry or what may more properly be termed Poor-houses for the lodgement of indigent persons, chiefly adults, and for dispensing charity in a systematic manner,

3rd. Eleven institutions for the lodgement, support and education of indigent orphans and neglected and abandoned children,

4th. An institution of a reformatory character, known as a Magdalen Asylum, for the sheltering and re-claiming of abandoned women.

The 24 institutions comprised in the above classes, situated in every section of the Province, received from the Provincial funds the sum of $40,260, and having thus ascertained what are their various objects, it only remains to enquire whether a proper and equitable distribution of Government aid was made to each class of Institution, and to each individual establishment under that class.[76]

Langmuir then proceeded to examine the basis on which grants were being paid to each of these types of institutions and, finding that no proper and equitable basis existed, proceeded to consider the principles upon which a system of provincial grants ought to be based.

The details of his findings and recommendations as they were set out both in the 1872 report and in the one for the following year[77] and as they affected the various programmes are examined in chapters 3 to 6. The broad principles enunciated in these reports were that: grants should be offered to those institutions whose programmes and standards made for the achievement of the charitable purposes they were designed to serve; the institutions receiving grants should be prepared to accept inspection and other forms of provincial supervision and direction; the amount of the grant to the institutions should be related to the amount of service provided by the institutions; the grants should be designed in such a way as to encourage financial support from sources other than the province.

In his attempt to develop a formula for the proper distribution of public funds to the institutions, Langmuir proceeded on the assump-

[76]*Ibid.*   [77]*Ibid.*, 1874 (vol. VI), no. 2, pp. 128, 134.

tion that he had to work within the existing appropriations. This may have been part of the terms of reference within which he was instructed to confine himself. And the fact that he succeeded in developing a formula which did not involve additional expenditures no doubt assisted in reducing possible opposition to his proposal in an economy-minded Legislature. By making this the sole basis on which to arrive at the specific amounts to be recommended for each of the classes of institutions, however, Langmuir failed to consider and discuss other possible approaches. He did not, for example, ask what amounts were needed to operate the institutions at an acceptable level of service or what was an appropriate proportion of provincial funds to other funds. His failure to ask such questions, if only to put them on the record, was unfortunate, and the failure to base his formula on the considerations that they implied resulted in long-standing defects in the grant formula —reaching, perhaps, to the present.

The government failed to act on Langmuir's proposals in 1873 and might have continued to draw back from a measure that was certain to be unfavourably received by those institutions which would suffer from the principle that the total grant be divided according to the services rendered. Other and stronger political considerations, however, appear to have operated in the opposite direction and led to the proposal for reforming the distribution of grants being added to the government's legislative programme in 1874. These considerations related to the pressure placed upon the government to grant incorporation to the Loyal Orange Order through the passing of special legislation, a step Mowat was reluctant to take because of the anticipated reaction of those opposed to the extension of Orange influence. His solution to this difficulty was to pass legislation making it possible for benevolent, provident, and like societies to be incorporated under a general act[78] rather than through separate legislation for each such society. It fitted well with his case for the adoption of this measure to associate it with the proposal to reform the distribution of grants to charitable institutions. There was no necessary connection between these two matters, but they were referred to in the same sentence in the speech from the throne, were placed side by side in the statutes, and were generally treated as related measures for tidying up provisions touching on private societies and associations.

The reference in the throne speech to the proposed legislation on grants to charitable institutions was to a bill "for regulating the

[78]An Act respecting Benevolent, Provident, and other Societies. Ontario, *Statutes*, 1874 (1st sess.), c. 34.

distribution of the money voted out of the public funds for charity, by proportioning the payments as far as may be to the results accomplished by the respective institutions aided."[79] The act, as passed, referred in its preamble to the aim of having the distribution of "public funds in aid of charitable institutions . . . made upon some properly arranged and equitable system."[80] It also stated a second objective—one which Langmuir had particularly emphasized—"that municipal and other corporations, as well as private individuals, should be stimulated and encouraged to give a liberal support to such institutions."[81]

The means employed in the act to achieve these purposes were ingenious. Langmuir's plan of identifying categories of institutions in terms of their purposes was followed, but no attempt was made to define the categories. Instead, three schedules were attached to the act, giving the names and locations of the institutions which were eligible for the provisions under each schedule. Schedule A contained the general hospitals, together with a lying-in hospital and an eye and ear infirmary. Schedule B contained houses of refuge, and schedule C orphanages and homes for unmarried mothers. Grants were provided for each day of "actual treatment" in institutions listed under schedule A, for "each day's actual lodgement and maintenance therein of any indigent person" in the institutions under schedule B, and for "each day's actual lodgement and maintenance . . . of any orphan and abandoned child" in the homes listed in schedule C. The grant comprised a basic amount and an amount which was contingent upon the institution receiving aid from sources other than the province (Table III). The latter portion of the grant could not exceed one-fourth of such funds, and as in the case of the basic amount a per diem limit was established for all institutions in each of the three groupings.

The institutions in the lists appended to the original act and immediately eligible under its terms were those "hitherto receiving public aid." The act also provided for the addition of other institutions, a step which could be taken only "upon report of the Inspector . . .

[79]Ontario, *Journals*, 1874 (1st sess.), p. 3.

[80]Ontario, *Statutes*, 1874 (1st sess.), c. 33. See also Charles Clarke, *Sixty Years in Upper Canada* (Toronto, 1908), p. 203. Clarke notes that "prior to the passage of this resolution each particular hospital grant instead of being a sum fairly earned, was the result of a sort of grab-game wherein the stronger party prevailed. There is little wonder that the adjustment thus alternating between Protestant and Catholic institutions, as change or adroit scheming directed, was deemed an unfair one, and that Mr. Fraser and the Government did wisely in arranging a method of distribution based on work done."

[81]Ontario, *Statutes*, 1874 (1st sess.), c. 33.

TABLE III

AMOUNTS PAYABLE PER DAY UNDER THE
CHARITY AID ACT, 1874

Schedule	Basic grant (in cents)	Maximum contingent grant (in cents)
Schedule A	20	10
Schedule B	5	2
Schedule C	1½	½

SOURCE: Ontario, *Statutes*, 1874 (1st sess.), c. 33.

showing that the institution named . . . has all the usual and proper requirements for one of its nature and objects, and . . . ought to be aided under this Act," and through an order-in-council ratified by a resolution of the Legislative Assembly.

In addition to this function of reporting upon and recommending additional institutions for inclusion under the act, the inspector was given more specific inspectional duties and powers relating to this group of private institutions than he had been granted under the Prison and Asylum Inspection Act of 1868. These responsibilities were set out in section 12 of the Charity Aid Act:

The said Inspector shall, from time to time, visit and inspect every such institution, and make all proper enquiries as to the maintenance, management, and affairs thereof; and by examination of the registers and such other means as he may deem necessary, particularly satisfy himself as to the correctness of any returns made under this Act, or under any Order in Council in that behalf, as aforesaid; upon all which matters he shall make report to the Lieutenant-Governor in Council.[82]

Where the inspector found an institution to be "unsufficient, or without the necessary and proper accommodation or requirements for one of its nature and objects," he was to report this to the lieutenant-governor-in-council and this body was thereupon required to direct by order-in-council that no further aid be given to the institution until the inspector, "upon good and sufficient grounds," recommended that the order be revoked.

The province's supervisory relationship to the institutions was not limited to the periodic visits of the inspector. The final section of the act, section 14, gave the province broad powers over the management of the institutions listed under the first two of the three schedules:

The directors or managers, or other body or persons having the control or management of any such institution named in Schedules A and B shall,

[82]*Ibid.*

within six months after the passing of this Act, enact by-laws or regulations for the government and management of such institution, prescribing the method and terms of admission thereto, and defining and regulating the duties and powers of all officers and servants of such institution, and the salaries (if any) of such officers and servants, and shall immediately thereafter submit such by-laws or regulations to the Lieutenant-Governor in Council for approval, and no such by-laws or regulations shall have force or effect until the same, upon report of said Inspector, shall be so approved of.[83]

This strong assertion of the province's right to exercise a decisive measure of control over internal policies of the private institutions remained undiminished throughout the period under review here. If anything, the versions of the act which appear on the revised statutes of 1877 and 1887 express this control with even greater vigour. They also retained, as a further indication of the serious view the province took of the responsibility of the institutions to provide full and honest reports, the penalty of $1,000 which could be imposed on anyone making a false return under the Act.[84]

In its revised as in its original version, however, the act continued to make the curious distinction between institutions in schedules A and B on the one hand, and those in C on the other. The failure to assert the same measure of control over institutions for children and unmarried mothers as that applying to hospitals and houses of refuge appears both as an oddity and a weakness in the act.

There were no amendments to the act during the period save those made in the decennial revisions of the statutes, and with a single exception these changes were largely by way of clarification or the removal of aspects of the act of 1874 which derived from it being a new act. The exception was the addition of a section taken from an old statute[85] dealing with hospitals. It provided that no public grant be paid to a hospital which admitted smallpox patients unless it had a totally separate ward for such patients.

Generally speaking, the Charity Aid Act encouraged the expansion of existing private institutions and the development of new ones, and assisted in the establishment and maintenance of good standards. There is, of course, no way of knowing how many institutions would have developed or what their standards would have been had the Charity Aid Act not been passed, but the actual increases, over a period of twenty years, as shown in Table IV, are impressive. While the number of institutions under schedule C doubled, those under schedule A more than tripled, and there was an eightfold increase of

83*Ibid.*
84*Ibid.*   85Canada, *Statutes,* 1861, c. 24.

TABLE IV

DATA ON INSTITUTIONS UNDER THE CHARITY AID ACT, 1874 AND 1893

Type	Number	Persons receiving care	Total days care	Total expenditure (in dollars)	Total grants payable* (in dollars)
Hospitals					
1874	10	3,466	127,160	62,337	32,684
1893	32	12,392	389,700	297,660	107,312
Refuges					
1874	4	793	100,445	23,799	7,072
1893	32†	3,483	639,206	179,960	53,548
Orphanages					
1874	14‡	1,846	367,280	50,200§	7,346
1893	28‡	4,125	694,089	112,846	14,925

SOURCE: Ontario, *Sessional Papers*, 1874 (vol. VII), no. 2; 1894, nos. 28, 29.
*Amounts shown are those payable in the next fiscal year on the basis of service given and revenues received, other than from the province, in the years indicated.
†Includes six institutions for incurables or convalescents.
‡Includes two homes for unmarried mothers.
§Expenditure data not available; the figure shown is total revenue.

TABLE V

PROVINCIAL GRANTS AS A PERCENTAGE
OF THE COMBINED EXPENDITURES OF
THE INSTITUTIONS, BY TYPES,
1874 AND 1893

Type of institution	1874	1893
Hospitals	52.4	36.1
Refuges	29.7	29.8
Orphanages	14.6	13.2

SOURCE: Ontario, *Sessional Papers*, 1874 (vol. VII), no. 2; 1894, nos. 28, 29.

the houses of refuge and institutions associated with them.[86] There were roughly proportionate increases in the numbers of persons served and in the extent of the provincial grants.

There can be little doubt of the importance to the private institutions of the financial assistance provided by the province, although its significance for their support varied widely as between institutions. Table V provides an indication of the total effect of the provincial grants and shows that each of the three classes of institutions was materially helped, with the hospitals benefiting most, and the

[86]See chapter 3 concerning the addition of convalescent hospitals and hospitals for incurables to schedule B but at a higher rate of fifteen cents per day—a rate not authorized by the legislation.

orphanages (together with institutions for unmarried mothers which were grouped with them) receiving decidedly less favourable treatment than the other two types of institutions.

The administration of the grants went through a somewhat critical period in the early years after the passage of the Charity Aid Act because of the opposition to reduced aid by the institutions unfavourably affected by the grant formula. The old rate was therefore continued for an interim period. The combined effect of this failure to enforce rigorously the financial terms of the act and the rapid inclusion of new institutions within its schedules was, of course, an increase in provincial expenditure. The resultant criticism was met by Langmuir's spirited assertion of what neither he nor those who have come after him have been able to prove conclusively, namely, the nature and extent of the contribution to human well-being that is made by social welfare institutions or programmes:

While the operations of the "Charities Aid Act" has removed many anomalies in the distribution of aid to the local charities of the Province, it has to some extent increased the amount of the appropriation that it is necessary to ask from Parliament on that account. It cannot, however, be urged that a small additional sum expended in the relief of the sick or destitute, or in the reclamation of vagrant children, who would doubtless otherwise add to the criminal population of the country, is either ill-bestowed or extravagant. Were complete statistics published of the good work annually accomplished by the local charitable institutions of Ontario, the history would surprise the friends and confound the enemies of those institutions.[87]

In assisting the "good work" of the institutions, the inspectors achieved varying degrees of success. In general, they were successful in improving the statistical and accounting procedures of the institutions and in working for safe and comfortable buildings, adequate diets, and good sanitation. They were less successful in promoting or stimulating programmes to enrich the quality of life within the institutions' walls. Throughout the period, however, the Charity Aid Act was administered by the provincial officials in such a way as to encourage the humane and considerate treatment of the thousands of persons annually receiving care in the participating institutions.

[87]Ontario, *Sessional Papers*, 1877, no. 2, p. 4.

3

The Care of the Poor

Rejection of the English Poor Law

THE FIRST STATUTE adopted by the Legislature of Upper Canada in its first session was an act to introduce the main body of English civil law into the new province. The act, however, did not extend to one area which had an important bearing on social welfare: the final clauses stated "that nothing in this Act . . . shall . . . introduce any of the laws of England respecting the maintenance of the poor. . . ."[1] Neither John Graves Simcoe, the first lieutenant-governor of the province, nor William Osgood, his attorney-general and the probable author of the statute,[2] appear to have left any account of their reasons for excluding so important an English institution as the poor law. On Simcoe's part, the exclusion is surprising because of his insistence that he had a mission "to render the Province as nearly as may be a perfect Image and Transcript of the British Government and Constitution."[3] Furthermore, the English poor law had been adopted in most of the

[1]Upper Canada, *Statutes*, 1792, c. 1.
[2]W. R. Riddell, *The Life of John Graves Simcoe, 1792–96* (Toronto, 1926), p. 176.
[3]E. A. Cruikshank, *The Correspondence of Lieutenant-Governor John Graves Simcoe, with Allied Documents Relating to His Administration of the Government of Upper Canada* (Toronto, 1929), vol. IV, p. 115. This initial enthusiasm of Simcoe for British, or rather English, institutions was commented on by Simcoe's Canadian contemporary Richard Cartwright who referred to him as thinking that "every existing regulation in England would be proper here" (*ibid.*, vol. I, p. 57). S. R. Mealing ("The Enthusiasms of John Graves Simcoe," *Canadian Historical Association, Annual Report, 1958* (Ottawa, 1959), p. 60), however, suggests that Simcoe preached the following of English models but did not practise it.

other British colonies in North America, including both those that had rebelled and those that had remained loyal. There was, moreover, an expectation on the part of at least some of the early settlers in what was to become Upper Canada that a poor law would be enacted as soon as a constitution for the area was framed and in force. For example, the magistrates who wrote the Cataraqui Memorial, which was forwarded to the Governor in Quebec in 1786, indicated their concern about measures for the poor, commenting that "humanity will not allow us to omit mentioning the necessity of appointing Overseers of the Poor, or the making of some kind of provision for Persons of that description, who, from Age or Accident, may be rendered helpless."[4]

In default of clear evidence on why the kind of action recommended by the magistrates was not taken, two or three possible explanations suggest themselves. One is that Simcoe, who in the early part of his régime entertained wildly idealistic expectations about Upper Canada, may have felt that poverty would not be a problem in the new province or, at any rate, not a problem amenable to the types of measures taken to deal with it in England. Another possibility is that Simcoe may have seen the introduction of a poor law, involving the appointment, or perhaps the election, of overseers of the poor, as strengthening local as opposed to centralized government and, therefore, as containing the seeds of democratic and rebellious action.[5]

Whether Simcoe saw the administration of the poor law in Upper Canada in these terms, he is likely to have been conscious of the practical difficulties of transplanting the English poor law administration, which was based on the English parish and on a society whose members had well-defined social rôles, into a new colony where settlement was just beginning, where the structure of society was inchoate, and which, at the outset at least, manifestly lacked the ability to undertake the responsibilities associated with an English-type poor law. Among such responsibilities would have been that of providing from local sources sufficient funds to maintain any persons who became destitute and who applied for public assistance. The obstacles to the levying and collecting of a poor rate would have been formidable in the extreme. Even if there had been taxable cash

---

[4]Adam Shortt and Arthur G. Doughty, *Documents Relating to the Constitutional History of Canada, 1759–1791* (Ottawa, 1918), p. 943.

[5]Adam Shortt, "Municipal History, 1791–1867," in Adam Shortt and Arthur G. Doughty (eds.), *Canada and Its Provinces*, vol. XVIII (Toronto, 1914), p. 410. Shortt takes the view that "although there proved to be but few points on which Dorchester and Simcoe could agree, they were at one at least in their determination to obstruct and discourage the tendency towards local self-government."

resources on the typical pioneer farm, the settlers were adamantly opposed to direct taxation. When Simcoe resisted the strong desire of the members of the Legislature to secure funds from customs duties for the construction of gaols and court houses in the four initial districts and attempted to convince them "that a County rate was the natural supply for the Discharge of all expenses contracted by the County . . . the answer was that the smallest tax on real property would prevent Emigration."[6] Simcoe tried to present evidence to show that this would not be the result of direct taxation, but, as he noted, "the House of Assembly consisted entirely of Landholders," and "all arguments were useless to persons actuated by their fears." The intensity of the prevailing antipathy towards taxation on property suggests that even if the English poor law had been nominally brought into the province by the act of 1792, it would have remained, for lack of local tax support, a dead letter for an indefinite period.

A further factor affecting Upper Canadian attitudes towards the meeting of material needs in the early years of the colony was the strength of the view that any necessary assistance, not merely for the survival of the population but also for the economic development of the province, should come from the British government. This is not surprising. The province began as a great refugee project for the resettlement of the dispossessed and largely impoverished Loyalists[7] who were provided not only with food and clothing for survival, but with tools, implements, building materials, firearms, livestock, grist mills, and, of course, land. Although the refugee phase of development was largely over by 1792, relief continued to be provided to meet extreme hardship for a number of years. One of the centres of conflict between Simcoe and the Governor-General, Lord Dorchester, was, in fact, Simcoe's authorization of the use of army stores to meet "contingencies" that continued to arise in the province throughout his régime.[8]

The decision to exclude the English poor law in 1792 (whatever the actual basis for it may have been) can be regarded as the deliberate rejection of a method of assisting the poor which could not have worked well in the pioneer conditions of the province. It cannot justifiably be regarded as the outright rejection of the principle of public support for the maintenance of those in acute need. That could

---

[6]Cruikshank, *Simcoe Correspondence*, vol. I, p. 250. The term "emigration" referred to immigration into Upper Canada.

[7]"Nearly all were depending upon the bounty of government." William Canniff, *History of the Province of Ontario* (Toronto, 1872), p. 183.

[8]Cruikshank, *Simcoe Correspondence*, vol. IV, pp. 207, 242, 274. The issue seemed to come to the point of conflict in 1796.

hardly have been conceivable in a colony whose birth and early survival, until well after 1792, were dependent upon extensive measures of public assistance granted by a public body—the only one capable of providing it, the British government. Yet the decision in future years was to lend itself to this false interpretation, for while the memory of the extent of the public aid given to the Loyalist settlers faded and was all but forgotten, the first volume of the provincial statutes stands out as apparent evidence of the decision of the pioneer residents of the new province to renounce public responsibility for the support of the poor. Such an interpretation of the decision is highly questionable; but the practical effect was an absence of public responsibility for the poor for many years after the decision was taken.

The immediate effect of the rejection of the poor law by the Upper Canada Legislature was to shift the responsibility for the poor from the public authority to the individual, the family, and private philanthropy. But this abdication of responsibility could not endure indefinitely: the years from 1792 to 1867 were to see a gradual and piecemeal assumption of public responsibility for those in need, as well as the adoption of various expedients from which was to emerge a sharing of responsibility between public and private bodies that was to become an enduring characteristic of social welfare organization in Ontario. The methods used to meet the needs of the early decades included some sporadic assistance by the British authorities where there were acute emergency situations, such as crop failures or epidemics; similar assistance by the province itself, largely through grants to voluntary associations; the use of gaols as refuges for the poor; provincial support of voluntary institutions when local public action in the institutional field failed to materialize; and the gradual growth of municipal responsibility for assistance to persons in their own homes.

Gaols as Congregate Institutions

The burden fell first upon the gaols, which were the earliest institutions created by the new province.[9] They were destined to be put to a number of uses other than the primary one of detaining persons charged with or convicted of crime. Among those who were soon crowded into them were persons whose only crime was their inability to care for themselves.

This use of the gaols to house those who were in poverty was not,

[9]Upper Canada, *Statutes*, 1792, c. 8. Under this legislation gaols were established in each of the districts into which the province was initially divided.

however, foreign to the prevailing and traditional ideas about the nature of poverty. Poverty was normally associated in the public mind with vagrancy and the wilful refusal to work and to save. The poor, or at any rate the able-bodied poor, were accordingly thought to be in need of correction and discipline which could best be imposed in special houses of correction, but until such institutions could be established there was held to be a case for using the gaols as a substitute. Legislation to this effect was therefore passed in 1810—the act providing that until houses of correction could be erected "in the several districts of this province . . . the common gaol be held and taken to be for certain purposes a house of correction . . . and that all and every idle and disorderly person, or rogues and vagabonds, and incorrigible rogues, or any other person or persons who also may by law be subject to be committed to a house of correction, shall be committed to the said common gaols . . . any law or usage to the contrary in any wise notwithstanding."[10] Similarly, legislation was enacted some twenty years later[11] to give authority for the practice, all too prevalent during the period,[12] of housing the destitute insane in the local gaols.

Early Municipal Programmes

One of the most important means of filling the vacuum created by the initial exclusion of the English poor law was through the evolution of local government and the assignment to the local authorities of responsibilities for the care and maintenance of the poor. This was to be a gradual process, characterized by reluctance on the part of the province to authorize local governments to grant direct or outdoor relief, and hesitation on the part of municipal bodies to take action of any kind on behalf of the poor. Yet, by 1867 very considerable progress had been made and positive measures had largely reversed the negative decision of 1792.

In the early years of the province, limited assistance was given by the courts of quarter sessions to a few persons whose needs demanded attention. Records of the sessions show payments for the care of

[10]*Ibid.*, 1810, c. 5.
[11]*Ibid.*, 1830, c. 20. The preamble of the act noted that several insane persons, destitute of any provision for their maintenance, had been "charitably received into the gaol of the Home District."
[12]William Kilbourn, *William Mackenzie and the Rebellion in Upper Canada* (Toronto, 1956), p. 58. Mackenzie called for an investigation concerning "female lunatics chained together in the filthy cellar of the County jail."

orphan children or the children of persons in gaol, for the care of the destitute ill, the maintenance of unmarried mothers and burial expenses of deceased immigrants.[13]

The increasing problem of destitution in the 1830's, associated mainly with immigration, might have led to an extension of action by local government had it not been for the strength of the movement towards institutional care and away from outdoor relief that was gaining ascendency on both sides of the Atlantic[14] and which won its most notable victory in the new poor law passed in England in 1834. The view, which was to prove illusory, that by the erection of a house of industry or a combined house of industry and farm the poor could be made to support themselves, spread to Upper Canada and became the subject of considerable public discussion in 1836 and 1837. The idea received the support of a group of citizens of Brockville who in 1836 recommended public and voluntary co-operation in building houses of industry throughout the province.[15] The idea was also endorsed by a general meeting held in Toronto in December 1836 to discuss poor relief.[16]

House of Industry Act

As a result of these representations, the Legislature, in 1837, passed an act[17] which seemed about to create a system of local institutions under public auspices. The act authorized the erection and maintenance of houses of industry in each of the districts into which the province was then divided. Action to establish the institution, however, could be taken by the justices of the peace of a district only "after the presentment of three successive grand juries" recommending the move to the general quarter sessions of the district. The justices were then to secure plans, acquire a site, and contract for the erection of a suitable building. The cost was not to exceed £1,000, and construction and maintenance were to be financed by taxation on the

[13]Upper Canada, *Journals*, 1839–40, Appendix, pp. 541, 552, 555; also J. H. Aitchison, "The Development of Local Government in Upper Canada, 1783–1850" (unpublished Ph.D. dissertation, Dept. of Political Economy, University of Toronto, 1954), p. 644.

[14]Upper Canada had been treated during the previous decade to a dramatic and highly publicized attack on England's poor laws by Robert Gourlay whose massive plan for their reform involved, as one stage, a grand system "of immigration from England to Upper Canada." Robert Gourlay, *General Introduction to Statistical Account of Upper Canada Compiled with a View to a Grand System of Emigration in Connection with a Reform of the Poor Laws* (London, 1822).

[15]Aitchison, "Local Government in Upper Canada," p. 649.

[16]*Ibid.*, p. 650.　　　　　　　　　　[17]Upper Canada, *Statutes*, 1836–37, c. 24.

ratable property of the district. On the completion of the institution, the justices were to appoint five inspectors who were to constitute a board of management who would be responsible for appointing a master, mistress, and other staff. The inspectors were to meet as a board at least once a month to formulate the necessary orders and regulations for the operation of the institution.

The types of persons to be accommodated in the house of industry were "all poor and indigent persons who are incapable of supporting themselves; all persons, able of body to work and without any means of maintaining themselves, who refuse to or neglect to do so; all persons living a lewd, dissolute vagrant life or exercising no ordinary calling or lawful business sufficient to procure an honest living; all such as spend their time and property in Public Houses to the neglect of their lawful calling." Persons could be committed to the house of industry and, when committed, they were to be "diligently employed in labour." They could be punished for failure to work or for breaches of the rules established by the board of inspectors. The house of industry was therefore expected to house a congregate population, including those regarded as deserving of sympathy and those for whom a punitive régime was considered appropriate. Thus, as well as being a house of refuge, it was to have something of the character of a house of correction.

The passing of legislation, in this instance, as in many others in the social welfare history of Ontario, did not produce the intended effect. The act, indeed, was never implemented. In part, this was because its enactment occurred in the year of the rebellion. It was attacked by the Reformers as a Tory measure and one which would prove to be permanently costly. It would, moreover, serve not merely to pander to the idle and profligate then in the province, but to encourage an influx of "thousands of miserable people . . . from the old country."[18] Because of the widespread opposition, no three successive grand juries in any district recommended establishment of a house of industry during the pre-Union period. When popular support developed in some districts in the Union period, changes in the form of municipal government put the legal means of applying the legislation in question.[19] None the less, the act of 1837 was of importance both for the influence it was to have on later legislation and as a declaration of public responsibility for relieving the poor.

[18]Brockville Recorder, April 13, 1837, quoted in Aitchison, "Local Government in Upper Canada," p. 651.
[19]Aitchison, "Local Government in Upper Canada," p. 653.

The failure of local governments to implement the act resulted in some action on the part of voluntary groups in the centres most affected. A committee appointed by the general meeting on poor relief held in Toronto in 1836, for example, took the initiative in establishing a house of industry and refuge through voluntary subscriptions. The city assisted by providing a grant as well as the premises for the institution.[20] The province, having endorsed the principle of houses of industry, could not deny the request of the new institution for grants, and these were paid in varying amounts on an annual basis from 1839.[21] The court of quarter sessions for the Home District, however, upon which responsibility for establishing a house of refuge would have fallen had the necessary preliminary steps been taken, made no contribution to the institution other than to bear the expense of bastard children born in it.[22]

The House of Industry in Toronto, from the outset, provided outdoor as well as institutional care, thus drawing attention to the necessity of non-institutional relief. It was this form of assistance which, during the Union period, was to be developed at the municipal level, though always on a limited scale and unevenly as between different municipalities. Throughout both the pre-Union and Union periods the institutional emphasis remained strong.

Other Provisions for Institutional Care

Evidences of the institutional emphasis in the care of the poor are also to be found in the early acts of incorporation of the towns and cities of the province. The council of the city of Toronto under its Act of Incorporation of 1834, for example, was given authority to establish and maintain alms-houses or other places for the relief of the poor.[23] This appears to have been the first reference to provision for the poor in legislation defining municipal responsibilities and the only one to be found in provincial statutes in the pre-Union period. Hamilton was the first city to be incorporated in the Union period, and we find the responsibilities of its council defined in precisely the terms used in relation to Toronto fourteen years earlier. Both of these acts of civic incorporation gave the city council authority to set up and provide for a "work house, gaol, Bridewell or House of Cor-

[20]*Ibid.*, p. 657.
[21]Upper Canada, *Statutes*, 1839, c. 63. Until well into the Union period, grants were made through separate acts each year.
[22]Aitchison, "Local Government in Upper Canada," p. 657.
[23]Upper Canada, *Statutes*, 1834, c. 23.

rection"[24] and empowered the mayor to arrest rogues, vagabonds, drunkards, and disorderly persons and have them committed to the institution for a period of a month.

In 1846, Toronto's Act of Incorporation was amended to permit the city to establish an industrial farm which was to serve the same general purpose of control, correction, restraint, and punishment that had been envisaged for the work-houses referred to in the earlier legislation.

During the same period, provincial acts incorporating towns also limited the provision for the poor to institutional care, and again the belief that poverty could be dealt with through corrective or disciplinary measures was evident. An act respecting the town of Cornwall, for example, gave the council power to establish and support a house of industry, and enforce labour and discipline therein.[25]

Municipal Poor Relief

Although the District Councils Act of 1841, which marked the first step in the fundamental reconstruction of local government in Upper Canada, had no immediate effect on social welfare, an amendment to the act in 1846[26] became the first important poor relief measure not limited solely to institutional care. It provided that, where application was made by a majority of those qualified to vote at the election of township officers in any township in a district, the township could adopt a by-law raising funds from the taxable property of the township "for the purpose of affording relief to indigent, sick or infirm persons." Unlike the act of 1837 and the later provisions in municipal legislation which gave towns and cities the right to establish institutions for the poor, the amendment of 1846 did not become a dead letter. Professor Aitchison, noting that the measure "was contrary to the prevailing theory of poor relief which had been imported from England and which held that the most economical manner of dealing with the poor was to put them in a house of industry,"[27] commented that it is "astonishing" how often the power of levying a tax for the poor was invoked.[28] Although the measure fell far short of constituting

---

[24]Canada, *Statutes*, 1846, c. 73. In the Toronto act of 1834, the term "work house" was not used in the listing, but appears later in the legislation as the general term for all such institutions.
[25]*Ibid.*, c. 72.
[26]*Ibid.*, c. 40.
[27]Aitchison, "Local Government in Upper Canada," p. 656.
[28]*Ibid.*, p. 659.

a universal provision for the poor, its passage and its implementation represent a clear indication that by the mid-1840's the province was beginning to concede the necessity of public support for those in need.

The township by-laws adopted under the amendment of 1846 usually provided for raising a specified sum of money, although a general rate was levied at least once. The funds obtained were generally handled by the township wardens, but there were instances of administration by designated commissioners or the councillors resident in the district, or by township boards set up by district councils to manage various matters assigned to the township. The right of townships to tax themselves for the support of their poor seems to have been placed in some question in 1849[29] and not restored to them unequivocally until 1853, when an amendment to the basic municipal act then in force gave the township the authority, where the majority of freeholders and householders requested it, to levy, collect, and appropriate "such moneys as may be considered necessary for the support of any indigent, infirm or helpless persons resident in such townships."[30]

The Municipal Corporations Act of 1849[31] did not advance, and in the case of the townships may even have restricted, existing municipal powers relating to the care of the poor. It served, however, to create the basis on which future progress in this, as in many other areas, could be made. Its sections dealing with the township[32] and incorporated villages made no reference to poor relief, although towns and cities were assigned the powers relating to alms-houses, houses of refuge or industry, work-houses, and industrial farms that had been granted to them in their individual acts of incorporation. Furthermore, in its creation of the county as the upper level of the new two-tier system, this act provided a unit of municipal government capable of assuming social welfare responsibilities that could not, in general, be carried effectively by the individual towns, incorporated villages, and townships. The county, rather than the district, became responsible for the establishment and maintenance of gaols, and the care of the poor was to be accomplished through the establishment and main-

[29]Canada, *Statutes*, 1849, c. 80, 81.

[30]*Ibid.*, 1852–53, c. 181.

[31]*Ibid.*, 1849, c. 81. For structure of municipal government provided by this act, see page 29.

[32]Aitchison, "Local Government in Upper Canada," p. 807, takes the view that while "townships and villages were given no specific powers to relieve the poor . . . there was nothing to prevent them from spending money on poor relief or even to levy a special rate for the purpose." The fact that specific amendments granting powers to assist the poor were passed in later years does not lend support to this view.

tenance of a county house of industry, essentially as provided under the terms of the House of Industry Act of 1837.

Between 1849 and Confederation, as the machinery of municipal government became more effective in its operation, there were a number of amendments affecting poor relief. As noted above, an amendment to the Municipal Corporations Act in 1853[33] affirmed a township's authority to pass a poor relief by-law, although the levying of the tax was contingent upon agreement by a majority of the taxpayers. A revised act in 1858[34] dropped the latter proviso, and a further revision of the act in 1866[35] made it possible for funds for the support of the poor to be appropriated from the general revenue of the municipality. The revision of the act undertaken in 1858, and better known in a somewhat revised form in the consolidated statutes of 1859,[36] at last gave cities and towns the authority to grant "out of door" relief to the resident poor and also allowed them to aid charitable institutions.

The Municipal Institutions Act of 1866 is notable for its provisions concerning the county houses of industry or refuge. The act made it mandatory for all counties with a population of over 20,000 inhabitants to establish an institution within two years. Where the population of a county was below that figure, it was to combine with contiguous counties in the erection and operation of a house of refuge until such time as its population reached the number required for the independent establishment of an institution. This mandatory provision, which was destined to be removed shortly after Confederation, represented the closest point to the endorsement of the principle of public responsibility in meeting the needs of the poor that the province was to reach at any time during the period under review.

It will be apparent that on the eve of Confederation the vacuum created in 1792 by the rejection of the English poor law had been largely filled. Counties were under instruction to establish houses of refuge and cities and towns were empowered to do so. These three types of municipal governments could also make grants to charitable institutions. They could, moreover, grant direct or outdoor relief, a power which had earlier been extended to townships. The stage seemed to be set for the rapid expansion of public provisions for the care of the poor in the post-Confederation period.

[33]Canada, *Statutes*, 1852–53, c. 181.
[34]*Ibid.*, 1858, c. 99.
[35]*Ibid.*, 1866, c. 51, s. 279.
[36]Canada, *Consolidated Statutes of Upper Canada*, 1859, c. 54.

Provincial Aid to Private Charity

In the absence of public provisions for the care of the poor through much of the pre-Confederation period, the conscience of the Upper Canadians found expression in various private charitable ventures. Relief of need was undertaken by religious, fraternal, and patriotic organizations, and from the 1820's by a few organizations whose sole purpose was to meet the needs of the poor. It was through these organizations that demands upon the government for public aid for the poor began to be channelled. The demands took the form of insistent pleas for grants to assist the work of various organizations. Apart from special relief measures arising out of the War of 1812, however, this form of public aid did not appear until around 1830. In that year, a sum of one hundred pounds sterling was granted to the Female Benevolent Society of Kingston, an agency which had been formed in 1821 for the relief of the destitute sick and for nine years had been "wholly supported by the contributions of benevolent individuals."[37] The society again petitioned successfully for a grant in 1834 because of "the great and numerous losses incurred by fire in the Town of Kingston" and because "the voluntary contributions of individuals were nearly exhausted."

If a special claim could be made on public funds to deal with the results of a disaster such as a fire, a strong case could also be made by communities bearing the brunt of the care of newly arrived immigrants. Thus, the citizens of Prescott, which was then an important port of entry, could argue that, because of the sickly and destitute state in which immigrants found themselves on arrival, "some relief should be afforded to persons of this description over and above what may arise from the Christian feelings and benevolence of the people residing at that place of general disembarkation."[38] Their petition resulted in a provincial grant of £250 in 1832 and again in 1833.[39]

Provincial grants to relieve distress in Toronto began in 1837[40] when a sum of £250 was made available for distribution by the Receiver-General without designation of the organization through which it was to be administered. This practice was followed the next year when the amount was £350 which was granted because, in the words of the act's preamble, "the high price of provisions and the increased number of paupers arising from various causes has rendered the efforts of private charity insufficient for the relief of the sick and destitute

[37]Upper Canada, *Statutes*, 1830, c. 32.
[38]*Ibid.*, 1832, c. 34.
[39]*Ibid.*, 1833, c. 52.   [40]*Ibid.*, 1836–37, c. 104.

poor in the City of Toronto."[41] From 1839[42] grants were made directly to the privately established House of Industry in the city.

Grants to hospitals, which began in 1830, are also to be regarded largely—and in the first few years perhaps exclusively—as assistance to the indigent.[43] The grounds on which the first grant was made to the York Hospital provide evidence of this conception of the rôle of the hospital: its "useful and beneficial operation" was described in terms of the numbers of "sick, destitute, and unfortunate subjects, and emigrants" who had received "medical and surgical assistance" in its wards.[44] The maintenance grant to the Toronto hospital was followed two years later by a capital grant of £3,000 to a hospital being built in Kingston, and once again reference was to provision "for the destitute sick within this Province."[45] Further grants to these two hospitals were made prior to the Union of the two Canadas in 1841 and represented the principal provincial expenditures in the fields of health and welfare during this period.

Each grant made to a hospital or charitable institution before the Union was the subject of a separate act of the Legislature. In the Union period, this practice was abandoned and grants were made from general funds, usually for predictable amounts given on a regular annual basis. During this twenty-six-year period there was a notable increase in the number of voluntary institutions assisted. By 1866, as shown in Table II, orphanages, maternity homes, hospitals, and houses of refuge were included. Although all of these types of institutions were to a greater or lesser extent designed to deal with poverty either as the principal or as an associated problem, the houses of refuge were the most closely identified with the poor. Three such institutions in Canada West were in receipt of public grants during the final year of the Union period.

Other Provisions to Meet Need

In view of the very limited means possessed by most of those who settled in Upper Canada, it is remarkable how restricted was the

[41]Ibid., 1837–38, c. 55.
[42]Ibid., 1839, c. 63, and 1840, c. 67.
[43]Provision for patients who paid ward rates and for private patients developed at different times, and as late as 1868 the question of whether patients able to pay for their care should be provided accommodation in the hospitals was a matter for discussion; see the inquiry concerning the Toronto General Hospital, Ontario, Journals, 1867–68, pp. 177–78.
[44]Upper Canada, Statutes, 1830, c. 31.
[45]Ibid., 1832, c. 28.

extent of public aid to arriving immigrants. Public measures, however, were taken when the problems presented by the immigrants were extreme or when they seemed to endanger the colony. The arrival of sick immigrants, for example, was found to pose the threat of disease of epidemic proportions and led to the adoption of quarantine procedures and provisions for medical care to sick immigrants. Funds to defray the costs of such care and to assist indigent immigrants to reach their place of destination were raised through a rate payable by shipping companies for all immigrants brought into the country.[46] Following the arrival of thousands of ill and impoverished immigrants in 1847, the shipping companies were also required to give bond with sureties to meet the costs incurred in the event that immigrants brought in by the companies became public charges within a year.[47] In 1851 the immigration legislation was amended to permit payment of money from the fund collected from the shipping companies to any charitable institutions affording relief to sick or destitute immigrants.[48] Under this measure some £900 were distributed to four institutions in Upper Canada in 1852.[49] The public accounts for that year show how the penalties under the legislation were imposed on the shipping companies; for example, an item of £12/3/4 was paid by the Captain of the *Janet* as "commutation money on account of D. M'Cavanagh, an Insane Passenger."[50]

The principal forms of aid to needy immigrants, however, were granted upon their arrival and shortly thereafter by immigration agents located at the major centres. The assistance consisted primarily of passage money, with small amounts given for "provisions" and medical aid. In 1860 the agent at Toronto, in addition to providing bread and temporary shelter in the immigrant sheds, helped some 970 with passage money and food, although the average cost of this relief was only 93 cents. The agent at Ottawa in the same year granted assistance to 113 persons at an average cost of $2.24.[51] In addition to furnishing relief when it proved necessary, the immigration agents provided many other services to the new arrivals. They offered information on employment and settlement prospects, helped the newcomers to find relatives and friends, and took what measures they could to prevent their exploitation. Accounts of the work of the

[46]Canada, *Statutes*, 1841, c. 13.
[47]*Ibid.*, 1848, c. 1, and 1849, c. 6.
[48]*Ibid.*, 1851, c. 78.
[49]Canada, *Journals*, 1852–53, Appendix B.
[50]*Ibid.*
[51]Canada, *Sessional Papers*, 1861, no. 14, n.p.

immigration agents suggest that within the limits of their time and resources they served in a most praiseworthy manner.[52]

A type of agricultural aid designed to prevent poverty through assisting farmers to continue in production was provided by legislation in Upper Canada during certain years when crops were poor in parts of the province.[53] The legislation authorized the counties to raise money and lend it to the townships in which the need existed. The townships could, in turn, either lend the money to needy farmers for the purchase of seed, or purchase the seed and make the loans in the form of seed grain. Provision was made for the enforcement of repayment. The terms of the legislation indicate that although the programme served to alleviate a crucial form of rural need—that of ability to resume production—it is more aptly described as a farm loan scheme than as agricultural relief.

POST-CONFEDERATION PERIOD, 1867–1893

The Legislative Amendments of 1867–68

Because the pre-Confederation period ended with a legislative assertion of the principle of public responsibility for the care of the poor, the province of Ontario might have been expected in the new era to extend the concept even further, clarifying municipal responsibilities and taking the additional step of ensuring that the municipalities had the necessary financial resources to support adequate measures to meet the needs of the poor without prejudice to their other responsibilities.

The province did, in fact, proceed one pace in this direction when, in the act of 1867–68 which amended the Municipal Institutions Act of 1866, it completed the work of the pre-Confederation legislation by giving to an incorporated village council the same authority to provide for the resident poor as it had conferred earlier upon a township council; that is, the village could raise money for poor relief by a special tax rate or through appropriations from its general funds.[54]

In the amending act, however, the mandatory provision of the legislation of 1866 respecting houses of industry and refuge was

[52]Frances Morehouse, "Canadian Migration in the Forties," *Canadian Historical Review*, Dec. 1928, p. 315.
[53]Canada, *Statutes*, 1859, c. 7; 1863 (1st sess.), c. 1; 1865 (1st sess.), c. 24.
[54]Ontario, *Statutes*, 1867–68, c. 30.

removed. Whereas the act of 1866 had required the establishment of such institutions within two years, the new amendment, in a curious provision, made their establishment permissible within four years. The time limit could have little meaning divorced from a mandatory requirement, and the promise of a rapid development of county homes died with this amendment. Over twenty years were to pass before the province would put effective weight behind the establishment of municipal institutions for those in need.

The Charity Aid Act

With the act of 1867–68, the province turned its attention from the question of direct public responsibility for the poor to other pressing social welfare matters, including the development of correctional establishments, hospitals, and institutions for the mentally ill, the mentally retarded, the deaf and the blind. The next significant move towards improved provision for the poor was to come through provincial support and supervision of private care of the poor—action taken through the medium of the Charity Aid Act of 1874, for which Langmuir was largely responsible.

In his initial review of private charitable institutions being aided by the provinces, Langmuir unaccountably dealt with only two houses of industry, the House of Industry, Toronto, and the House of Industry, Kingston, even though the House of Providence, Toronto, and the House of Refuge, Hamilton, had previously received provincial grants. Of some aspects of the two institutions that he did study, Langmuir made little attempt to conceal his disapproval. To begin with, he disapproved of the name "House of Industry" because there was, he pointed out, no industry of any description except ordinary housework carried on in either.[55] They were "in reality Poor-houses and nothing but that." Having reached this conclusion, Langmuir asked why these institutions were singled out for special attention, and, of much more significance, why the problem of indigent care was not being dealt with as a public responsibility to be assumed by the municipality.

It becomes the more necessary to make this enquiry since both the law and the genius of our Municipal Institutions require that every Municipality shall take care of its own poor; and the enactment of the statute of 1868 by the Ontario Legislature in respect to poor houses[56] confirms this well-

[55]Ontario, *Sessional Papers*, 1873, no. 2, pp. 69–70.
[56]This would seem to suggest that there was a special statute on the matter; actually there was only the amending act referred to above (Ontario, *Statutes*, 1867–68, c. 30).

understood wish of the people. And it is to be regretted that so wholesome and necessary a law should through the operations of the *permissive* in place of a *compulsory* clause remain practically inoperative upon the Statute Book.[57]

Langmuir was, it appears, asserting the case for public responsibility more strongly than the facts of the case justified. The law did not actually require the municipalities to care for their poor; it merely permitted them to do so. Nor was the wish of the people as clear and insistent that local governments should establish poor houses, as he suggested; had it been so, there would have been more than one such institution established between Confederation and 1872. What can be said for Langmuir's comment, however, is that it pointed, at least by implication, to the problem which would arise if the care of the poor under private auspices was subsidized by a provincial grant while no similar provision was made for institutions under public, that is, municipal auspices.

Langmuir proceeded to argue that if poor-houses were established in various parts of the province in conformity with the spirit of the statute[58] the problem of caring for the poor would be largely, though not wholly, met in the locality in which it presented itself, and the tendency of the poor to wander to the cities would be reduced. This basic though not fully formulated principle was behind Langmuir's first recommendation on the matter to the government. He would have excluded from the basis of provincial payment to the private institutions those persons in the institution who were residents of the municipalities and thus, as he saw it, the responsibility of the local authorities. Having thus removed from his proposed formula of provincial aid those whom he regarded as municipal charges, he argued further that the grants could legitimately be based on the number of immigrants and foreigners cared for by the institutions. He admitted another consideration: that in spite of attempts to deal with indigency on a local basis "pauperism has a tendency to centralize itself, and . . . cities and towns are apt to be burdened with the support of a greater number of paupers than legitimately belong to them."[59]

As an additional prerequisite of provincial support, he placed considerable emphasis upon the principle of strong local support of the institution. He was highly critical of the House of Industry, Kingston, which had been subsisting almost wholly upon its provincial grant. Of its total revenue of $2,669 in 1871, $2,400 was from the

[57]Ontario, *Sessional Papers*, 1872–73, no. 2, p. 70.
[58]*Ibid.*   [59]*Ibid.*

province. Not only was the province, in this case, providing the major share of the institution's revenue; it was doing so quite unconditionally, with no control or participation in its management.

With these several considerations in mind, Langmuir formulated his first and second recommendations:

1st. That the sum at present appropriated by the Legislature, with whatever additions may hereafter be made to it in aid of poor-houses, shall be distributed amongst all the poor houses in the cities of the Province, in proportion to the number of immigrants and foreigners admitted into the house, and the population of each city. Such annual Government grant not to exceed in amount one-third of the sum received the preceding year from Municipal grants, private subscriptions and all other sources.

2nd. The Government to appoint not less than three of the local Directors as Managers of every poor-house in receipt of such Government aid. The Government to approve of the buildings and site used for the purposes of the poor-house, as well as the by-laws and regulations framed by the Directors for its Government, and the general management of its affairs.[60]

In his next report, that for 1873, Langmuir presented statistics on the four poor-houses then receiving provincial support (Table VI). He also indicated that there were wide variations in the extent to which

TABLE VI

PROVINCIAL GRANTS TO THE HOUSES OF REFUGE, 1872

Institution	Provincial grant (in dollars)	Collective days' stay	Grant per inmate day (in cents)
House of Industry, Toronto	2,900	27,863	$10\frac{1}{2}$
House of Providence, Toronto	1,000	45,722	$2\frac{1}{5}$
House of Industry, Kingston	2,400	10,268	$23\frac{1}{3}$
House of Refuge, Hamilton	720	12,673	$5\frac{3}{4}$

SOURCE: Ontario, *Sessional Papers*, 1874 (vol. VI), no. 2, p. 133.

the provincial grant met the institutions' maintenance costs. As a solution to the problems represented by these differences, Langmuir re-stated part of his formula of the previous year. He abandoned, however, the attempt to restrict the basis to one involving support of immigrants, foreigners, and the wandering poor. Still recommending the appointment by the province of three or more members of the boards of management of the poor-houses, he amended his central proposal to the suggestion that the institution "be entitled to receive aid from the Government in proportion to the number of poor persons they receive and support."[61]

60*Ibid.*, p. 71.   61*Ibid.*, 1874 (vol. VI), no. 2, p. 134.

When finally passed in 1874, the Charity Aid Act[62] adopted as the principal basis of payment the number of indigent persons cared for in the institution in the preceding calendar year. An unconditional five cents "for each day's actual lodgment and maintenance"[63] constituted the major payment, with up to a further two cents a day per inmate. This amount was payable depending on the funds received by the institution from sources other than the provincial government. The full two cents per day per inmate were payable when one-quarter of the revenue received by the institution from sources other than the province exceeded the aggregate amount computed on the two-cent basis. When the non-provincial revenue was less than this aggregate amount, the province paid the equivalent of one-quarter of the non-provincial revenue actually received. It was rare for an institution to fail to qualify for the full two-cent supplement. The inducement which the supplement offered may have discouraged the continuation of situations such as that discovered by Langmuir in relation to the House of Industry, Kingston, in 1872, although that institution twice failed to qualify for the full amount.

Langmuir expressed his approval of the act's affirmation of the principle of local support as a prerequisite to full support:

Fault cannot be found with the principle that has been adopted by Government in apportioning aid to these local institutions. For it will not be denied that if Poor Houses and local charities are to be assisted at all by the Government, the extent of such aid must be proportionate with the work they perform. And, unless we desire to see local Poor Houses *mainly* supported by Government but *entirely* controlled by municipalities or private boards, the principle that further Government aid to such establishments should depend upon the amount they obtain from the general public, cannot be yielded.[64]

The act did not incorporate Langmuir's recommendation for provincial appointment of a number of the members of the boards of management. It did, however, give the inspector much stronger powers of supervision than those conferred by the act establishing the office of inspector.[65] In this way, the interest and responsibility of the province was given recognition.

If the financial terms of the Charity Aid Act had immediately been applied to the institutions without regard to consequence, the effect

---

[62]Ontario, *Statutes*, 1874 (1st sess.), c. 33.
[63]*Ibid.*
[64]Ontario, *Sessional Papers*, 1874 (vol. VII), no. 2, p. 122.
[65]Ontario, *Statutes*, 1867–68, c. 7.

would have been to cut the grant to the House of Industry in Kingston to a third of the amount paid prior to the passage of the act. The grant to the House of Industry, Toronto, would also have been reduced by about $1,000 from the figure of $2,900 at which it stood in 1874. Not until 1880, however, were the financial provisions of the act rigorously carried out in relation to the first four institutions, although from 1877 the grant to the Kingston House of Industry was reduced from $2,400 to $2,200. The other two institutions gained under the terms of the act, the House of Refuge in Hamilton receiving $1,154 in 1875 compared with $720 in 1874. The House of Providence, Toronto, profited most, its grant rising from $1,000 in 1874 to $3,299 in the following year. By 1880, its population entitled it to $4,618.

Despite the mixed financial effect on the institutions previously receiving provincial grants, the Charity Aid Act was a boon to institutions which had not, up to 1874, received provincial aid. Moreover, the assistance it made available was undoubtedly a factor in the establishment of new institutions. By 1893, the number of institutions classed as houses of refuge had risen from the initial four to thirty-three,[66] an eightfold increase. The remarkable rate of expansion is shown in Table VII, and the continuous growth of the service the refuges provided is indicated in Table VIII. Table IX suggests the financial effect of the act on the various institutions coming under schedule B in 1893. By this time, the grant represented as much as 53 per cent of the annual expenditure of St. Peter's Home, Hamilton, and 45 per cent in the case of St. Charles Hospice, Ottawa, whereas, at the other extreme, it amounted to less than 10 per cent of the expenditures of the Roman Catholic Refuge, London, and the Old Ladies Home, Galt. It constituted between 30 and 39 per cent of expenditures in nine of the thirty-one institutions for which expenditure figures are presented, between 20 and 29 per cent in an additional eleven, and between 10 and 19 per cent in the remaining seven.

The reports of the inspector indicate that there were wide differences in the organization, programme, and quality of care of the various institutions coming under the terms of the act. The institutions with the most marked differences in programme were the homes for incurables and the convalescent homes. The Home for Incurables, Toronto, was admitted in 1876 under schedule B on the same basis as other institutions and received the seven-cent grant until 1882. In that

[66]This number includes the incurable ward of the House of Providence, Toronto, and a number of refuges which were administratively associated with orphanages or other types of institutions.

TABLE VII

NUMBER OF INSTITUTIONS COMING UNDER
SCHEDULE B OF THE CHARITY AID ACT
FOR THE FIRST TIME*

Year	Number of institutions
1874	4
1876	4
1877	3
1878	1
1879	2
1880	1
1883	1
1884	4
1886	1
1888	5
1891	6
1892	1

SOURCE: Ontario, *Reports of the Inspector of Prisons, Asylums and Public Charities,* 1875–94.
*The figures shown do not necessarily indicate the years in which new houses of refuge were established. Some were refuge branches of institutions already established, while others did not apply immediately for grants under the act.

TABLE VIII

RESIDENTS OF INSTITUTIONS RECEIVING GRANTS UNDER
SCHEDULE B OF THE CHARITY AID ACT, 1874–1893

Year	Inmates on September 30	Inmates during year	Aggregate days care
1874	272	793	101,024
1875	292	939	109,956
1876	398	1,114	149,160
1877	511	1,313	185,314
1878	579	1,300	213,196
1879	613	1,351	234,642
1880	686	1,468	259,028
1881	717	1,551	273,256
1882	756	1,572	281,888
1883	817	1,641	309,375
1884	888	1,952	339,665
1885	978	1,857	362,167
1886	1,034	2,016	388,530
1887	1,062	2,026	399,290
1888	1,196	2,362	433,379
1889	1,260	2,585	477,845
1890	1,339	2,728	494,394
1891	1,349	3,086	556,396
1892	1,463	3,252	598,017
1893	1,706	3,483	639,206

SOURCE: Ontario, *Reports of the Inspector of Prisons, Asylums and Public Charities,* 1875–94.

TABLE IX

INSTITUTIONS RECEIVING A PROVINCIAL GRANT UNDER SCHEDULE B OF THE
CHARITY AID ACT IN 1893

Institution	Location	Expenditures (in dollars)	Provincial grant Total (in dollars)	Percentage of Expenditure
House of Industry	Toronto	19,318	2,604	13.5
House of Providence	Toronto	26,267	4,436	16.9
House of Providence incurable ward*	Toronto	†	8,729	—
Home for Incurables*	Toronto	17,635	5,979	33.9
Aged Women's Home	Toronto	‡	493	—
St. John's Hospital*	Toronto	7,345	1,127	15.3
Convalescent Home*	Toronto	3,764	1,002	26.6
Church Home	Toronto	1,375	329	23.9
House of Refuge	Hamilton	6,729	2,196	32.6
Home for Aged Women	Hamilton	2,076§	577	27.8
St. Peter's Home*	Hamilton	2,168	1,153	53.2
House of Industry	Kingston	3,525	1,363	38.7
House of Providence	Kingston	11,063	3,452	31.2
Roman Catholic House of Refuge	London	16,344	1,599	9.8
Aged People's Home‖	London	4,583	1,206	26.3
Convalescent Home*	London	791	104	13.1
St. Patrick's Refuge	Ottawa	9,880	3,329	33.7
St. Charles' Hospice	Ottawa	4,506	2,023	45.0
Home for the Aged	Ottawa	2,634	758	28.8
Orphans' Home (Refuge Branch)	Ottawa	2,076§	470	22.6
Home for Friendless Women	Ottawa	4,114	638	15.5
Refuge of Our Lady of Charity	Ottawa	11,606	2,952	25.4
House of Providence	Guelph	3,365	1,005	29.9
Thomas Williams' Home	St. Thomas	1,360	420	30.9
House of Providence	Dundas	9,515	2,995	31.5
Home for the Friendless	Chatham	1,731	450	26.0
Widows Home	Brantford	821	276	33.6
Home for the Friendless	Belleville	506	181	35.8
Protestant Home	Peterborough	1,559	454	29.1
House of Providence	Peterborough	2,603	594	22.8
Old Ladies Home	Galt	2,210	187	8.5
Home for the Friendless	Windsor	2,641	376	14.2
Protestant Home (Refuge Branch)	St. Catherines	496§	87	17.5

SOURCE: Ontario, *Report of the Inspector of Prisons, Asylums and Public Charities*, 1893.

*Institutions receiving fifteen cents per inmate per day for inmates in the incurable, chronic, or convalescent categories.

†Expenditures combined with those of the House of Providence, Toronto.

‡Expenditures combined with those of the House of Industry, Toronto.

§Estimated expenditure of refuges combined with orphanages; estimate based on relative numbers of inmate days and average costs per day for all institutions under schedule B and all institutions under schedule C in 1893.

‖Separate institutions for men and women were combined in 1892.

year the rate was raised to the equivalent of one-half the hospital rate, making it fifteen cents a day, provided that its income from sources other than the province entitled it to this amount.

Langmuir did not discuss this new basis of payment other than to note that the change was made "under instruction of the Government."[67] It was not until 1884, two years after Langmuir's resignation, that the question of making special provision for institutions for incurables was discussed in an annual report. In that year, Inspector Christie referred to and recommended favourably upon the application by the House of Providence to have its incurable ward placed on the fifteen-cent basis. At the same time he suggested a number of rules which formed the basis of an order-in-council. The order set out the following conditions: that the institution keep a separate register for incurable patients; that certification be given by two medical practitioners, one to be the institution's regular physician, stating that the person applying was "afflicted with incurable disease requiring active medical treatment or supervision"; that the increased rate would not apply to persons who were insane, or blind, or suffering from venereal disease or epilepsy or "from mere functional disease," or who were "merely infirm from old age or debility or senile decay."[68] This basis appears to have been employed in the case of the other institutions for incurables. No legislation was passed to re-define schedule B which in the revised statutes of 1887[69] remained unchanged.

The Convalescent Home in Toronto was also admitted to the fifteen-cent basis on the recommendation of Christie. The trustees of the home, in their submission to the government in 1887, had requested that the grant to the home be the same as that to hospitals, but Christie pointed out that its costs were much less than those of an active treatment hospital and recommended the fifteen-cent rate. He further recommended that the grant be limited to thirty days per patient. These provisions were incorporated in the order-in-council which brought the home under the terms of the act.[70] A similar policy was adopted in relation to the Convalescent Home, London, in 1891.[71]

Of the thirty-three institutions (counting the incurable ward of the House of Providence, Toronto) listed under schedule B of the act in 1893, there were thus six receiving a different rate of provincial aid

[67]Ontario, *Sessional Papers*, 1882, no. 8, p. 269.
[68]*Ibid.*, 1885, no. 40, p. 10.
[69]Ontario, *Revised Statutes*, 1887, c. 248.
[70]Ontario, *Sessional Papers*, 1889, no. 11, p. 21.
[71]*Ibid.*, 1892, no. 6, p. 58.

than the other twenty-seven. Their programmes, especially those of the convalescent homes, were necessarily different from the other institutions. A good case might therefore have been made for amending the act to place them in a new schedule, especially because the payment to them of a rate not authorized in the act would seem to have been of highly questionable legality.

An anomaly of a different character is to be noted respecting the inclusion of the Home for Friendless Women, Ottawa, under schedule B of the act.[72] The purpose of this institution was stated to be the reclamation of fallen women. Its inmates and programme were thus indistinguishable from the magdalen asylums which were included under schedule C of the act and which therefore received a grant of only two cents per inmate per day.

Private Houses of Refuge

ORGANIZATION

A number of the houses of refuge were organized and administered by women, either from the Protestant groups acting in concert or, in the case of institutions under Roman Catholic auspices, by one of the religious orders. However, not all the institutions were so administered. The board of directors of the House of Industry, Toronto, for example, consisted of "forty gentlemen,"[73] and the institution of the same name in Kingston had an all male board of four men appointed by the city council and eight by the subscribers.[74] The House of Refuge, Hamilton, was administered in the same way with the real control apparently residing in the city council. The Church Home for the Aged, Toronto, was under the auspices of the Church of England, with the Bishop of Toronto at the head of its board of trustees.[75]

FINANCING

The various auspices just referred to give some indication of the financing of the institutions. Data on the sources of revenue of the institutions were collected by the Inspector according to the following breakdown: the province, the principal municipality, other municipali-

---

[72]*Ibid.*, p. 56.
[73]*Ibid.*, 1893, no. 10, p. 7.
[74]*Ibid.*, 1872–73, no. 2, p. 71.
[75]*Ibid.*, 1889, no. 11, pp. 22–23. When the Church Home applied for inclusion under schedule B of the Charity Aid Act as a home associated solely with the parish of St. George's Church, the request was denied and the home was admitted only when its scope was extended from the parish to the diocese.

ties, income from property, payments from inmates, subscriptions and donations, and other sources. The proportion of revenue from these sources varied widely as between institutions. In the report for 1888, for example, the House of Refuge, Hamilton, was shown to have no revenue whatever other than that from the province, the city of Hamilton, and other municipalities, together with a small amount from the payments of inmates.[76] At the other extreme, the House of Providence, Kingston, received no municipal aid, but had considerable voluntary support, some income from property, and payments by inmates amounting to about 13 per cent of its revenue.[77]

After the first five or six years of experience under the Charity Aid Act, the Inspector made few references to the financing of the institutions. During that initial period, the House of Industry, Kingston, had been urged to secure more local support, especially from the municipalities benefiting from its services,[78] and the House of Refuge in Hamilton had drawn unfavourable comment from him because, in terms of admissions, financing, and control, it gave every evidence of being a municipal institution. In noting that admission seemed to be awarded only to the poor of the city and that the establishment was "owned and maintained by the Corporation of the City of Hamilton," Langmuir commented that "it becomes a question whether it should receive aid from the Government at all, as it certainly can only be classed as a Corporation Poor House, of the same description as the one in the County of Waterloo."[79]

The Inspector also raised a question on one occasion about the propriety of the provincial grant applying to the care of inmates who were in a position to pay a significant amount towards their maintenance.[80] His own answer, or that of the government, appeared to be in the affirmative, and the point was not referred to again. In his next report, in fact, he is found speaking with approval of a method employed by the Home for Aged Women, Hamilton, by which the application for admission of a person to the institution was accompanied by the payment of $50 by a sponsoring church, organization, or individual. Subject to approval by the lady managers, the applicant was thus entitled to "remain in the institution during life."[81] Langmuir recommended the practice to other refuges. Subsequently, there were

[76]Ontario, *Sessional Papers*, 1889, no. 11, p. 25.
[77]*Ibid.*, p. 29.
[78]*Ibid.*, 1880, no. 8, p. 258; and 1881, no. 8, p. 247.
[79]*Ibid.*, 1877, no. 2, p. 192.
[80]*Ibid.*, p. 189.
[81]*Ibid.*, 1878, no. 4, p. 218.

occasional references by the Inspector to the extent of private payments by inmates, but such references were not related to the payment of the provincial grant.

Apart from the early difficulties of the House of Industry at Kingston and certain problems concerning outdoor relief which are referred to later, the houses of refuge do not appear to have encountered serious financial difficulties, nor did they, during the period, make any appeal for more substantial grants. In one report in the mid-eighties, Christie expressed his concern at the falling off in the revenues of the refuges at a time when their population was rising,[82] but this stands as the only comment of its kind in the reports relating to the institutions' financial needs.

BUILDINGS, LAND, AND FACILITIES

Buildings and land were accorded a high degree of importance in the establishment and administration of the houses of refuge. Many of their buildings were of substantial construction and built at considerable cost[83] on architectural advice.[84] Other institutions were, for at least part of the period, housed in makeshift and inadequate buildings which subjected their inmates to varying degrees of danger and discomfort.

The Inspector played an important part in relation to building standards. Where buildings were unsuitable, he made every attempt to secure alterations and improvements, or, where necessary, completely new construction. Notable among the institutions which required such attention were the House of Industry, Kingston, and the House of Refuge, Hamilton, two institutions which seemed to earn the disapproval of the Inspector on a number of counts. On his first visit to the House of Industry, Kingston, Langmuir remarked on the unsuitable state of the buildings,[85] and the following year he reported that "every part of the Establishment was inspected, and every part of it was found in a dilapidated, disorderly, and untidy state . . . utterly unfitted for the purposes of the Charity."[86] A year later, he was able

[82]*Ibid.*, 1887, no. 21, p. 6.

[83]*Ibid.*, 1884, no. 32, p. 10. Between 1856 and 1883, the House of Providence, Toronto, expended over $104,000 on its building.

[84]*Ibid.*, 1881, no. 8, p. 241. More than a full page of the report is given to the architect's description of the new Home for Incurables, Toronto, which was apparently built to the highest contemporary standards. The architect was chosen following a special competition for the best design, a premium being offered for the most suitable plan.

[85]Ontario, *Sessional Papers*, 1870–71, no. 6, p. 76.

[86]*Ibid.*, 1871–72, no. 4, p. 118.

to announce that the "premises having been found to be unfitted, both from their condition and situation for the purposes of the charity, a very eligible property has been acquired."[87] The new premises had not been occupied when Langmuir made his statutory visit the following September, and, seeing the opportunity to have the institution adopt a better programme coincident with its occupation of new quarters, he recommended to the board that it should have its superintendent visit the Toronto House of Industry "so that the order, regularity and comfort that prevails there [Toronto] may be introduced and maintained in the House [Kingston] that is about to be opened."[88] In his next report, he noted that the internal arrangements of the building were "very well adapted for the purposes of the charity, containing the requisite domestic offices, sitting rooms and dormitories for at least forty inmates," and he drew the moral that "the whole arrangement and surroundings of the house are such that any further mismanagement, untidiness, or discomfort will admit of no excuse on the part of the Superintendent and Matron."[89]

For some years thereafter, the improvement of both the accommodation and the general care of inmates in the home won Langmuir's general commendation, although in 1877 he pointed to the "great want of press and lock-up accommodation . . . giving some portions of the house an untidy appearance."[90] This deficiency, he remarked, "could be remedied at a trifling cost." From 1879, the inspectors' reports mention overcrowding and poor ventilation. On his first visit Christie found that thirteen beds were crowded into a room the dimensions of which were seventeen feet by twenty-seven feet and commented that "under such circumstances it is not difficult to imagine the foul and impure character of the air which the inmates are obliged to breathe."[91] In 1883 the institution added a verandah which Christie noted afforded "airing room to those of the inmates who, from feebleness and other causes, cannot be moved to a greater distance from their beds."[92] Christie was pleased to be able to report in 1886 that the institution was adding a new wing to the building at a cost of from $3,000 to $4,000 to provide accommodation for about twenty-five additional persons, sixteen in double rooms and the remainder in a dormitory.

[87]*Ibid.*, 1872–73, no. 2, p. 86.
[88]*Ibid.*, 1874 (vol. VI), no. 2, pp. 151–52. The new building, together with the twelve acres of land on which it was situated, were donated by the city of Kingston. The buildings were valued at $9,000 before being altered to meet the institution's needs at a further cost of $3,000.
[89]Ontario, *Sessional Papers*, 1874 (vol. VII), no. 2, p. 143.
[90]*Ibid.*, 1878, no. 4, p. 209.   [91]*Ibid.*, 1884, no. 32, p. 17.   [92]*Ibid.*

His suggested change in the provisions for ventilation was also adopted.[93] In spite of the new addition, however, the institution once again fell into a state of dilapidation which was reported on by Hayes in 1888.[94] The repairs and renovations he recommended were carried out, and Christie, the next year, was able to speak with praise of improvements which added much "to the comfort and appearance of the institution." The principal halls had been "neatly and chastily papered," the floors painted, and the walls kalsomined. New bedding was to be obtained, and when this was done the home would be, in Christie's words, "in an excellent condition for the class for which it is provided."[95]

An even more prolonged attempt on the part of successive inspectors to have the House of Refuge, Hamilton, provide adequate buildings was not crowned with success during the period covered here. Langmuir's early reports were consistently critical of the dilapidated old frame buildings in which the institution was housed. In 1877, finding that the buildings which he was later to describe as "mere sheds"[96] were in an advanced state of decay, with their floors falling away and their heating presenting an almost impossible problem, he was on the point of applying the one means he possessed of bringing more than moral pressure to bear on an institution. He informed the civic authorities, under whose direction the institution operated, that he would "have to recommend that any future Provincial appropriation, to which the Institution might be entitled, under the Charity Aid Act, be withheld until a proper structure be provided for the purpose of the charity, or at any rate, until a commencement be made in that direction."[97]

This warning was apparently not without effect, for shortly thereafter, as related in Langmuir's report, "a deputation consisting of the Mayor and two members of the Corporation of Hamilton, waited upon me in regard to this matter."[98] They told of plans to obtain a site for a new building and made certain other suggestions about the accommodation of men in an outbuilding of the General Hospital. To this Langmuir assented and agreed also "not to recommend the withholding of Government aid, provided that a complete change were made next year." He then suggested that the city give first priority to erecting a new hospital building, the existing one being unsuitable for treatment

[93]Ibid., 1887, no. 21, pp. 17–18.
[94]Ibid., 1889, no. 11, p. 28.
[95]Ibid., 1890, no. 15, p. 30.   [96]Ibid., 1881, no. 8, p. 244.
[97]Ibid., 1878, no. 4, p. 211.   [98]Ibid.

purposes, and "use the Hospital structure for a House of Refuge, for which both in respect to site and structural arrangements it is well adapted." Although Langmuir and future inspectors may well have regretted this suggestion in later years, it is to be borne in mind that Langmuir's rôle as inspector of hospitals, as well as of houses of refuge, made it possible and indeed necessary for him to make comparative assessments of the need for the two types of care, and his suggestion in this case may well have promoted the general well-being more effectively than would have the prior construction of a new house of refuge.

The programme to carry out the plan, however, was painfully slow, and in spite of pressure by Langmuir the hospital was not completed nor the move of the refuge into the old building made during Langmuir's tenure as inspector. The account of the move did appear in Dr. O'Reilly's first report, but the picture he gave of the new situation was far from cheering. In describing it, he contrasted unfavourably the care provided by this publicly directed institution with that of other institutions in Hamilton operating under private boards, such as the Home for Aged Women: "Everything in this building is of the roughest description in all respects. The poor of Hamilton, so far as the city has charge of them, are the worst lodged of any in the Province, while in the same city the institutions managed by private persons compare favourably with the best."[99]

The new Inspector then described the serious fire hazard which the building constituted in its existing state and recommended "that Government aid be withheld from this institution until some efficient provision be made for the safety of the inmates in the event of fire." The following year Dr. O'Reilly found that his "previous remarks in reference to the necessity for a fire escape from this building has led to the erection in the front and rear of alleged fire-escapes."[100] Of these, particularly the one at the rear of the building, he was critical, stating that as an escape for any old and infirm person it was "simply an absurdity."[101] When, a year later, he found that the necessary changes in the escape had not yet been made, he asserted that he had no recourse "but to withhold my recommendation for the payment of the usual annual grant to this Refuge until the work be done."[102] The government was apparently not disposed to take so drastic a step as withholding the grant, and Dr. O'Reilly was found in his next report

---

[99]*Ibid.*, 1882–83, no. 8, p. 13 (refuge and orphanage report).
[100]*Ibid.*, 1884, no. 32, p. 15.
[101]*Ibid.*   [102]*Ibid.*, 1885, no. 40, p. 15.

expostulating: "I shall consider that, in calling attention to this matter for the last time, I, at least, have done my duty; the rest I presume must be left to chance."[103] When Hayes inspected the institution in 1886, some improvements to the fire escapes had by then been made; a telephone had been installed in the institution; an alarm box had been erected nearby; and some "hand grenades" were hung in the halls.[104]

In succeeding reports, Dr. O'Reilly resumed his indictment of the institution. In commenting in 1887 that the house was in "its usual untidy, unsatisfactory condition," he made it clear that he did not blame the staff, "as it is simply impossible to have such a building as this otherwise."[105] And in his last report, he drew attention to the specifics of the overcrowded and inadequately equipped state of the building in the following terms: "There is no such thing as a dining-room, or a table off which the patients can take their meals, the prisoners in the gaol are accorded this latter privilege. It seems hard, therefore, that people whose only crime is their poverty, should be forced to live in the way these do."[106] As the period under review closed, Chamberlain had assumed the burden and reported that he had again called "the attention of the authorities of the City of Hamilton to the necessity for a new building for this Charity, the present structure being in a very dilapidated condition and a menace to the lives of inmates if a fire should occur."[107]

The kinds of problems encountered by the inspectors in the House of Industry, Kingston, and the House of Refuge, Hamilton, were not found to any comparable degree in the other institutions. In general, relationships were cordial, and the inspectors' criticism of institutional plants relatively infrequent. Their influence appears none the less to have been both considerable and beneficient. They drew the attention of all institutions to the need for adequate safety measures against fire, frequently combining the question of safety with that of comfort and urging institutions to remove the usual wood stoves located throughout the buildings and replace them with a system of hot water heating. The latter, as they frequently pointed out, would also provide "the steady and generous heat"[108] that old people require. The provision of good ventilation and of adequate bathing and lavatory facilities and the avoidance of overcrowding were other matters the inspectors kept

103*Ibid.*, 1886, no. 14, p. 14.
104*Ibid.*, 1887, no. 21, p. 15.
105*Ibid.*, 1888, no. 40, p. 15.
106*Ibid.*, 1890, no. 15, p. 27.
107*Ibid.*, 1894, no. 28, p. 20.   108*Ibid.*, 1888, no. 40, p. 34.

to the fore, and their reports indicate a substantial measure of success in securing action on them.

STAFFING

The inspectors' reports give a less than adequate picture of the staffing of the institutions. It appears that an institution's board usually hired a man and wife to occupy, respectively, the positions of super-intendent and matron. It was customary to offer the couple a combined salary, usually around $400 or $500 per annum, together with living-in accommodation and food. In some institutions they seem to have been the only paid staff, it being left to them to organize the inmates as best they could into work units capable of assisting in the various house-keeping operations. There are, however, a few references in the reports to additional staff. It was noted, for example, that the House of Providence, Guelph, which had considerable land, kept a hired man who was generally responsible for the gardens and for directing the work of inmates able to assist in gardening activities.[109] There were, as well, references to some of the institutions having one or more general assistants. It appears also to have been the practice of the institutions to have the services of a local physician on an annual retainer basis, the physician to the Toronto House of Industry receiving $200 annually for his services.[110]

In general, the inspector's relations with the institutions' staffs appear to have been cordial. He frequently pointed out that where the building or facilities were inadequate it was impossible for the staff to maintain high standards of order and comfort. At the same time, however, where he felt the fault to lie at the door of the superinten-dent, as Langmuir did during the tenure of one superintendent at the House of Industry, Kingston, he let this appear in his report.

Rarely was the name of a superintendent or matron mentioned, and at no point did the inspector discuss, in other than the most general terms, the qualifications which were possessed or which ought to be possessed by institutional staff. Salaries too were a matter on which reporting on the houses of refuge is all but silent. On one occasion, however, Langmuir commented on the reduction made in the salary of the superintendent of the House of Industry, Kingston, when that institution was undergoing financial difficulties. It was, he remarked, "an act of rather doubtful economy, as that officer appeared to be an efficient one."[111]

109*Ibid.*, 1882, no. 8, p. 281.
110*Ibid.*, 1870–71, no. 6, p. 75.   111*Ibid.*, 1881, no. 8, p. 246.

PROGRAMME

With populations made up of the aged and the crippled, and with limited staff, it is obvious that the houses of refuge could offer little more than custodial care. Inmates were expected to assist in household duties, and where there were extensive grounds and gardens they were encouraged to help in planting and maintaining them. In a few instances measures were considered for finding some type of remunerative employment for the inmates, but these attempts appear to have been abandoned. The references in two or three reports to the men being engaged in "breaking stones" have an ominous sound, but there is little suggestion of a punitive enforcement of onerous, unpleasant, or dangerous work.[112] Religious services and observances were mentioned in some reports as playing an important part in institutional programmes, especially those under Roman Catholic auspices. It was noted in connection with one large Roman Catholic institution that its chapel was located centrally so that persons in all wards had ready access to it.

The quality of the routine care given to the inmates appears, in general, to have been at an acceptable level. References to good food, well served, were frequent in the reports. The few comments about clothing and bedding suggest that the institutions generally found it possible to provide these in sufficient quantity. Where they were inadequate or the standard of their cleanliness was low, these facts drew comments from the inspector and remedial action appears to have been taken.

The practice of separating the sexes was followed in some of the institutions. Where such segregation was practised, the inspector might refer to it in the reports, but he never commented on the desirability of the policy. Another type of segregation was mentioned in relation to the Home for the Friendless, Chatham. On this, Dr. O'Reilly reported noncommittally that "some of the inmates are white and some are coloured, and as a rule they are kept in separate rooms and have different tables for their meals."[113]

Specific indications of the philosophy or basic points of view about the rôle of the institutions, either on the part of their boards of directors or of the inspector, are infrequent. The institutions were regarded as providing a service of obvious value which required little in the way of defence, elaboration, or evaluation. "As regards these Refuges," Christie remarked in one of his early reports, "there is really

[112]*Ibid.*, 1879, no. 8, p. 222.
[113]*Ibid.*, 1886, no. 14, p. 30.

nothing much to be said . . . except that in a quiet way they relieve a great deal of distress and afford places where many of the aged and infirm can pass away the last years of their lives in comparative peace and comfort."[114] Although this remark points to a lack of insight into the possibilities which existed for the enrichment of institutional programmes, it also indicates that there was no disposition to operate the institutions in the spirit of "less eligibility." If there was any tendency to keep standards at or near a poverty level, it found no reflection in the reports. If such an attitude had support in any board or institutional staff, the influence of the inspector would have served to minimize it.

The reports abound in commendations of institutions which were providing a homelike atmosphere,[115] devoted care under trying circumstances,[116] extra comforts,[117] or attractive surroundings.[118] They also showed a consistent appreciation of life and of health. Dr. O'Reilly, for example, reported of the House of Providence, Dundas, in 1885 that its health record had been excellent, "there having been almost no sickness during the past two years except that which is incidental to the very aged people who are accommodated in the House, one of whom is said to have reached the age of 107 years."[119] Other successful records in achieving low mortality rates received approving comment in the inspectors' reports. These reports, when read by institutional boards and staffs, could not have failed to influence and encourage them in the provision of programmes characterized not only by order, cleanliness, and efficiency, but also by kindness, consideration, and humanity.

[114]*Ibid.*, 1884, no. 32, p. 2.

[115]An example, in spite of its size, was the House of Industry, Toronto, the management of which usually won Langmuir's highest commendation. In his report of 1873 (*Sessional Papers*, 1874 (vol. VI), no. 2, p. 153), he refers to the dormitories having "an air of comfort and cheerfulness about them that is seldom found in a poor house." Again in relation to the institution with the bleak title of "Home for Incurables," Langmuir noted in his 1876 report (*Sessional Papers*, 1877, no. 4, p. 194), that "the wards were very cheerful and homelike in their surroundings."

[116]Referring to the twenty-five bedridden patients in the House of Providence, Toronto (*Sessional Papers*, 1879, no. 8, p. 220), Langmuir commented that "these poor helpless people appeared to be well looked after and kindly treated by the sisters in charge of this excellent charity, although in many cases their care is attended with great trouble and responsibility."

[117]The Inspector referred, for example, to the collection of feathers by the sisters in charge of the House of Providence, Kingston, and the provision of feather beds for the women residents (*Sessional Papers*, 1879, no. 8, p. 225).

[118]Ontario, *Sessional Papers*, 1878, no. 4, p. 218. The report commends the superior appointments and the associated air of neatness and comfort of the Home for the Aged, Hamilton.

[119]Ontario, *Sessional Papers*, 1886, no. 14, p. 29.

County Houses of Refuge

By making the establishment of county houses of refuge permissive rather than mandatory, as it had been in the pre-Confederation statute of 1866, the 1867–68 amendment of the Municipal Institutions Act had the effect of handing the initiative for public provisions for the care of the poor back to the municipalities. Although Langmuir indicated on a number of occasions that he would have liked to see public institutions developed throughout the province, the administration did not adopt any special measures to bring this about. What happened, in fact, was that institutions under voluntary auspices were placed in a preferred position through the maintenance grants which were paid to them under the Charity Aid Act. No comparable provision was made for public institutions established under the Municipal Act. Moreover, the effect of the Charity Aid Act in encouraging the development of voluntary institutions may well have removed the pressure for the establishment of public institutions in many communities. If and where such was the case, the act may be said to have retarded the development of public institutions.

The first indication of renewed interest by the province in encouraging the development of public institutions was the passage of the Municipal Amendment Act in 1888, which extended to all types of municipalities the right to combine for the establishment and maintenance of houses of refuge.[120] The new amendment seems not to have been in response to any actual demand for the change because no municipality took advantage of it during the period.

The next year, a further indication of interest in the question appeared in the Legislature with the request of two members, Charles Clarke of Wellington and Thomas Gibson of Huron, for extensive information about municipal institutions then in existence. This produced a forty-page return[121] giving construction and maintenance costs, the value of the products of the institutions' fields and gardens, information on the staff and the salaries paid, and data on the inmates and how they were treated. The latter included information on age and sex and on the number of inmates who were "regarded as imbecile, idiotics, or insane, and of the blind, epileptic or deaf and dumb."[122] The return also contained figures on the number of inmates committed to detention in the institutions for short periods and on the use of solitary confinement as a punishment of inmates for acts committed

[120]Ontario, *Statutes*, 1888, c. 28, s. 18.
[121]Ontario, *Sessional Papers*, 1889, no. 61.
[122]*Ibid.*, p. 1.

while in the institutions. A final point concerned the supposed causes of the pauperism which was itself the reason for the inmates' presence in the institutions.

Aside from their intrinsic interest, the data contained in the return were no doubt of value to the administration in the preparation of the Houses of Refuge Act. The introduction of this measure was foretold in the speech from the throne in 1890 in a paragraph which put the legislation in its setting in terms of existing needs and available resources and also revealed something of the administration's approach to the care of the poor:

Public attention has of later years been directed to the inadequate provision by County Municipalities for the care and support of the aged, helpless and poor within their boundaries, only nine Counties having yet availed themselves of the provision of the law authorizing the establishment of Industrial Farms, and Houses of Industry and Refuge in connection therewith. Organized philanthropy in the larger centres of population, has provided institutions for the aged of such persons in these localities; and the Provincial aid to many of these institutions has been extended under our Charity Aid Act. With a view of encouraging the erection of County Houses of Refuge in connection with Industrial Farms and of thereby relieving the gaols of this unfortunate class of their inmates, a measure will be submitted for your consideration, providing for a grant from Provincial Funds of a sum not exceeding four thousand dollars towards the cost in any County or Union of Counties availing itself of the Act, the grant to be subject to such conditions as you may deem fitting. The Bill will also provide for the case of Counties which have already established a House of Refuge.[123]

The act took the form outlined in the throne speech, its preamble stating that its aim was "to encourage the erection and establishment by county municipalities of houses of industry or refuge for the care and custody of the aged, helpless and poor."[124] The encouragement offered was a grant towards the cost of acquiring land and erecting buildings, which would meet up to a quarter of the actual cost but would not exceed $4,000. Where the institution was built by two or more municipalities (the preamble was inaccurate in suggesting that the act applied only to counties), the grant was to be distributed between them according to their population.

The other important provision of the act was that it placed the public houses of refuge under the scrutiny of the inspector of asylums and public charities, though not so comprehensively as did the Charity Aid Act in the case of the private houses of refuge receiving aid under that act. The new act required the public institutions to be open to inspection

123Ontario, *Journals*, 1890, p. 4.
124Ontario, *Statutes*, 1890, c. 78.

and required the inspector to report to the lieutenant-governor-in-council on any matter which he considered should be drawn to the cabinet's attention. Regular annual reporting, however, did not seem to be envisaged and was not, in fact, instituted. A specific responsibility assigned to the inspector was that he examine the land and buildings, and certify their suitability for the purposes intended and their readiness for occupation. Such certification was required before an order-in-council could be made authorizing the payment of the funds, and the order-in-council, in turn, did not become operative until ratified by a resolution of the Legislative Assembly. The terms of the act also extended to municipal houses of refuge already in existence, and the first task of Inspector Chamberlain was to look into and report on them. He was to report, in particular, on the cost of their land and buildings, the value of which would determine the extent of their eligibility for the grant. The resultant report, prepared by Chamberlain and entitled "County Houses of Refuge," was attached to his annual report for 1888 on houses of refuge and magdalen asylums under the Charity Aid Act.

Table X shows that of the nine institutions then in operation six were eligible for the maximum grant of $4,000. Their land and build-

TABLE X

COUNTY HOUSES OF REFUGE ELIGIBLE FOR A PROVINCIAL CONSTRUCTION GRANT
UNDER THE HOUSES OF REFUGE ACT, 1890

Institution	County	Year founded	Population on the day inspected	Grant payable (in dollars)
House of Industry	Waterloo	1869	90	4,000
House of Industry	Elgin	1875	70	3,000
House of Industry	Wellington	1878	59	4,000
House of Industry	Norfolk	1879	50	2,250
House of Refuge	Middlesex	1880	96	4,000
House of Industry	York	1883	91	4,000
House of Refuge	Lincoln	1887	41	4,000
House of Industry	Brant	1888	38	3,500
House of Industry	Welland	1889	40	4,000

SOURCE: Ontario, *Sessional Papers*, 1889, no. 61; 1892, no. 6.

ings, that is, were judged to have a value of $16,000 or more. The House of Industry for Brant County would have qualified for the maximum but for the fact that the land had been donated and the act specified that the basis of payment be the "amount actually expended by the municipality." Chamberlain seems, however, to have deviated from this basis in placing a lesser value on some of the properties than that certified as the actual cost by the municipal officials. Apparently, he was making a deduction for depreciation. Thus, although the cost of the House of Industry of Elgin County was stated by county officials to be $13,783, Chamberlain named $12,000 as its present value and made that the basis of the grant. Similarly, he placed the valuation of the Norfolk County institution some $450 below its stated cost.

Chamberlain sketched a very favourable picture of the institutions. A number of them had cost about $30,000 and were well constructed and well maintained. They all appeared to operate under a committee of the county council acting primarily through an inspector who received a salary of from $100 to $150 annually. Internal management was, as in the case of the private houses of refuge, usually carried by a married couple who filled the positions of superintendent and matron. The salaries for the two positions seemed to be combined in most cases and were from $450 to $760 annually. Some other help was normally provided. In the cases of the Wellington County institution, which was the best staffed, there was an establishment for five women servants at $7 per month each, and one part-time man servant at $18 per month. The Middlesex institution, which Chamberlain described as "the best of the kind in Ontario,"[125] had steam heating and employed an engineer at an annual salary of $400. Chamberlain also mentioned that most of the institutions had made arrangements for a physician's services at an annual retainer of from $100 to $200.

Few of Chamberlain's comments related to the programme of the institutions. Farming and gardening were carried on by all the institutions, but how the inmates were involved, if at all, in these operations was not indicated. The Middlesex institution which Chamberlain described most fully was reported to have a library, to receive visits each week from a committee of ladies from the town of Strathroy, and to have religious services on Sunday conducted by the ministers of the different denominations.

Chamberlain's over-all estimate of the public houses of refuge appeared in his discussion of the county gaols. Through the use or misuse of "vagrancy" as the grounds for detention, persons without means of support but in no other sense guilty of an offence were still being sent to the local gaols in many communities in default of other means of caring for them. In attacking this practice, Chamberlain advanced a strong case for establishing county houses of refuge:

I am pleased to be able to report that during the year some of the counties in the west have provided industrial homes, and many other counties throughout the Province are moving in that direction, and I am in hope that

125Ontario, *Sessional Papers*, 1892, no. 6, p. 100.

in the near future every county or group of counties will have provided suitable accommodation for their poor people. In my report on the gaols last year I called the attention of the counties to this matter, stating that having visited all the industrial homes in the Province and carefully observed their management, I was convinced it was the most economical and at the same time the most humane way of maintaining their poor. All the county officers and others with whom I conversed, assured me that since the establishment of county poor-houses there had been a feeling of satisfaction among the people from the knowledge that the aged and poor people were more comfortably and respectably cared for, and at no greater cost than under the old system of farming them out or committing them to gaol.[126]

Chamberlain also put pressure on those counties where the gaols were being used for maintaining old persons. In his inspection of the gaol in Peterborough in 1892, he found that no less than seventeen of the twenty-seven prisoners had been charged as vagrants, "being destitute poor people who had committed no crime and were only fit subjects for the care of an Industrial Home or Poor House."[127] He insisted that such persons should not be compelled to wear prison clothing, and that they be allowed a more liberal diet than other prisoners. He also stated that where steps were not being taken to provide a county home he would be compelled to require the county authorities to build additions to the gaols for the special care and comfort of these indigent people.[128] The cost of such an addition, as Chamberlain pointed out to the officials in Peterborough, would have to be borne totally by the county, whereas the provincial construction grant would be available to assist in the establishment of a county house of industry.

Chamberlain did not, however, discuss in his reports the exact rôle that the province believed the county houses of refuge should play. The province assumed about half the costs of the maintenance of persons in the county gaols, and it had shared in the initial construction costs of the gaols in exactly the same proportion that it was now offering to the county houses of refuge. The assistance in the construction of the county homes, moreover, was not as favourable as the continued assistance the province gave the voluntary houses of refuge through the Charity Aid Act. Thus, the province, though urging the counties to establish homes, was not giving them the support or attention it was giving the gaols or the private refuges, either in terms of financing or supervision. In default of a more definite indication of the province's conception of the part to be played by the county homes,

126*Ibid.*, 1893, no. 9, p. 5.
127*Ibid.*, p. 67.   128*Ibid.*, p. 5.

one is left to infer that this rôle was seen as residual. Where there were needs that were not being met by voluntary institutions or where needs were being inappropriately met such as through the incarceration of the aged poor in gaol, the county should establish a public institution. This seemed to be the extent of the province's position on the matter in the early 1890's.

The Royal Commission on the Prison and Reformatory System in its report in 1891 called for a more definite policy—actually for the return to the legislative position of 1866:

It is urgently recommended that, in order to abolish completely the inhuman system of committing homeless and destitute men, women and children to common gaols, many of whom are from old age or physical incapacity unable to earn a living, the establishment of a poor house be made compulsory (instead of permissive as at present) on every county in the Province; or where the population and requirements of a county in respect to its poor do not seem to warrant such an expenditure, that two or more counties be grouped for that purpose; every poor house to have attached to it a sufficient quantity of land to furnish employment for the inmates. . . . That it shall be unlawful when a poor house is established in a county, or group of counties, for a magistrate or justice to commit to a common gaol as a vagrant any homeless and destitute person who seems to be physically incapable of working, unless such person has committed some offence.[129]

By the end of the period under review, however, there was little to suggest that the administration was prepared to move from exhortation and encouragement to the stronger measures implied in the commission's recommendations.

Private Outdoor and Casual Relief

In the years following the passage of the Charity Aid Act, Langmuir advocated additional provincial grants to the institutions which were giving outdoor relief as well as providing long-term boarding care. His discussion of the question centred principally on the outdoor relief programme of the House of Industry, Toronto, to which he referred in each of his reports from 1872. In 1874, he outlined its outdoor operations as follows:

1st. The distribution of bread, corn meal, groceries and fuel to 586 poor families and 255 casual callers, representing a total of 2,308 souls who received relief in this manner.
2nd. Giving supper, bed, and breakfast to 4,550 casuals during the six winter months of the year.

[129]*Ibid.*, 1891, no. 18, p. 220.

3rd. The distribution of 100 gallons of soup daily during winter months to the poor of the city.

The operations are conducted under a well-devised and well-supervised system and are calculated to benefit the greatest of the most deserving poor that come within the knowledge of the Directors of the Charity.[130]

Langmuir argued that if such operations were carried out "in a judicious manner and under proper supervision" they were "quite as worthy of Government aid as indoor relief."[131] Moreover, assistance granted in this way would win the approval of the "many who entirely deprecate the establishment of Poor Houses in this Country," and he therefore suggested that, "in apportioning Government aid to Poor Houses, some consideration should be afforded for expenditures incurred in this manner."[132]

Langmuir continued to praise the outdoor programme of the Toronto institution and similar activities carried on elsewhere. In relation to persons helped in their own homes, he referred to the "wise discrimination"[133] displayed by the House of Industry "based upon the observation and personal knowledge of the members of the Visiting Committee." He commented further that this system "is the only wise and proper one; for while well-organized relief is a duty well performed, it is clear that indiscriminate and unsystematic relief fosters a spirit of dependence and begets pauperism."[134]

Langmuir returned to the question of government support for the outdoor relief programmes of the institutions in his report for 1877. Affirming his view that this work merited the assistance of the public body no less than did resident care, he stated that he proposed "making enquiry into this phase of poor relief during the present winter, reporting the result of my enquiries for the consideration of the Government."[135] The results of his study and the nature of his recommendations do not appear in the reports in any detail. If he was able to suggest any basis for remuneration for the institutional assistance to the locally resident poor, either in their own homes or through the availability to them of outdoor aid on the premises of the institution, no indication either of his proposal or of the government's reaction to it is reported. Perhaps a sufficient indication that there was no change in policy, however, is provided in his disposition of a problem he encountered in his inspection of the Home for Aged Women, Hamilton. On this question (with its incidental side-light on problems of adjustment in an institution), Langmuir commented that "there

130*Ibid.*, 1874 (vol. VII), no. 2, p. 140.   131*Ibid.*, p. 122.
132*Ibid.*
133*Ibid.*, 1877, no. 2, p. 186.
134*Ibid.*
135*Ibid.*, 1878, no. 4, p. 173.

were then 18 women in residence and the name of another was on the register, but being of a troublesome disposition she had been removed, but was supplied with rations. I informed the manager that she must be a resident of the House if they applied for Government Aid in respect to her maintenance."[136]

Although Langmuir thus appears to have been unsuccessful in formulating any method that was feasible, or at any rate acceptable to the government, for provincial grants relating to the outdoor relief given by the private institutions, he did make a recommendation for provincial support on the somewhat related matter of casuals receiving institutional help. This appears in part of his report for 1878 on the House of Industry, Toronto:

At this visit, I made particular inquiry into the method adopted by the managers of the Institution for the relief of the necessities of casuals. As the result of such inquiry, I found that every casual asking admission was received into the House, unless some good reason such as previous bad conduct in the Institution necessitated refusal; that such casuals come from all parts of the Province; that they invariably received supper, bed, and breakfast, and the majority of them returned at noon, when they received dinner, consisting of a pint of soup and half a pound of bread. In fact, in most cases a full day's lodgment and maintenance was given. In view of these facts, I expressed the opinion that the wording of the Charity Aid Act would admit, certainly without doing any violence, to the spirit of the law, of aid being given to the House of Industry in respect of such casuals who receive the entire day's board and lodging as above indicated, and made a recommendation to that effect to the Government. No decision, however, was arrived at.[137]

Only limited support for Langmuir's case can be found in terms of the Charity Aid Act. Payment to an institution under the act was based on "each day's actual lodgment and maintenance therein of any indigent person,"[138] and although not explicit on the point it appeared to envisage care of some duration. Pay for the day of departure was to be excluded in calculating the number of days' stay and thus the act was clearly not applicable to the casual who remained only one night. It is equally hard to uphold Langmuir's stand on the basis of the aims and purposes of the act, for these were expressed not in social welfare terms (though they were in some contemporary legislation), but in terms of the desirability of making provincial appropriations to institutions on a "proper and equitable basis" and of encouraging other

[136]Ibid., 1880, no. 8, p. 256.
[137]Ibid., 1879, no. 8, p. 219.
[138]Ontario, Statutes, 1874 (1st sess.), c. 33.

bodies and individuals to give "liberal support" to such institutions. The act contained no general statement about the kinds of need it proposed to relieve and hence offered no guidance for broader interpretations of its provisions.

The government did not act on Langmuir's recommendations, perhaps because of the weaknesses in the case he was able to put forward, or perhaps because it might involve administrative problems and create a precedent applicable to municipal outdoor relief programmes. Nothing more is heard of the proposal during the period.

One aspect of the problem of casual relief was the division of opinion on whether the applicants should be treated as in need of assistance or whether they should be regarded as vagrants subject to punishment or correction—the correction to take the form of hard work designed to form "habits of industry." The problem presented itself most acutely in Toronto where, during the 1880's the number of casuals seeking aid from the House of Industry reached numbers which taxed the resources of the institution. In 1886, a labour test was applied by which the "able-bodied and physically strong" were required to saw wood in payment for their lodgings and meals.[139] Wood sawing presented some difficulties because of the limited capacity of the institution to use or dispose of fire wood, however, and in 1888 the institution considered, but apparently rejected, oakum picking as an alternative.[140] It decided, instead, to meet the problem by erecting additional sheds and a new casual wing, requiring applicants to take a bath before going to bed and "to saw one and a quarter cords of wood as compensation for their keep."[141]

The Royal Commission of 1890 also gave serious attention to the problem of what it called "tramps and vagrants," and about which it received a good deal of testimony. Part of the commission's review of the problem appears in the following paragraph:

"What shall we do to repress vagrancy" is still a question that perplexes statesmen and magistrates, and strange to say it seems most difficult of solution in the United States and Canada in which it was almost unknown until the great civil war disturbed all the social elements and created a liking for an idle shiftless life. To-day vagrancy is perhaps as great a nuisance in Ontario as in any state of the Union. Many of the lazy and worthless amongst our own people have adopted it as a profession. Under the system of assisted passages many have been brought to Canada from Europe who never intended to make a living by honest labour and a large

139Ontario, *Sessional Papers*, 1887, no. 21, p. 8.
140*Ibid.*, 1889, no. 11, p. 12.
141*Ibid.*, 1890, no. 15, p. 15.

number of inveterate vagrants still drift from the United States into the Province.[142]

The commissioners found that the gaols provided the principal form of shelter for this group. The numbers of such persons confined in the county gaols had risen from 783 in 1869 to a high of 3,888 in 1877, and although the figure had then progressively decreased to 1,554 in 1883 it increased again in 1884 and between then and 1889 fluctuated between 2,100 and 2,450. The commission was concerned with the fact that the gaols were regarded by large numbers of the vagrants as places of free board and lodging. Frequently they appeared at the gaols bearing their own commitment, procured "from some accommodating justice of the peace or constable." Many were received overnight in police stations and lock-ups without a record being kept.

The directors of the House of Industry of Toronto indicated in their testimony to the commission that a major purpose of their programme for casuals was to prevent them from going to the Toronto gaol. This was partly "in order that those who are honestly seeking work and willing to labour may not undergo the degradation and loss of self-respect which are usually the consequences of imprisonment in a gaol," and also because they would "find the gaol ten times more comfortable than our quarters."

Testimony differed on the rôle to be played by gaols, houses of refuge, and a third type of institution, houses of correction. Although the last mentioned had found a place both in the thinking and in the legislation of the province from its earliest years, none had been established. Now the proposal was raised again before the Royal Commission by Goldwin Smith and Rev. Arthur H. Baldwin, both members of the board of directors of the House of Industry, Toronto. They recommended that the house of industry, as a private institution, should provide refuge only for the old, feeble, and disabled, and that its casual ward should be turned into a house of correction operated by the city.[143] It would be distinguished from a gaol by having somewhat less stigma attached to it, but primarily it would be devoted to the task of keeping its inmates at hard and, if possible, productive labour. This approach, it was felt, would reduce vagrancy which the commissioners regarded, in spite of some evidence to the contrary, as a matter of individual choice and a condition which could be successfully dealt with through the enforcement of labour upon all

[142]This and the following references to vagrancy are from Ontario, *Sessional Papers*, 1891, no. 18, pp. 111, 112.
[143]*Ibid.*, pp. 684–86.

able-bodied applicants for care in houses of refuge, as well as upon those who made the gaols their winter quarters.

In their final summary of the evidence as they saw it, the commissioners referred to three groups within the transient population who, they said, should be carefully distinguished and appropriately dealt with. One consisted of "those who are willing to work, who go from place to place honestly looking for work, and who are unable to find steady employment."[144] A person in this category "should be assisted in his efforts to find employment, and nothing should be done that would tend to degrade him or to destroy such self respect as he may be able to retain when compelled to seek relief." The second group was made up of "those who are willing to work and who do work occasionally, but who are dissolute or improvident, indulging in what they call sprees whenever they earn a few dollars, and finding themselves without money or resources of any kind at the beginning of winter." The commissioners felt that there was little reason to fear that men in this grouping "would be degraded by being sent to a gaol or to a house of correction where they would be kept under strict discipline and compelled to do a full day's work every day." The third group was described by the commissioners as professional tramps who disliked and avoided work and who procured food in the summer by begging and stealing and in the winter frequently sought the protection and care of houses of refuge and gaols. These, the commissioners felt, should be treated with more severity. If they were addicted to drink, they should be sent to an industrial inebriate reformatory[145] for terms of not less than six months. Others "who do not settle down to some regular steady employment" should be treated as dangerous and sentenced for a like term to the central prison.[146]

Although the commissioners referred to a house of correction in relation to the second of their three categories of transients, there was no reference to this type of institution in their concluding recommendations.[147] Presumably, in their final judgment, they saw no need to establish a new type of institution which would be only slightly distinguishable from the gaols and prisons. Rather, they called for the enforcement of hard labour in the gaols and the commitment to the

[144]*Ibid.*, pp. 113, 114.
[145]The reference would seem to suggest that an inebriate reformatory was actually in being. In fact, the establishment of inebriate institutions was a recommendation of the commissioners which was destined to wait some sixty years for implementation.
[146]Ontario, *Sessional Papers*, 1891, no. 18, p. 114.
[147]*Ibid.*, pp. 219–20.

central prison of those receiving a third or subsequent sentence for vagrancy.

The commissioners made no further reference to the needs of persons in the first category who, on the basis of their analysis, required kind and charitable treatment and assistance in finding employment. This silence can perhaps be accounted for by the fact that the focus of the inquiry was primarily upon the penal system. Their failure, however, to suggest resources that would meet the needs of those transients who required help during a period of involuntary unemployment and assistance in finding new jobs constitutes a gap in the recommendations and makes them notably less constructive and far-seeing in this matter than on many others in the report.

Municipal Outdoor Relief

After 1868 when incorporated villages were added to the types of municipalities empowered to give relief to needy persons, the province appeared to take little further interest in the matter of municipal aid to the poor. Only twice during the next quarter of a century, in the years 1875 and 1889, did it collect and publish statistics relating to it.

The statistical inquiry of 1875 was conducted by the Inspector "under instructions from the Government." To the clerks of all the municipalities entitled to give direct relief, Langmuir forwarded forms that were designed to show the numbers of physical defectives, mental defectives, and others who were "poor and destitute," together with the expenditures on each group. Few municipalities were able or willing to provide this three-way breakdown, however, and Langmuir was obliged to present tables showing only the combined figures.[148] These, too, lacked completeness because 60 of a total of 575 municipalities failed to make the return. Moreover, the returns from two of the four cities that did report included aid granted through "established houses," and that of the county of Waterloo applied to the inmates of the county House of Industry. The data reported, therefore, do not represent non-institutional relief exclusively. None the less, the figures do indicate that the granting of municipal relief was remarkably widespread and involved a considerable expenditure. Although the year covered, 1874, was one of reasonable prosperity, no fewer than 418 of the 515 municipalities reporting had relief recipients. The reports they presented showed 10,976 persons relieved at a cost of $110,210, and Langmuir estimated that had the returns been complete the

148*Ibid.*, 1875, no. 4, pp. 186–200.

figures would have indicated that 12,230 persons were covered at an expenditure of $123,050.[149]

Langmuir's support of the outdoor relief operations of the privately sponsored houses of refuge might have led one to expect his approval of the extent of outdoor relief being granted by the municipalities. Instead, he referred to it as "unsystematic charity" and showed his preference for a publicly sponsored institutional programme. He contended that the money expended on outdoor relief would more than "suffice to maintain an Industrial Farm or House of Refuge, where the infirm, or physically or mentally defective classes could be permanently maintained, and the destitute poor temporarily lodged, at a less cost than is now paid for mere temporary assistance."[150]

Langmuir may have been prompted to depreciate the value of outdoor municipal relief because he was anxious to have county houses of refuge established to deal with types of problems which were being referred to other institutions under his jurisdiction. Thus he accompanied his comments on municipal relief with a discussion of the kinds of persons being sent to gaol, pointing out that the gaols were housing many "vagrants and unfortunates who are committed for no offence save that they are homeless and destitute." In addition, the gaols received many persons "as being insane and idiotic, a great many of whom were fitter subjects for a House of Refuge than an Asylum." Thus linking the problem of the gaols and asylums with that of local relief, Langmuir proceeded to offer his conception of the rôle of the county houses of refuge. He saw them assuming most, if not all, of the burdens of municipal relief. They would utilize the work of the relatively able-bodied vagrants who were currently obtaining "immunity from labour" in gaol.[151] They would be productively employed in the farming and other activities to be carried out in the county home and would thus help to support the "non-productive or helpless class of indigents who are now a charge upon the municipalities."[152]

Another possible key to Langmuir's attitude towards municipal relief, however, may have lain in his preference for large units of administration. The organization of a system of county homes, parallel to the structure of county gaols, and like the gaols probably subject to provincial inspection, appealed to him as a "systematic" way to meet a welfare need. Small amounts of money spent on relief by over five hundred municipalities on a basis so casual that simple statistics on numbers and expenditures could not be provided by many of them

[149]Ibid., p. 200.   [150]Ibid., p. 201.
[151]Ibid., p. 3.   [152]Ibid., p. 201.

were bound to seem to Langmuir to be inefficient and wasteful. In his view, such haphazard action represented an impediment to the development of a network of county homes which he regarded as an essential element in the pattern of provincial and provincial-municipal institutions.

The second of the two occasions on which the province collected statistics was in 1889 when data on municipal relief were requested in a motion[153] proposed in the Legislature by Charles Clarke, the member for Wellington, and Thomas Gibson who represented Huron. The two members seem to have been consistent supporters of the government, and it therefore seems probable that the government welcomed and perhaps prompted this legislative initiative on a matter that was likely to be unpopular with municipal officials for whom it meant additional work. And because the same two members submitted a second motion[154] requesting data on the county homes then in existence, it appears that, as in 1875, the information was being sought in connection with the formulation of policy on institutional care for the poor. The introduction, in 1890, of legislation to make grants for the establishment of county homes would seem to uphold this supposition.[155]

The statistics secured appeared as a separate return in the form of a table which ran to some twenty pages and which was presented without any comment or explanation. The data showed the amounts paid in 1887 and 1888 for relief to both permanent and temporary indigent persons directly as well as through the remission of taxes. Much of the significance of this information was concealed, however, because the figures were listed municipality by municipality and no totals were taken to provide the over-all provincial picture. Only when added and presented as in Table XI do the statistics take on some meaning. For example, the number of persons aided appears to be significantly lower in 1888 than in 1874, although the figures cited above for the earlier year were undoubtedly inflated by the inclusion of those assisted casually in the private houses of refuge in the cities. Numerous additional limitations in the statistics for both years make

153Ontario, Sessional Papers, 1889, no. 77 (appears in pt. IX of the Papers as no. 85).
154Ibid., 1889, no. 61. See also above, page 98.
155Ibid., 1891, no. 18, p. 665. Further support was provided on this point by Christie in his testimony before the Royal Commission in 1890 when he stated that "we had a statistical return prepared which was submitted to the Legislature showing that the expenditure was greater in distributing charity in small sums through the municipalities than it would have been, provided there had been erected in these countries poor houses."

TABLE XI

MUNICIPAL RELIEF, 1888

Type of municipality	Persons assisted			Amount of assistance (in dollars)		
	On a temporary basis	On a permanent basis	Total	Through direct payments	Through remission of taxes	Total
Cities	859	111	970	9,192	775	9,967
Towns	1,317	267	1,584	25,708	2,659	28,367
Villages	374	44	418	4,834	590	5,424
Townships	1,307	761	2,068	55,285	2,572	57,857
TOTAL	2,857	1,183	5,040	94,029	6,596	100,625

SOURCE: Ontario, *Sessional Papers*, 1889, no. 77 (appears in pt. IX of the *Papers* as no. 85).

it perilous to draw definitive conclusions or to make comparisons between the two years. In each case the total figures stand as little more than rough approximations. They undoubtedly testify, however, to the widespread and continuing provision of assistance by the municipalities, at a considerable expenditure of public funds.

The work of administering poor relief in the municipalities throughout the province was normally carried out by the municipal clerk or by someone designated by the municipal council to perform the function on a part-time basis. The council itself usually considered the applications case by case. Thus the administration of assistance did not, during the period under review, become a specialized function, and it continued to reflect popular attitudes to poverty and the appropriate modes of dealing with it.

These attitudes and the manner in which they found expression in the granting of assistance are perhaps typified in the *Upper Canada Sketches* of Thomas Conant, written in the 1890's:

The burdensome tax which the people of England pay for the support of the poor we know nothing of in Canada. True, we have a poor-rate, but it sits so lightly upon us we do not heed it very much. For example, in the rural township of East Whitby, in the county of Ontario, there is a population of three thousand. The township is assessed at one and one-half million dollars. Among these people an annual tax is levied of about $8,000; for the poor, $400 out of the total tax levied. There is no poor-house in this locality. The really deserving poor are given an allowance of money weekly for their maintenance—what would be called "out-door relief" in England. It is not to be supposed that this sum is ample for all relief, but in this land of greatest abundance the people give and give liberally, and no further charge is made upon the authorities. Again, we take the ground that when food is cheap and fuel plentiful scarcely any should be so poor as to be unable to support themselves, where the opportunities have always been sufficient to enable all to earn enough from which to save a small competency. There are, of a truth, cases of unfortunate and honest poverty, and such we do not demur at relieving. . . .

It has been a mooted question in Canada whether we ought to erect county poor-houses for the care and provision of the poor and infirm or leave such matters to the ordinary township councils to deal with. In a land of plenty like ours, where there is abundance of food and constant demand for work-people, there should be no need for such persons to become a charge upon the bounty of the public; and it is absolutely certain that if we erect poor-houses there will always be poor to fill them. Such a class of population will come to us, if not already here, and having provided a place for them in the erection of poor-houses, we shall never get rid of them.

There are, of course, objects of charity scattered throughout the country, but they bear an infinitesimal proportion to the whole population, and can be provided for at small cost to the local community. In a country where everyone who will can provide for an inclement season or against the needs of age and infirmity, it becomes a very serious question whether the hardworking and thrifty ought to be taxed to provide for the lazy and thriftless. Or again, is it wise to foster the growth of a class of persons whose filth and foul diseases are the result of laziness and their own vices?[156]

One sees in these comments a number of popular attitudes towards the granting of assistance: few persons should need aid because it is easy to provide oneself with the essentials of life; if aid were given on any but the most restricted basis, it would foster dependency; some "unfortunate and honest poverty" does exist, but public aid, even to such cases as these, should be on a limited scale, with additional help sought from private sources.

Conant's sketches also provide an indication of a widespread view of the effect of establishing county houses of refuge; they would not, as had been supposed in England, restrict the increase of those seeking help by imposing the poor-house test—"enter the poor-house or starve"—but rather they would become repositories of the slothful. Thus it was better to let the township deal with the requests for aid to the poor by methods which, in the view of rural Ontario, placed an effective check upon dependency and its attendant costs.

Similar attitudes towards the needs of the poor and the problems which were thought to result if responsibility for meeting them were fully assumed by the government were to be found in the larger centres. The cities appear, in fact, to have made only very limited

156Thomas Conant, *Upper Canada Sketches* (Toronto, 1898), pp. 193–95.

use of the legislative authority they, as well as the towns, had acquired in 1858[157] for direct relief to the poor. Of the eleven cities in existence at the time of the survey summarized in Table XI, only five reported the number of persons they had assisted, and in the case of two of these the numbers given were obviously rough estimates.[158] It is clear that the cities had left the problem of relieving the poor, as far as possible, to voluntary associations which had developed in response to various welfare needs that had called for organized action. The rapid growth of the cities and the occurrence of periods of economic depression, however, began to place a burden on the private agencies which became increasingly harder to carry.

The advent of the ideas and practices of the charity organization movement, which began to make themselves felt in the province around 1880, led to greater collaboration between the agencies and made for improved efficiency in their operations. The movement, however, was characterized by widely differing views on the extent and proper auspices for the granting of outdoor relief. The "almost superstitious fear of relief giving"[159] in any form, although apparent in some centres in the United States, did not make itself felt to the same extent in Ontario where the division of opinion developed mainly on the question of public as opposed to private administration of relief measures. In Toronto the leadership in favour of the public assumption of responsibility for poor relief was provided by Goldwin Smith who over many years was able to present increasingly convincing evidence for the primary rôle of the public authority:

. . . where over-population is gathered in large masses, there must be a certain amount of failure, infirmity, disease, decrepitude and intemperance; the vicissitudes of commerce and industry on a large scale must give birth to cases of individual misfortune. The length of the close season in this climate presses hard on industry; and a summer's improvidence, which is almost pardonable, often leads to winter suffering. Moreover, the pauperism of the Old World is being constantly thrown upon our shores. There is happily no need for darkening the smiling prospects of our land with the Bastiles, as they are somewhat unjustly nicknamed, which mar the loveliness of the English landscape. But there is need, and in our great cities pressing need, for the institution of some relieving agency more regular, more certain, and more responsible than private charity, whether it be that of individual citizens or of charitable corporations. . . . Private

157Canada, *Statutes*, 1858, c. 99.
158Ontario, *Sessional Papers*, 1889, no. 77 (appears in pt. IX of the *Papers* as no. 85).
159Margaret E. Rich, *A Belief in People: A History of Family Social Work* (New York, 1956), p. 64.

charity will go on: it is the most suitable as well as the most Christian, way of dealing with a multitude of cases, including that bitterest of all kinds of indigence, the indigence of those who have known better days, and to whom to beg is as hateful as death. It is with waifs, hopeless wrecks, and castaways who might otherwise starve on the street that the relieving officer will have to deal. He will have, with the aid of the police, to maintain order, which no private person can maintain, among the inmates, often rough and turbulent, of a casual ward. He will also have to forward wanderers to their homes or destinations, which there are at present no regular means of doing, though that duty, and indeed the duties of a relieving officer in general, are incongruously cast upon the Chief Magistrate of a great city. But here the action of the legislature will be needed to prevent the country districts from shipping off their pauperism to the cities, and to compel each county to take care of its own poor. To talk of making the Churches the organs of charity, in such cases as the Conference has in view, is surely futile. How are you to inquire into the Church membership of a waif who presents himself late at night and famishing at your door?[160]

Goldwin Smith made many of the same points in a public address[161] delivered in 1889, but on that occasion he emphasized the need "of a more regular and more skilled administration . . . in regard to the relief of destitution," comparing the need for a high degree of knowledge and ability in this matter to that which had already been recognized and accepted in the civic departments of health and engineering. He also added to his earlier list of necessary welfare functions which could not be performed by volunteers or private associations. "What is to be done, for example, where chronic destitution is the consequence of mental disease or infirmity, and where a private individual or charity can have no right to interfere? Besides a centre of guidance, information and observation is needed, and this nothing but a public office can supply."[162] The case Goldwin Smith made for a city welfare officer was finally and hesitatingly accepted by Toronto and an appointment was made in 1893.[163] For two years, however, the officer's salary was paid by Smith,[164] who thereby demonstrated his conviction about the value and necessity of public welfare through a particularly imaginative and generous private action.

Toronto's appointment of a relieving officer in 1893, if it did not constitute a general acceptance on the part of the urban centres of

[160]*Bystander*, July 1883, pp. 206–7.
[161]Goldwin Smith, *Social Problems: An Address Delivered to the Conference of Combined City Charities of Toronto* (Toronto, 1889), p. 3.
[162]*Ibid.*
[163]Elisabeth Wallace, *Goldwin Smith: Victorian Liberal* (Toronto, 1957), p. 105.
[164]*Ibid.*

Ontario of civic responsibility for poor relief, was, at least, prophetic of such an acceptance. The period covered in this study thus closed on a note of promise. The cities which, in terms of acting on their legislative authority to grant relief, had lagged behind the towns, villages, and townships, had been given, however belatedly, a lead which they would have to follow. The metropolis of the province had taken an historic step in implanting the nucleus of what would grow in succeeding decades into the extensive civic welfare departments of the mid-twentieth century.

4

The Development of Correctional
Programmes

ALTHOUGH THE MAINTENANCE of law and order does not, in itself, come within the scope of social welfare, the causes of crime and, more particularly, the treatment of the offender do. Social welfare is concerned both with the failure of some men, women, and children in every generation to conform to those contemporary standards of conduct that are enforced by law, and with the parallel failure of traditional methods of law enforcement to achieve their supposed objectives of preventing and controlling crime.

Upper Canada, immediately upon its creation, had to face the question of maintaining law and order, and it was not long before the means adopted in the province began to reveal their limitations and, indeed, to contribute to and magnify the problems they were intended to solve.

PRE-UNION PERIOD, 1791–1840

English Criminal Law

A complicating factor in the maintenance of law and order was that the new province had inherited English criminal law as the latter stood at the beginning of the last quarter of the eighteenth century. It had been introduced into the whole of the geographic area covered by the Quebec Act in 1774 and continued to prevail in Upper Canada following the passage of the Constitutional Act. In 1800, however, the Upper Canadian Legislature, noting that "divers amendments have since been made in the same by the mother country, which it is expedient to introduce and adopt in this Province,"[1] enacted that the criminal law of England be introduced as it stood on September 17, 1792.

This statute also indicated the growing feeling in Upper Canada that more moderate forms of punishment ought to be employed in preference particularly to the form of gross physical punishment, that is, "burning in the hand," that appears to have been applied rather frequently in the early years of the colony before the gaols were ready to receive prisoners. The act noted that laws requiring this punishment for certain offences were "often disregarded and ineffectual," and that as a form of punishment it "sometimes may fix a lasting mark of disgrace and infamy on offenders, who might otherwise become good subjects and profitable members of the community." "Instead of such burning or marking," the act suggested that the court might impose upon the offender "such a moderate pecuniary fine as . . . in its discretion shall seem meet." If a fine did not seem sufficiently severe, the act provided for public or private whippings and, of course, imprisonment. The legislation also removed the penalty of transportation from the armoury of punishments inherited with the English criminal law. This seems to have been done, however, for reasons of administrative practicability rather as an expression of a more humane attitude to the offender, for although transportation was for the time being[2] excluded as a form of punishment, banishment as a less costly and less troublesome equivalent was substituted and appears to have been employed rather extensively for many years.[3]

English criminal law continued, over the years, to be modified through legislation[4] and practice but there is no evidence of any serious attempt to create a system of criminal law for Upper Canada that would reflect the special circumstances of the province and the character and habits of its people. In some matters, indeed, it proved more difficult for Upper Canada to qualify the application of English criminal law as it stood in the late eighteenth century than was the case in England. When, for example, an attempt was made to bring

[1]Upper Canada, *Statutes*, 1800, c. 1.

[2]Transportation was resumed in 1837 when it was enacted that "the transportation of offenders to such place or places in His Majesty's dominions as may be assigned for the reception of convicts" could be substituted for banishment (*ibid.*, 1836–37, c. 7).

[3]An interesting example of banishment for a sex offence which was protested by the friends and neighbours of the one banished is recorded in Upper Canada Sundries, Nov. 29, 1829.

[4]Notably, Upper Canada, *Statutes*, 1833, c. 4, which reduced to twelve the number of offences for which capital punishment could be inflicted. This statute also abolished the antiquated defence known as benefit of clergy.

the law relating to an unmarried mother convicted of causing the death of her child into line with that obtaining at the time in England, the legislation was disallowed when it was initially passed in 1826[5] and received royal assent only after it was re-enacted in 1831.[6]

A further legacy of the English criminal law was the penalties imposed against debtors, involving their imprisonment until they or their friends paid their debts or until their creditors withdrew charges against them. To carry out this law in the manner traditional in England it was necessary to provide special quarters in the gaols distinct from and less restrictive than those for persons charged with other crimes. This made for extra costs in the construction of the gaols,[7] complicated their management,[8] and made classification of other prisoners even more difficult than it would otherwise have been.[9] The presence of debtors in the gaols, however, may have had one compensating value in that the debtors frequently drew attention to conditions in the gaols and in so doing gained a more sympathetic hearing from the public than might other classes of offenders on the matter of the standards of care in them. Nevertheless, the improvement of the gaols of Upper Canada was doubtless advanced when in the mid-thirties the Legislature began to move away from the English criminal law on insolvent debtors, a process that was not completed for many years even though the folly of imprisoning persons for debt was recognized and explicitly stated in the preamble to the statute of 1835 called "An Act to Mitigate the Law in Respect to Imprisonment for Debt."[10]

The Establishment and Maintenance of Gaols

Noting in its preamble that "great inconveniences have been suffered by the inhabitants of this Province, from the want of Prisons and

[5]*Ibid.*, 1826, c. 2.
[6]*Ibid.*, 1831–32, c. 1.
[7]The Clerk of Prince Edward County, in describing the new gaol (Upper Canada Sundries, Jan. 22, 1834) reported that "six cells in the basement, for criminals and two commodious apartments for debtors in the second story are furnished and fit for the reception and security of Prisoners."
[8]When the state of the Home District gaol was unfavourably reported on by a grand jury in 1834 the magistrates of the district replied that a great improvement in the gaol would be possible if provision could be made for debtors away from the gaol (Upper Canada Sundries, July 26, 1834).
[9]William Lyon Mackenzie, while mayor of Toronto, made a surprise visit to the Home District gaol to see if the sentence of hard labour he had imposed on two prostitutes was being carried out; he found them at large in the debtors' quarters. (Upper Canada Sundries, Nov. 23, 1834).
[10]Upper Canada, *Statutes*, 1835, c. 3.

Court Houses in the several Districts thereof," the last statute passed in the first session of the Legislature of Upper Canada enacted that each of the four districts then in existence should establish a gaol and court house and that the same measure should be taken by new districts when they were formed.[11] The act delegated full responsibility to the magistrates in quarter sessions to finance, build, and maintain the gaols, although the sheriff of the district was given the authority to appoint and, where necessary, to discharge the gaoler and was expected to maintain a general oversight of the gaol. This delegation of responsibility for the gaols to the local level of administration proved to be a decision of enduring significance, for although some measure of central control had to be asserted over the gaols even before the end of the pre-Union period, municipal operation of local gaols became solidly embedded in the governmental structure of the province.

The reluctance of the members of the first session of the Legislature to enact that the gaols and court houses be financed by local direct taxation was based on their fears that the resources which could be directly taxed in the new province were too limited to make this a suitable way to raise the necessary funds. Although Simcoe regarded these fears as groundless, the securing of sufficient money to construct and operate the gaols and court houses was to prove, in fact, to be very difficult throughout all of the pre-Union and much of the Union period. Professor Aitchison has described it as "the most serious governmental problem the magistrates had to face."[12]

An early example of the financial and other difficulties encountered in the establishment of a local gaol is offered by the Eastern District which undertook to build its court house and gaol at Cornwall,[13] the principal centre in the district. The magistrates authorized the collection of funds for the enterprise to begin in 1793, but before a sufficient sum had been raised a substantial amount had to be surrendered to a new district which was carved out of the western townships of the old. Thus it was not until 1801 or 1802 that a wooden gaol, with an associated court house, was ready for occupancy.[14]

The slow pace at which district gaols were being established and the financial burdens that they were imposing caused the Legislature in 1822 to extend to the districts the power to borrow the necessary

---

[11]*Ibid.*, 1792, c. 8.

[12]J. H. Aitchison, "The Development of Local Government in Upper Canada, 1783–1850" (unpublished Ph.D. dissertation, Dept. of Political Economy, University of Toronto, 1954), p. 619.

[13]Then known as New Johnstown.

[14]John G. Harkness, *Stormont, Dundas and Glengarry: A History, 1784–1945* (Oshawa, 1946), p. 77.

funds. This right was first granted to the Midland District[15] and it became a precedent for other districts engaged in building or rebuilding their gaols. In 1824 the Legislature acknowledged the need of additional taxation to support gaols and court houses and authorized the District of Johnstown to levy an assessment of a penny on the pound for a specified period.[16] A few years later the province recognized that a gaol and court house were part of the essential equipment that a group of townships should possess before they were collectively given the status of a district, and from 1831[17] these two institutions had to be completed before a new district could be proclaimed.[18]

The financial burdens of the gaols did not end with their initial erection. Because some of the early gaols were poorly constructed, new or reconstructed buildings were often required within a few years. As early as 1825, for example, "the Magistrates, Grand Inquest and other Inhabitants of the Eastern District" forwarded a petition to the provincial government stating that the inmates of the old gaol were made to "suffer the most dreadful privations as it is impossible, particularly during the Winter Season to make the cells fit for their reception," and asking for the right to borrow £4,000 for the construction of a new gaol and court house.[19] There were numerous other instances during the pre-Union period of the magistrates' failing to provide adequately for the proper administration of the gaols and care of the inmates, and this situation, in part at least, was a reflection of the limited resources of the districts to meet the costs of even this basic service. As late as 1834 the magistrates of the Home District, perhaps the wealthiest district in the province, answered the charges of a grand jury concerning the deplorable state of the gaol, with the contention that they lacked funds for such improvements as a wall for an exercise yard, better salaries for the gaoler and other staff, more frequent cleansing of the interior, and more adequate clothes and bedding for the inmates.[20]

[15]Upper Canada, *Statutes*, 1822, c. 21.
[16]*Ibid.*, 1824, c. 35.
[17]Aitchison, "Local Government in Upper Canada," p. 620.
[18]Upper Canada Sundries, Jan. 22, 1834.
[19]*Ibid.*, Jan. 29, 1825.
[20]*Ibid.*, July 26, 1834. The case of the Home District magistrates was that "these evils, however, are beyond the power of the magistrates to remove until the funds at their disposal warrant their incurring a very large expenditure and until the laws under which the District funds are collected and expended are in some degree modified. Sensible of the latter necessity an application was made by the Magistrates by petition to the Legislature in 1827 praying for authority to levy an increased rate for a limited period, and for a repeal of the enactment which restricted them from laying out more than £50 at any one time on any object of improvement other than the Gaol and Court House."

Although this claim by the districts that they lacked funds to operate the gaols at an acceptable standard had much to support it, especially in view of the limitations placed on their taxing and spending powers under provincial legislation, it is also clear that the magistrates often neglected their responsibilities. They appear in many cases to have refused to take any responsibility for providing food and other necessities to the debtors,[21] to have neglected to ensure adequate medical attention,[22] to have been unprepared to pay adequate salaries for the gaolers, to have neglected their responsibility to frame rules and regulations for the operation of the gaols, and in some instances to have condoned harsh and repressive treatment of prisoners. Their failures were on a scale that drew complaints from the prisoners[23] and outcries from the humane and thoughtful members of society both in Upper Canada and in England, as well as the censure of average citizens acting in their capacities as grand jurors in carrying out periodic inspections of the public institutions of the district.

The maintenance of the gaols was complicated not only by limited funds and by the necessity of providing special quarters and procedures for insolvent debtors but by the lack, during almost all of the pre-Union period, of any alternative resources. Because of this latter deficiency, the gaols were required to act as houses of correction[24] for any homeless or needy person for whom there was no other place, and, more serious, they were made to serve as institutions for the insane.[25] The combined effect of these factors inevitably created such

[21]*Ibid.*, Feb. 1, 1827; also Upper Canada, *Journals*, 1830, Appendix (Report of the Committee on the Petition of Prisoners in the Gaol of York). The latter refers to debtors being dependent "on the humanity of the jailer and other debtors."

[22]This was the subject of a letter by Dr. William Rees to the Lieutenant-Governor (Upper Canada Sundries, March 8, 1836). Dr. Rees asserted "that in all civilized communities the benefits of a regular medical attendant is afforded the unfortunate Inmates of Prisons, and perhaps this city forms the only exception to any in His Majesties colonies in which such appointment does not exist. That the attention of the public has been repeatedly called to the subject and very recently by the Grand Jury of the District wherefore your memorialist respectfully represents that the Gaol of this city being the only receptable for Insolvent Debtors Criminals and Insane Persons with whom it is frequently crowded to excess requires such an appointment as well for the security of their lives as for enforcing sanitary regulations."

[23]Including a complaint from prisoners which resulted in the formation of a committee of the Assembly in 1830, of which W. L. Mackenzie was chairman (Upper Canada, *Journals*, 1830, Appendix (Report of the Committee on the Petition of Prisoners in the Gaol of York).

[24]Upper Canada, *Statutes*, 1810, c. 5.

[25]*Ibid.*, 1830, c. 20. This statute provided for the "relief of insane destitute persons" only in the Home District, but there is no doubt that other gaols were used similarly.

poor standards of treatment in the gaols that official attention was drawn to them. Measures for reform were advocated with growing insistence until, finally, in a piecemeal way and to a partial extent they were adopted.

Professor Aitchison has referred to "the function performed by grand juries of persistently calling attention . . . to the inadequacy of the state of the gaols during the whole period."[26] The reports of the grand juries were doubtless of importance in improving many situations in local gaols and in creating an atmosphere favourable to more fundamental measures by the province. Perhaps more immediate spurs to provincial action came from the members of the ruling oligarchy who, from their own experience and through prompting from the Colonial Office, became convinced that remedial measures were required. Such action by the Colonial Office was a reflection of the prison reform movement which was then current in England and which had gained expression in the appointment of prison inspectors in 1835.[27] The government was making a determined attempt to improve the gaols in the United Kingdom and to exercise a reforming influence on the prison systems in the colonies. Thus when a petition was received by the British government in 1835 from a person complaining of the bad conditions to which he was subjected during confinement in the Hamilton gaol, Lord Glenelg, the colonial secretary, although professing to assume that "a matter so essentially connected with a merciful and just administration of the law"[28] could not have been overlooked by the government of Upper Canada, none the less asked for a report on the matter and for information on "whether any and what regulations are established for securing a frequent . . . visitation of all places of confinement by the Provincial Magistracy."[29]

Supporting the impetus towards reform that came in this way from the Colonial Office was the action taken later in 1835 by the judges of the Court of King's Bench within the province. In a printed memorandum to the Lieutenant-Governor the judges referred to the failure of the magistrates in some districts, notably the Home District, to provide adequate food. Although often limited to bread and water, the diet in all gaols, in the view of the judges, should contain meat and vegetables. Medical attendance, fuel, bedding, and clothing should also be provided in all cases "to such an extent as to prevent absolute suffering, and the danger of permanent injury to the health of the

26Aitchison, "Local Government in Upper Canada," p. 619.
27Great Britain, *Statutes*, 1835, c. 38.
28Public Archives of Canada, G. ser., vol. 73, p. 268.
29*Ibid.*, p. 269.

prisoner."[30] In considering the question of remedial action on the situation, the judges noted that "it may probably be difficult, or impossible, for the Magistrates in some of the Districts to defray, out of the present rates, all the charges to which the District funds are liable; but it appears to the Judges that there can be no claim upon these funds entitled to take precedence of the indispensable charge of providing whatever may be necessary for preserving Prisoners from absolute suffering." In viewing the acute and immediate need of prisoners in the Home District gaol the judges remarked "that private charity might, and would, if appealed to, extend its aid to these miserable objects; but besides that such a resource is precarious and unsteady, it is already heavily burthened by other claims; and the proper maintenance of prisoners seems to us to be a charge peculiarly incumbent upon the Civil authority." In directing their memorandum to the Lieutenant-Governor, the judges implied that they expected the province to assume more of the responsibility which it had up to that time delegated completely to the districts.

The Act of 1838

Notwithstanding the pressure for remedial action in the gaols,[31] no legislation other than that relating to the establishment of a penitentiary was enacted by the province until the act to regulate the erection or reconstruction of the gaols and the framing of rules for their government was passed in 1838.[32] The board created by the province to achieve these purposes[33] was to exercise control over the plans adopted in the building of new gaols and the rebuilding of old ones, keeping in mind a long list of details relating to the location, construction, and inner layout of the buildings. Consideration of the latter point was to be aimed particularly at the proper classification of prisoners and at the "provision for the reformation of convicts, so far as may be practicable, and for their employment, in order that the

[30]Upper Canada Sundries, Dec. 22, 1835.
[31]See Upper Canada, Gazette, Jan. 14, 1836, for an indication in the speech from the throne that the government intended that year to take action on the gaols. "The state of the Gaols, and the treatment of the Prisoners confined in them, I shall have occasion to bring to your notice: for it appears to me that to relieve the Magistrates from an undue responsibility, as well as to ensure the humane care and safe custody of the prisoners, it is desirable to frame more particular provisions than have hitherto been made; and render this department in every respect complete."
[32]Upper Canada, Statutes, 1837–38, c. 5.
[33]For composition of the board, see above, page 26.

common gaols may really serve for places of correction according to the intention of the law." The act instructed the board to meet without delay and to "frame a set of rules and regulations for the government of common gaols in this Province, extending to the maintenance of the prisoners in regard to diet, clothing, bedding and other necessaries; medical attendance; religious instruction; the conduct of the prisoners and the restraint and punishment to which they may be subjected; and also to the treatment and custody of the prisoners generally, and to the whole internal economy and management of the gaol, and all such matters connected therewith, as shall be thought by them expedient." These comprehensive terms seemed to offer an opportunity for the board to set standards on all the questionable aspects of correctional care. The resultant rules were to be laid before each house of the Legislature at its next session and were to take effect after the termination of the session.

The Board of Gaol Commissioners appears to have set about its double assignment with reasonable faithfulness but with some delay, due perhaps to the effect of the rebellion. It was able to report[34] in 1839 that it had carefully examined and approved plans for proposed gaols in Woodstock, Peterborough, Guelph, Barrie, and London. It had, moreover, drawn up some thirty-one regulations for the gaols together with two extensive statistical forms which were to be filled out by the sheriff and gaoler and forwarded to the secretary of the province during the month of January each year. The proposed regulations covered virtually all aspects of the internal management of the gaols and represented important forward steps in the treatment of prisoners over the practices which had generally been characteristic up to that time. Adequate food, clothing, bedding, medical care, and religious counsel were set out as essentials; attention was drawn to the legal requirement that gaolers be paid adequate salaries; the use of irons for the restraint of prisoners was severely limited; and the gaoler and his assistants were required to "treat the several prisoners under their care with the utmost tenderness and humanity as far as may be consistent with the safe custody of such prisoners."[35]

The work of the board, covering what proved to be most of its effective life, was assessed in one of the examinations of public departments which was undertaken through a royal commission in 1839. In commenting on the implementation of the act of 1838, the committee examining the gaols and their administration noted that the

[34]Upper Canada, *Journals*, 1839–40, Appendix, vol. I, p. 320.
[35]*Ibid.*, p. 324.

provisions of the act had not, up to the time of the review, "been regularly complied with,"[36] a fact which it ascribed, in part, to the lack of a paid secretary or clerk to assist the commissioners. The committee held the appointment of such a secretary to be "an indispensable preliminary to the usefulness of the enactment." Much more fundamental, however, were the committee's recommendations concerning "the imperative necessity that exists of placing those receptacles for crime and misfortune under a well-regulated and wholesome discipline, and subject to the constant superintendence of some active and efficient inquisitorial power." To this end the committee suggested that "the Executive Government should be authorized by the Legislature to appoint a Commissioner . . . to prosecute a system of local investigation of every Gaol in this Province now in use." The investigation ought to be thorough, touching not only on the physical layout, accommodation, management, and staffing of the gaols but also on "generally every thing relating to the moral and physical condition of the inmates." It was suggested that this commissioner should transmit to the executive government a copy of his report "respecting each separate Gaol—and therein suggest any improvement of which the existing system could be found susceptible." The report should also be transmitted to the Board of Commissioners who, when changes in or enlargement of the structure of the gaol were involved, "should forthwith return their written opinion on the propriety and practicability of the alterations suggested." A final suggestion of the committee was that "the Executive Government should then have the power to direct the Magistrates of the District in general Quarter Sessions assembled, wherein the proposed alterations are required, to proceed to the carrying into effect the same, and they should be empowered and required, if necessary, to impose a rate not exceeding a certain fixed amount on the District, to defray the expense of the meditated improvements."

In addition to making these broad recommendations, the committee presented a brief review and assessment of the adequacy of the existing gaols, basing their findings on the visits of its members, all of whom were judges who travelled on circuit through the province and who "frequently, though not uniformly, visited the several Gaols." Their assessment of the gaols was as follows:

SANDWICH: The Gaol . . . is reported by the Sheriff as too small and insecure. But it has always been considered to be well managed by its old and

[36]This and the following references to the committee's report are from Upper Canada, *Journals*, 1839–40, Appendix, vol. II, pp. 10–13.

respectable keeper, and has been found clean and in apparently good order on personal inspection.

LONDON: The Gaol . . . is small, incommodious, and as the Committee believes, unsafe, and so inadequate that the complaints of persons therein confined, of the loathsome cells in which they are incarcerated, need create no surprise in those acquainted with its actual condition. A new Gaol is, however, about being erected.

SIMCOE: The Gaol . . . is new, and sufficient for the wants of that District.

HAMILTON: The Gaol . . . is much too small for the accommodation of the numbers therein confined, so much as to preclude any attempt at classification. Its management has been generally represented as tolerable.

NIAGARA: The Gaol . . . is offensive and insufficient; the site may be considered as ineligible, making drainage difficult if not impossible. It is remote from the Town. The Committee is of opinion that a new Gaol on a well-designed plan and favourable situation, is highly desirable.

TORONTO: A new Gaol is being erected in the Home District; the present one is quite insufficient for the proper accommodation of its numerous prisoners. There is reason to believe, however, that under the present keeper it is well managed, and the comfort of the prisoners as carefully attended to as circumstances will permit.

NEWCASTLE: The Gaol . . . is new, sufficiently commodious, and well managed.

PICTON: The Gaol . . . is reported as sufficient for the wants of the District of Prince Edward.

KINGSTON: The Gaol . . . is reported as sufficiently large to accommodate the average number of persons confined; clean, well ventilated, and healthy; but of such defective construction as to preclude proper classification.

BROCKVILLE: The Gaol . . . has been always well managed, but its accommodations are much too limited, and the erection of a new one is much to be desired.

L'ORIGNAL: The Gaol . . . is small; sufficient for the present accommodation of prisoners, though represented by the Sheriff as being insecure.

CORNWALL: The Gaol . . . is reported by the Sheriff as sufficient for the accommodation of prisoners.

PERTH: The Gaol . . . is reported to be sufficient for the proper accommodation of prisoners.

It will be observed that, of the thirteen gaols, eight were considered to be defective in some important respect, and only two of these had plans for replacement.

The state of the gaols at the end of the pre-Union period was thus far from ideal. There is little doubt, however, that the mounting criticism that had been directed against them during the thirties had resulted in significant improvements and that the work of the Board of Commissioners in drawing up rules and in approving plans had exerted a reformative influence. It had, none the less, become apparent that the board could not bring about reforms on the scale required unless its work was supported by an inspector capable of working systematically for the implementation of the standards that the board had formulated.

Even if the Board of Commissioners had been supported with the necessary staff, its efforts to reform the gaols could have had only limited success as long as the gaols remained, in default of other types of institutions, the dumping ground for persons who were not criminal offenders within the proper meaning of that term. It was increasingly recognized during the pre-Union period that there should be other ways to deal with debtors, that there should be refuges for those needing merely shelter, and that there was an acute need for asylums for the mentally ill. It was also increasingly apparent that the local gaols should not be used for the custody of those sentenced to long terms of imprisonment.

Some progress was made in each of these directions: by way of ground work towards the removal of debt as an offence punishable by imprisonment and hence the removal of debtors from the gaols;[37] through legislation designed to encourage the founding of refuges;[38] through legislation and executive action towards the establishment of a provincial asylum;[39] and, much more successfully, in the planning, building, and operation of a provincial penitentiary.

Establishing the Penitentiary

Other than the measures that the central government of Upper Canada had taken from time to time to deal with the epidemics of cholera, the establishment of the penitentiary represented the first undertaking of any magnitude in the field of social welfare. Although a good case could perhaps have been made for the establishment of a penitentiary from as early as 1820 and although the arguments in favour of such an institution would have merited increasing considera- tion as the population of the province and its penal problems mounted through the twenties and early thirties, it none the less seems remark-

[37]Upper Canada, *Statutes*, 1835, c. 3. Although this act went only part way in removing insolvent debtors from the gaols, the movement to carry that objective further, which had been in evidence from at least as early as 1827, was making itself felt towards the end of the period.

[38]*Ibid.*, 1836–37, c. 24. Although this act was not implemented it indicated public policy in the matter. In Toronto, where the need was greatest, a refuge under private auspices came into being at about the same time.

[39]*Ibid.*, 1839, c. 11. Three years earlier, commissioners had been appointed to explore the means of establishing an asylum. See Upper Canada, *Journals*, 1836, no. 30.

able that the question of building a penitentiary became a matter of legislative concern and action as soon as it did. The major credit for launching and pursuing the project to the threshold of completion belongs to H. C. Thomson, the founder and editor of the *Upper Canada Herald* of Kingston and the member for Frontenac in the Legislative Assembly from 1825 until his death in 1834. During each session beginning with that of 1826–27, Thomson introduced resolutions advocating an inquiry concerning "the propriety of erecting a penitentiary within this province,"[40] and each year he appears to have had better success in gaining attention and support for the project. It was not until 1831, however, that an inquiry was actually undertaken by a legislative committee.[41] The committee seems to have done little more than receive a statement on penal institutions from an unidentified "gentleman whose practical knowledge of the subject entitles his opinion to a respectful consideration."[42]

This statement, which began with the assertion that "the necessity for a penitentiary must be obvious to everyone who has ever attended a court of justice in the province,"[43] presented the case Thomson had been making for such an institution over the years. Basic to the case was the view that English criminal law sanctioned the death penalty— a penalty which juries and the judiciary in Upper Canada were increasingly reluctant to see exacted and which was increasingly being set aside through the lieutenant-governor's exercise of the prerogative of mercy. Of the four remaining types of penalty—the payment of fines, imprisonment in the local gaols, corporal punishment, and banishment—the statement to the committee found that each had serious weaknesses. The sentence of banishment for life, or for a specified term of years, which was frequently inflicted for the more serious crimes, was particularly criticized because, among other reasons, this form of punishment was frequently flouted entirely or violated through the return of the sentenced person before the expiration of the required period. Similarly, the remaining alternatives were held to be inadequate and defective as legal sanctions, the common gaols because of their failure to classify and separate the inmates and hence their tendency to become what the statement described as "seminaries kept

---

[40]Upper Canada, *Journals*, 1826–27, p. 23.
[41]*Ibid.*, 1831, p. 32.
[42]*Ibid.*, Appendix, pp. 211–12. The committee was supposed to consist of Christopher Hagerman, the solicitor-general, and a member of the Assembly, Donald McDonald, but while Thomson was not mentioned as a member of the committee, it was he who signed the report as chairman of the committee.
[43]*Ibid.*, p. 211.

at the public expense for the purpose of instructing his majesty's subjects in vice and immorality, and for the propagation and increase of crime."[44]

The principal conclusion and recommendation of the report—that the province build a penitentiary essentially on the lines of the state penitentiary at Auburn, New York—may have been made palatable to the Legislature by the accompanying contention that a provincial penitentiary could be erected for approximately £10,000 and, once built, would be self-sustaining.

The report was accepted, and in the following year Thomson moved a resolution "that the sum of one hundred pounds be granted for the purpose of procuring Plans and Estimates of a Penitentiary to be erected in this Province, and to enable Commissioners to collect information respecting the management of such Institutions."[45] A vote was called, the only one recorded on the project during its formative stage, and carried by twenty-three in favour to eighteen opposed. On January 28, 1832, an act[46] was passed embodying the intent of the resolution and naming Thomson and John Macaulay as the two commissioners to carry out the assignment. Macaulay was an able, wealthy, and public-spirited Kingston business man[47] who was later to become successively, surveyor-general, civil secretary, and inspector-general in the provincial administration, and a member of the Legislative Council during the Union period.

The two commissioners visited three penal institutions in New York State and one in Connecticut and returned convinced that the system employed in the penitentiary at Auburn, New York, should be adopted in the establishment of an Upper Canadian penal institution.[48] In their report to the Legislature they described the essential principles of the Auburn system to be the solitary confinement of prisoners while not at work, silence in the sense of severe restraint upon speech, strict discipline, and collective employment at industrial pursuits designed to provide hard labour and to make the institution self-sustaining. In this

[44]*Ibid.*, p. 211. In the report this view of local gaols in general was attributed to Lord Brougham.

[45]Upper Canada, *Journals*, 1831–32, p. 94.

[46]Upper Canada, *Statutes*, 1832, c. 30.

[47]In a return attached to a letter of the Lieutenant-Governor to the Colonial Secretary in 1834 (Upper Canada, *Journals*, 1836, Appendix 28, p. 6) Macaulay is described as "an opulent merchant, of Kingston, and a large proprietor of land— a native of the Province, and a son of a U.E. Loyalist; and from his character, intelligence and acquirements, possesses great influence."

[48]Upper Canada, *Journals*, 1833, Appendix, pp. 26–41. They had planned also to visit Boston and Philadelphia but returned in haste because of the outbreak of cholera in Kingston.

report the commissioners went beyond their terms of reference and argued that if the Legislature planned to proceed with a penitentiary it would "become requisite to make great and corresponding alterations in the criminal law of this Province."[49] The case they made for modification of the criminal law appears to have been accepted because the Legislature proceeded soon after to pass an act[50] to reduce substantially the number of cases punishable by death and to substitute other forms of punishment, notably terms of imprisonment.

The project to establish a penitentiary passed from the stage of planning to that of development on February 13, 1833, when an "Act granting to His Majesty a sum of money to defray the expense of erecting a Penitentiary in this Province"[51] was passed. This statute provided for the appropriation of £12,500 over a period of three years and authorized the appointment of three commissioners to secure a site for the institution and to manage and superintend its erection. The commissioners chosen were Macaulay and Thomson together with Henry Smith, another prominent citizen of Kingston. More than two years were to pass from the enactment of the legislation authorizing the building of the institution to the reception of its first prisoners in June 1835. Under the act of 1833 the commissioners acquired a site[52] for the institution near Kingston and secured as superintendent of construction William Powers, who had been deputy warden at the Auburn penitentiary and who had drawn the plans which the commissioners had submitted in their report to the Legislature. Other staff was acquired but by the time construction was well started the commissioners found that the first instalment of funds appropriated for the institution had been largely exhausted, so the project had to mark time until action was taken in 1834[53] to make the remainder of the initial

[49]*Ibid.*, p. 29. Noting that the provincial law continued to be limited to that of England, the commissioners extended their exhortations on the matters of legal and penal reform to the mother country, remarking that "it is indeed full time that England should act truly in the spirit of the statute passed in the year 1779, in consequence of the united efforts of Sir William Blackstone, Mr. Howard and Mr. Eden, and adopt a proper system of prison discipline, whereby 'offenders shall be placed in solitary imprisonment, accompanied by well regulated labour, and religious instruction, thus deterring others from the commission of crimes, and also reforming the individuals, and inuring them to habits of industry.'" England would accordingly do well to investigate and imitate the "penal codes and prison discipline of the United States." (*Ibid.*, p. 30.)

[50]Upper Canada, *Statutes*, 1833, c. 4. The report of the commissioners was dated Nov. 12, 1832, and the legislation on capital punishment did not begin its course through the Assembly until December.

[51]Upper Canada, *Statutes*, 1833, c. 44.

[52]The land consisted of 100 acres, one mile west of Kingston and was purchased on June 10, 1833, for £1,000 (Upper Canada, *Journals*, 1833–34, Appendix, p. 103).

grant available. During the summer and fall sufficient progress was made that prisoners could have been accepted but for the further failure of the Legislature to make funds available for their maintenance.

In the same year a comprehensive act was passed for the maintenance and government of the penitentiary, including the appointment of a board of five inspectors with "full power and authority to make all necessary rules and regulations respecting the discipline and Police of the said Penitentiary."[54] The legislation also provided for the appointment by the lieutenant-governor of a warden, chaplain, physician, and deputy warden and the appointment by the Board of Inspectors of a clerk and up to twenty keepers. The appointment of guards was, for some reason, retained as a responsibility of the lieutenant-governor. The warden was required

to exercise a general supervision over the government, discipline, and police of the said penitentiary; to give the necessary directions to the keepers, and to examine daily into the state of the Penitentiary, and the health, conduct and safe keeping of the prisoners; to use every proper means to furnish such prisoners with employment the most beneficial to the public, and the best suited to their various capacities; and to superintend all the manufacturing and mechanical business that may be carried on within the Penitentiary; to receive the articles so manufactured, and to sell and dispose of the same for the benefit of the Province, when the labour of the convicts is not let out by contract.[55]

It had been the intention of the government to appoint Thomson as warden of the penitentiary but his death in April 1834 made it possible for Henry Smith to press his claim for the position,[56] and on July 28, 1834, he received the appointment. Simultaneously, the new board was named with Macaulay as its first chairman.

Following Thomson's death, Macaulay and Smith continued as the commissioners for building the institution until 1835 when an act for

[53]Upper Canada, *Statutes*, 1834, c. 38.   [54]*Ibid.*, c. 37.   [55]*Ibid.*
[56]He had done this prior to Thomson's death (Upper Canada Sundries, April 10, 1834) when, in a letter to the Civil Secretary, he had said that he intended to petition for the appointment unless the Government planned to give it to Thomson "whose claims upon His Excellency for the appointment are, I conceive, paramount to those of any other person." A few days later Smith wrote (Upper Canada Sundries, April 26, 1834) a second letter stating that "the lamented death of my friend Mr. Thomson leaves me at liberty to forward to you the accompanying Petition." The petition, containing the names of some fifteen prominent citizens of the Midland District, was also supported by letters from John S. Cartwright and Robert S. Cartwright. The letter from the former referred to Smith as "a most correct and religious person—of mild and conciliatory manners and a most excellent temper added to which he possesses good judgment and I do not know any person in this place so likely to discharge with effect the arduous duties of the office."

the further completion of the penitentiary[57] provided that the duties of the commissioners be assumed by the Board of Inspectors and the warden. This step, together with the appointment of the senior staff of the institution, completed the initial phase of the institution's establishment, though the continued construction of the buildings and the surrounding walls was to be a principal concern in the operation of the penitentiary during the remaining years of the pre-Union period. The continued needs of the penitentiary for capital as well as maintenance funds, the salary and perquisites of the warden, and the salaries of the chaplain and surgeon were the major matters still involving consideration by the provincial government and requiring action by the Legislature. Acts respecting the penitentiary, largely concerning its further erection and support, were passed in each of the remaining years of the pre-Union period,[58] and the members of the Legislature became increasingly aware that the early estimates of the cost of the penitentiary had been well short of the amounts that they were actually called upon to appropriate.[59]

Macaulay resigned as a member of the Board of Inspectors towards the end of 1836 when he moved to Toronto to become surveyor-general.[60] While in this latter position, and in others that he was to occupy in the provincial government during the period, he became, unofficially, the adviser to the government on the penitentiary. Although this arrangement resulted in at least one instance of the government taking his advice against that of the Board of Inspectors,[61] there is no doubt that he brought to the highest level of government an informed opinion supportive to the continued development of the penitentiary.[62]

[57]Upper Canada, *Statutes,* 1835, c. 42.

[58]*Ibid.,* 1836–37, c. 90; 1837–38, c. 53, 54; 1839, c. 65; 1840, c. 59.

[59]It may have been concern about the cost of the institution which lead to the consideration from 1837 to 1839 of a project to remove the penitentiary from Kingston to Marmora with the object of employing the convicts in mining and processing iron ore. Although the project received considerable support from the commissioners appointed to investigate the matter it was opposed by Henry Smith and nothing came of it (Upper Canada, *Journals,* 1839, Appendix, p. 237).

[60]Upper Canada, *Gazette,* Oct. 13, 1836.

[61]This was on the matter of the relative levels of the surgeon's and chaplain's salaries. On the grounds that the chaplain had to spend more time at the institution than the surgeon Macaulay, as opposed to the board, thought his salary or retainer should be higher.

[62]Following his move to Toronto there were no further instances of the kind of obstruction that had occurred in 1836 when a bill providing £5,000 for the support of the penitentiary, which passed on March 4, was reserved by the Lieutenant-Governor and did not become law until the end of September. This of course delayed construction as well as the payment of salaries and the meeting of other obligations.

In general the Board of Inspectors was given both the authority and the means to develop the penitentiary in the manner that early reports had envisaged, that is, along the lines of the Auburn penitentiary, with perhaps somewhat more stress upon religious influences. In addition, in order to affirm the principles on which the penitentiary was to operate, the inspectors, in 1836, formulated rules and regulations on discipline and policy.[63] These regulations set out the duties of each of the officers of the institution and laid down in considerable detail the daily routines that were to be followed in its administration. Particular emphasis was placed on the rule of silence because of the firmly held belief that "the preservation and due effect of the whole system of discipline depends upon the absolute prevention of intercourse among the Convicts." The keepers, accordingly, were required to show the utmost diligence in "preventing any such intercourse or communication." They were, moreover, "to hold no unnecessary conversation with convicts, nor to allow them to speak on any other subject but such as is absolutely necessary." The convicts were not to "exchange looks, wink, laugh, nod, or gesticulate," or to "make use of any signs, except such as are necessary to explain their wants to the waiters." The principle of keeping the convicts "constantly employed at hard labour during the day time" was also emphasized. It was clearly assumed, however, that the employment they were given would be useful and indeed profitable to them following their release.

Religious training, as set out in the initial rules and regulations, consisted only of a Sunday service and individual counselling by the chaplain. Both before and after the appointment of the chaplain, however, a short period each day was devoted to the reading of religious material by those who were literate. Those unable to read were "divided into classes, and taught to spell and read by qualified teachers, selected from amongst the other convicts, under the immediate eye of the Keepers and superintendence of the Warden or Deputy Warden." This practice, which was at variance with the principle of non-communication between the convicts, was discontinued, but in his last report during the pre-Union period the chaplain expressed the hope that a sabbath school on a similar basis could be established.[64]

In drafting the rules for the penitentiary the inspectors were completely convinced of the soundness of the Auburn principles and were confident that the rules based on them, if rigorously adhered to,

[63]The following references to the regulations are from Upper Canada, *Journals*, 1836–37, Appendix 10, pp. 2, 19–27.

[64]*Ibid.*, 1840, Appendix, vol. I, pt. I, p. 93. The inspectors, however, indicated that they would not approve the proposal until a chapel was erected (*ibid.*, p. 61).

would achieve the intended purpose of reforming the convicts. It was thus with some concern that they viewed the return to the institution of a growing number of those who had been discharged in the early years of its operation. As a solution to this problem their main suggestion was longer prison sentences. They felt that no sentence should be for fewer than three years. Based on their observation of the first recidivists they also formulated a second and more imaginative recommendation. This took note of the fact that discharged prisoners tended to remain in the immediate locality where, meeting with associates from the penitentiary, they fell once more into intemperate and criminal habits. Because this practice could be partly attributed to the prisoner's lack of sufficient funds at the time he left the institution, the inspectors suggested that the discharged prisoner be placed "in a state of probation, under some sort of surveillance after his discharge,"[65] and given some reward for continued good behaviour. Their specific proposal was that "one third of the convict's earnings . . . be paid to him in annual installments, on his producing to the treasurer of the District in which he resides, satisfactory certificates of good conduct, signed by any two magistrates of that District, together with a certificate of some resident Minister of Religion; that he, (the convict) had been a regular attendant on his ministry during the year, and that to the best of his knowledge and belief, his character among his neighbours for honesty, sobriety and industry had been irreproachable."[66] This plan was put forward hesitatingly by the inspectors, however, and it appears not to have received serious consideration.

If such a plan, involving the payment to the convict of much of his earnings, had been adopted, it would, of course, have reduced further the income of the penitentiary. The extent of the income was already failing to justify the early predictions that the institution would be financially self-sufficient and, although this was largely attributable to the extensive use of convict labour in the construction of the prison buildings, it was also due, in part, to the opposition that was immediately encountered to the penitentiary's engaging in any activity which would be in competition with business and labour operating outside its walls.[67]

As the period closed, however, the penitentiary seemed to be firmly

[65]*Ibid.*, pp. 58–59.   [66]*Ibid.*, p. 59.

[67]A decision was made in 1838 to establish a rope works in the penitentiary and in 1839 it was decided to enlarge it on the grounds that it would not interfere with established industry but on the contrary would promote it. "The Inspectors had two objects in view in commencing this work. It in no degree interferes with any of those mechanic arts against the introduction of which so much opposition has been made; and it may also afford encouragement to the growth and cultivation of hemp within the Province" (*ibid.*, p. 60).

established, with modern buildings and a system of prison administration and discipline which was held to incorporate the best and most modern penal practices of the time; it seemed also, in a manner generally regarded as satisfactory, to be accomplishing the purposes that the Legislature had assigned to it. The tests of the soundness of the principles on which the institution was based and the efficiency of its administration were to come in the next period.

UNION PERIOD, 1840–1867

The prospects for rapid progress in the field of corrections looked bright as the Union period opened because the groundwork seemed to have been laid for the improvement both of the local gaols and of the penitentiary. But the appearances proved deceptive. When action was not taken to re-establish the Board of Gaol Commissioners which had operated briefly before the Union, the Upper Canadian legislation became a dead letter. Nearly two decades were to pass before measures were finally adopted of the kind recommended by the committee which had examined the question in 1839. In the case of the penitentiary there was a gradual decline in its administrative efficiency and discipline during the forties until, at last, the resulting scandals and dissension led to the appointment of a royal commission of inquiry.

The Penitentiary to 1849

One of the acts passed during the first session of the new Legislature was "an Act to render the Penitentiary erected near Kingston in the Midland District, the Provincial Penitentiary for Canada."[68] This measure did not, however, result in an immediate flow of prisoners from the lower province. Even though Canada East did, after a few months, begin to commit prisoners in considerable numbers, Upper Canada always provided a disproportionate percentage of the inmates, and the penitentiary continued to be essentially an Upper Canadian institution.[69]

The admission of Lower Canadians to the penitentiary, its use to

[68]Canada, *Statutes*, 1841, c. 69.

[69]In 1860, for example, only 63 came from Lower Canada while 167 came from Upper Canada; in 1865 the figures were 70 and 203. Few provisions were made for French-speaking inmates. It would be interesting to explore whether this fact together with the location of the penitentiary in Canada West affected the sentences imposed by French-Canadian magistrates and judges on their compatriots.

imprison soldiers courtmartialled for military offences, the tendency of the courts to issue longer sentences, and the increase of crime associated with the expanding population, together constituted the major factors in the fivefold increase in the population of the penitentiary during the Union period (Table XII). This increase affected

TABLE XII

NUMBER OF PERSONS IMPRISONED IN THE PENITENTIARY AT
THE END OF EACH FISCAL YEAR, 1835–1866

Year	Number	Year	Number	Year	Number	Year	Number
1835	55	1843	256	1851	448	1859	801
1836	81	1844	384	1852	463	1860	784
1837	123	1845	478	1853	496	1861	764
1838	154	1846	480	1854	512	1862	765
1839	148	1847	468	1855	557	1863	823
1840	153	1848	454	1856	668	1864	729
1841	151	1848	410	1857	683	1865	774
1842	164	1850	397	1858	778	1866	815

SOURCE: Canada, *Journals*, 1849, Appendix B.B.B.B.B., n.p.; also Canada, *Journals*, and *Sessional Papers*, 1850–67.

many aspects of the institution's administration. It involved the continued construction of cell blocks, workshops, and other facilities, and because a large proportion of the convicts were employed in these building activities the type of discipline and routine which had initially been envisaged proved difficult to apply, and the amount of income from the sale of prison-made articles was reduced. More important, perhaps, was the effect that the expanded numbers of inmates had in placing pressures on the administrative and custodial staffs and in heightening the tensions normally characteristic of penal institutions.

The growing responsibilities and intensified pressures associated with the expansion of the institution, particularly after 1842, seem to have brought to the fore certain characteristics of the warden, Henry Smith, which adversely affected his ability to administer a large penal institution. Smith had shown a disposition soon after his appointment to seek to eliminate, by direct or indirect means, all limitations upon his absolute mastery of the penitentiary. When opposition appeared, either from his subordinates or from members of the Board of Inspectors, he set about to rid himself of it and to become the dominant figure not only in the day to day administration of the institution but also in the formulation of its policies. Thus he sought and finally brought about the dismissal, or at least the departure, of William Powers, the first deputy-warden, and then of Edward Utting, Powers' successor. Similarly, he appears to have employed his considerable influence with the provincial government to secure the replacement of inspectors who expressed opposition to his plans. His first such action occurred prior to the Union period when he found himself in dispute with the majority of the members of the board, principally on matters of the relationship between himself and the deputy wardens. When all the members except one who had consistently supported Smith were replaced, the resulting board was quite tractable until its members were confronted in 1846 with a new penitentiary act. Not having been consulted about this legislation, which was obviously inspired by the warden and promoted in the Legislature by his son Henry Smith Jr. (Conservative member for Frontenac), and being opposed to a number of its provisions, this board resigned.

The board appointed to replace it proceeded, during the next two years, to act in harmony with the warden whose position for some time seemed stronger than ever. An early act of the new board, however, was to promote the officer in charge of kitchen stores to the position of head-keeper (the position initially established as the deputy-warden-ship) and to appoint Francis Smith, one of the warden's sons, to the post of kitchen-keeper. This step together with the subsequent dismissal of certain members of the custodial staff resulted in considerable public criticism with which was linked a growing concern about the extensive use in the institution of corporal punishment.

The criticism of the operation of the penitentiary was augmented from an unexpected quarter in 1847 when the surgeon, Dr. James Sampson, directed a number of serious charges against Francis Smith. These were dismissed by the Board of Inspectors, and some time later countercharges were levelled against the surgeon. Dr. Sampson refused to have these dealt with by the board, and both he and the board referred the matter to the provincial government.[70]

Royal Commission of 1848–49

The government responded by appointing the five-member Royal Commission of 1848–49 to conduct an investigation of the charges

[70]It has been suggested that the Reform government that came to power in March 1848 was eager to find abuses associated with the previous government and Tory officials to sack (D. G. Creighton, *John A. Macdonald: The Young Politician* (Toronto, 1952), p. 159). Although this may well have been the case, it is difficult to see how any government could have ignored the deep division between Dr. Sampson and the Board of Inspectors which reached a point of crisis just as the old government was leaving office. Letters from the board and Sampson were dated March 8 and 9, 1848, respectively. The new government took office on March 10. Sampson was himself a Conservative, and by this time those with whom the warden had quarrelled included many of the most prominent citizens and leading Conservatives of Kingston and the Midland District.

and countercharges and of "the whole conduct, economy, system of discipline and management, pursued in or with respect to Our said Penitentiary."[71] In the course of a very thorough inquiry[72] the commissioners made certain findings, on the basis of which the government discharged the warden.[73]

The commissioners also submitted a second report[74] on measures to improve the penitentiary system. This report was to influence the development of penal policies for many years and is thus to be regarded as one of the more significant documents in the history of social welfare in the Union period. It reflected the considerable study of penal matters made by the commissioners, particularly by William Bristow and George Brown[75] who, like Macaulay and Thomson fifteen years earlier, visited some of the major penal institutions of the northeastern United States and discussed correctional questions with members of the prison discipline societies in Boston, New York, and Philadelphia. The report accordingly incorporated the best in contemporary North American ideas of the purposes of penal programmes and of how these could be achieved through the physical design, internal discipline, and day-to-day administration of a prison, and through the type of influences which could be brought to bear on its inmates. The commissioners also stressed that well-conceived and well-administered correctional programmes directed towards the reformation of the prisoner were, or should be, matters of concern to philanthropists, statesmen, and the general public. They pointed out that although great progress in penal reform had been made much still remained to be done.

[71]Canada, *Journals*, 1849, Appendix B.B.B.B.B., n.p.

[72]*Ibid.* The report of the inquiry is voluminous and indicates an approach to the assignment on the part of the commissioners which probably justified some of the criticism made against it by Smith and John A. Macdonald, who served as his principal champion. The report begins with a useful history of the institution and of the troubles which developed within it, and then moves into an account of the more recent incidents through the introduction of parts of the evidence taken. It then examines some twelve charges against the warden and certain other officials, introducing some evidence verbatim and other evidence in summary form. If indicating, at times, a less than judicial approach to the inquiry, the commission none the less brought out evidence of maladministration and of brutal and excessive punishment of prisoners that was conclusively damning. In the interests of humanity and efficiency alike the penitentiary had to be given a new administration.

[73]Dr. Sampson was cleared of the charges made against him.

[74]Canada, *Journals*, 1849, Appendix B.B.B.B.B., n.p.

[75]Bristow, the editor of the Montreal *Times*, and Brown of the Toronto *Globe* were able, as a result of their experience as commissioners, to bring an informed and highly influential point of view to penal matters in Canada for many years. See J. M. S. Careless, *Brown of the Globe*, vol. I (Toronto, 1959), pp. 77–87, 101–3.

The time has been when the Prison was regarded as a mere place of punishment, when fear was deemed the only passion by which prisoners could be swayed, and the law of terror the only rule of discipline; when a discharged Convict, no matter what his crime, was shunned as the leper, and driven by the cold unpitying cruelty of his fellow-beings to despair, too often sought revenge by plunging into the lowest abyss of guilt. But the labours of the great and good men who have devoted their lives to the cause of the outcast of society, have not been fruitless; public attention has been gradually awakened to the errors of the prevailing systems of prison discipline, and great ameliorations have been effected. The dungeon gave way to the well regulated apartment—healthful labour has replaced vicious idleness —and now the general aim is to find in what manner the security of the public, the prevention of crime and the reformation of the criminal can be best obtained without the appearance of revenge. And when it is considered that a large proportion of the inmates of prison are the victims of circumstances; that many are condemned for the first act of crime, and many more for the act of a moment of passion or intemperance; and that the great majority of prisoners have been born and reared in ignorance of everything but vice—how strong is the claim on a Christian people to see well that their prisons shall not become the moral tomb of those who enter them, but rather schools where the ignorant are enlightened and the repentant strengthened— in which expiation for crime is not lost sight of, but the permanent reform of the Convict is the chief aim.[76]

In applying the results of their study to the provincial penitentiary, the commissioners recommended that the institution modify its existing congregate system through subjecting all new convicts to separate confinement for a period of up to six months.[77] The commissioners

[76]This and the following references to the commissioners' reports are from Canada, *Journals*, 1849, Appendix B.B.B.B.B., n.p.

[77]This recommendation comes as a somewhat surprising conclusion to the account the commissioners presented of their visits and discussions. In reporting on the Cherry Hill Penitentiary, Philadelphia, where the separate system was employed, they noted that "insanity, to a fearful extent, is to be found within the walls" and that "the prisoners, as a class, have a sallow, worn-out appearance, and while the eyelids have a heavy, languid appearance, the eyeballs glare with a feverish brightness." They regarded this to be the result of protracted separation, and it is therefore odd to find them assuming that up to six months of this type of confinement would be beneficial when longer periods were clearly harmful. Conversely, the commissioners had seemed to be favourably impressed with the Massachusetts Penitentiary at Charlestown where "everything is done to make the prisoners comfortable and happy and remove from his mind all feeling of degradation." They agreed that "the general principle of kindness . . . is the only one which will ever obtain high success in the moral reformation of the criminal, for any institution." They seemed to fear, however, that the Charlestown system would not have the value of deterrence. In any case they felt that while it might work in Massachusetts "where the theory of equality is perhaps nearer realization than among any other people, where much light has been spread abroad on the subject of prison discipline, and where active benevolence is at work to find employment for the prisoner and strengthen his resolution the moment he is discharged," it would not be successful in other places, like Canada, where these conditions did not obtain.

believed that "in many cases where mitigating circumstances existed," this relatively brief period of separate confinement would prove sufficient to achieve the aim of reformation and the prisoner might, accordingly, be pardoned "with benefit to society and to the criminal."

The commissioners affirmed the importance of industrial labour in the penitentiary both for the discipline and training of the prisoners and for reducing the costs of the institution. They saw "no reason why the labour of able-bodied men should not produce sufficient to pay for their sustenance" and felt that a penitentiary ought to be able to "make its revenue nearly equal to its expenditures." At the same time they were insistent "that the pecuniary interests of the penitentiary should, in no manner stand in the way of the reformation of the criminal; and that, desirable as economy is, it is a sad mistake to sacrifice for that consideration, all the higher objects of such an institution." Thus the commissioners recommended "as of first importance . . . that the means of moral, religious and secular instruction, shall occupy much greater prominence than they at present do in our own or any of the American Penitentiaries." In addition to the important rôle to be played in the institution by the chaplains and schoolmaster, the commissioners emphasized the necessity that all the officers of the prison be men of "high moral character" and "general attainments" such as to warrant the respect of the prisoners. With staff of this quality and a programme strongly directed towards reformation there would be little need for the harsh punishments that had been so much in evidence prior to the inquiry. "With proper management," in the view of the commissioners, "the punishments in a Penitentiary may be few in number and mild in character." Without ruling out the necessity of the use of the dark cell and the "cat" for the few "who are only to be ruled by bodily fear," the commissioners held that "the deprivation of comforts, and solitary confinement, and as little of these as possible, will be found sufficient aids to kindness and reason for the maintenance of good discipline."

The core of the report as it related to the administration of the institution concerned the Board of Inspectors and the office of warden and the relations between the two. The commissioners examined the working of the voluntary local board as constituted under the existing legislation and concluded that it could never succeed in ensuring efficient supervision and control. What was required was to bring "the direct action of the Executive Government to bear on the management of the Penitentiary" through the appointment of two inspectors who would be salaried officials of the province and who would, ideally, carry other duties relating to corrections. They would have all the responsibilities of the existing inspectors including that of formulating the rules and regulations for the institution, and in addition they would be expected to undertake quarterly a much more careful inspection of the penitentiary, including its financial operations, than had been carried out by the voluntary board. They would also be responsible for reporting periodically to the government on various aspects of the affairs of the institution and for preparing comprehensive annual reports. These would "be replete with the statistics of crime and punishment" which the commissioners described as "a species of information difficult to be procured and arranged, except through some such medium, and which is most useful to the statesman, from its bearing on the principles of penal legislation." The commissioners anticipated that, through the exchange of annual reports with other jurisdictions and through related means, the inspectors would place themselves in "communication with those philanthropic associations and individuals in other countries, now so actively and zealously engaged in the amelioration of prison discipline." Thus "valuable information on every subject connected therewith, would be received and imparted and a spirit of emulation excited to elevate and maintain the character of our Institution to a level, at least, with those of a similar nature elsewhere."

Although asserting that the proposed inspectors should carry more earnestly and efficiently than the previous board the responsibilities of formulating regulations, carrying out inspections, and reporting, the commissioners were insistent that the inspectors should not infringe upon the authority and responsibilities of the warden. On the basis of their analysis of the location and exercise of authority in the government of the institution, the commissioners concluded that "the safest depositary of power and responsibility . . . is the Warden." The essentials of "uniformity of discipline—prompt and decided action on emergency—proper control over the subordinate officers—and active, business-like management of the financial and other affairs" would be secured through the concentration of executive action in the warden's hands. To exercise such extensive authority, the warden needed to possess outstanding abilities, and, "to fulfil the benevolent object of the penitentiary—the reformation of the unfortunate men committed to his care," he needed to be "thoroughly imbued with the spirit of philanthropy, and deeply interested in the moral welfare of those under his charge."

The commissioners took note of questions that went beyond the internal management of the institution. They advocated, for example, the formation of private prison societies to assist the discharged prisoner and to promote public discussion of penal matters. They also suggested the establishment of an asylum for the criminally insane to be associated with the penitentiary. And they placed strong emphasis on the need for refuges for juvenile offenders and for radical improvements in the county gaols. They felt that the latter objective could best be achieved by making the inspectors of the penitentiary also responsible for the inspection and supervision of the gaols.

The Commissioners as Inspectors

The board of inspectors which was in office when the inquiry began resigned in November 1848. In the following month the commissioners were given the task of serving as the board of inspectors until the investigation was completed and new policies for the penitentiary were formulated. This arrangement was to last longer than originally expected,[78] indeed until new legislation came into effect on October 1, 1851. Vacancies occurred in the board during the interval, however, and these were not filled. During most of the period only Bristow and Brown made up the board, and thus the commissioners' recommendation that two inspectors be appointed to constitute the permanent board was put to a partial test.

Although the interim arrangement under which the provisional inspectors operated left them powerless to adopt measures that went beyond those authorized by the act of 1846, they were able, none the less, to effect what they referred to, in the first of their two reports, as "very great improvements . . . in the administration of the Financial, Industrial, and Disciplinary Departments of the Institution."[79] They were able to pay off outstanding debts, to reduce the cost of operating the institution, to enter into more extensive and more favourable contracts for using the labour of the convicts in industrial production, and to ameliorate the punishments and deprivations to which the prisoners were subjected.[80] They were also able to carry forward

[78]The speech from the throne in May 1850 (Canada, *Journals*, 1850, p. 3) suggested that action was planned for that year: "A measure will be submitted for your consideration founded on the Report of the Commissioners appointed to enquire into the conduct, discipline and management of the Provincial Penitentiary. The increasing wealth and population of the Province, and the growing aversion to capital punishment, render it highly important that the system of discipline established in the Provincial Penitentiary and Gaols should be made as far as possible effectual for the prevention of crime and the reformation of offenders."

[79]Canada, *Journals*, 1950, Appendix R.R., n.p.

[80]*Ibid.*

extensive additions to the penitentiary buildings and to achieve, as one result of the more extensive accommodation, a complete separation of military prisoners from the rest of the prison population.[81]

Penitentiary Act of 1851

In August 1851 the Legislature finally passed an act[82] for the better management of the provincial penitentiary, incorporating the principal recommendations of the Royal Commission. One notable change in the new act, was the provision for the gradual construction of up to fifty cells "with a workshop attached to each cell, adapted to carry out the 'separate' or 'solitary' system of discipline." This was doubtless in implementation of the commissioners' proposal that all new prisoners be subjected to an initial period of separation from the main body of the inmates. The new legislation attempted to prevent excessive use of punishments and privations by establishing specific safeguards governing the circumstances under which they could be imposed. It also reduced the use of the penitentiary for sightseeing by fee-paying visitors. Although the act failed to implement the recommendation of the commissioners for an insane asylum attached to the penitentiary, it did provide for the inmates' removal to the Lunatic Asylum of Upper Canada for the duration of their illness.

The principal change in the act from the earlier legislation was in the appointment of two non-resident inspectors at an annual salary of £400. The act sought to define the duties and responsibilities of the inspectors and of the principal officers of the penitentiary in such a way as to minimize conflicts and gaps in authority. Thus while it confirmed the warden's full executive power and defined in considerable detail the duties of other officers, the legislation clearly established that the inspectors were responsible in the event of any "detrimental incapacity, inefficiency or negligence, on the part of any officer . . . not removable by the said Inspectors . . . to represent to the Governor-in-Council without delay, that such is the case, and what is the nature

[81]*Ibid.*, 1851, Appendix W. The temporary inspectors did not enjoy a régime unmarred by difficulties. They encountered, for example, the problem of the contractor's agents' introducing tobacco and other bribes to the prisoners for "extra industry." They were also disappointed by the moral progress of the prisoners and attributed this in part to the deficiencies they said they found in the performance of the Roman Catholic chaplain. The reports, particularly that for 1851, are enlivened by an outspoken exchange between the inspectors and chaplain. The chaplain, who had the last word, referred to the inspectors as "a queer set of beings."

[82]Canada, *Statutes*, 1851, c. 2.

of their complaint against such officer, and what is the injurious effect produced upon the Institution, and to recommend, if they see fit, the removal of such officer."[83] Because the inspectors would be making only periodic visits to the institution, the act also provided for the appointment of three persons to form a board of visitors with authority to visit the penitentiary at specified times "to see that the reformatory objects of the institution are carried out, and that the convicts are humanely and justly treated."[84]

The Penitentiary, 1851–1859

The inspectors appointed under the act of 1851 were Dr. Wolfred Nelson, the Lower Canadian rebel of 1837, who had returned after the Union to represent Richelieu in the second and third legislatures,[85] and Andrew Dickson, who was an Upper Canadian Reformer and a pioneer merchant, miller, and sheriff in the District of Bathurst in the upper Ottawa valley. D. A. MacDonell, who had been appointed as acting warden at an early stage in the inquiry, was confirmed in his position. During most of the period from 1851 until the appointment of the Board of Inspectors of Prisons, Asylums and Public Charities in 1859, the penitentiary was presided over by these three officials. In general, they appear to have acted in harmony,[86] the inspectors with each other and with the warden, and the warden with the officers and staff of the institution. They appear to have provided sound administration. Construction continued at a good pace, and by 1859 the institution had most of the facilities it required including chapels, a hospital, a library, and extensive workshops. A relatively humane system of discipline was in force although the "cat" was still used occasionally, and during 1858 punishment by water showers was inflicted forty-four times and two convicts were being kept in chains.[87]

The confident hope of the Royal Commission that the penitentiary could engage in industrial activities which would make it largely self-sufficient without adversely affecting the reformative programme of

[83]*Ibid.*, s. IX.

[84]*Ibid.* There is no evidence that the board of visitors was ever established.

[85]J. O. Cote, *Political Appointment and Elections in the Province of Canada from 1841 to 1865* (Ottawa, 1866), p. 77.

[86]The report for their first full year as inspectors, however (Canada, *Journals*, 1853, Appendix I.I.I.), revealed a division on the extent of the education and training the convicts should receive while in the penitentiary. Their contending reports seemed to indicate an ominous incompatibility but there was no further evidence of it in later reports.

[87]Canada, *Journals*, 1859, Appendix 29, n.p.

the institution was, however, not realized. In successive reports the inspectors and the warden referred to difficulties in securing acceptable contracts for penitentiary labour and in having the contractors honour the agreements into which they had entered. Thus, although by 1857 the penitentiary had workshops which "for design, convenience, and salubrity, are perhaps unequalled on the American Continent,"[88] the financial returns from the labour of the convicts fell far short of earlier expectations. The inspectors sometimes accounted for this disappointing result by implying that the institution would have been more successful financially if it had been prepared "to forego those noble ends for which such establishments are now erected . . . [that is] the reformation of the offenders." There was ample evidence, however, that these ends were already being sacrificed in the attempt to make the contract system as lucrative as possible. In 1852 the warden, in commenting on the clandestine introduction of tobacco and other inducements to greater productivity by the prisoners, remarked that "the greed and impatience of the Foreman employed by the Contractors, has given me a very great degree of uneasiness and trouble."[89] The Roman Catholic chaplain referred to another aspect of the matter, the trifling amount of time allowed for a mid-week service of instruction, and concluded that the "worldly interests of the Penitentiary" were being "considered of greater value than the reformation of the Convicts."[90] The first Protestant chaplain in his last report also expressed the view that "the moral well-being of the prisoner, is seriously interfered with by the present arrangements with the Contractors." He observed that "an interest has been created, separate and distinct from the duties of the Penitentiary, which, if it do not militate with, yet does in no way subserve the great ends of the institution—the reformation of the unhappy inmates."[91] A similar conclusion was reached by his successor who noted, as well, that the contract system, because of its use of the division of labour, was not succeeding even in teaching the prisoners a trade which they could follow on their release. This chaplain was prompted to ask if it was "not possible that the Convicts could be instructed in trades under some system which would tend to enlighten and exalt their minds rather than to deprave them."[92] It is clear that in the opinion of those who gave primacy to the reformative purpose of the penitentiary, the contract system stood condemned.

[88]Ibid., 1857, Appendix 7, n.p.
[89]Ibid., 1852, Appendix III, n.p.   [90]Ibid., 1858, Appendix 11, n.p.
[91]Ibid., 1851, Appendix W., n.p.   [92]Ibid., 1857, Appendix 7, n.p.

In their annual reports the two inspectors accepted with evident relish the view of the Royal Commission that they should discuss, in addition to the immediate concerns of the penitentiary, the broader aspects of penal administration and the causes of crime. They frequently presented lengthy statements of their views on penal matters, as did the officers of the institution, particularly the warden, the Protestant chaplain, and the schoolmaster. Their reports indicate a growing appreciation of the nature of the human problems with which the penitentiary was confronted and of the importance of attacking them vigorously and imaginatively both within the penal system and beyond it. Thus the reports explored such possible root causes of criminal behaviour as alcoholic addiction, the early social conditions of the convicts, and the lack of education, poverty, and squalor. Although the inspectors and the officers of the penitentiary felt obliged to support the doctrine of individual moral responsibility, they came increasingly to the view that crime sprang, in a very large measure, from social causes. They concluded therefore that "if society were more mindful of its obligations and interests, there can be no doubt that the amount of crime would be much smaller."[93] Dr. Nelson developed this theme in a special appendix to the report for 1853 in which he discussed the relation of crime and poverty.

Poverty in the lower classes is very generally the parent of every deviation from right and order, leads to the commission of all description of crimes, and these are in one way or another visited upon all indifferently. . . . The welfare and consequent happiness of the poor thus becomes the protection and security of the wealthy. . . . Let us elevate the poor in their own estimation, let us as far as possible raise them to the common level, and ere long their very nature will change with their altered condition.[94]

The inspectors thought of their reports as vehicles for public education. They hoped that they would be widely read and discussed and that, through this means, "every member of the community may understand his position and the very serious obligations that rest upon him as a man and a Christian."[95] Nevertheless, the advocacy by the inspectors and officers of the penitentiary of various specific penal reforms seemed, for some time, to be productive of rather meagre results. With increasing insistence they advocated the establishment of special accommodation for prisoners suffering from insanity, the establishment of reformatories for young offenders, and the bringing of the local gaols under a provincial system of control and inspection.

[93]*Ibid.*, 1858, Appendix 11, n.p.
[94]*Ibid.*, 1854, Appendix D.D., n.p.   [95]*Ibid.*, 1859, Appendix 29, n.p.

All of these matters, however, were finally dealt with in the Prison Inspection Act of 1857[96] and the statutes of 1859 which derived from it.[97] One of the latter, in making effective provision for the appointment of the Board of Inspectors, became the vehicle through which, in the remaining years of the Union period, a notable contribution was made in the fields of both corrections and public charities.

Asylum for Insane Convicts

Action to provide for all mentally ill prisoners in the penitentiary seemed imminent as a result of the act of 1857 when a medical superintendent of the criminally insane was appointed and property, in the form of the Rockwood estate near the penitentiary, was acquired in 1858 on which to establish an asylum. The estate provided some buildings, but these proved to be capable of accommodating only the female insane from the penitentiary, and plans had to be made to establish suitable buildings for the accommodation of the men. In the apparent belief that these would be speedily erected, the practice of sending the mentally ill from the penitentiary to the asylum in Toronto was discontinued, and convicts suffering from insanity began to be confined in the basement of one of the penitentiary buildings where they received such care from the medical superintendent of Rockwood as the circumstances permitted. This deplorable arrangement, recalling the situation in the Home District gaol in the 1830's, resulted in a mortality rate which was three times as high as that among the women residents in Rockwood.[98] The situation, moreover, persisted from some time in 1857 to the early months of 1865,[99] illustrating the proverbial longevity of temporary expedients.

Prisons for Young Offenders

A more immediate benefit to the penitentiary deriving from the act of 1857 was the removal in 1858 of the first group of youthful offenders. Some forty-seven young prisoners were dispatched in that year under the direction of Andrew Dickson who gave up his position as inspector of the penitentiary to become the warden of the new reformatory. Their destination was Isle aux Noix on the Richelieu River near the

[96]Canada, *Statutes*, 1857, c. 28.
[97]*Ibid.*, 1859, c. 107, An Act respecting Prisons for Young Offenders; c. 108, An Act respecting a Lunatic Asylum for Criminal Convicts; c. 110, An Act respecting Inspectors of Public Asylums, Hospitals, the Provincial Penitentiary of Canada and of all common Gaols and other prisons.
[98]Canada, *Sessional Papers*, 1865, no. 14, p. 147.   [99]*Ibid.*

American border in Lower Canada where they were to occupy the buildings of a former garrison until new buildings could be completed. This initial exodus represented a start in terminating the confinement of children in the penitentiary, a practice which had been recognized as undesirable from its earliest days and which had drawn unfavourable comment in most of the reports on the institution, including that of the Royal Commission. The reports of the inspectors, for example, upheld the view that if the sentencing of young offenders to penal servitude was necessary, and no one seemed to argue otherwise, the youths should be received in juvenile reformatories where they would not be associated with the more hardened criminals, where they would not be subjected to so unnatural a sanction as the rule of silence and its related restrictions, and where a reformative programme emphasizing education, training, and religious instruction could be undertaken. Nevertheless, despite these sentiments, a total of 683 persons from ten to twenty years of age were sentenced to the penitentiary between 1835 and 1857.[100]

The establishment of reformatories first in Lower Canada and later in Upper Canada was, accordingly, widely regarded as an important penal reform, and the two institutions were launched with enthusiasm and high expectations. The early days of the Canada East reformatory were fraught with numerous misfortunes, most of which were the products of seriously inadequate planning. This indictment applied to the choice of the warden and staff of the institution, its location, and certain of its initial policies.[101] The mistakes were perhaps attributable to the absence of adequate administrative machinery within the provincial government to deal with the greatly expanded social welfare responsibilities of the late 1850's. The consequences of the mistakes, however, drew attention to the need for the appointment of the board of inspectors which had been authorized in the statute of 1857 but not acted upon. When the board became operative in 1860 it found that it was faced with an accumulation of problems respecting the institution and that it had, indeed, "to reform a Reformatory."[102] The experience gained in the administration of this reformatory had the further effect

---

[100]Canada, *Journals*, 1858, Appendix 11, n.p.
[101]Canada, *Sessional Papers*, 1860, no. 32, pp. 20–21, 23–36.
[102]*Ibid.*, 1861, no. 24, n.p. This was the comment of Dr. J. C. Taché who, among other indictments, referred to the lack of French-Canadian members on the initial staff of the reformatory. An appendix to the report is an account of a special investigation of the board into charges that had been made against the second warden of the institution, who was a French Canadian. The board concluded that the charges were baseless. A second appendix presents the findings of Frances G. Johnson who had been appointed a commissioner by the provincial

of indicating that it was unwise for an institution for young offenders to accept both boys and girls. The reformatory in Upper Canada was, therefore, organized exclusively for boys, and, as alternative provisions for delinquent girls in the province, the inspectors recommended that the government undertake to pay any voluntary institution which would provide care and training for such girls at a rate equivalent to the cost of caring for boys in the provincial institutions.[103]

The reformatory that was established in Upper Canada in 1859, unlike its Lower Canadian counterpart, had a felicitous beginning and throughout the remaining years of the Union period it developed in a manner that was generally satisfactory to the inspectors. It was given vigorous leadership by William Moore Kelly who, with the other officers of the institution, administered it with competence and with a degree of co-operation which led one of the inspectors to remark that "an air of universal harmony seemed to prevail throughout the administrative machinery of the entire institution."[104]

The site of the new institution, as in the case of the reformatory for Canada East, was selected principally because of the availability of unused military barracks which could be employed as temporary quarters until more adequate accommodation could be constructed. The site near the village of Penetanguishene included a rocky plateau which offered a magnificent view of the waters and islands of Georgian Bay. It was here that permanent buildings were erected over a period of five or six years beginning in 1861. The institution started out with a group of some 40 boys, rose to over 90 in the third year of operation, and remained between 90 and 100 until 1864 when new quarters made possible its expansion to over 130 in that year and to over 150 at Confederation. The programme of the reformatory placed a strong emphasis upon work. The inspectors continually remarked upon the success that was attained in organizing the boys in construction activities, road-building, quarrying, lumbering, farming, and brick-making as well as in such trades as tailoring and cabinet-making.

---

government in 1859 to inquire into complaints that Andrew Dickson had attempted to seduce the matron of the reformatory and her sister. The commissioner found that the evidence supported the charges. On the second question, the conduct and management of the reformatory, the commissioner found "that punishments of great severity, in some instances upon mere children, and in one case upon an idiot—known to be such at the time—have been inflicted." Noting that "enough . . . has been adduced to convince me that scenes of the most revolting description have taken place, more than once, at the infliction of corporal punishment," the commissioner remarked that this was "very contrary" to the expectations of the members of the Legislature when they established the institution.   [103]*Ibid.*, 1860, no. 32, p. 20.
[104]*Ibid.*, 1863, no. 66, n.p.

Military drill was also introduced with apparent success. Academic training, however, was rather neglected, and as the period closed facilities for proper schooling were still lacking.[105]

Although the warden of the reformatory and the provincial inspectors felt confident that the institution was achieving its objective of reformation with a high degree of success, they were convinced that improvements were needed in the legislation to increase its effectiveness. They found that the sentencing of young men in their late teens or early twenties was destructive of the institution's programme, and accordingly they recommended that no boy over sixteen should be sent to the institution. They were also critical of short sentences, both because these failed to bring about the hoped for changes in attitudes and outlook, and because they allowed very young children to be released before they were old enough to have become self-supporting. On the other hand, although recommending long sentences of five to seven years (the inspectors more frequently suggested that the minimum be three or four), Kelly was of the opinion "that it would have beneficial effects were the good conduct of a convict to have an influence in shortening the duration of his sentence, and if an amount of his earnings during his confinement were to be kept aside, to make up a small capital upon which to commence whenever his sentence expires."[106]

In the same way that the penitentiary had come to be regarded by those closely identified with it as an unsuitable place for young offenders, the reformatory began to be looked upon by the inspectors as an inappropriate and costly way to meet the needs of the increasing numbers of children being sentenced to it who were more neglected than delinquent. Beginning with a reference by Meredith to the newly established Boys' Home in Toronto in the report for 1861,[107] the inspectors came to the view that the work of the reformatories should be supplemented by refuges which would be organized under voluntary auspices but with financial support from the municipal and provincial governments.[108]

The Penitentiary, 1859–1867

During the period from 1858 to Confederation the operation of the penitentiary benefited from the removal of most of the younger offenders and from the transfer of the mentally ill to the neighbouring

[105]*Ibid.*, 1866, no. 6, pp. 97–100.
[106]*Ibid.*, 1863, no. 66, n.p.
[107]*Ibid.*, 1861, no. 24, n.p.
[108]*Ibid.*, 1865, no. 14, p. 76; 1866, no. 6, pp. 71–72.

asylum. In addition, the construction of the Rockwood Asylum proved beneficial in providing useful work for a large group of the prisoners at a time when industrial contracts fell short of providing employment for all the convicts.

The penitentiary also seems to have profited from the reforming zeal of one or two of the members of the Board of Inspectors, notably Meredith and Taché, who had the courage to be critical of its existing programme and system of discipline and who were able to secure agreement on the adoption of a number of significant changes. Their success is the more remarkable because two of the other members of the board were closely identified with the penitentiary, Dr. Wolfred Nelson as one of the two inspectors since 1851 and MacDonell as its warden since 1849. The appointment of MacDonell to the board while he continued as warden of the penitentiary must be regarded as highly questionable, even though the appointment was on a part-time basis and was made as a temporary expedient destined to terminate after a year and a half. Inevitably it made for difficulty in the assessment of the programme and administration of the penitentiary and might well have inhibited improvements in the institution had it not been for the pertinacity of Meredith in pressing for reform.

In his separate report for 1861 Meredith remarked that after "a few months insight, as Inspector, into the inner life of the Penitentiary," he had concluded "that the system of discipline there pursued, however admirable for the purpose of order was nearly, if not altogether ineffectual, for the reformation of the convicts brought under its influence."[109] He described its system of discipline "as one of rigid repression, of uncompromising coercion . . . which admits of no change or improvement in the condition of the convict in consequence of his good conduct." As such it must inevitably fail "to make convicts good and useful men, or prepare a convict to take his place again as a freeman among his fellows."[110] As a remedy to this egregious lack in the existing system, Meredith advocated the introduction of a number of the principles and procedures that were employed in the Irish prison system as established by Sir Walter Crofton in 1854. He listed three in particular which he felt would create a truly reformative programme in the institution:

1. A scheme of conduct classification of the convicts, accompanied by distinctive badges and money gratuities.
2. Every convict should be able to earn, by continued good conduct in the Penitentiary, the remission of a certain fixed portion of his sentence.

[109]*Ibid.*, 1862, no. 19, n.p.   [110]*Ibid.*

3. Convicts who by their steady good conduct have risen to the highest class in the Penitentiary, should enjoy certain advantages in the institution. They should, for example, be entitled to a small portion of their earnings; but above all they should be, if possible, employed outside the institution in important public works, and while so employed they should be allowed greater freedom, and be exposed to more of the ordinary temptations of the outer world—the main object of this phase of their convict life being to prepare them for their return to social life.[111]

Meredith was able to secure the concurrence of the board in placing these recommendations before the government, and some internal measures by way of classification and rewards for good conduct were adopted. These together with renewed instructions that convicts were not to be treated with harshness or severity and that punishments should be as humane as circumstances would permit appear to have produced a worthwhile improvement in the institution's morale and discipline. In their report for 1864 the inspectors remarked that "the feelings of irritation and discontent which prevailed so unmistakeably among the convicts, male and female, some few years ago, have gradually subsided and given place to a general feeling of resignation and even of contentment."[112]

As the period closed, however, the more important reforms advocated by Meredith, including his second and third recommendations above, were unrealized. MacDonell was showing increasing resistance to change, supporting his views with the defence, cited by conservative prison administrators in every era, that the order and discipline of the institution and the very lives of its officers required the continuance of existing methods.[113] Also, constitutional questions dominated the political scene during the closing years of the Union period, so the question of whether far-reaching measures were required to achieve the reformative purpose of the penitentiary was to be left to the parliament and government of the new Dominion.

The Gaols, 1840–1867

Although some of the pre-Union reforms affecting the local gaols of Upper Canada carried over into the Union period, they were not sustained by further legislation until the act of 1857, and there was no effective administrative action until the Board of Inspectors was able to turn its attention to the gaols early in 1860. During the intervening twenty years the operation of the gaols by the district councils

[111]*Ibid.*
[112]*Ibid.*, 1865, no. 14, p. 16.   [113]*Ibid.*, 1866, no. 6, pp. 69, 76.

until 1849 and the county councils thereafter was characterized by varying degrees of interest but nowhere was this sufficiently pronounced or sustained to produce a good standard of penal administration. Criticism of the gaols by the circuit judges[114] and more frequently by the grand juries seems to have had little effect on the situation and the conclusion that had been so emphatically reached in the later 1830's, that reform could be achieved only through provincial action, was, for nearly two decades, lost sight of or ignored by the Legislature and government of the United Province. Furthermore, when the inspectors addressed themselves to the problem in 1860, they indicated no knowledge of the work done in the closing years of the pre-Union period; thus deprived of the advantages that a review of the earlier efforts might have had, they exemplified the lack of historical perspective which has been a persistent and lamentable characteristic of those working in the field of social welfare in Canada from the days of the pioneers to the present.

The act of 1859[115] set out in considerable detail the duties and powers that the inspectors were to perform and exercise in relation to the gaols. As in the statute of 1838[116] the inspectors were to place particular emphasis on seeing that new gaols were planned and old ones reconstructed, with due regard to a variety of factors relating to the security, healthfulness, and efficiency of the gaols, the safe custody of the prisoners (to be attained "without the necessity of resorting to severe treatment"), and their classification, correction, and reformation. The act of 1859, however, went beyond the earlier statute in one important respect, namely, that the province agreed to share equally in the cost of the alterations or additions to the gaols up to an amount of £1,500.[117] Thus the province indicated in a tangible manner its concern about the state of neglect into which it believed the local gaols had fallen and its recognition of the necessity for decisive action by the way of remedy.

The view that the gaols were in a deplorable condition was supported all too conclusively by the answers to a questionnaire that the inspectors had sent out early in 1860 to the sheriffs of the counties

[114]Canada, *Provincial Secretary's Letter Book*, Nov. 18, 1843, for example, contains the government's acknowledgment of a letter from Hon. J. B. Macaulay which had enclosed presentments on the state of the gaols in Niagara, Talbot, Brock, and Gore and had called for remedial action.
[115]Canada, *Consolidated Statutes*, 1859, c. 110.
[116]Upper Canada, *Statutes*, 1837–38, c. 5.
[117]Canada, *Consolidated Statutes*, 1859, c. 110, s. 21.

and to the chaplains and medical attendants of all the gaols. The hundred or more replies revealed, in the words of the inspectors, "defects . . . of every possible kind . . . defects in superintendence, defects in discipline, defects in construction, in the internal and external distribution of the buildings, defects in the sanitary arrangements, defects, above all, in the means of reforming; defects everywhere."[118]

Later that same year, as a major means of removing the weaknesses in the internal management of the gaols, the inspectors drew up detailed regulations touching on all aspects of the operation of the gaols and sent these to all the gaols in the province for implementation by the sheriffs and staffs.[119] Vigorous effects on the part of the inspectors were required in support of the regulations. That they were, on the whole, rewarded by a fair measure of success was beginning to be apparent by the end of 1863 when the inspectors reported that "it is with satisfaction that the Board are enabled to state that the rules drawn up by the Inspectors are gradually coming to be better observed at the various gaols. They have felt some delicacy in enforcing a sudden change from the old management of the prison to the more strict exactions of the new and have proceeded by advice and persuasion, . . . so far, with cordiality."[120]

In these regulations the inspectors placed considerable emphasis on the securing of more adequate staffs, the development of better sanitary arrangements, and the provision where necessary of prison clothing.[121] They also sought to improve the statistical records of the gaols, and before the period closed were able to secure from the provincial government and distribute to all the gaols standard record books setting out the kinds of data they required.[122] They also stressed the provision of a simple, healthful standard diet in the gaols and the procurement of the necessary supplies through outside contracts rather than arrangements entered into with the gaoler. By requiring the adoption of these principles, the inspectors caused the average daily cost of the prisoners' rations to drop from 14.8 cents per head in 1860 to 9.0 cents per head in 1864.[123]

[118]Canada, *Sessional Papers*, 1860, no. 32, p. 9.
[119]*Ibid.*, 1861, no. 24, n.p.
[120]*Ibid.*, 1864, no. 39, n.p.
[121]*Ibid.* As late as 1863, the inspectors on a visit to the gaol in Kingston cited "the case of a poor idiot who was lying in his own filth on a heap of straw, destitute of the slightest article of clothing."
[122]*Ibid.*, 1866, no. 6, p. 36.   [123]*Ibid.*

The inspectors' work with the county councils concerning the alterations or additions needed to raise the physical accommodation of the gaols to a satisfactory level proved a much more difficult matter than that of securing the adherence of the staffs of the gaols to the new regulations. A number of the counties responded positively and undertook the necessary improvements without delay but in other instances the inspectors encountered indifference or resistance so pronounced that their best efforts during the remainder of the pre-Confederation period were without avail. The inspectors came increasingly to attribute this problem to the limited powers of the board under the statute[124] As members of the board they could "reason and remonstrate with the County authorities: and when their reasoning and remonstrances prove unavailing they can refer the matter to the Executive Government."[125] But this was not enough. At the end of 1863 when fourteen counties had still taken no action to improve their gaols, the inspectors expressed the hope that "the Government will not hesitate to avail itself of those powers which the law gives it, so as to prevent such recusant municipalities from practically annulling the provisions of a wise and salutary Statute, by their ignorance and short-sighted parsimony."[126] In the belief that the government would take action to force the counties to undertake the measures recommended, the inspectors then identified for the cabinet a number of the recalcitrant counties. The government, however, appeared reluctant to take vigorous action, and although it was induced to call upon certain councils to proceed with the work of altering their gaols,[127] it stopped short of effective measures of enforcement.

By 1866 the inspectors no longer believed that the existing legislation was capable of achieving its intended purpose, and accordingly they "strongly represented to the government the expediency of amending the present law so far as it relates to the alteration and improvement of defective Gaols, so as to provide some summary means of enforcing compliance with its salutary requirement."[128] Under the political and constitutional circumstances of the closing years of the Union period the government was not easily convinced that it should pass legislation to coerce a group of Upper Canadian municipalities on a matter which doubtless seemed at the time to be of marginal importance. The political influence of the municipalities, moreover, was by no means negligible and it may well have been a contributing factor in at least

[124]*Ibid.*
[125]*Ibid.*
[126]*Ibid.*, 1864, no. 39, n.p.
[127]*Ibid.*, 1866, no. 6, p. 33.
[128]*Ibid.*, p. 36.

two attempts that were made during the 1860's to abolish the Board of Inspectors or to reduce drastically its size and effectiveness.[129]

Partly because of the difficulties in securing the physical improvements to the gaols which the inspectors regarded "as the first step in the work of prison reform,"[130] the inspectors began urging the establishment of central prisons "intermediate between the Common Gaol and the Penitentiary."[131] These prisons should be operated by the province with a system of discipline resembling that of the penitentiary and they should receive "all prisoners whose term of sentence exceeds 30 or 40 days, and is less than three years."[132]

In contrast to this forward-looking recommendation and to the ideas expressed by Meredith on the programme of the penitentiary, the inspectors also put forward certain rather dubious ideas on corrections which appeared to have gained currency in the British Isles. Thus they suggested that whipping "should be resorted to as a punishment for such offences and for such offenders as may now, under the recent Imperial Statutes, be punished in that way in England, Ireland and Scotland."[133] The inspectors also expressed support for separate confinement as "the basis of the system of discipline in all prisons" and penal labour as distinguished from industrial labour as part of the sentence of all persons in the longer-term institutions.[134] It thus appears that in their disappointment at not achieving their objectives in relation to the local gaols the inspectors, like their contemporaries in other countries, were inclined to advocate various alternative means of correction which, when tested in later periods, were to prove to have very different degrees of merit.

PERIOD OF LANGMUIR'S INSPECTORSHIP, 1868–1882

In terms of its institutional resources in the field of corrections, Upper Canada entered the Union in 1841 with thirteen gaols and a penitentiary, and left it in 1867 with thirty-seven gaols and a prison for young offenders. Under the terms of the British North America

129Canada, *Journals*, 1863, p. 34; 1864, pp. 129, 218.
130Canada, *Sessional Papers*, 1864, no. 39, n.p.
131*Ibid.*, 1866, no. 6, p. 37.
132*Ibid.*
133*Ibid.*
134This suggestion also reflected British influences. Great Britain, *Public General Statutes*, 1865, c. 126, s. 19, provided that hard labour of two types be provided in all prisons. One type involved "Work at the Tread Wheel, Shot Drill, Crank, Capstan, Stone-breaking, or . . . other like Description of hard bodily labour."

Act the penitentiary became an institution of the Dominion government, and as such would receive prisoners sentenced to terms of more than two years from Ontario as well as from other parts of Canada. For the administration of the penal institutions that were left within its jurisdiction, the new province made legislative provision through the Prison and Asylum Inspection Act[135] of 1868. This statute required the inspector "to visit and inspect every Gaol, House of Correction, Reformatory and Prison . . . at least twice in each year." He was to examine all aspects of the institutions and their programmes, and on the state of each he was to "make a separate and distinct report in writing to the Lieutenant-Governor."[136]

The Local Gaols

The inspector's duties in respect to the common gaols were set out in considerable detail. Subject to the approval of the cabinet, he was given the power to make rules and regulations on all matters relating to their internal economy and management and to the maintenance and treatment of prisoners including their employment, medical care, religious instruction, and the restraint and punishment to which they could be subjected. The inspector's powers in respect to the planning and construction of gaols were also very extensive. No gaol could be built except on plans which he approved. He received detailed guidance in the legislation, however, for no less than thirteen subsections of the act were devoted to matters to be considered in the gaol's design, location, and construction. He was given similarly broad powers to require a county or city to make any necessary repairs and additions to its gaol. In this he was placed in a stronger position than the inspectors in the Union period. The new statute provided that if the municipality failed to act on his recommendations the matter could be referred to the lieutenant-governor-in-council. A decision by the cabinet was then binding upon the municipal council, which, if it defaulted, "could be proceeded against by mandamus." Thus the powers of the province to secure municipal conformity to the provisions of the act were greatly strengthened, although as under the old act enforcement would depend on the will of the provincial government to take action against the recalcitrant municipalities.

In his first report Langmuir found that he had some praise but more criticism for the system of local gaols.

[135]Ontario, *Statutes*, 1867–68, c. 21.
[136]*Ibid.*

While it may fairly be claimed for the Province of Ontario, that Gaol construction and administration, as well as the observance of Prison discipline, have in many respects kept pace with the rapid strides that have been made in this important branch in the science of government . . . it must be admitted that there are many painful defects and imperfections in our system, and its practical working, which have a tendency to counteract and destroy the benefits that society has a right to expect from the establishment and maintenance of penal institutions.[137]

In discussing specific defects, Langmuir referred first to the partial failure of the programme of gaol construction. He pointed out that although the act of 1859 had been explicit in the requirements it laid upon county councils concerning the erection and alteration of common gaols, and although the act was "framed to meet the peculiar circumstances and financial ability of the different counties," it had been "utterly disregarded and ignored" by a number of the local councils.

But it was upon other deficiencies of three or four of the gaols that Langmuir placed the strongest emphasis. He condemned the practice, which had not been wholly eradicated in the Union period, by which county councils contracted with the gaoler for the "dieting of prisoners." In inspecting the accounts of the province's thirty-seven common gaols, he found that this method was invariably much more costly than that laid down in regulations of having "the keeper of the Gaol . . . purchase what is required, and charge the same to the County at *cost price.*" He pointed out, as well, that there were two sound principles involved: "that the keeper of the Gaol should have no pecuniary interest in the prisoner's rations, and that a uniform system should be adopted and carried into effect in every Gaol in the Province."

Langmuir also had criticism for those gaols which made little or no attempt at proper classification or at employment of their inmates:

It must be admitted, that under the most favorable circumstances, with well planned and properly constructed Prisons, this is a most difficult matter to accomplish, and at best can only be of a partial character, but the *indiscriminate* mixing together, of the inmates of a Gaol without the slightest regard to classification, which is so painfully apparent in the gaols before enumerated, is an evil that no civilized community should tolerate, and if the county councils, who are responsible for the existence of the evil, persistently refuse to apply the remedy, by furnishing proper and adequate accommodation, then, the Government cannot too soon apply the law. A visit to many of the Gaols in question, will convince the most unbelieving

[137]This and the following references to Langmuir's first report are from Ontario, *Sessional Papers*, 1868–69, no. 3, pp. 2–22.

of the necessity that exists for even a partial separation, and of the positive crime of bringing the thoughtless juvenile offender into contact with the hardened criminal; the untried and possibly innocent man, with the sentenced felon; the unfortunate female convicted of her first offence, with the shameless and debauched prostitute.

The inadequacies of the design, the equipment, and above all of the administration of most of the gaols were, in Langmuir's opinion, revealed with equal force in their failure to provide suitable work for the inmates and particularly to enforce the carrying out of sentences of hard labour.

This most important branch of Prison discipline, is almost, if not altogether, a *dead letter* in the common gaols of this Province; with the exception of what may be termed "occasional jobs" there is no recognized or defined system of hard or penal labor. Notwithstanding this, in our Recorder's and Police Courts is daily witnessed the solemn farce of sentencing criminals to confinement for a certain period to the Common Gaol *with hard labor*. That this unfortunate state of things in our prison administration is productive of the very worst results, does not admit of a doubt. It is only necessary to pass through the over-crowded Gaols of our cities, large towns and populous localities, in order to witness the lamentable spectacle of able-bodied, healthy men, who have been convicted of crime, lounging about in *utter idleness*, with plenty of time on their hands to devise and concoct other ways of breaking the laws of their country, when released.

Because Langmuir could see no satisfactory solution within the county gaols to these problems of classification and employment, he believed that three additional types of institutions were needed to deal with them. His principal recommendation was that intermediate prisons be established in the west, centre, and east of the province. He suggested that these should be under the control of the provincial government and that they should receive all prisoners sentenced to periods between sixty days and two years (those exceeding that period being received by the federal penitentiary) as well as the habitual drunk and disorderly "class of prisoners" after their third conviction. "These prisons," he felt, "should be eminently 'hard labor' institutions, every prisoner being employed in some mechanical or industrial employment, the religious and secular instruction of the prisoners being also properly provided for."

The second type of institution that Langmuir recommended, and for which he was able to make out a powerful case, was a reformatory for girls. He provided statistics to show

that of the 8,015 commitments for the fifteen months ending 1st October 2,530 were females; of this number it is quite safe to say that three-fourths were prostitutes of all ages, and representing every stage of prostitution, infamy and shame. By far the most painful fact revealed by these statistics being, that 340 of them were girls under sixteen years of age.

It is, beyond dispute, that the incarceration in our common Gaols of this class of unfortunates, for short periods, without any means of employment or instruction is attended with little or no good to the offender, and very often, through contamination, the evil sought to be remedied is aggravated and increased. That it is no manner of punishment, is very evident from a perusal of the gaol records, by which we find that a large proportion of females of this class are committed to Gaol from twenty to twenty-five times before they attain the age of twenty-five.

Commitment to a reformatory was one of Langmuir's recommendations for solving the problems presented by the female offender. But it was to apply only to girls under sixteen. For those above that age he suggested longer sentences in the common gaol, "with proper means of employment." The latter is a rather surprising suggestion in view of the conclusion which had led to his recommendation for intermediate prisons—that the county gaols had demonstrated their inability to provide programmes of employment.

Another type of institution which Langmuir found was acutely needed for the effective operation of the prison system was the mental hospital. He noted that on an average day during the period under review there were "no less than 73 Lunatics"confined in the common gaols. Steps had been taken to remedy this situation by having Rockwood Asylum, Kingston, which had been taken over by the Dominion government as part of the arrangements at Confederation, receive 100 to 150 of these mentally ill gaol inmates. Langmuir described this as a temporary measure adopted until such time as permanent provisions could be made for this "unfortunate portion of our population." To meet the long term need he recommended the acquisition of Rockwood by Ontario and its use as an asylum for the eastern part of the province. Similarly asylum facilities should be developed in western Ontario and expanded in the Toronto area.

Langmuir continued to explore the strengths and weaknesses of the local gaols in subsequent reports. In 1869 he referred to the situation he found at the Barrie gaol which had fourteen inmates on the day of his inspection:

. . . only three of them were charged with crime; of the remainder no less than eight were committed as dangerous lunatics, idiots, or imbeciles incapable of taking care of themselves, the rest vagrants; in fact the establishment had much more the appearance of a Poor House, insane asylum and Hospital combined, than of a Common Gaol. One poor creature has been here for eight years, who, in addition to being afflicted with idiocy and epilepsy is now becoming quite blind, another quite imbecile has been in Gaol for over three years, and the rest for periods varying from six months to two years, the sadest case of all being that of an unfortunate woman of weak intellect who had two illegitimate children by her side, one, an infant born in the Gaol.[138]

In the following year Langmuir commented, in connection with the Kingston gaol, that the most of the inmates were vagrants and that "a poor house would have been a fitter place of residence for nearly half the number found in Gaol."[139] Speaking more generally in 1871, he remarked that many of the inmates of the gaols were:

. . . committed as vagrants who neither committed nor had any intent to commit an offense, and whose only crime was homeless poverty and old age, very often conjoined with physical disease. The commitment of this kind of *vagrants* to prison is not only at variance with the dictates of humanity, but at once turns the Gaol into a Poor House and Hospital, and very often seriously interferes with a proper classification of criminal prisoners.[140]

By this time Langmuir was convinced that the gaols, even if ideally administered, could not operate effectively if they continued to be used as congregate institutions. The gaols, he continually asserted, should be used only for persons who were being held in custody because of crimes. For all other persons different types of institutions were needed, and as noted above he employed his position as the chief executive officer for the prisons, asylums, and public charities of the province to promote the development of a broad range of institutions.

As he began to attack the problems of improving the gaols themselves he found it necessary to take up the struggle for the physical improvement of the gaols where his predecessors had left off. He was determined that every gaol should be physically adequate in the sense of being healthful, permitting of some classification of prisoners, and being secure against escape. In his relations with the group of counties which had refused to take action to improve their gaols before Confederation, Langmuir soon found that exhortation had little effect. He accordingly undertook to report the recalcitrant municipalities to the government and to recommend that the Attorney-General apply to the Court of Queen's Bench for writs of mandamus requiring the municipal officials, on pain of imprisonment, to take the necessary steps for the repair or reconstruction of the gaols in question. The counties of Perth and Lindsay and the city of Hamilton were municipalities against

[138]Ontario, *Sessional Papers*, 1869, no. 4, p. 11.
[139]*Ibid.*, 1870–71, no. 6, pp. 13–14.   [140]*Ibid.*, 1871–72, no. 4, p. 5.

which the device of mandamus was employed,[141] apparently with some success, for by 1880 Langmuir was able to remark during his speech at Cleveland that "the good effects of this authority are shown by the fact that all the gaols of the Province, with one or two exceptions, are structurally up to approved modern requirements."[142] In addition to the pressure of mandamus, the province undertook in 1879 to offer a more positive inducement through a continuation of the pre-Confederation grant for repairs and alteration. As in the Union period, the province agreed to share in the cost of repairs on new construction, limiting its contribution, whether made before or after Confederation, to six thousand dollars.[143]

In contrast to the experience of the inspectors of the Union period, Langmuir encountered more difficulty in raising the internal standards of the gaols than in securing structural improvements. He remained dissatisfied throughout the period with the measures taken in most of the gaols in the matters of work and classification, but his most severe criticism was directed at the defects in their administration. He found these to be so numerous and so hard to remedy that he came to feel that provincial inspection could not correct them. Weakness in staffing was among the defects he examined. He was frequently critical of the failure of the counties to pay salaries sufficient to attract and retain competent personnel. He found instances of salaries that were less than "the compensation given to a common laborer,"[144] and he concluded that there could be no substantial improvement in the gaols "so long as the present mode of appointing and paying gaolers and turnkeys is persisted in."[145] Largely as the result of the poor quality of personnel recruited to the staffs of the gaols the Inspector found during the early years of his tenure of office that "instances of gross carelessness and dereliction of duty" were of "constant occurrence."[146] Even in 1881, which he described as a comparatively good year, there were at least two major scandals within the gaols. One at Barrie indicated "great waste and extravagance, if not positive dishonesty,"[147] and one at Belleville involved extreme laxity of régime, characterized by a free movement of goods and persons in and out of the institution, "singing, dancing and unseemly conduct" in the women's corridors and—as a suitably shocking climax—the elopement of the matron with one of the prisoners.[148]

141Ibid., 1870–71, no. 6, p. 8.   142Ibid., 1881, no. 8, p. 9.
143Ontario, Statutes, 1874 (1st sess.), c. 31.
144Ontario, Sessional Papers, 1870–71, no. 6, pp. 6–7, 10.
145Ibid., p. 10.   146Ibid., 1882, no. 8, p. 2.
147Ibid., p. 73.   148Ibid., p. 74.

In the financial management of the gaols Langmuir found a further illustration of the weaknesses of local administration. Here it was both a matter of narrowness of conception and confusion of responsibility. In his third report he outlined his criticisms and his proposed solution in a manner which may be taken as representative of the position he normally held throughout the period:

In fact, the whole administration of Gaol affairs throughout the Province is devoid of *system*, owing to the division and variety of authority having control, and hence the confusion and want of uniformity in expenditures, which will continue to exist as long as direct authority and supervision is not vested in the Government, who alone should be responsible to the people for the effective management of this branch of service.[149]

There could be little doubt of what Langmuir meant when he said that the government alone should be responsible to the people for the administration of the gaols, but it was not until 1879 that he put his position unequivocally, expressing his trust that "the Legislature will soon see its way to follow the example of England and assume the entire management and control of the Common Gaols of the Province."[150] The government of Oliver Mowat was not prepared, however, to place such a measure before the Legislature. The long tradition of local management of the gaols, dating, as we have seen, from the very beginning of the corporate life of Upper Canada, could not be swept aside merely by the presentation of evidence that the existing system was defective and that the operation of the gaols in England had been assumed by the central government. The local management of the gaols (even though it was often known to be mismanagement) was to prove too deeply rooted to be displaced solely by argument however cogent and well supported.

If Langmuir was denied the satisfaction of seeing the entire gaol system become provincial, he did have the pleasure of directing the development of three institutions which relieved the gaols of a number of the categories of persons with whom they were least able to deal effectively. The new institutions were a central prison for men and the two Mercer institutions, one for women and one for girls.

The Central Prison

In his second report Langmuir pursued the argument of his first report for the establishment of an intermediate provincial prison in

[149]*Ibid.*, 1870–71, no. 6, p. 7.
[150]*Ibid.*, 1879, no. 8, p. 6.

each of the eastern, central, and western sections of the province. In a way reminiscent of H. C. Thomson's advocacy of a penitentiary forty years earlier, he contended that such prisons would have, among their other advantages, that of being wholly or nearly self-support-ing.[151] The government appeared to be convinced that it should proceed with the establishment of one or more intermediate prisons, for the speech from the throne, in echoing Langmuir's case for such institutions, strongly recommended legislative action:

I cannot avoid bringing under your special notice the state of our prisons, at once the receptacles of the hardened offender and the novice of crime, generally huddled together without regard to their classification. The latter surely ought not to be exposed to influences calculated to stifle the disposition to reform, when again at liberty. The objection is still more obvious in the case of untried prisoners, who may not be found guilty of the crime for which they are committed. Still more is it clear in the case of females of a like class. I recommend to you strongly the erection of institutions in central localities, to which those sentenced for periods less than two years, may be transferred from the surrounding gaols, to undergo their term of punishment under a system of rigid discipline analogous to that of penitentiaries, and where their labour can be utilized toward defraying the cost of their own maintenance.[152]

The proposal encountered criticism, however, and was not proceeded with during the session. Langmuir undertook to answer the arguments of the opponents of central prisons in his third report, and the government included the project in its legislative programme for the following year, still as a measure which might involve "the establishment of one or more Central Prisons."[153] In his fourth report Langmuir was able to announce that $150,000[154] had been appropriated by the Legislature and plans were being prepared in accordance with the "Act to provide for the establishment and government of a Central Prison for the Province of Ontario."[155]

The terms of the act as they related to the staffing, maintenance, inspection, and control of the new prison had much in common with the provisions in the legislation governing the penitentiary during the latter part of the Union period. In addition to the powers that the former inspectors had exercised over the warden and staff of the penitentiary, however, the inspector for Ontario had the right to

[151]*Ibid.*, 1869, no. 4, p. 6.
[152]Ontario, *Journals*, 1868–69, p. 2.
[153]*Ibid.*, 1870–71, p. 2.
[154]Ontario, *Sessional Papers*, 1871–72, no. 4, p. 15.
[155]This and the following references to the Central Prison Act are from Ontario, *Statutes*, 1870–71, c. 17.

impose a fine of up to one month's pay upon any officer or servant of the prison for "any act of negligence, carelessness or insubordination." Respecting the programme and discipline of the prison, the act provided that the institution should "be furnished with all the requisite means for enforcing the performance of hard labour by the inmates" and that solitary confinement should "form part of the discipline thereof." The act also authorized the maintenance of records of the conduct of every inmate with a view to permitting a prisoner "to earn a remission of a portion of the term for which he is sentenced to be confined" where his record of industry and good conduct merited such a remission. The act again differed from the legislation governing the penitentiary in that it provided that contracts and other business transactions should "be entered into and carried out in the corporate name of the . . . inspector on behalf of Her Majesty" rather than by and in the name of the warden. Langmuir was soon to be deeply involved in the business operations of the new institution and the capabilities which were later to make him one of the country's leading financiers were to be fully tested.

The planning, staffing, and construction of the central prison were matters of major importance from 1871 to 1874 when the institution, located in the west end of Toronto, was ready to receive prisoners. Considerable attention was also directed towards the kind of industrial employment that would be provided. In his report for 1872 Langmuir recommended against contracts involving supervision by the contracting manufacturers because of the objectionable features which had usually been associated with such arrangements.[156] In the following year, however, he reported that the institution was, for various reasons, preparing to adopt this method.[157] The precipitating cause for this decision arose from the chance circumstance that the Canada Car Company held a lease on some of the land which the province planned to acquire for the prison. The company happened to be on the point of undertaking a large-scale project for manufacturing railway cars and other industrial products on an adjoining property and hence was about to need a large and varied supply of labour. The company and the province seemed, therefore, to have needs that were complementary, and it occurred to Langmuir "that an arrangement might be entered into with the Company for the lease of the prisoners' labour, on terms equally advantageous to them and to the Government."[158]

[156]Ontario, *Sessional Papers*, 1871–72, no. 4, p. 19.
[157]*Ibid.*, 1872–73, no. 2, p. 2.
[158]*Ibid.*, p. 91.

Accordingly, a seven-year contract was entered into between the province and the company under which the prison's workshops would be fitted up in a way suited to the production of the cars with the labour being provided by the prisoners under the direction of the company's foremen and technicians. The company was to pay a daily rate for the labour of a prisoner during a ten-hour day.

What appeared, at its inception, to be a highly promising arrangement, however, was to prove within a few months to be a costly disappointment. The chief reason was the "almost complete stagnation in railway affairs,"[159] as a result of which the original contract was terminated early in 1875. Although a new contract was entered into with the Canada Car Company for the manufacture of other types of articles, "the uninterrupted depression in every trade"[160] and the weak financial position of the company led to the failure of this project as well. A new approach had then to be made on the basis of "the Government undertaking to manufacture all the wares for an individual or corporation, upon the system known as piece-work prices, such individual or corporation to furnish all the raw material, the Government only manufacturing the wares by the prison labour."[161] Under this method the prisoners were supervised by qualified prison officers rather than by employees of the manufacturer. Langmuir saw this as making it possible for the government "to introduce a system of rewards, in the way of shortening sentences and giving small gratuities for industrious conduct and good behaviour."[162]

The employment of the prisoners continued to present formidable problems, and there appears to have been a gradual transition away from production for sale towards production of items for use by departments of the provincial government. The central prison was, in fact, finding out by experience what had already been established in the case of the penitentiary, that profitable production for the general market through the use of prison labour is more difficult and hazardous in practice than it appears in the planning stage.

Notwithstanding the difficulties respecting labour, the central prison under its capable warden, James Massie, offered a correctional programme that was a great improvement over that of the county gaols. The prison operated from the beginning in an efficient and relatively humane manner and appeared to be achieving its stated

[159]*Ibid.*, 1878, no. 4,,p. 73.
[160]*Ibid.*, p. 77.
[161]*Ibid.*, p. 80.
[162]*Ibid.*

purposes. In 1880 Langmuir was able to give the following outline of its activities and achievements:

The establishment is provided with the means of keeping every person committed to it employed at hard labour, having attached to it, along with other industries, a brickyard, wherein upwards of one hundred prisoners are kept at work, a broom factory for one hundred more, and a shoe and tailor's shop, where all the boots and shoes and clothing required for the common gaols and all the public institutions of the Province are made. Notwithstanding the short-period sentences of the prisoners committed, which, of course, very seriously affect the financial results of the prison labour, the Central prison is fast approaching a self-sustaining basis. Altogether, after an experience of seven years, the Central Prison may be reported to have been eminently successful in all respects in accomplishing the objects of an intermediate prison between the common gaols and the Penitentiary, and is now one of the most important links in our prison system.[163]

Reformatories for Women and Girls

Langmuir soon moved beyond the position he had taken in his first report when he had advocated reformatories for girls under sixteen and longer sentences in the gaols for females over that age. In most of his next nine or ten annual reports he stressed the desirability of separate institutions for females of all ages. The government, however, failed to act on his recommendation, presumably for reasons of cost, until 1878 when a unique situation developed which gave Langmuir an opportunity to suggest the establishment of a reformatory for women at relatively little capital cost to the province. The province had acquired some $100,000 from the intestate estate of a wealthy Toronto citizen, Andrew Mercer, and had asked Langmuir to submit a scheme for the expenditure of these funds. After expressing the view that "the project most worthy of consideration is the expenditure of the sum in founding an entirely new Institution which would be not only a noble and permanent benefaction of a Provincial and undenominational character, but at the same time, a lasting monument to the memory of the deceased,"[164] the Inspector then presented the case that could be made for four types of institutions which he believed were needed in the province.[165] After weighing various arguments he recommended the expenditure of $10,000 for an eye and ear infirmary and $90,000 for a reformatory for females which would include, as a separate unit, a refuge for girls.

[163]Ibid., 1881, no. 8, pp. 9–10.   [164]Ibid., 1879, no. 8, p. 105.

[165]These were a training school for idiots, a hospital for inebriates, an industrial reformatory for females, and an eye and ear infirmary.

In considering the case for the new reformatory Langmuir discussed the nature of female crime, its trends within Ontario, and the effect of the common gaols in increasing it through the lack of classification and work programmes. He argued strongly against the suggestion that the institution should be part of the central prison, and, basing his stand, in part, on the Declaration of Principles of the National Congress on Penitentiary and Reformatory Discipline, asserted that "the buildings, their interior arrangements, the disciplinary management, industrial pursuits and general surroundings of a Reformatory for females" should be "altogether different from those for males."[166] He also contended that it was "of paramount importance" that there be complete separation in the institution between girls under fourteen years of age and the older offenders. The Inspector's recommendation was adopted by the government in 1878 and embodied in two acts in 1879, one establishing the Andrew Mercer Reformatory for females[167] and the other providing that a portion of the institution be set apart for the reception of girls under the age of fourteen years.[168]

THE MERCER REFORMATORY

Prior to the enactment of the legislation Langmuir was requested by the government to visit a number of penal institutions for women in the United States. Among these was the reformatory at South Framingham, Massachusetts, which was generally considered at the time to be a model. Langmuir, however, felt that the lessons provided respecting its structure and internal arrangements were largely "of a negative character,"[169] and he recommended a quite different type of construction and basic plan for the new institution.

Among his major proposals, the Inspector suggested that the building be planned to accommodate about 150 inmates, "the dormitories to be graded from cells to single and associated rooms, so that the inmates might be advanced from the lower class of prison surroundings to the better and higher, as evidences of reformation may be given; complete isolation, if possible, to be observed between the grades."[170] In 1879 Langmuir was able to report that the building was proceeding in conformity with this proposal. He referred to the construction of twelve distinct wards, each with its own workroom. In addition there was a general workshop "divided into two flats and five distinct

166Ontario, *Sessional Papers*, 1879, no. 8, p. 107.
167Ontario, *Statutes*, 1879, c. 38.
168*Ibid.*, c. 39.
169Ontario, *Sessional Papers*, 1879, no. 8, p. 108.
170*Ibid.*, p. 107.

compartments."[171] Provision was being made for serving meals either separately or in partial association, and there were four distinct yards for airing and exercise. Langmuir thus felt justified in making the claim that "the structural arrangement of the building secures . . . the means for as perfect a system of classification of the inmates as can be obtained under the partially associated system, and as effective and practical a method of separation as under the silent, or solitary system, without its bad effects.[172]

The Inspector advocated a diversified labour programme within the institution to avoid over-dependency on any one product and to reduce the opposition of manufacturers and labourers affected by the competition from the products or services produced in the reformatory. He also held that it was desirable "for disciplinary reasons that there should be a variety of labour, commencing with that of a more menial order, such as washing, etc., so that continued good conduct of an inmate might be rewarded by advancement to a higher grade of work, such as machine-sewing."[173] This approach to employment, in addition to his proposal for the organization of the prison, indicates that Langmuir had come to consider a certain measure of individual treatment as a desirable criterion in the function and operation of a reformatory. "It will be apparent," he stated, "that entire uniformity of discipline cannot be observed throughout the Reformatory, and to all inmates alike."[174]

Langmuir was able to observe the operations of the Mercer reformatory for only a little over a year during his inspectorship. In his final report he felt "warranted in reporting that the Institution is fulfilling the objects designed in its establishment in a very satisfactory way."[175] He had reached the conclusion, however, that the hope of reforming women offenders was vain unless they were sentenced for longer periods than the average of eight months established during the first year. He urged the courts to take advantage of a recent federal amendment to the Vagrancy Act increasing the maximum sentence for vagrancy from six months to two years. He summed up his position on the matter as follows:

The lives of most of these women having from childhood been spent in criminality and vicious indulgence, it is the design of the Reformatory, and the object of its training and discipline, to break up the evil habits so engendered, and to substitute in their place moral control and restraint. To this end I would strongly recommend that no woman be sentenced to the

171*Ibid.*, 1880, no. 8, p. 188.
172*Ibid.*
174*Ibid.*

173*Ibid.*, p. 190.
175*Ibid.*, 1882, no. 8, p. 3.

Reformatory for less than a year; and that, if it should appear that a woman has been committed to a Common Gaol oftener than three times, the longest term of sentence allowed by law should be imposed.[176]

THE MERCER REFUGE

Because of the inherent difficulties in achieving the aim of reformation in a reformatory for female adults, Langmuir began to emphasize the rôle of the Mercer Refuge to receive and reform the young female offender before she could become a confirmed delinquent. Just as the legislation under which the female reformatory was founded was patterned closely on the Central Prison Act, so the principles that were expressed in the statute establishing the refuge for girls[177] reflected some of the experience gained during the previous years in the administration of the boys' reformatory at Penetanguishene. On the other hand, the act for the Mercer Refuge differed in many important respects from other legislation in the corrections field. For example, it provided that the refuge, in addition to being available to receive any girl under the age of fourteen who was convicted of an offence for which a common gaol sentence might be imposed, was also to receive any girl who was committed by a warrant of a county or district, or police magistrate, and who came within five "descriptions." These included begging, being without a home, being a destitute orphan or a child whose surviving parent was in gaol, being beyond parental control, or being a child who "by reason of the neglect, drunkenness, or other vices of her parents . . . is suffered to be growing up without salutary control and education, or in circumstances which render it probable that such girl will, unless placed under proper control, lead an idle and dissolute life." The period of detention for a girl in the refuge was normally between two and five years, with the objective of having each girl learn "some proper trade, or be taught some other means of earning her livelihood, or for the formation of industrious habits."

It is apparent that, in accepting into the refuge girls who were in need of protection as potential rather than convicted offenders, and in undertaking to maintain and train them, the province had moved beyond any position it had previously taken. To prevent delinquency and to deal with the potential offender at a time when it was believed she could be helped with the best prospect of success, the Legislature had undertaken to set aside the established jur lical principle of

[176]*Ibid.*, p. 180.
[177]Ontario, *Statutes*, 1879, c. 39.

imprisoning only persons who were convicted of or involved in criminal activities.

The legislation establishing the refuge was further distinguished from former legislation in that it authorized the superintendent of the institution, with the consent of the inspector, to release any girl in the refuge under an indenture of apprenticeship in the home of a "respectable and trustworthy person" willing to undertake her charge.

At the end of the first year of its operation Langmuir was disappointed to find that the refuge was operating at less than half its capacity notwithstanding a circular which had been issued to all judges and magistrates informing them of the provisions of the legislation under which the refuge had been established. He remained convinced that the use of the refuge and the associated plan of placing the girls who had received its training in respectable families would "in all human probability, result in saving the largest proportion of them from disgrace and ruin."[178]

The Reformatory for Boys

On the subject of the boys' reformatory at Penetanguishene Langmuir, almost from the first, failed to share the satisfaction that had been, in general, expressed by the inspectors during the Union period. He was critical of the design of the main building which had cost $120,000 and which, though "really elegant" in appearance, had much waste space and was ill adapted for the residential and work needs of a boys' reformatory.[179] He also commented unfavourably on the remoteness of the location of the institution especially because of the difficulty of carrying on trades which would provide training and prove financially profitable.

He agreed, however, with the former inspectors and the warden that the upper age of those committed to the institution should be lowered. In his first report he noted that 54 of the 173 boys in the reformatory were over the age of eighteen, and he doubted whether an institution could achieve its objectives respecting the younger boys when it was also called on to receive the young adult. Similarly, the Inspector shared the views of his predecessors that the sentence of two years should be replaced by indefinite sentences of up to a maximum of five years.

The evolution during the 1870's of Langmuir's ideas concerning the

---

[178]Ontario, *Sessional Papers*, 1882, no. 8, p. 183.
[179]*Ibid.*, 1868–69, no. 3, p. 22.

kind of programme which should be adopted for a boys' reformatory and the efforts he made to put his ideas into effect form one of the most interesting chapters in his inspectorship—the more so because they involved the clash of two strong personalities, Langmuir, on the one hand, and William Moore Kelly, the warden of the reformatory, on the other. The Inspector's reports indicate the stages by which he began to question, to criticize, and finally to condemn Kelly's philosophy and methods. It became increasingly obvious to Langmuir that Kelly was operating the reformatory essentially as though it were an adult institution. It appears that Kelly, like many other prison administrators, had become progressively more conservative and security-minded. Langmuir found, for example, that it was Kelly's practice to keep the boys locked in their cells much of the time, including all of Sunday other than for meals and divine service.[180] Furthermore, Kelly sought to replace the fence surrounding the institution with a high wall and his principal aim seemed to be to develop a system of discipline which would keep the boys "docile and obedient."[181] Accordingly, he resisted Langmuir's pressure for a non-penal and less restrictive programme.

The Inspector's dissatisfaction with the institution was restrained in most of his early reports, but in 1874 he gave vent to the feelings he had built up about it:

Though for years I have accepted the situation, it has been at the expense of my judgment, my convictions, and I may almost add, of my duty towards Government. . . . The rescue of each lad from evil courses is an economy to the state, and is a direct benefit to society. What wonder then, that I should feel and write strongly, when I see that, from the very principles of its establishment and discipline, the Provincial Reformatory is unfitted for the work it should perform, and is wrong in principle and faulty in practice.[182]

As a follow-up to this adverse criticism, Langmuir presented in detail the principles which he believed should govern the work of rescue and reformation of delinquent youth. The first step was to remove the boy from want because "the half-starved, ill-clad and badly-treated boy is not susceptible of moral improvement." The next reforming influence was industry. In teaching the boy to be industrious, Langmuir emphasized not only that the tasks "should be apportioned to his strength and his capacity," but also with "due

[180]*Ibid.*, 1870–71, no. 6, p. 30.
[181]*Ibid.*, 1869, no. 4, p. 82.
[182]This and the following references to Langmuir's opinions on the reformatory are from Ontario, *Sessional Papers*, 1874 (vol. VII), no. 2, pp. 59–60.

regard being given to his predilections." The third element was education and instruction, both religious and secular. An additional principle was classification, with the complete removal from the reformatory of those who could not respond to its programme and who had to be regarded as incorrigible. For the care and reformation of the remainder "the next step should be to render the Institution attractive, and, in the true sense of the word *home-like*, furnishing every means of innocent amusement for the hours of recreation, affording good educational advantages, requiring just enough of labour to teach habits of industry, and by firm though kindly discipline to induce regularity and obedience to orders." With a system based on these principles complemented by "a carefully devised and extensive system of rewards for good behaviour" there would, in the view of the Inspector, "be no need of locks and bars." By 1874 Langmuir was convinced that the adoption of these principles was necessary before the institution could become truly a reformatory "instead of a Prison for Juvenile offenders." He was equally convinced that their adoption "would require a complete revolution of the present system."

Langmuir's critical reports on the reformatory brought him into open conflict with Kelly who was able to present his case in the appendices to the Inspector's reports. The warden's principal defence of his programme was that few ex-reformatory boys were to be found in the central prison or the penitentiary. In addition, Kelly, who had been involved in public controversy before he became warden,[183] did not hesitate to attack the Inspector and to seek to block Langmuir's efforts to change the programme which he had developed and with which he was so closely identified.

Kelly resigned in 1879 and his successor was sent to visit some of the better reformatories in the United States before taking up his new duties. In announcing the change, Langmuir stated that it was the government's intention that the institution, "instead of being a penal establishment . . . with all the objectionable features and surroundings of a penitentiary, shall become a Reformatory school, in the most liberal sense of the term, for the education, industrial training and moral reclamation of juvenile delinquents."[184] The government's position was expressed in the speech from the throne in 1880:

The attention of my Government has recently been directed to the duty of bringing the management of the Reformatory for Boys at Penetanguishene more thoroughly into harmony with the original design and intention of such

[183]Canada, *Journals*, 1856, pp. 387, 431.
[184]Ontario, *Sessional Papers*, 1880, no. 8, p. 176.

an institution. The system it is proposed to pursue is modelled on the improved method adopted at the most successful establishments of this kind elsewhere, and with the view of substituting for penal discipline treatment and influences of a strictly reformatory character. A Bill will be submitted to you for this object, and your assent will be asked to an appropriation to cover some necessary outlay in connection with the changes contemplated.[185]

The resulting legislation[186] replaced the existing act (the old pre-Confederation statute transferred to the provincial setting) and changed the designation of the institution from "reformatory prison" to "reformatory for boys." In some ways this new legislation was similar to the act establishing the refuge for girls, for it provided that a boy could be detained for a period of five years and that, under certain conditions, the superintendent of the reformatory could place a boy as an apprentice to a suitable person who would teach him a trade. In contrast with the refuge act, however, the new act made it possible for a boy to earn a remission of a portion of the term of his sentence through "good conduct, proficiency in school, and industrious habits" together with "evidence of being reformed." Remission could be granted on the recommendation of the superintendent and inspector, the boy being "discharged on probation for a stated period."[187] On evidence that a boy had "violated the conditions of his discharge," a judge or a magistrate could order him to be returned to the institution for the remainder of the original sentence.[188] Also unlike the refuge act, the new legislation did not adopt the provisions for preventive detention through the use of a judicial warrant, although it did allow that a boy between the ages of ten and thirteen years could be confined to the reformatory on a complaint by a parent or guardian that the boy's conduct was incorrigible or vicious.[189]

Before the new legislation was passed, Langmuir had outlined a number of methods and procedures designed to ensure that the principles he had formulated would be expressed in all aspects of the institution's programme. He was insistent, for example, that the old terms and expressions be replaced by new ones free of the odium of the penal tradition. He expressed the view that the use of the terms "convict" and "prisoner" could "inflict incalculable injury on the boys and cruelly burden their future with a stigma which may irretrievably

[185]Ontario, *Journals*, 1880, p. 5.
[186]Ontario, *Statutes*, 1880, c. 34.
[187]This was a complicated matter, however, involving the provincial attorney-general and the Dominion government which, by virtue of its jurisdiction in matters of criminal law, held that it had the authority respecting remission.
[188]Ontario, *Statutes*, 1880, c. 34.
[189]*Ibid.*, c. 34, s. 27.

ruin them."[190] Thus the inmates of the reformatory were to be "simply called 'boys' officially, and in all their relations with the officers and each other." The warden was to be called "superintendent," and the guards "overseers" or "instructors." The Inspector also ordered that "the objectionable word 'gang' must never be used."

Langmuir recognized the importance of the feelings of the boys when they first entered the institution, and he gave instructions that "on no account should a boy be stared at or rendered uncomfortable when admitted." The superintendent was to "take the earliest opportunity of conversing with each boy alone" and to "use every means" to gain the boy's confidence. The superintendent and the chaplain were to be readily accessible "to every lad . . . on all reasonable occasions." The Inspector was insistent that the officers of the institution "exercise the greatest kindness, patience, forbearance and well-directed zeal in the performance of their duties." If any officer lacked the "intelligence to appreciate the importance of these qualities, in proportion to the position he holds and the responsibility placed upon him," he was, in the opinion of Langmuir, "unfit to be on the staff of a Juvenile Reformatory." The superintendent was to suspend any officer displaying harshness towards a boy, whether "in demeanour, conduct or speech" and report the case for the action of the inspector.

The new programme of the reformatory, involving changes in its methods of discipline and extensive alterations and expansion of its buildings was not carried out without considerable difficulties. By 1882, however, these were largely overcome and Langmuir had the satisfaction of seeing the reforms he had advocated being progressively put into operation.

Encouragement of Prisoners' Aid Associations

Notwithstanding his success in developing public programmes in the field of corrections, Langmuir believed that these programmes could achieve their objectives only with the assistance of private individuals and associations. He developed this view in his sixth report, referring to the problems which faced discharged prisoners in finding work and accommodation and in forming social relationships other than those which had initially brought them into conflict with the law. They needed help in the form of "money, employment, advice and above all sympathy to encourage them in the right path."[191] In Great Britain

[190]This and the following references to Langmuir's views are from Ontario, *Sessional Papers*, 1880, no. 8, pp. 177–78.
[191]Ontario, *Sessional Papers*, 1874 (vol. VI), no. 2, p. 75.

and the United States assistance of this kind was being provided by prisoners' aid societies, and Langmuir asked if the establishment of such associations was not a question for "the practical philanthropists of the Province"[192] to consider. He indicated that if a prisoners' aid association was formed in Toronto he would recommend financial support for it by the provincial government.[193]

In 1874 Langmuir was able to announce that "the suggestion made in my last Report" had been carried into effect and that "a Prisoners' Aid Association has been established in this city, whose labours deserve every encouragement from the community."[194] He proceeded to outline the functions the organization might be expected to perform: "To visit every convict previous to his discharge, to ascertain from him his necessities, the state of his clothing, where he proposes to go when liberated, what are his wishes, prospects, plans &c., and having gained the necessary information, to supply his needs, procure railway tickets to send him to his home, if he so desire; procure employment if he wishes it, and give him counsel and sympathy."[195]

The account of the meeting at which the new association was organized showed clearly that Langmuir's report of the previous year was the precipitating cause of the meeting, but it also revealed that the association was more interested in evangelical work than in the kinds of activities Langmuir had in mind. This tendency was perhaps not surprising because many of those participating in the meeting had been associated with a mission sunday school conducted in the Toronto gaol for some seven years. The meeting decided that the new association would continue with this enterprise and undertake similar work in the central prison.[196] Although the emphasis during the proceedings was on bible classes, preaching services, and personal evangelism, reference was made to securing a "missionary agent" whose services were described as indispensable in organizing the religious work and

[192]*Ibid.*
[193]*Ibid.*
[194]*Ibid.* (vol. VII), no. 2, p. 46.
[195]*Ibid.*
[196]*Ibid.*, pp. 217–20. The meeting, an account of which was included as an appendix to the Inspector's report, was held in June 1874 in Shaftbury Hall, under the chairmanship of "Sheriff Jarvis." Most of the resolutions were moved by clergymen. The officers appointed were president, Dr. George Hodgins, and vice-presidents, R. W. Laidlaw, Dr. A. M. Rosebrugh, and George Hague, Bank of Toronto, who also served as treasurer. Membership was open to all who subscribed to its funds. A curious feature of its organization was that its board of managers was to consist of "all the teachers engaged in the Mission." Following the meeting the President wrote to every clergyman in Toronto asking for the names of suitable and experienced teachers for the sunday school to be conducted on alternate Sunday mornings.

in promoting "the welfare of the well disposed prisoners when discharged."[197]

An agent was appointed by the association during the first year of its operation but the work of the organization fell far short of what Langmuir had hoped for and he felt called upon again in 1881 to state that "there is the greatest need for the organization . . . of associations for the aid of discharged prisoners and for providing them with work, in order that the good effects of the moral, disciplinary, and industrial training which they have received in the Prisons and Reformatories may not be lost."[198] He proceeded to add to his previous list of functions for such associations "the care of the families of prisoner's undergoing sentence" and "the apprenticing or employment of the youth of both sexes discharged from the Reformatories."[199] These were duties which Langmuir felt "came within the sphere of private benevolence" and he made a strong appeal for the organization of prisoners' aid associations "in all of the cities in the Province, with agencies in the rural districts."[200]

This hope was not to be realized in the nineteenth century although the Prisoners' Aid Association of Toronto was to assume in the 1880's most of the functions he had outlined. It was to become, as well, an important agency for the promotion of social welfare objectives in the province, contributing to advances in penal reform, provisions for the poor, and measures for the protection of neglected children.

PERIOD 1882-1893

The inspection of the correctional institutions following Langmuir's resignation was performed by Robert Christie until 1890 and from then until the end of the period covered in this study by Dr. T. F. Chamberlain assisted, beginning in 1891, by James Noxon. Christie and Chamberlain appear to have been fairly capable administrators with a desire to promote the objectives that had been pursued by Langmuir. Christie's period as inspector, however, saw little added to the correctional institutions he had inherited, and the most important advances in the field of corrections—the development of an industrial school for boys and the growth of public understanding of penal problems—were the product of others' work. Christie was, moreover, unable to arrest

[197]*Ibid.*, p. 220.
[198]*Ibid.*, 1881, no. 8, p. 3.
[199]*Ibid.*   [200]*Ibid.*

the tendency of some of the institutions to become complacent and conservative. Because Chamberlain received his appointment shortly after the naming of the Royal Commission on the Prison and Reformatory System, he took up his duties at a time when reform was in the air and when the provincial government was under strong pressure to adopt constructive measures in the corrections field. He was therefore assured of more support for a vigorous approach to penal problems than Christie may have enjoyed.

The Common Gaols

The gaols continued throughout the 1880's and early 1890's to present essentially the same problems that had been the focus of the critical concern and earnest efforts of the Board of Inspectors prior to Confederation and of Langmuir thereafter. The municipalities continued to be grudging in their support; the quality of administration of the gaols by the sheriff and gaolers remained mediocre; constructive employment for the prisoners was limited or non-existent; classification was inadequate even where the conditions existed to make it possible; and persons continued to be committed to the gaols who required a different type of care or treatment.

Although the numbers committed to the gaols had fallen off by the year 1881 to about 9,200 from the record of nearly 13,500 in 1877, they began to rise again in the mid-1880's reaching some 12,500 in 1899.[201] Thereafter they began once again to decline and by 1893 had dropped to around 8,600, the lowest figure in twenty years.[202] The overcrowding that resulted from the increased commitments in the mid-1880's led the government to consider resuming the strong line with the municipalities that had been taken during the early years of Langmuir's inspectorship. Thus the Provincial Secretary in 1888 stated in a memorandum that "the authority vested in the Inspectors by statute should be invoked where negotiation fails to compel the council, upon whom the responsibility rests to make proper provision for classification where the structural accommodation is not at present sufficient for that purpose."[203] It does not appear, however, that the device of mandamus was employed, perhaps because of the decline, referred to above, in the numbers committed.

In addition to pressing for increased accommodation where this was required, Christie and Chamberlain urged the gaols to install furnaces,

[201]*Ibid.*, 1894, no. 27, p. 7.
[202]*Ibid.*   [203]*Ibid.*, 1889, no. 2, p. 12.

running water, and where possible gas lighting; in these efforts the inspectors achieved a fair measure of success.

The Central Prison

Commitments to the central prison, which with some fluctuations had risen from 370 in 1874 to 767 in 1882, reached a peak of 862 in 1887; by 1893 they stood at 632.[204] At any one time the number of prisoners ranged between 250 and 445.[205] The programme of the prison continued along the lines developed during the first few years of its operation, with a continuing emphasis on industrial labour. The buildings of the prison were enlarged and more modern industrial machinery was introduced.

The discipline of the institution continued to be strict: the rule of silence was generally enforced, and there appears during the mid-1880's to have been some increase in the severity of punishments. The latter became the subject of a newspaper attack which led the government to appoint a commission to investigate the matter.[206] The commission with Langmuir as one of its three members received testimony locally and also visited a number of institutions in the United States to study their methods of discipline. The commission's report, which supported the warden on the matter at issue, seems to have had some effect on the disciplinary arrangements of the prison. In 1893 Noxon reported that "while discipline has been strictly maintained the privations visited upon prisoners have been trifling and corporal punishment seldom inflicted."[207] The report also appears to have led to the introduction of a policy of paying prisoners for work done beyond a prescribed amount.[208]

The matter of prison labour continued to present difficulties and in 1888 Christie and James Massie, the warden, visited eleven American prisons to obtain "expert testimony upon the manner in which the prison labour question is being considered and dealt with in the States, in its various relationships to the Government, the free labourer and the prisoner himself."[209] On the basis of their report the government finally decided to abandon the contract system entirely in favour

---

204Ibid., 1894, no. 27, pp. 142–43. Commitments would have been higher in 1893, in the view of the warden, except "that a considerable number, even of Canadian crooks, went west to operate at the World's Fair" (ibid. p. 138).
205Ontario, Sessional Papers, 1891, no. 18, p. 678.
206Ibid., 1886, no. 10, p. 69.
207Ibid., 1894, no. 27, p. 138.
208Ibid., 1891, no. 18, p. 154.   209Ibid., 1889, no. 2, p. 78.

of "the piece-price plan for disposing of the products of the prison labour.[210]

By the late 1880's the central prison under Massie had settled into established practices characterized by strictness of discipline, denial of such privileges as the use of tobacco, and hard work. As a result, persons convicted by the courts requested longer sentences in the penitentiary rather than shorter sentences in the prison, a situation which Massie regarded with satisfaction.[211]

The Mercer Reformatory

The Mercer Reformatory was rapidly utilized and had an average occupancy during its first eight years of 114.[212] There was a decline in the numbers confined around the end of the 1880's and early 1890's but 1893 witnessed an increase to a daily average of 126 inmates.[213]

The main elements in the reformatory's programme were hard work, restraint, and closely ordered routine. Supervised work, supervised religious services, and silent, supervised meals made up most of the long day which began at 5.30 A.M. during the summer and 6.00 A.M. in the winter.[214] For inmates who had completed the work assigned them, two hours of recreation consisting of walking in the corridors or grounds was permitted.[215] Conformity to the discipline of the prison was emphasized, not only because it made for the smoother operation of the institution but because it was thought that the habits of conformity and docile obedience would be productive of enduring reform. Some doubt about the validity of this view was expressed in the superintendent's annual report for 1890: "It appears almost incredible that so many women who keep all the rules and regulations of the Reformatory, always conducting themselves in a quiet orderly manner doing their allotted portion of work diligently and well should on regaining their liberty so soon fall back into their old ways of living, many of them, I feel, are quite sincere at the time in making good resolutions; but they are weak and unable to resist the temptations that are ready to meet them on their discharge."[216] There is, however,

[210]*Ibid.*, 1890, no. 11, p. 75.
[211]*Ibid.*, 1891, no. 18, p. 681.
[212]*Ibid.*, no. 7, p. 101.
[213]*Ibid.*, 1894, no. 27, p. 86.
[214]*Ibid.*, 1889, no. 2, p. 103.
[215]*Ibid.*, 1891, no. 18, p. 735. "They walk around the corridors. We call this recreation, and in fine weather we allow them to go out on the grounds under close supervision; we allow them to walk up and down the grounds."
[216]Ontario, *Sessional Papers*, 1891, no. 7, p. 101.

nothing to indicate that this observation led to any diminution of the reformatory's dependence upon a rigid programme. What was advocated, in fact, was an extension of the inmates' exposure to it. The superintendent, in the report quoted above, commented enviously upon the long sentences being served in women's prisons in the United States where the women found "it to their best interests to conduct themselves in a quiet orderly manner."[217] She pointed out that the average sentence in Mercer during the year under review was nine months and she held that "very little in the way of reformation can be done with a woman in this short time."[218]

A similar emphasis on docility and obedience in the institution, notwithstanding the admitted lack of a direct relationship between such conduct within the reformatory's walls and acceptable behaviour beyond them, is to be seen in the superintendent's advocacy of remission of sentence for good conduct. In the event of the necessary legislation being passed, she asked that "this clemency be extended only to those who have never been reported for any infringement of the Reformatory rules."[219]

Throughout the period, the institution was under the direction of the same superintendent, Mrs. M. J. O'Reilly, who appears to have been able to operate the institution largely as she saw fit. When the Royal Commission received testimony concerning the reformatory it found that the initial plan of classification had been set aside, that instead of diversified industrial employment there was only laundering, sewing, and domestic work, and that no regulations or by-laws were in effect governing the operation of the institution.[220] It was obvious to Langmuir, in his capacity as chairman of the commission, that the hopes he as inspector had held for the institution were far from realization.

The Mercer Refuge

The utilization of the Mercer Refuge was slower than in the case of the reformatory but by the end of the 1880's occupancy was approaching the institution's capacity of fifty girls. With the establishment in 1891 of the Alexandra School for Girls in East Toronto, under the Industrial Schools Act, there was a decline in the number sentenced to the refuge from the Toronto courts.[221] Although the refuge was

[217]Ibid., p. 103.
[218]Ibid.
[219]Ibid., 1887, no. 12, p. 104.
[220]Ibid., 1891, no. 18, pp. 730–35.
[221]Ibid., 1894, no. 27, p. 92.

under the general direction of the superintendent of the reformatory, throughout the period its day-to-day operation was carried by Miss Martha Elliott who had a teaching background and who seems to have developed a relatively non-penal programme designed to provide a good elementary education as well as competence in the simpler domestic arts. The refuge seems to have been reasonably successful in placing children in homes on an apprenticeship basis and some efforts appear to have been made to keep in touch with the girls discharged by this and other means. It is difficult to believe, however, that the follow-up could have been sufficiently thorough to justify the contention of the officials that they had knowledge that 90 per cent of the former inmates had "not relapsed into vice and crime."[222]

By the time of the hearings of the Royal Commission, public concern had been voiced about existing methods of meeting the problem of neglected children, coupled with the knowledge that most of the girls in the refuge were neglected rather than delinquent. Questions had then been raised about the propriety of having the refuge housed under the same roof as the reformatory for women. It was not difficult to foresee, therefore, that the commission would recommend that this association of the two institutions should be terminated.

The Reformatory for Boys

In his early reports on the boys' reformatory at Penetanguishene, Christie traced the remaining stages of the process by which the prison procedures and attitudes that had prevailed under the Kelly régime were being replaced by the programme introduced by Langmuir and carried into effect by Thomas McCrossan, the new superintendent. "On entering the building," he wrote, "there may be seen the effects of introducing the modern and humane system which looks upon . . . a boy as needing moral training and influence more than rigorous discipline; interesting and useful work, with proper recreation, more than hard tasks; home comforts and surroundings more than the solitary cell; healthy food more than prison diet; a respectable dress rather than prison uniform."[223] In commending the new programme and recommending its extension, Christie suggested that the "home influence" of the institution could be increased "by the appointment of a lady holding the position of matron or one somewhat analogous, who, assisted by others, would counsel and instruct the lads, many

222*Ibid.*, 1891, no. 18, p. 736.
223*Ibid.*, 1882–83, no. 8, p. 80 (prison report).

of whom could be much benefitted by female influence."[224] Nothing, however, seems to have come of this admirable suggestion.

The reformatory, with its new approach, entered upon a period during which it appears to have achieved a reasonable measure of success. McCrossan's annual reports indicated that a much improved atmosphere was being created. In 1884 he noted that while each year "a larger measure of personal liberty has been accorded" there were, none the less, progressively fewer attempts at escape.[225] Two years later he commented on the "reduced number of punishments" and "the trivial nature of the offenses,"[226] and in 1891 he remarked that "a boy unworthy of being reasonably trusted is now rare, and the sly tyranny hitherto commonly practiced by the larger over the smaller boys has now little if any existence."[227] The work of the reformatory towards a more individualized approach was assisted during the later part of the period by the steady decline in the numbers in residence. By 1893 the figure had fallen to 173 from the high of 263 reached in 1882.[228]

The handicaps under which the institution operated, however, continued to be formidable. Its remoteness from the centres of population and industry led to the abandonment of the attempts to carry on industrial activities on any significant scale. Farming and gardening, though carried on to some extent, were also made difficult by the poor quality of the land surrounding the institution. In addition to these activities some lumbering, carpentry, shoe-making, and tailoring together with the maintenance of the property and the institution's internal services made up the work programme.

McCrossan felt that more serious problems for the institution arose from weaknesses in the processes of imposing and remitting juvenile sentences. In many of his reports he commented on the failure of the Bench to use the authority it had been given in 1880, by both the provincial and federal legislation, to impose indefinite sentences.[229] Because less than 20 per cent of the boys arriving at the reformatory had received such sentences, it was considered too impractical and invidious for the reformatory to seek to discharge the boys with indefinite sentences, while the majority had to depend on the royal

224*Ibid.*, p. 85.
225*Ibid.*, 1885, no. 12, p. 139.
226*Ibid.*, 1887, no. 12, p. 128.
227*Ibid.*, 1892, no. 8, p. 134.
228*Ibid.*, 1894, no. 27, p. 119.
229*Ibid.*, 1886, no. 10, p. 133. The acts referred to are Ontario, *Statutes*, 1880, c. 34, and Canada, *Statutes*, 1880, c. 39.

prerogative of pardon.[230] It was the procedures surrounding the exercise of this prerogative which drew the sharpest criticism from McCrossan and others interested in the reformatory. In spite of Ontario's attempts to have the prerogative transferred from the federal to the provincial executive, it continued throughout the period to be exercised by the Dominion government. The machinery employed was slow, cumbersome, and unpredictable. It included referring the question back to the sentencing judge, whose decision might reverse the plan of the executive to grant a pardon. Therefore, the wish of the reformatory to base a system of incentives to improved behaviour mainly on the hope of remission was largely set at nought and the effectiveness of its whole programme seriously affected.

During the 1880's the question first asked by Meredith and others before Confederation was raised again with more insistence. Was it necessary to put boys, many of whom were mere children and who were more often neglected than delinquent, through the formal processes of law and send them to a remote institution? Meredith, now living in Toronto, was among a number of prominent citizens who felt that there were better answers to the question than those embodied in current practice. Among the measures that were called for was the establishment of industrial schools under legislation which had lain dormant since its enactment in 1874. Such action was taken, at last, in 1887 when the first industrial school in the province was built at Mimico and began to receive children who might otherwise have been sent to Penetanguishene.[231] This development, which is discussed more fully in chapter 6, indicated the government's recognition that there were often more suitable ways of dealing with children who were creating a problem in the community than through correctional processes which, though somewhat reformed from earlier years, were essentially the same as those applied to adults.

The Prisoners' Aid Association

Action to encourage the development of industrial schools for boys and girls was a reflection of the public concern over social problems that developed during the mid-1880's, particularly in the larger centres and notably in Toronto. Another important manifestation of this concern was the broadening range of interests and activities of the Prisoners' Aid Association. Beginning in 1883 the government made

[230]Ontario, *Sessional Papers*, 1886, no. 10, p. 134.
[231]*Ibid.*, 1888, no. 7, pp. 253–62.

an annual grant of $1,000 to the association "with the understanding" that the funds would be used "toward assisting discharged prisoners in various practical ways to enable them to earn an honest living and lead an honest life on leaving the prisons."[232] The grant provided a strong impetus to the association to supplement its evangelical and teaching activities with the type of work envisaged earlier by Langmuir.

The work of the association was also given new life by the election to its presidency of Samuel Blake who replaced W. H. Howland in the post and who appears to have been able to devote more attention to the work than Howland, who was mayor of Toronto during this period. From about 1883 the association had one paid agent who carried out social work functions and three others principally engaged in teaching or evangelical activities.[233] In addition to work carried on in the prisons, assistance of various kinds was given to the families of prisoners and a broad after-care programme was developed. To help the newly discharged prisoners, the association opened a lodging house for men and later for women and established workshops in connection with each. Discharged prisoners were provided with clothing, tools, and furniture, and money was given for board and railway fares. The ex-prisoners were also assisted in finding work—the association reporting that it seldom failed in getting employment for discharged prisoners of both sexes.[234] The association also had a loan fund that worked well. Its activities in 1885 were summed up in a statement by the President who reported the provision of various types of aid to "726 discharged prisoners last year, nearly all of whom must otherwise have been a heavy financial charge upon the country, and out of this number found employment for 384; gave furniture to 68 families; gave food and board to 380; sheltered 250; paid rent for 24; paid fares to homes or to where work was offered for 29; distributed 339 articles of clothing, and 59 tools; lent $552.34 and received repayment of $416.91."[235]

The breadth of the whole programme of the association and the vigour with which it was carried on won the commendation of English and American visitors interested in corrections and led Blake to conclude that "the work of this Society is the most effective of any organization of its kind on this Continent."[236]

[232]Ibid., 1884, no. 8, p. 111.
[233]Ibid.
[235]Ibid., 1886, no. 10, p. 92.

[234]Ibid.
[236]Ibid., 1887, no. 13, p. 91.

The Congress of the National Prison Association

The extensive use of volunteers by the Prisoners' Aid Association, largely in connection with its teaching and evangelical work, and the broad participation in the development of the boys' industrial school by outstanding community leaders in the fields of business, government, religion, education, and law were indicative of the growing interest in corrections in the mid-1880's in Toronto. This reached a high point in mid-September 1887 when the annual congress of the National Prison Association convened in Toronto.[237] The invitation for this meeting, the first such to be held in Canada, had been extended by James Massie on behalf of the province of Ontario[238] with the support of Howland for the city of Toronto. The meetings, which lasted a week, attracted particularly wide attention because the president of the congress was Rutherford B. Hayes, a former president of the United States.

The proceedings of the congress allowed Canadians to hear the views on penal matters of distinguished American penal authorities including F. H. Wines, Z. R. Brockway, General Roeliff Brinkerhoff, A. G. Byers, Warren F. Spalding, and Professor Francis Wayland. It also gave Canadian leaders in the field an opportunity to gain public attention for the advancement of current ideas on penal problems as they applied to Canada. In formal papers read before the congress, Meredith strongly condemned county and city gaols as then conducted[239] and Howland discussed the problems of discharged prisoners.[240] There were shorter speeches by Goldwin Smith, Samuel Blake, G. W. Ross (provincial minister of education), Sir Alexander Campbell (lieutenant-governor), and James Massie.

The congress gave currency to a number of ideas relating to child welfare as well as to corrections, and stimulated thought and action in these fields. In particular it prompted the members of the Prisoners' Aid Association to make the advocacy of penal reform a more important part of its programme. And it appears to have been the pressure of the association which led the government in 1890 to appoint

[237]National Prison Association of the United States, *Proceedings of the Annual Congress, Toronto, 1887* (Chicago, 1889).

[238]*Ibid.*, pp. 316–17. Massie referred to the kindness of the Provincial Secretary, Hon. A. S. Hardie, "whereby, in the most liberal manner, he has afforded us facilities for defraying the expenses of the Congress, and his kindness in entertaining the delegates."

[239]*Ibid.*, pp. 242–56.

[240]*Ibid.*, pp. 286–97.

the Royal Commission on the Prison and Reformatory System of Ontario.[241]

The Royal Commission

The general scope of the commission's work and its review of certain problems respecting the poor have been noted earlier in this study and its consideration of alcoholism and child welfare is discussed in later chapters. The commission's major focus, however, was upon corrections and it explored this field much more thoroughly than had any previous commission, including that of 1848–49.

The recommendations of the commission were the product of a selective review of the literature on crime and its treatment, carefully prepared interviews with Canadian and internationally recognized authorities in the field of charities and corrections, visits to institutions in four states of the United States, an inspection of all the provincially operated penal institutions together with a number of local gaols in Ontario, and interviews with most of the gaolers of the county gaols of the province as well as with many sheriffs, gaol surgeons, and gaol chaplains.

The extensive material on correctional and other problems secured in this way was presented and analyzed in some two hundred pages of the eight-hundred-page report and formed the basis of the commission's forty-eight recommendations. In their analysis, the commissioners reviewed various theories and opinions on the causes of crime and later explored certain of these with greater care—notably the relation of crime to the conditions under which many children were being raised, the effect of alcohol on crime, and vagrancy as a penal problem. The remainder of the analysis was largely a consideration of the rôle played in the treatment of offenders by the various existing types of correctional institutions and by such aspects of their programmes as prison labour and prison discipline. The commissioners also reviewed the existing federal-provincial arrangements respecting corrections and the impact of these arrangements, constitutional and otherwise, on the important matter of sentencing.

Several of the recommendations referred to the existing correctional

---

[241]Ontario, *Sessional Papers*, 1891, no. 18, pp. 8, 12. Many references are made in the report to the recommendations of the association, witnesses frequently being asked by the commissioners to express an opinion concerning one or more of the recommendations.

institutions for the juvenile offender. It was suggested, for example, that the refuge for girls be removed from association with the Mercer Reformatory and that one or more industrial schools for girls should be established. Similarly, the reformatory for boys should be moved from its remote location and reconstructed on a cottage plan; its programme should emphasize industrial training and employ the mark system in association with the indeterminate sentence. The provincial attorney-general should be empowered to liberate juvenile offenders from both the existing and the proposed institutions either "unconditionally or conditionally and on parole as may seem best calculated to promote the welfare of the offenders and the interests of the state."[242]

The commissioners also recommended that between the boys' reformatory and the central prison or the penitentiary there should be established a separate industrial reformatory for first offenders from the ages of seventeen to thirty. Such an institution would incorporate "all the best features of the Elmira system"; that is, the programme would be one in which "the matter of retribution is left out and the whole treatment of the prisoner is remedial." Specifically, it would consist of a variety of activities and incentives designed to improve the prisoner physically and educationally and to develop his ability to work.

Respecting the existing intermediate institutions the report contained recommendations concerning Mercer directly and the central prison indirectly. Having urged the removal of the refuge for girls from its connection with the Mercer Reformatory, the commissioners recommended the re-arrangement of the total space of the building to "provide for a perfect classification of the inmates in the corridors, workshops, dining rooms and other departments." Thus the institution would at last be organized on the lines initially proposed in 1879. The central prison was affected principally by recommendations in the report relating to the treatment of inebriates, vagrants, and young first offenders. The last mentioned would no longer be sentenced to the central prison and the first two groups would be only after other methods of dealing with them had failed. The commissioners did not recommend the indeterminate sentence for Mercer or the central prison because most of the persons committed to them were sentenced for short terms. The report suggested, however, that the "good time"

[242]This and the following references to the commission's report are from Ontario, *Sessional Papers*, 1891, no. 18, pp. 163–66, 218–25, 774.

system be adopted by which prisoners, through "observance of the rules, diligence at work and general good conduct . . . could earn . . . a remission of some portion of their sentence."

As in the case of the intermediate institutions, the common gaols were affected chiefly by the commissioners' proposals for the removal of groups with which the gaols could not properly deal. Thus the mentally ill, when at all possible, were to be sent to an asylum and placed in a common gaol only "in case of absolute necessity." Similarly, juvenile offenders would no longer be sent to the gaols, and "a very considerable number of the drunkards now committed to gaols" would "be sent to an industrial reformatory for inebriates" or, if that failed, to the central prison. Those who were homeless and destitute would be cared for in the county houses of refuge. These measures, if fully implemented, were intended to remove from the gaols over 50 per cent of their existing population so that they could become what "the most advanced prison reformers claim they should be; that is, safe places of detention pending trial for persons charged with the commission of offences, and of punishment only for those sentenced to imprisonment for very short periods."

The commissioners did not recommend in favour of the policy that Langmuir had advocated when he was inspector, that is, the assumption by the province of the entire control of the gaols, at least "until it is fully ascertained what effect the changes [recommended by the commission] . . . will have on the management and discipline of the common gaols and the classification of prisoners therein." Meanwhile, the commissioners recommended that, in addition to the powers the provincial government already possessed to build new or repair existing gaols, "the inspector of prisons be empowered to order inexpensive structural changes necessary for health or safety to be made promptly."

The commissioners also devoted some thought to the structure through which the province administered its own penal institutions and supervised the county gaols. They seem to have limited their consideration, however, to a comparison of administration effected through an independent board of the type they had observed in a number of the American states and administration as provided for in Ontario through the office of the inspector. Noting that in Ontario the inspector was appointed by the government "under whose control that officer always is," and that the government is "responsible to the representatives of the people in the legislature" for all of the inspector's official acts, they concluded that Ontario's type of administration was "more in harmony with the spirit of responsible government." They then proceeded to the further conclusion that "if the Inspector be competent and energetic, and clothed with sufficient authority, this system should be thoroughly effective."

What the commissioners failed to consider, perhaps because their terms of reference limited them largely to corrections, was whether the office of inspector in its divided form and with its limited staff possessed the capacity to develop integrated social welfare policies and whether two or three senior officers with a few clerks could deal effectively with operational and policy-making responsibilities of the range and magnitude characteristic of the work of the office. Between 1882 and 1891, Christie, as the inspector in charge of correctional institutions and the non-medical institutions under the Charity Aid Act, had been able to discharge little more than the operational aspects of the office. He had been unable to develop and effectively recommend new policies in the correctional field—a failure that was obliquely referred to during the hearings of the Royal Commission. It was implied, indeed, that it was the fact of this failure that had made the commission necessary.

Although Langmuir, as chairman of the Royal Commission, was able to preside over the formulation of the comprehensive and challenging programme of reform and development embodied in the commission's recommendations, he may not have been capable of realizing that the office which had been so productive of social welfare advancement when it was held by him could not in its existing divided state and confronted by the more complex problems of the 1890's perform its functions merely through a slight augmentation of senior staff. Whether or not this situation was perceived by him and his fellow commissioners, the report carried the question of provincial administration no further than to decide in favour of the office of inspector and against the independent administrative board.

Implementation of the Recommendations to 1893

The impact of the recommendations of the Royal Commission on the penal system during the short period from the presentation of the report in 1891 to the end of the period covered in this study is rather hard to gauge. All the existing institutions were affected by the report in some degree, but there were few profound changes to be observed by the end of 1893.

Even though the most significant contribution of the report was to be its stimulation of child welfare programmes, the existing correctional institutions for children were still operating at the close of the period in much the same ways as they had been during the hearings of the commission. The superintendent of the boys' reformatory did welcome the report of the commission with enthusiasm, particularly the recommendations relating to the indeterminate sentence and the removal of the institution from Penetanguishene to a more central location,[243] but in November 1893 he reported that the question of having boys released on the recommendation of the institution was still unresolved;[244] nor was action on the part of the government to move the institution in sight. Similarly, the Mercer Refuge was still associated with the adult reformatory, and girls of nine and ten, including some with "respectable" parents, from whom, in the view of the superintendent, they should not have been taken, were still being sent to the institution, the opening of an industrial school for girls notwithstanding. And in 1893 the Inspector, in his visits to the county gaols, found numerous instances of the incarceration of children, of which the case of a ten-year-old girl in the company of an insane woman[245] in the Owen Sound gaol was not exceptional.

There was likewise little evidence of change in the central prison, even in the matter of prison labour. The commissioners had been critical of the piece-price method of employing the prisoners in production for the open market and had recommended increased production of goods for provincial institutions through what was described as the "provincial account system."[246] As the period closed, however, the prison was engaged in expanding its twine-making facilities for marketing by a private industrialist. As for its general programme, this showed little evidence of being influenced by the commission.

More evidence of the effect of the report could be seen in the supervision of the county gaols. Backed by the recommendations of the commissioners, Chamberlain was able to take a firm attitude with any county or city council which failed to carry out necessary alterations or repairs to its gaol.[247] It was in the furtherance of a recommendation in the report, moreover, that Chamberlain encouraged the gaols to develop wood-cutting and stone-breaking projects on which all able-bodied vagrants could be required to work, and he credited a

[243]Ontario, Sessional Papers, 1892, no. 8, pp. 132–33.
[244]Ibid., 1894, no. 27, p. 114.
[245]Ibid., p. 64.
[246]Ibid., 1891, no. 18, p. 223.
[247]Ibid., 1894, no. 27, p. 59.

marked decline in the number of this type of prisoner in 1892 and 1893 to the growth of this practice.[248]

Chamberlain's own moral indignation was, as we have seen, added to that of the commissioners concerning the use of the gaols to house the aged and the poor. By requiring the gaols to provide special and more costly treatment for such persons, in the form of better accommodation, diet, and clothing, he sought through economic pressure to bolster the humane case for the establishment of county houses of refuge. In this endeavour he was able to achieve some success by the end of the period and in 1893 he was able to report, as one of a number of similar instances in the west of the province, that "hereafter the gaoler will not be allowed to receive any poor persons residing in the city or county . . . committed under the Vagrant Act on account of their poverty."[249]

Thus Chamberlain seemed to be making useful, if limited progress in his work with the local gaols. However, the gains made by the end of the period in improving the gaols, though somewhat more substantial than that in the other correctional institutions, still fell far short of the prescription for the reform of the gaols as set out in the recommendations of the Royal Commission. By 1893 the province had begun to take action for the protection of children regarded by the commissioners as potential delinquents but it had not yet taken up the commission's challenge to make a broad frontal attack on the correctional system.

[248]*Ibid.*, p. 3.
[249]*Ibid.*, p. 76.

5

The Development of Health Services

THE PIONEER FAMILY of Upper Canada, though obliged to meet many of its health needs on a self-help basis, followed well-established North American and English practice in supplementing its own efforts and resources through the purchase of medical services and drugs as soon as these were available and within its means.[1] Upper Canadians had, in fact, no alternative to the purchase of health care on an individual and family basis because the machinery of government in the province was unfitted for public action in a matter of this kind, and the Loyalists and other early settlers, being largely Protestant, did not bring with them religious orders that had traditions of developing hospitals and providing nursing care.

Although the purchase of health services on an individual and family basis was to predominate, not only in the early years but throughout the whole history of the province, public action in a variety of matters vital to the health of the people did have to be taken as the province developed, especially when considerable numbers of people began to live in close contact in the villages, towns, and cities. Public measures on a significant scale were undertaken to prevent or limit the spread of communicable diseases, to aid in the treatment of the sick poor, to provide treatment and custodial care for the mentally ill and the alcoholic, to care for and educate the deaf, the blind, and the mentally retarded, and to protect the public against the prescription or sale of drugs and against the provision of medical treatment by ill-qualified practitioners.

[1]Medical services were often paid for by goods and services, and even by the ceding of land until currency became more plentiful.

Professional Services in the Health Field

It was the last mentioned of these types of action—the protection of the people against "quackery"—that was taken first by the province. At its fourth session the Legislature of Upper Canada, following closely an ordinance that had been adopted by the province of Quebec in 1788,[2] passed "an Act to regulate the Practice of Physic and Surgery"[3] which was designed to limit practice to persons who were graduates of universities within the Empire or who had held commissions in the armed forces as surgeons or surgeons' mates. The act proved premature, for the province found that the aim of achieving high professional standards could not proceed more rapidly than the supply of qualified practitioners. The lack of educational and training facilities in the province, together with the unattractiveness of practice,[4] limited the supply of doctors both from within the province and from abroad. Thus, because it was unenforceable, the act was repealed in 1806,[5] making "the practice of medicine free in the Province."[6]

Increased settlement, however, and the growing accumulation of wealth with which Upper Canadians could purchase drugs and medical treatment appear to have attracted considerable numbers of ill-trained practitioners to the province. Their activities became a matter of concern to those capable of assessing their work, including the small group of qualified physicians, mostly army surgeons, who had settled in Upper Canada. Representations led to new legislation in 1815[7] and in 1818,[8] with the latter, as amended in 1827,[9] providing the basis for the licensing of medical practitioners throughout nearly all of the pre-Confederation period. This act provided for a board of physicians to meet periodically in the capital to examine and license all persons wishing to practise in the province.[10] The work of the board proved

[2]Quebec, *Ordinances*, 1788, c. 8. This ordinance appears to have applied to Upper Canada both before 1795 and after 1806.
[3]Upper Canada, *Statutes*, 1795, c. 1.
[4]Robert Gourlay, *Statistical Account of Upper Canada*, vol. II (London, 1822), p. 364. Gourlay remarked that "nobody above the rank of a common cowleech would travel around a circle of forty or fifty miles, in the wilderness, for the pittance which could be collected long after this law was made; and, save in the large villages, Kingston, Niagara, and York, nothing like a genteel subsistence could be obtained." [5]Upper Canada, *Statutes*, 1806, c. 2.
[6]William Canniff, *The Medical Profession in Upper Canada, 1783–1850* (Toronto, 1894), p. 24. [7]Upper Canada, *Statutes*, 1815, c. 10.
[8]*Ibid.*, 1818, c. 13. [9]*Ibid.*, 1827, c. 3.
[10]In 1839, a college of physicians and surgeons of Upper Canada was incorporated (*ibid.*, 1839, c. 38) and the responsibilities of the board were transferred to it. In 1841, the act was disallowed, however, and the medical board resumed its previous functions.

moderately successful, although the lack of good basic educational resources and the difficulties encountered in developing medical training facilities[11] contributed to limiting the supply of qualified physicians. These factors prolonged the period in which Upper Canadians were exposed to the work of those with inferior medical qualifications and to the activities of patent medicine salesmen whose work was much assisted by advertising in the growing numbers of local newspapers.

By Confederation, however, a strong medical profession had developed in the province and had been given control of medical education and registration.[12] Medical education, though still riddled with rivalries and dissension, was by then largely carried on within the universities, and relatively high standards of training were being required. In the post-Confederation period, continued medical progress was associated with the rapid development of hospitals and the improvement of nursing. By 1883, three hospitals had developed training facilities for nurses,[13] and thus a foundation had been laid for a nursing profession.

Meanwhile, dentistry[14] and pharmacy[15] had made remarkable strides and had achieved professional status, both having been given statutory control of their standards of practice and of the entry into their professions. Complementing the improvements in medicine and nursing, the emergence of these professions added greatly to the quality of the health services available in the province.

Prevention against Contagious Disease

Although the wide dispersal of the population of Upper Canada in the early years of its history offered some protection from communicable diseases, it was not enough in itself to provide immunity from contagion, and during the 1820's summer fevers of varying intensity

[11]This reflected the difficulty of getting an institution of higher learning established in the province, the initial refusal of King's College to establish a medical school, and the rivalry between the schools finally established in connection with the university and that of Dr. John Rolph.

[12]Canada, *Statutes*, 1865 (2nd sess.), c. 34. The act "to regulate the Qualifications of Practitioners in Medicine and Surgery in Upper Canada" established a council consisting of twelve medical practitioners elected in twelve specified regions by their medical colleagues, together with a representative from each of the University of Toronto, Queen's, Victoria, and Trinity colleges, and the Toronto School of Medicine.

[13]Ontario, *Sessional Papers*, 1884, no. 16, p. 2.

[14]Ontario, *Statutes*, 1867–68, c. 37; 1877, c. 23.

[15]*Ibid.*, 1870–71, c. 34; 1884, c. 22.

appear to have spread through many parts of the province, including the countryside as well as the towns.[16] No action was taken by the government for their control, and public health measures were adopted only after the province had been stricken by the cholera epidemic of 1832. The approach of cholera up the St. Lawrence in the early summer of that year caught the provincial government without any legislation with which to meet the threat, and the Lieutenant-Governor had to take emergency action under his executive powers. He called upon the magistrates in each of the districts to form boards of health and placed the sum of £500 at their disposal "to defray the expense of the disbursements that may become necessary for providing Hospitals and Medical attendance, and for making the arrangements that the Medical Board of each District . . . may suggest."[17] Despite the commendable and often heroic efforts to deal with the epidemic, the lack of administrative preparedness and the deplorable conditions throughout the province, and particularly in "muddy York,"[18] resulted in a heavy loss of life and left many women and children without support.

The legislative committee appointed to review the manner in which the emergency had been handled warmly supported the Lieutenant-Governor's actions, but strongly recommended the enactment of "a law to enable the Executive Government, in the event of a future visitation, to act with energy and without embarrassment in every possible case that may occur."[19] Accordingly, the Legislature passed "an Act to establish Boards of Health and to guard against the introduction of Malignant, Contagious and Infectious Diseases."[20] It gave the lieutenant-governor authority to appoint "three or more persons in each and every town in the province and in such other places as may be deemed necessary to Act as Health Officers." The officers were given authority, backed by police power, to inspect premises and order them to be cleansed and all dangers to health removed. The Legislature, however, showed no disposition to establish permanent public

[16]William Perkins Bull, *From Medicine Man to Medical Man* (Toronto, 1934), pp. 56–58.
[17]Upper Canada, *Journals*, 1832–33, Appendix, p. 83.
[18]C. Dade, *Notes on the Cholera Seasons of 1832–4* (Pamphlet #1428, P.A.C. Catalogue of Pamphlets, vol. I), p. 18. Conditions in York were described as follows: "The genius of filth, if such there be, reigned predominant both in public and private. Crowded and loathsome hovels, cellars with putrid and stagnant water, dunghills with animal and vegetable garbage reeking in the scorching rays of the summer's sun, these deadly agents everywhere spread their contaminating influence."
[19]Upper Canada, *Journals*, 1832–33, Appendix, p. 206.
[20]Upper Canada, *Statutes*, 1833, c. 48.

health services, and the act was placed on a year-to-year basis. It was re-enacted in 1835[21] with the addition of a section, found necessary from the experience of the second cholera epidemic in 1834, giving the board of health authority to move persons from unsuitable quarters to "sheds or tents or other good shelter, in some more salubrious situation." This act, too, was initially on a temporary basis, but in 1839 a statute[22] was adopted to make it permanent, though its provisions continued to be enforceable only on the proclamation of an emergency.

During the Union period, public health problems applying to both Upper and Lower Canada were dealt with by the government of the United Province. Thus, the improvement of the quarantine facilities and the action taken during the typhus epidemic of 1847 related to the province as a whole and rather more to the lower St. Lawrence than to the upper region. The epidemic, however, exposed limitations in the act of 1839, which had continued to apply in Canada West, so in 1849 a new measure was adopted covering Upper Canada.

The new Public Health Act[23] constituted an elaboration and extension of the previous measure and, like it, was designed to have effect only when the province, or some part of it, was "threatened with any formidable epidemic, endemic or contagious disease." Under such circumstances, the governor could appoint a central board of health and require the municipalities to establish local boards of health which would act on directions from the central body and take specified sanitary and other measures to control and prevent the spread of disease.

Baldwin's great Municipal Corporations Act for Upper Canada,[24] passed in the same year, was also of importance for public health. It provided that incorporated villages, towns, and cities could make by-laws for the general health of the municipality "and against the spreading of the contagious or infectious diseases," as well as for the interment of the dead, the provision of public cemeteries, and the recording of mortality statistics. The Public Health Act of 1849, however, provided that such by-laws would be set aside whenever its emergency clauses were in force. Thus, although the Municipal Corporations Act made it possible for urban municipalities to take such public health measures as they saw fit, the Public Health Act continued to give support to the view that public health was a matter of concern only when disease of epidemic proportions had struck or was threatening. This continued to be the provincial approach through the

[21]Ibid., 1835, c. 10.   [22]Ibid., 1839, c. 21.
[23]Ibid., 1849, c. 8.   [24]Ibid., c. 81.

remainder of the Union era. For example, the province was able, with the existing legislation, to deal with an outbreak of cholera in 1854 and to organize against a threatened epidemic in 1866, but it was not able to create strong permanent public health programmes within its boundaries.

The same attitude was revealed in the first Public Health Act passed by Ontario after Confederation—that of 1873—which was basically the same as the earlier measures. Before the end of the 1870's, however, support began to be expressed for the creation of some permanent central health organization. This goal was partly achieved with the Public Health Act of 1882[25] under which a provincial board of health was established with strong medical representation. Although the board achieved some success, its powers were largely advisory, and it had only part-time professional staff. In 1884 these limitations were removed with the passage of a comprehensive new act[26] which was based on the English consolidated Public Health Act of 1875[27] and which contained detailed provisions in respect to the organization and responsibilities of local boards of health. The appointment of such boards was mandatory upon townships and incorporated villages, towns, and cities, and in each case was to include the chief elected official, a number of ratepayers to be appointed by the municipal council, and the municipal clerk who was to act as secretary. The act contained, as an appendix, a comprehensive local by-law which, until altered by the municipal council, was deemed to be in force in all municipalities in which a medical officer of health and a sanitary inspector had been appointed.[28]

To administer the new legislation, the province appointed Dr. Peter H. Bryce as full-time secretary to the provincial board of health. He brought to the post excellent qualifications, including a deep conviction about the rôle of public health in the welfare of the people of the province. He placed strong emphasis upon the formation of local boards of health, and by 1890 these had been formed in 576 municipalities, 356 of which had appointed medical health officers. The soundness of the new programme was indicated in the control of an epidemic of smallpox in one county of the province in 1884 and in preventing the introduction of the disease from Quebec in the following year. Steady improvement in public health programmes under strong provincial leadership continued from the mid-1880's to the end

---

[25]Ontario, *Statutes*, 1882, c. 29.
[26]*Ibid.*, 1884, c. 38.
[27]Great Britain, *Statutes*, 1875, c. 55.   [28]Ontario, *Statutes*, 1884, c. 38, s. 69.

of the period and contributed greatly to reducing illness, death, and dependency.

Measures for the Deaf and Blind

In a brief report on a petition from upwards of a hundred residents of the Eastern District in 1839, a select committee of the Legislature of Upper Canada drew eloquent attention to the deprived state of the deaf child, the effect special education could have on his life, and the strong desirability of securing such education for the deaf children of the province:

Separated from their fellows by the dispensation of Providence; cut off from the ordinary means of intercourse from almost every pleasure or enjoyment, whether of infancy, youth or manhood; they pass a cheerless existence, and in the midst of human society and surrounded by the activity and intelligence of manhood, they are as solitary as the recluse of the cloister or the desert.

Worst of all . . . it . . . shuts them out from the consolations of religion, leaving their minds a wilderness in which neither hope nor faith can find a place to take root.

A casual consideration of this destitute condition must excite an anxious wish in the breast of every philanthropist to rescue, from such a state of misery and degradation, this unfortunate class of our fellow beings; and it is gratifying to reflect that means have been discovered and have been applied to the practical utility of which successful results bear abundant testimony.

Institutions for the instruction of the deaf and dumb have been formed in various parts of Europe and America, and by a well organized system the minds of the pupils have been enabled to receive knowledge and have developed powers of imagination, thought and reflection, of as high an order as belong to their fellow creatures.[29]

The members of the select committee, noting that there were some two hundred "sufferers" in the province "for whose education there is not the slightest provision,"[30] recommended

that steps should be taken to establish one or more schools for the instruction of the deaf and dumb in this Province, and that, for this purpose, a sum of money should be granted . . . in the same manner as for the Common Schools . . . to pay an annual salary to one or more teachers properly qualified for this duty, and to establish one or more institutions where these unfortunate sufferers may be educated.[31]

The petition dealt with by the select committee was one of a number which had been addressed to the government on the same subject

[29]Upper Canada, *Journals,* 1839–40, Appendix, vol. I, pt. II, p. 7**.
[30]*Ibid.*   [31]*Ibid.,* pp. 7**–8**.

during the 1830's.[32] Throughout the Union period, many more were to follow, often with requests for educational facilities for the blind,[33] and it was frequently proposed that the two types of training might be offered in a single institution. At times the establishment of a public institution seemed imminent, but no definite action was taken until after Confederation.

The first separate institutions were opened early in the history of the new province, one for the deaf and dumb at Belleville in 1870, and one for the blind at Brantford in 1872. They were established without the enactment of special legislation, and only in 1873 was an act[34] passed indicating the objectives of the institutions and the ways in which they were to be managed. The act stated that the institutions were "for the purposes of educating and imparting instruction in some manual art" to deaf and blind residents of the province. Though emphasizing the educational nature of the institutions, the act placed them under the control of the inspector of prisons, asylums and public charities rather than under the superintendent of education. The inspector was to make rules for the management of the institutions, including the conditions of admission, but the appointment of staff was left to the lieutenant-governor.

In planning and developing the institutions, the province followed the customary practice of borrowing heavily from American experience. In 1870 Langmuir visited institutions for the deaf in three states and attended the annual convention of principals and teachers of the deaf and dumb institutions at Indianapolis where he secured the services of the first principal of the school at Belleville.[35] A somewhat similar course was followed respecting the school for the blind.[36] The principals and staffs of the two schools made vigorous efforts to interpret the work of the schools to the public. They attempted, wherever possible, to have direct interviews with the parents of the

[32]See *ibid.*, 1832–33, p. 63; 1833–34, p. 10; see also Upper Canada Sundries, July 21, 1835; Feb. 8, 1836; Aug. 7, 1836. The first and last of the sundries are petitions of residents of the township of Waterloo, on behalf of two deaf children of a fellow resident, requesting that the government provide aid to send "these two very interesting but unfortunate children" to a school in New York or in Canada if there was one. The other was a letter from a former King's Printer, John Corey, referring to the extent of deafness among children and suggesting that a proper instructor be attached to Upper Canada College which "would add to the respectability of the institution" and honour to the government.
[33]Canada, *Journals*, 1848, p. 40; 1850, p. 190; 1858, p. 384; 1861, pp. 24, 57, 65, 75, 116, 125, 130, 321.
[34]Ontario, *Statutes*, 1873, c. 32.
[35]Ontario, *Sessional Papers*, 1870–71, no. 6, p. 53.
[36]*Ibid.*, 1872–73, no. 2, p. 55.

handicapped children.[37] This was often found to be the only way to remove the misunderstandings and fears about the schools and to convey to parents the changes in the lives of their children that the educational programmes of the schools would make possible.[38]

Attendance at both of the schools increased in a fairly satisfactory manner, but it was adversely affected in the early years by the refusal of many municipalities to concur in sending indigent children to the schools as long as the municipality had to make a payment towards the maintenance of these children.[39] This requirement was removed in the act of 1873, making the cost of the institutions wholly provincial except in the case of the few parents able to pay the annual fee of $50.00 per child.[40] To send a child to the schools without payment of this fee, however, a parent was required to make a declaration to the mayor or reeve of his municipality that he was unable to afford the expense. Because some parents in these circumstances were unwilling to take the declaration, their children were withheld from the schools.[41] Attempts by the schools and the inspectors to have the ruling set aside, however, were unsuccessful, and it continued throughout the period to stand as a barrier to the education of some children.[42]

Enrolment at the school for the deaf increased steadily from 1870 to 1882 when the number reached 303, declining in subsequent years but remaining above 275 in all but three of these later years.[43] The number attending the school for the blind reached the highest point of just over 200 in 1880 and thereafter dropped to between 140 and 170.[44]

[37]*Ibid.*, 1875, no. 4, pp. 257–58. The zeal of one of the officers of the school for the blind probably cost him his life. During the summer of 1875, J. M. Brown travelled some 2,000 miles in the eastern part of the province, including 800 miles on foot, visiting the families of blind children. He returned to the school "jaded and emaciated and he was only two weeks in the classroom when he fell an easy victim to typhoid fever, which was prevailing in that portion of Brantford where he resided."

[38]*Ibid.*, 1874 (vol. VI), no. 2, pp. 200–1. Even personal interviews were not without their difficulties. The principal of the school at Brantford referred ruefully to the attitudes of "some mothers who seem to imagine me a sort of sharper who only needed the assistance of their sightless children to complete my fortune."

[39]*Ibid.*, 1872–73, no. 2, p. 47.

[40]*Ibid.*, 1874 (vol. VI), no. 2, p. 37. Referring to the regulation which, prior to the enactment of the statute, had required the municipality to bear the cost of indigent children maintained at the school for the deaf, Langmuir remarked that "the illiberality of many Municipal Councils, and the indifference of others, soon made it apparent that the working of the regulation would leave the indigent deaf-mutes of many counties without the benefits of an education."

[41]*Ibid.*, 1882, no. 8, pp. 483–84.

[42]*Ibid.*, 1894, no. 31, p. 22.

[43]*Ibid.*, p. 27.

[44]*Ibid.*, no. 30, p. 31.

The schools appear to have been successful in attaining high standards of academic education and of training in the industrial skills and arts, and in helping the children live full lives, their handicaps notwithstanding. By 1893, both schools could point to mounting evidence that their graduates were enjoying both happy and productive lives, thereby justifying the establishment and maintenance of the institutions, and making the fate of those so long deprived of similar advantages seem the more tragic and needless.

Care of the Mentally Ill

No public measures to provide for the mentally ill were taken in Upper Canada until 1830 when the Legislature, noting that many destitute insane persons had been "charitably received into the Gaol of the Home District," gave statutory approval to this action, which had been taken without legislative authority.[45] The practice adopted in the Home District was undoubtedly widespread, because the same right was extended to the other districts in later legislation.[46] However, the confinement of the insane in the common gaols was generally recognized as unsatisfactory, and continuous efforts were made by those chiefly concerned to have a provincial asylum established. The project was before the Assembly each year during the 1830's, mainly as a result of the mounting pressure for legislative action from families faced with the problem of caring for a member who was mentally ill[47] and from the magistrates in the various districts who were having to meet the problem of the indigent insane. In 1839, for example, the justices of the District of Ottawa, in petitioning the Lieutenant-Governor, stated:

That for a number of years past, the peace of the said District has been repeatedly disturbed and the moral feelings of its inhabitants shocked, by the appearances among them of maniacs, and insane persons, for the most part strangers to the country, or to the district.

That although the magistrates have, in every case, promptly interfered, both to protect the public, and to secure the unfortunate beings in question, yet their measures have been unavoidably attended with great public expense and inconvenience, owing to the necessity of confining and maintaining the deranged persons in the Common Gaol of the District.[48]

[45]Upper Canada, *Statutes*, 1830, c. 20.
[46]*Ibid.*, 1833, c. 46; 1836–37, c. 29.
[47]Upper Canada Sundries, Aug. 3, 1831. An example is provided in a letter from the wife of an insane and dangerous man pleading for his confinement in a secure place.
[48]*Ibid.*, Feb. 16, 1839.

The magistrates, accordingly, felt justified in forcefully expressing their belief

that it has become a solemn and imperious duty on the part of the Legislature to provide for the reception and accommodation of insane destitute persons in this Province, one large establishment worthy of the public character of Upper Canada, and of so just and philanthropic a cause.[49]

Within a few months, the Legislature did pass "an Act to authorize the erection of an Asylum within this Province, for the reception of Insane and Lunatic persons,"[50] but more than ten years were to pass before a hospital specially designed for the mentally ill was finally opened in 1850.[51] During this long interval use was made of the old Home County gaol from which all its occupants except the insane were removed in 1841. Although at the outset the old gaol building was deemed "very little adapted for a Lunatic Hospital,"[52] it did provide an opportunity to Dr. William Rees, who was the gaol physician and a strong advocate of the establishment of a mental hospital, to remove the insane prisoners from the basement, where they had long been confined, to the upper floors of the building and for the first time to offer a sustained programme of treatment. Here he was able to develop remarkably advanced methods which produced dramatic results.[53] His treatment served to indicate at once the tragic cruelty and waste of the previous handling of the insane and the prospect which was held out for better results when a well-adapted and suitably staffed institution would be established. Rees had a somewhat unstable temperament,[54] however, and, after sustaining an injury from an inmate, was removed from his post in 1844. His régime and those of his successors throughout the 1840's were beset by difficulties[55] which reflected, in part,

[49]Ibid.   [50]Upper Canada, Statutes, 1839, c. 11.

[51]During this period two acts were passed to provide funds to carry on the erection of the asylum: Canada, Statutes, 1846, c. 61, and 1850, c. 68.

[52]Canada, Journals, 1841, Appendix L.L., n.p. This is a report to the Under-Secretary by Robert S. Jameson who was one of the commissioners appointed to build and operate the asylum.

[53]Ibid. Jameson reported that "many who had long been confined as confirmed Lunatics were found to be labouring, not under mania, but under derangement arising from physical causes and yielding to physical remedies. Several have completely recovered, who, but for this treatment, would probably never have exhibited another gleam of reason."

[54]Canniff, The Medical Profession in Upper Canada, p. 572, refers to his appointment to the superintendency of the asylum being on the principle "of setting a madman to watch a madman." Although there was some basis for the quip, Dr. Rees was a brilliant contributor to many aspects of Upper Canadian society.

[55]Dr. George Park, the third superintendent, was involved in a prolonged quarrel with the board of commissioners, culminating in his dismissal by the government.

weaknesses in the type of board charged with the direction of the institution and, in part, the lack of experience and competence of the executive branch of the provincial government to deal with matters as complex as the development of institutional programmes for the mentally ill.

The appointment of Dr. Joseph Workman as superintendent in 1852 finally placed the asylum under strong and able direction and initiated an era of expanding facilities and improved treatment. In the following year, "an Act for the better management of the Provincial Lunatic Asylum at Toronto"[56] vested the asylum in the Crown, abolished the board of commissioners, and placed its "financial business and affairs" under an appointed bursar and its general management and operation under the medical superintendent. The act provided for the quarterly appointment of four or more commissioners who were to inspect the institution and to frame by-laws which, when assented to by the governor, were to take effect.[57] This arrangement was superseded by the establishment of the Board of Inspectors, and from the end of 1859 Dr. Workman found that his efforts both in the administration of the programme and in its interpretation to the government and public were strongly reinforced by the "intelligent, humane and vigilant supervision"[58] of the Board of Inspectors.

By 1859, Dr. Workman had under his direction the main provincial asylum and the university branch, both in Toronto, as well as the newly opened Malden branch which occupied a former military barracks near Amherstberg in the southwest of the province. In the nineteen years during which the asylum had been in operation since its commencement in the old gaol, it had received some 2,244 patients[59] and, at the end of 1859, was caring for 524 persons[60] distributed among its three establishments. In 1861 a branch was established at Orillia, and the Rockwood Asylum for the criminally insane, which was opened at Kingston in 1858 as part of the penitentiary, began to be used in the 1860's as a general asylum for the eastern part of the province.[61] At the end of 1866, 828 patients were being cared for in the three regular institutions, and a further 132 were being treated in Rockwood.[62] Late in the Union period, Dr. Workman proposed "establishing in Upper

[56]Canada, *Statutes*, 1852–53, c. 188.
[57]*Ibid.*
[58]Canada, *Sessional Papers*, 1860, no. 32, p. 60. The words are those of Dr. Workman welcoming the new board.
[59]*Ibid.*, p. 46.
[60]*Ibid.*, p. 49.
[61]*Ibid.*, 1867–68, no. 40, p. 3. The use of Rockwood in this way involved some rather questionable commitment procedures.
[62]*Ibid.*, pp. 92, 109, 117, 134.

Canada several Secondary Lunatic Asylums for 'chronic insane or harmless incurables,' " but despite strong support from the Board of Inspectors action on this important and difficult question had to be left to the "philanthropists and statesmen" of the new province of Ontario.[63]

After Confederation, until his retirement in 1875, Dr. Workman worked closely with Langmuir in the further development of the mental hospitals of the province. The first phase of this expansion was marked by the completion of new wings to the asylum in Toronto and the establishment of a new asylum in London in 1870. By the mid-1870's, however, an acute shortage had once again developed, and Langmuir recommended a broad plan, the objective of which was not merely to meet the existing shortage, but to anticipate future needs through a statistical analysis of the growth of population and the existing trends in mental illness. The plan envisaged the extensive provision of chronic facilities and emphasis upon early admissions and treatment with a view to achieving the maximum number of cures.[64] The specifics of the programme involved conversion, into a mental hospital, of a building that the province was erecting in Hamilton for the treatment of inebriates; the acquisition from the Dominion government of the Rockwood institution with a view to its more complete development as an asylum which would serve the eastern portion of the province, and the creation of a programme for mental defectives at Orillia providing both custodial care for the older patients and training facilities for children. All aspects of this plan were carried into effect and towards the end of 1876 Langmuir remarked (somewhat pompously) "that only within the present year could it be truthfully said that we had liquidated the arrearage of dethroned reason that was bequeathed to the Province of Ontario by Canada."[65] Two years later, after reviewing the further expansion that had been achieved and the improvements in the administration of the institutions and in the quality of the care and treatment given, Langmuir felt justified in making the further claim that "in the Asylums of no other country does a more enlightened and humane system of treatment prevail, or is more administrative economy preserved."[66]

[63]*Ibid.*, p. 2.
[64]*Ibid.*, 1877, no. 2, p. 2. Langmuir urged "that speedy admission . . . be awarded to every case of insanity as soon as it develops itself, and that the accumulation of chronic cases from a lack of proper treatment may, in future, be reduced to a minimum."
[65]*Ibid.*, p. 11.
[66]*Ibid.*, 1879, no. 8, p. 5.

Langmuir appears to have been a ready convert to the humane school[67] respecting the care and treatment of the insane of which Dr. Workman was a leading exponent. He commended the absence of restraint on patients in the asylums,[68] advocated the maximum development of recreation and the employment of patients in useful activities whenever possible,[69] and cautioned against the development of excessively large institutions.[70] He placed strong emphasis upon the quality of staff, urging upon the government the payment of higher salaries for attendants and the introduction of a plan of superannuation which would attract and hold the "kind and intelligent men and women"[71] whose vital function it was to be "in constant attendance upon insane people, closely observing their habits and practices, looking carefully after their wants, and keeping them employed, interested and amused."[72]

In the last decade of the period under review, vigorous efforts continued to be made to develop accommodation to meet increased needs. Additions were made to the existing institutions, though none reached the excessive size that was in later years to contribute, in Ontario as in many other jurisdictions, to the deterioration of their programmes. The opening of a new institution at Mimico, which by September 30, 1893, was caring for some 559 patients,[73] had helped to arrest the pressure for the enlargement of the existing asylums. The total population of the mental hospitals numbered 3,727 while a further 513 patients were being cared for in the asylum at Orillia.[74] Thus, the province had been called upon to meet a fourfold increase in patients and appears to have responded in a creditable manner. The mental hospitals, however, were often having to receive persons who could appropriately have been cared for in homes for the aged,[75] and, as revealed by the Royal Commission of 1890, the mentally ill were still, in many cases, being confined for periods of time in the local gaols.[76]

[67]T. P. Rees, "Back to Moral Treatment and Community Care," *Journal of Mental Science*, April 1957, pp. 303–13.

[68]Ontario, *Sessional Papers*, 1875, no. 4, p. 21. Langmuir refers to finding, on a visit to the asylum in Toronto, "not a single case of mechanical restraint in the Asylum," and only three female patients being kept "secluded in single rooms, owing to destructiveness."

[69]*Ibid.*, 1879, no. 8, p. 21.

[70]*Ibid.*, 1874 (vol. VI), no. 2, p. 9. Langmuir held that the capacity of 700 represented the limit "beyond which dimensions no establishment of this kind should go."

[71]*Ibid.*, 1879, no. 8, p. 21.

[72]*Ibid.*

[73]*Ibid.*, 1894, no. 26, pp. 2–3.

[74]*Ibid.*

[75]*Ibid.*, p. 93.

[76]*Ibid.*, 1891, no. 18, pp. 121–46, 220.

Hospitals

General hospitals in Ontario during the period of this study were largely founded by private initiative and looked upon as community endeavours to be supported by voluntary giving and operated by private boards. They were, in the first instance, established chiefly for the sick poor and were thus "charitable institutions" in the truest sense. The first two permanent hospitals in the province—those in York and Kingston—however, were founded with the aid of public funds,[77] and later became recipients of grants for their maintenance from time to time through the 1830's and 1840's. By 1851 hospitals in Toronto, Kingston, and Hamilton were receiving annual grants, and in 1866 a total of eight hospitals throughout the province were in receipt of provincial funds ranging from $480 for the Lying-in Hospital in Toronto to $11,200 in the case of the Toronto General Hospital.[78] Yet despite this extensive programme of grants to hospitals, as well as to other charitable institutions, the province failed during the Union period either to supervise the institutions or to put the grants on a systematic basis.

Soon after Confederation, however, Ontario found it necessary to take a more direct interest in hospital matters, chiefly because of a financial crisis facing the Toronto General Hospital.[79] Within a year or two of his appointment, Langmuir was asked by the government to begin the inspection of the hospitals receiving public grants, and in 1872 he was further requested to prepare a report of the basis on which provincial grants were distributed to the various types of charitable institutions. Because Langmuir had some familiarity with the hospitals, he had already formed certain views on the nature of the case for public grants to hospitals and the standards with which the grants should be associated. Inevitably, he incorporated these opinions into

[77]York Hospital, though apparently built largely with funds from the Loyal and Patriotic Society collected during the War of 1812, also received a public grant of land. See Charles K. Clarke, *A History of the Toronto General Hospital* (Toronto, 1913), pp. 10–33; see also Upper Canada, *Journals*, 1839–40, Appendix, pp. 313–19, which refers to the development of the hospital and the lands with which it was endowed. Kingston Hospital received a capital grant from the province in 1832 for the sum of £3,000 to aid in the establishment "of the destitute sick within this Province" (Upper Canada, *Statutes*, 1832, c. 28).
[78]See Table II, p. 40.
[79]This occurred because the hospital did not receive the grant it had been accustomed to receive from the United Province of Canada (Ontario, *Journals*, 1867–68, Appendix, pp. 157–78). John Macdonald, the president of the board of the hospital, brought the most effective kind of pressure on the government by temporarily closing the hospital.

his report. He felt that the case for hospital grants was founded upon two bases: first, that hospitals were essential for the training of medical students, and that it was to the advantage of the whole population that "a well-educated and properly trained medical profession"[80] be created; and, secondly, that hospitals were devoted to the relief of suffering and the cure of disease of their patients, three-fourths of whom "if not in indigent circumstances, were of that class who have to work for the daily bread of themselves and their families, and who, if Hospital treatment had not been open to them, when overtaken by sickness or accident, might have been permanently withdrawn from the working and wealth-producing population of the Province, and placed upon the charity of friends or the public."[81]

Although he felt that hospital grants thus merited public support, Langmuir also believed that the payment of these grants should be associated with a number of important conditions. These would have included agreement by each hospital or group of hospitals to serve an assigned area of the province; provincial approval of all hospital buildings, sites, and equipment; the development by the hospitals of separate isolation buildings and separate accommodation for chronic and incurable patients; assurance that 60 per cent of a hospital's beds be reserved to indigent patients; and provision that its board of management have substantial provincial and municipal representation.[82] If these conditions were all met, Langmuir would have been prepared to see the province pay each hospital a grant equal to the "total amount received from municipal grants and private donations for *its actual maintenance and support during the preceding year.*"[83] The basis for the payment of grants to hospitals which emerged in the Charity Aid Act[84] was at once less demanding in respect to standards and less generous in terms of financial assistance than Langmuir had proposed. His proposal is of interest, however, both in its indication of the kind of objectives he would have in mind in carrying out his responsibilities under the Charity Aid Act, and in its anticipation of the degree of public control and responsibility that would ultimately be required to ensure hospital accommodation for all who needed it.

The inspection of the hospitals by Langmuir and his successors bore the same character as the inspection of the other types of charitable

[80]Ontario, *Sessional Papers*, 1872–73, no. 2, pp. 66–67.
[81]*Ibid.* [82]*Ibid.*, p. 69. [83]*Ibid.*
[84]The basic grant was 20 cents per patient, plus a supplementary amount of up to 10 cents a day depending on revenues received from sources other than the government of Ontario; the full grant of 30 cents a day was nearly always payable on this basis.

institutions considered earlier. Of special concern, however, were the policies of the hospitals on the admission and discharge of patients. Langmuir was called upon to deal with complaints against some hospitals concerning "unjust discrimination . . . in awarding admission only to residents of certain municipalities; through which the sick poor, in some instances, have failed to receive treatment."[85] He pointed out that "such action entirely defeats the object the Government had in view," which was to relieve the sick, and especially the sick poor, "in every part of the Province." He warned that continued discrimination would result in an amendment to the Charity Aid Act "so as to provide for a division of the province into hospital districts, and the setting apart of a certain percentage of the beds of every Hospital receiving Government Aid for the sick poor of such districts." On the other hand, Langmuir also noted that the basis of payment under the Charity Aid Act presented a "temptation . . . to Hospital authorities to admit unfit and improper subjects and to retain patients longer than treatment, with a view to restoration, is required." In respect to those being admitted with "very trifling ailments," he urged the development of out-patient services. Concerning long-term patients, he took a stronger line. Arguing that "one year's continued treatment in an Hospital should be sufficient for the most obstinate cases," he proceeded to reduce the grant from the hospital rate of thirty cents to the refuge rate of seven cents for all persons whose stay in hospital exceeded one year.

In their periodic visits to the hospitals, the inspectors attempted to exert a pressure for improvements of buildings,[86] facilities, and equipment,[87] and to encourage improvements in hospital practices.[88] They were outspokenly critical of poor conditions,[89] while warmly commending improvements and evidence of good management.[90] They praised especially hospitals that were providing nursing training and thus aiding the establishment of the nursing profession in the province.[91]

The period from the passage of the Charity Aid Act to 1893 was one of rapid development of hospitals in the province. The number receiving provincial grants increased from 10 to 32; the total amount of grants showed a proportionate increase from $32,684 to $107,312; and

[85]References in this paragraph are from Ontario, *Sessional Papers*, 1878, no. 4, pp. 167–69.
[86]*Ibid.*, 1879, no. 8, p. 202; 1882, no. 8, p. 241.
[87]*Ibid.*, 1874 (vol. VII), no. 2, p. 132.
[88]*Ibid.*, 1879, no. 8, p. 204; 1882, no. 8, p. 258.
[89]*Ibid.*, 1882, no. 8, pp. 239, 249.
[90]*Ibid.*, 1879, no. 8, p. 207.   [91]*Ibid.*, 1884, no. 16, p. 2.

the number of patients cared for during the year rose from 3,466 to 12,392.[92] Furthermore, as Chamberlain noted in 1893, increased numbers of "experienced nurses and medical men"[93] were being added to the staffs of the various hospitals, and "improvements are constantly being made . . . by the erection of 'lying-in' or maternity departments, isolated buildings for infectious diseases, morgues, laundries, separate rooms specially adapted for operations and anesthetic purposes; also, in renewing plumbing, heating and drainage arrangements."[94]

The substantial advances made during the period were undoubtedly attributable mainly to the voluntary community leadership and support, together with the work of the medical profession and of the emerging profession of nursing. Important contributing factors, however, were the assurance of provincial financial assistance, the incentive given by the Charity Aid Act for the mobilization of private and municipal contributions, and the inspectors' support of good standards in the development of hospitals and hospital practice.

Hospital for Inebriates

Heavy drinking was commonplace in Upper Canada and drunkenness became a problem of considerable concern throughout the province. It was regarded by those responsible for social welfare programmes as one of the principal causes of crime, insanity, and dependency.[95] Until the early 1860's, however, when attention was attracted to the work of inebriate hospitals in Europe and America, any solution to the problem was thought to lie wholly in the realm of morality. Reports that inebriate hospitals were achieving good results in the reclamation of their patients opened the possibility of a new line of endeavour.

The establishment of inebriate hospitals in Canada became the particular cause of a well-known Toronto physician, James Bovell, who discussed it directly and through correspondence with many of the public figures in both Upper and Lower Canada. In 1862, he published a book[96] of some fifty pages presenting the case for inebriate asylums. Addressed to the present and past premiers of the province, the book

[92]See Table IV, p. 63.
[93]Ontario, Sessional Papers, 1894, no. 29, p. 3.
[94]Ibid., p. 9.
[95]Canada, Sessional Papers, 1863, no. 66, n.p. E. A. Meredith remarked that "whatever . . . diminishes intemperance in the country must, pro tanto, diminish crime and insanity."
[96]James Bovell, A Plea for Inebriate Asylums (Toronto, 1862).

contained an architect's drawing of a proposed inebriate hospital in Toronto, together with layout drawings of its three floors and grounds, and suggestions on how it could be operated.

Nothing came of the proposal at the time, but wide attention had been directed to it, and it continued to attract interest and support. Accordingly, in 1872, when the province had completed the first phase in its development of new social welfare institutions, it responded to what were described as "unmistakable evidences of public opinion in regard to the matter, verified in the strongest manner by the observations and experience of all public men"[97] by instructing Langmuir to report on the practicability of establishing an inebriate hospital in the province. Langmuir reviewed available literature on the subject and visited two hospitals in the state of New York. His findings, including evidence that "cures" were of the order of 33 to 40 per cent of admissions, led him to conclude that "the plan of treating drunkenness as a *disease*, and of establishing hospitals for its cure and amelioration is not chimerical or impracticable, but is one which gives greater promise of success than any other that can be adopted, and which therefore demands the serious consideration of government."[98] He argued that "the establishment and maintenance of an Asylum of this character falls within the true sphere and work of the Government." It would, in the truest sense, be "an institution of *public utility*, as the evil against which it would contend is pre-eminently a public burden and calamity."

On the basis of Langmuir's further analysis of the kinds of inebriates who would be suitable for treatment in such a hospital, the type of institution which would be required, and the nature of the legislation needed in order at once to protect the patient's civil rights and to ensure the required time for successful treatment, the government decided to proceed with the project and to undertake it on a generous scale. Accordingly, in 1873 the government introduced a bill "to provide for the establishment of an Hospital for the reclamation and cure of Habitual Drunkards,"[99] and appropriated $100,000[100] for the construction of such a hospital in Hamilton to be completed in 1875. The building went forward as planned until a combination of second thoughts about the project, together with the urgent need to develop more accommodation for the mentally ill, resulted in its appropriation for the latter purpose. Although Langmuir recommended the change

[97]Ontario, *Sessional Papers*, 1872–73, no. 2, p. 2.
[98]*Ibid.*, p. 35.
[99]Ontario, *Statutes*, 1873, c. 33.   [100]*Ibid.*, c. 1.

in plans, he did so with reluctance, stating that he continued "to hold the opinion that an effort should be made to reclaim drunkards and cure the disease of drunkenness by special treatment, in an establishment provided for that purpose."[101] He expressed the hope that an inebriate hospital on a smaller scale might be established.

This did not take place, however, and some years later Langmuir himself discouraged consideration of a project to establish an alcoholic unit associated with the Toronto General Hospital.[102] No discussion of the question by the inspectors following Langmuir's retirement is to be found in the annual reports, but the subject received renewed attention and careful consideration during the hearings of the Royal Commission. Despite their observation that "the belief in the efficacy" of inebriate asylums "is neither so general nor so strong as it was a few years ago,"[103] the commissioners proceeded to recommend that "the Government, out of funds derived from the fees for Provincial licenses . . . shall erect in the centres of population one or more industrial reformatories for inebriates." Although each such reformatory "should be chiefly an hospital having as its main object the reclamation of drunkards and the cure of inebriety," admission, or rather committal to it, would be on a compulsory basis and would apply to those "who have been previously convicted of drunkenness three times within two years: such other persons addicted to the use of strong drink as in the opinion of the county judge may be reclaimed by timely restraint and judicious treatment: and those who may be compulsorily committed to an inebriate asylum under the provisions of the Inebriate Asylum Act." Committal should not be for less than six months and might be for as much as two years less one day.

These proposals made no reference to the alternative of voluntary admission as envisaged in the act of 1873,[104] perhaps because the commission's terms of reference centred on the penal system. Similarly, although the nature of the proposed cure for drunkenness was essentially medical, the context in which the treatment would be given was now wholly within the area of corrections. Whether this emphasis or other factors weakened the force of the commission's affirmation of public responsibility for developing a treatment programme for alcoholics by the end of the period or, indeed for the next half century, there was no action by the province to implement the commission's proposal.

---

[101]Ontario, *Sessional Papers*, 1875, no. 4, p. 8.

[102]*Ibid.*, 1878, no. 4, p. 183.

[103]*Ibid.*, 1891, no. 18, p. 105.   [104]Ontario, *Statutes*, 1873, c. 33, s. 13.

6

The Welfare of Children

IN CONCLUDING his testimony before the Royal Commission in 1890, J. J. Kelso, who for some years had been associated with various welfare endeavours in Toronto, remarked that "in this province we have been very negligent in the matter of children."[1] His evidence before the commission, and that of other witnesses, provided support for his comment and created a picture of a serious problem of neglected and delinquent children throughout the province, particularly in the large towns and cities.

If it was possible in 1890 to refer to public negligence in the welfare of children, a similar indictment could have been made with greater force at any earlier point in the province's history. For although some public and voluntary steps were taken on behalf of children fairly early in the history of the province and were augmented at an accelerating pace in the middle and later decades of the nineteenth century, only towards the end of the 1880's was there enough interest and concern to bring comprehensive public measures in "the matter of children" within the scope of legislative and executive action.

PRE-UNION PERIOD, 1791–1840

In the very early years in Upper Canada, children shared with their parents the hardships and privations of frontier life, and many of them doubtless suffered from poverty, isolation, and neglect. Life for the child on the typical pioneer farm, however, probably had its compensations. At an early age he was able to join in the work about the

[1]Ontario, *Sessional Papers*, 1891, no. 18, p. 729.

homestead and thereby earn the status of a productive member of the farm economy. By the 1820's or 1830's, he was probably able, as well, to gain the rudiments of an education in a local school and to prepare himself for wider opportunities. Compared with many of his European contemporaries, caught in the web of the industrial revolution and obliged to work in the mines or mills, his life was relatively healthy and secure.

Yet before Upper Canada had experienced the growth of towns to any significant extent and before war and expanding immigration had created additional problems affecting children, the province found it necessary to pass legislation for the protection of the child.

The Orphans Act of 1799

The measure that was adopted had the promising title of "an Act for the education and support of orphans or children deserted by their parents."[2] However, the sole means provided by the act for the attainment of this objective was that of binding the child as an apprentice. This action could be taken by the town wardens with the consent of two justices of the peace, or by a mother whose husband had abandoned her and left a child or children in her care. The indentures of apprenticeship were to be binding on a girl until she reached the age of eighteen and on a boy until he was twenty-one. Where a child was over fourteen, no indenture for his apprenticeship could be made without his consent.

The act was deficient in two important respects. It failed to indicate, even as a general principle, that the child be apprenticed in a home that would provide adequately for his care and development, and it failed to make any continuing provision to guard against the exploitation or abuse of the child. It lacked, moreover, any provision for public support of a child who could not be placed as an apprentice. Thus, although admitting public responsibility for protective action for the orphaned or deserted child, the Legislature neglected to provide any means for discharging the responsibility in the case of the child for whom no placement as an apprentice could be secured. The difficult position in which this placed the local officials was resolved in a few instances by the courts of quarter sessions' paying for the care of such children,[3] notwithstanding the courts' lack of authority for such action.

2Upper Canada, *Statutes*, 1799, c. 3.
3See, for example, Upper Canada, *Journals*, 1839–40, Appendix, pp. 541, 552.

The town wardens were not required to report the number of place-ments they made under the terms of the legislation, and accordingly no statistics were compiled that would indicate the extent to which the Orphans Act was implemented. Some doubt has been expressed "that the Act really accomplished what it professed to do,"[4] but there is evidence that the apprenticing of children became a rather widespread and well-established practice.[5] It appears, indeed, that there was a high demand for healthy children, particularly those old enough to be useful on a farm or in a village workshop and that those to whom the children were indentured were, in general, motivated to give them good care and useful training, not only because of considerations of common humanity, but also because of economic advantage in ensuring that the children would continue to serve until the termination of their apprenticeships.

There might have been no necessity for a statute dealing with orphans and abandoned children at this point in the history of the province had the colony not initially rejected the English poor law which contained provisions for the apprenticing of such children. It is worth noting, therefore, that the origin of separate child welfare measures in the province is thus another important consequence of the rejection of the poor law.

The Militia Pension Act

Because the limitations of the Orphans Act made it an unsuitable statute to deal with children who lost their fathers in the War of 1812, these children were included among those to whom war pensions were payable. An "Act to provide for the maintenance of persons disabled and the widows and children of such persons as may be killed in His Majesty's Service" was first passed in 1813 and frequently amended in later years.[6] The amount payable under the legislation was £20 per annum whether for a militia man sufficiently disabled to qualify for payment,[7] or for the widow or the child or children of a deceased soldier. A widow without children received as large a pension as one

---

[4]C. Owen Spettigue, *An Historical Review of Ontario Legislation on Child Welfare* (Toronto, 1957), p. 10.

[5]A memorandum on juvenile immigration prepared by the emigration agent for the province (Upper Canada Sundries, July 18, 1834) suggests this.

[6]Upper Canada, *Statutes*, 1813, c. 4; 1815, c. 6; 1816, c. 17; 1817, c. 5; 1821, c. 4; 1826, c. 6; 1837–38, c. 44; 1840, c. 27.

[7]Except for the period between 1817 and 1821 when a partial pension was paid for the loss of an eye.

with ten, and a single child left as an orphan through his father's death in action received as much as a group of brothers and sisters in the same circumstances.

The recognition of public responsibility for the support of children of deceased soldiers might have been expected to point to a similar if perhaps less compelling responsibility for other children without parents, but the fact that the annuity did not vary with the number of children requiring support reduced the payment to a token discharge of the province's responsibility. Because the Pension Act did not, therefore, represent a realistic attempt to provide for the material needs of the children coming within its terms, it did not constitute a strong precedent for public action in meeting the needs of the many children destined to be bereft of parents or parental support in the post-war period through such causes as the loss of life on immigrant ships, the devastation of periodic epidemics of cholera, and other contingencies associated with frontier life and with the growth of towns.

The Guardian Act

Although the Pension Act stated that a guardian could accept the pension of a child under sixteen, it did not indicate the basis for the recognition of a guardian. Because the Lieutenant-Governor subsequently received numerous petitions from persons seeking to be confirmed in this rôle,[8] legislative action was taken in 1827[9] to make better provision for dealing with the question of guardianship. The act noted in its preamble that "there are in all the respective Districts of this Province many infants within the age of twenty-one years, left by the decease of their fathers, subject to the disabilities of infancy, and destitute of guardians to act in their behalf, and to have the care of their persons and the charge of their estates." To remedy this situation, the act provided that a judge of a probate or surrogate court could appoint a guardian for a child until the child's twenty-first birthday unless the guardianship was terminated earlier by the same type of judicial procedure.

Guardianship action could be initiated on the written application of the infant or a friend as long as the child's mother was given twenty days' notice of the proceeding. Although the terms of the act seemed to take for granted that the mother would not be appointed

---

[8]See, for example, Upper Canada Sundries, Jan. 13, 1818; March 11, 1818; Oct. 15, 1818; Jan. 5, 1820; Sept. 30, 1821; Nov. 13, 1821; Dec. 26, 1821; Jan. 9, 1824; April 15, 1825.　　　　　[9]Ontario, *Statutes*, 1827, c. 6.

to the guardianship rôle, reflecting the contemporary approach of the English common law which accorded the mother few rights to her children, social practice in Canada had already begun to reject the traditional English approach, and it was quite common for the mother, whether or not she was married a second time, to be recognized as the obvious person to act as the guardian of her children. For example, in the case of Elizabeth Tipps, the pension board set up in the district ruled that she was the mother of the children in question, and that she was "a proper Person to be the Guardian of the Children."[10] Indeed, in only one of the petitions cited above was the step-father of the children designated as their guardian, and that was at the request of the mother.[11]

Although the Guardian Act seemed to emphasize the guardianship of property and could require a guardian to provide sureties that he would faithfully administer the child's property, it also made the guardian responsible for the child's "person and education."[12] He could discharge this responsibility directly, or he could exercise the same right as that possessed by the town wardens under the Orphans Act—namely, to place the child as an apprentice on the consent of two justices of the peace and of the child.

Like the Orphans Act, the Guardian Act represented a method of making some provision for fatherless children with a minimal commitment of public responsibility; in the 1827 legislation the public involvement was wholly that of action by the court, with this to be had, moreover, only on the payment of the prescribed fees.

Provision for Unmarried Mothers and Their Children

The pre-Union period witnessed some legislative action on problems relating to children born out of wedlock. In 1823, the case of Mary Thompson, sentenced to be hung for having caused the death of her illegitimate child,[13] drew attention to the position of the English law as it applied at the time in Upper Canada and led to the passing of legislation in 1826,[14] and again in 1831,[15] because the earlier act had been disallowed by proclamation.[16] The 1831 act provided that "the

[10]Upper Canada Sundries, Oct. 15, 1818.
[11]*Ibid.*, April 15, 1825.
[12]Upper Canada, *Statutes*, 1827, c. 6.
[13]Upper Canada Sundries, Oct. 25, 1823; Nov. 28, 1823.
[14]Upper Canada, *Statutes*, 1826, c. 2.
[15]*Ibid.*, 1831–32, c. 1.
[16]Upper Canada Sundries, March 14, 1827.

trial of any woman charged with murder of any issue of her body, male or female, which being born alive, would by law be bastard, shall proceed and be governed by such . . . rules of evidence and presumption as are by law used and allowed to take place in respect to other trials for murder."[17] Where the mother was found guilty of concealing the body of an illegitimate child, she could be imprisoned in a common gaol for a period of up to two years. The practical effect of this legislation was probably to make it possible for a jury, not wishing to find a mother guilty of murder, to convict her on the lesser charge of concealment of the child's body.

A further measure relating to the unmarried mother and her child was the act, passed in 1837, "to make the remedy in cases of seduction more effectual and to render the Fathers of illegitimate Children liable for their support."[18] The legislation gave the parents of an unmarried female who had been seduced the right to take action against the father of the illegitimate child, whether or not they could establish that the daughter's service to them had been affected by the seduction. The act also gave anyone who was providing "food, clothing, lodging or other necessaries" to any child born out of wedlock the right to "maintain an action for the value thereof against the father of such illegitimate child." Provision for the rights of the unmarried mother's parents and for the support of the illegitimate child was, however, only a partial solution to a serious social problem. Other aspects were ignored. For example, the act failed to indicate that the unmarried mother herself had any right of action against the father; nor did it offer an alternative means of support for her, or her child, in default of such action. Moreover, because of the difficulty with the limited law enforcement machinery of the time, there was little reason to suppose that the provisions to secure financial aid for the child from the father would be effective in the great majority of cases.

Apart from the benefit children derived from the grants extended to a small number of voluntary associations for the care of immigrants, the poor, or the sick, public action to meet the social welfare needs of children during the pre-Union period was limited to the few and manifestly limited statutes outlined above. The failure of the province to take more comprehensive measures at a time when it was beginning to develop programmes for the adult offender and the mentally ill is not to be accounted for by the lack of problems on which action was required or by the absence of at least some demand for public

[17]Upper Canada, *Statutes*, 1831–32, c. 1.   [18]*Ibid.*, 1836–37, c. 8.

measures. In 1828, for example, some ninety residents of the Bathurst District petitioned "that the laws of England making provision for the maintenance of bastard children may be extended to this Province,"[19] and in 1831 a similar petition was received from the citizens of Lanark.[20] There was also some advocacy of the establishment of a foundling hospital,[21] and for public measures to assist in the training of children who were deaf and dumb.[22] But whereas the provincial government could make provisions for the adult offender and the mentally ill through the establishment of centrally located institutions under provincial management, measures for children would have involved local initiative and action and at least some degree of local financing. The limitations of local governments in the pre-Union period and their unwillingness to make use of some of the social welfare powers that they did possess—notably the failure of the districts to establish houses of industry—appear to have prevented serious consideration to any additional public measures for local government action on behalf of children.

UNION PERIOD, 1840–1867

A census of Upper Canada taken at the beginning of the Union period revealed the remarkable fact that over half the population of the province was under sixteen years of age.[23] The proportion of children to adults fell as the period advanced, but it remained high, and despite the gradual improvement in conditions throughout the province the physical and social circumstances for adults and children alike, especially in the growing towns, were often bad. Inevitably, many of the large numbers of children were exposed to various forms of deprivation and neglect. As an indication of these conditions, juvenile delinquency made its appearance, and action was taken during the 1850's and 1860's to deal with it, but as in the case of other jurisdictions before and since the province acted largely to treat the symptoms rather than their causes. Thus the principal public actions taken during the period were in the corrections field, and consisted

[19]Upper Canada, *Journals*, 1828, p. 90.
[20]*Ibid.*, 1831, p. 17.
[21]*Ibid.*, 1831–32, p. 39.
[22]Upper Canada Sundries, 1829, n.d.; Feb. 8, 1836.
[23]*Censuses of Canada, 1665–1871*, vol. IV (Ottawa, 1876), p. 128. Of a total population of 432,159, some 220,022 or 51 per cent were children under the age of sixteen.

mainly in the establishment of prisons for young offenders. Bills were introduced into the Legislature in 1843 and 1857 "for further and better provision for the support of illegitimate children,"[24] but they were not enacted, and few new public measures, other than grants to certain voluntary institutions, were taken during the period to meet the fundamental needs of even the more exposed groups of children.

The Apprentices and Minors Act

For the care and support of children lacking an adequate home and parents of their own, the province continued to place almost total reliance on apprenticeship. In 1851 the Legislature passed "an act to amend the law relating to Apprentices and Minors"[25] that went considerably beyond the terms of the Orphans Act of 1799 and the sections of the Guardian Act of 1827 dealing with apprenticeship. It permitted any parent, guardian, or other person having the care or charge of a child fourteen years of age and over to have him bound as an apprentice, with his own consent, for any term of years up to the attainment of his majority. A child over the age of sixteen years without a parent or legal guardian could on his own initiative enter into an apprenticeship arrangement with a master, and thereafter he and his master would be bound by the terms of the legislation. In addition, a child of any age could, with his consent, be bound as an apprentice by specified public officials[26] if he had been orphaned or deserted, if his parents or guardian had been committed to gaol, or if he was "dependent upon any public charity for support."

The act contained safeguards for both the apprentice and his master, but those designed to protect the latter received much the greater emphasis. The apprentice could make a complaint against his master "for any refusal of necessary provisions, misusage, cruelty or ill-treatment," and where the charge was proved the master could be fined up to five pounds or imprisoned for up to one month in default of payment of the fine. Although any justice of the peace, mayor, or police magistrate could hear these proceedings, they appeared to have no authority to terminate the indenture, this power being restricted to

[24]Canada, *Journals*, 1843, pp. 56, 70; 1857, pp. 54, 549.
[25]Canada, *Statutes*, 1851, c. 11. The act applied only to Upper Canada. It was reorganized and the apprenticeship sections of the act of 1827 incorporated in the consolidation of 1859 (Canada, *Consolidated Statutes of Upper Canada*, 1859, c. 76.
[26]These included the mayor, recorder, or police magistrate in cities and incorporated towns and the chairman of a court of general quarter sessions in a county.

the courts of quarter sessions. Thus, an apprentice wishing to make a complaint against the treatment he was receiving would have encountered formidable difficulties and delays in being released from his indenture. The act took no account of the relatively unprotected position of the apprentice and the difficulties he would experience in securing, on his own, legal redress for ill-treatment or in gaining release from an apprenticeship arrangement which was damaging to his person or restrictive of his prospects. On the other hand, the master could be released from his obligations. He could, for example, "legally transfer his Apprentice to any person competent to receive or take any Apprentice; provided always, that no master shall transfer his Apprentice except to another carrying on the same kind of business as himself." The master could also, by publishing his intention to take such action, "avoid the indenture of Apprenticeship" where the apprentice had absconded or been committed to the penitentiary or had become insane. The master also had recourse to legal action against his apprentice for refusal to obey commands, for waste or damage to property, or "for any other improper conduct." On conviction of any of these offences, the apprentice could be imprisoned for up to one month in the common gaol. More rigorous action was taken against him if he deserted. On being apprehended, he could be sentenced for up to three months and required to make up to his master the time he had lost through his desertion and imprisonment.

Other Laws Affecting Children

The Apprentices and Minors Act, with its clarification of the relations of the apprentice and his master and the provision of legal sanctions supporting them, constitutes one of several examples of the Union Legislature's more careful consideration and elaboration of social relationships that had previously been governed by English common law or by a brief act passed during the pre-Union period. Among other enactments affecting children was a criminal law statute passed in 1841[27] for the purpose of indicating the penalties which could be inflicted against a person found guilty of attempting to procure an abortion, having carnal knowledge of young girls, abducting a female under the age of sixteen years against the parents' will, or decoying a child under the age of ten years from his parents. In the field of civil law, the Legislature passed an act in 1855[28] aimed at improving and extending the law on guardianship. It authorized the superior courts

[27]Canada, *Statutes*, 1841, c. 27.   [28]*Ibid.*, 1855, c. 126.

of the province to give a mother the care and custody of her child until he reached the age of twelve years and to require the father to contribute to the maintenance of the child. This legislation, however, fell short of giving the mother equal guardianship rights with the father and reflected a slower recognition of a mother's rights in the matter of children than she gained in 1859 in respect to property.[29]

The Development of Children's Institutions

In default of public measures other than the Apprentices and Minors Act for the care of children without parents or proper parental maintenance and control, private individuals and groups began to respond to needs which by the end of the 1840's were increasingly insistent. Thus, voluntary organizations were formed to develop programmes for children and unmarried mothers similar to those organized for the sick and the poor. Individuals and private associations once again assumed responsibilities which the community as a whole was unprepared to accept and act upon through the machinery of government. For example, the House of Industry in Toronto, which took the lead in providing institutional services for the adult poor, was also a pioneer in the care of children, operating for many years as a congregate institution for both young and old. At an early stage, it developed a programme for placing children as apprentices and by 1850 had placed 275 with good results.[30]

The movement to develop special institutions for children gained momentum in the 1850's. It appeared in the larger centres and represented mainly the work of women, many of whom came from the most prominent and influential families in the community. The initial members forming the Orphans' Home and Female Aid Society in Toronto in 1851, for example, consisted largely of the wives and daughters of the leaders of the Family Compact,[31] together with a few representatives of the newer professional and commercial families. However,

[29]Ibid., 1859, c. 34. This act gave the married woman the right to hold and control her own property, whether obtained before or after her marriage.

[30]Ian Bain, "The Role of J. J. Kelso in the Launching of the Child Welfare Movement in Ontario" (University of Toronto, unpublished M.S.W. thesis, 1955), pp. 20–22.

[31]Canada, Statutes, 1851, c. 34. Names of board members probably having an identification with the Family Compact families were: Mary G. Sherwood, Charlotte B. Rideout, Isabella Baby, Augusta Draper, Caroline Jarvis, Alice Clark, Emily M. Lefroy, Eliza Heward, Sarah Ann Boulton, Harriet E. M. Boulton, Sarah Spragge, Eliza Stanton, Sarah Nation, and Lilla Van Koughnet. On the boards of the agencies formed in Toronto in the 1860's, in contrast, few Family Compact names are to be found.

because the status of married women at the time raised some problems about their capacity in law to operate a corporate enterprise, it was deemed necessary to affirm in the act establishing the Orphans' Home that the validity of the actions performed by a member of the corporation who was a married woman did not depend on such actions being "specially authorized by her husband; any law, usage or custom to the contrary notwithstanding."[32] An act passed during the following year concerning an orphanage in Hamilton undertook to deal with the same problem through the rather indirect measure of incorporating seven men as the "Trustees of the Hamilton Orphan Asylum," though the essential work of the institution was carried out by a "Ladies' Committee of Management."[33]

The act incorporating the Orphans' Home and Female Aid Society of Toronto stated that its purposes were to offer "relief and support to friendless orphans and destitute females" and to afford "religious and moral instruction" to them. Although the institution did not originally include among its purposes the placement of children as apprentices, it took this step a year later.[34] A number of other children's institutions established in the 1850's and 1860's indicated similar intentions,[35] normally including in their acts of incorporation a section resembling that in the statute granting corporate status to the Hamilton Orphan Asylum. This provided:

That the said Ladies' Committee of Management shall, and may send out to service, and apprentice thereto, or to any healthy trade or business, all youths, male or female, having the protection or aid of the said Institution, to such person or persons, and upon such terms, as to the said Ladies' Committee of Management may seem fit and proper; and for that purpose shall have power, on behalf of and for such youths and themselves, to enter into and make with any person or persons with whom such youths may be placed . . . articles of apprenticeship of agreement: and that such articles of agreement may be enforced as well by action at law or in equity for breach thereof warranting any such action, as by summary application to a Magistrate or Justice of the Peace, (who is hereby authorized and empowered to act thereon,) on any such occasion as would, according to the laws of this Province, warrant the interference or adjudication of any one or more Justice or Justices of the Peace, in disputes between masters and apprentices: Provided always, that a copy of the articles of indenture apprenticing such youth shall, within three days from the time when such articles or indenture

32*Ibid.*
33*Ibid.*, 1852–53, c. 67.
34*Ibid.*, c. 71.
35For example, the Boys' Home, Toronto (*ibid.*, 1861, c. 114); the Girls' Home and Public Nursery, Toronto (*ibid.*, 1863 (1st sess.), c. 63); the Children's Industrial School of Hamilton (*ibid.*, 1864, c. 145).

were executed, be lodged with the Clerk of the Common Council of the City of Hamilton, who is hereby required to file such copies.[36]

That three or four children's institutions were incorporated with such provisions might seem to have indicated that the province was beginning, as a settled policy, to insist that incorporated institutions with apprenticeship programmes should administer them in a manner that gave some assurance that the indentures would be properly drawn and that they would be enforced. Other children's institutions, however, were incorporated without these provisions respecting their apprenticeship programmes. Thus, the reference in the section quoted above, and in parallel sections in the similar statutes, to the registration of the indenture of apprenticeship with the municipal clerk did not indicate a firm policy of active public involvement in the apprenticeship programmes of the voluntary institutions.

Certain of the institutions indicated in their acts of incorporation their intention to require that persons taking a child as an apprentice pay a fee to the institution. In two instances, it was stated that the payment was for the benefit of the child,[37] while in a third there was no indication of its purpose.[38] The figure mentioned in one act was "a sum of money not less in amount than two dollars,"[39] the reference being to a single payment made at the time the child was placed. Two of the acts specified that a minimum of three dollars was to be paid annually.[40]

Although apprenticeship continued throughout the period to be the principal method of providing for children who lacked parents or proper parental care, two other approaches were initiated: adoption and care in children's institutions. Adoption was mentioned as an alternative to apprenticeship in two of the statutes[41] incorporating institutions in the 1860's, but no separate legislation was passed governing it or indicating what legal status it had or what responsibilities it entailed. To the extent that adoptions were made, the relationships they involved and any legal problems they may have created were left to the common law for definition and resolution.

The establishment of institutions in which children were maintained and cared for apart from adults in need of similar provision and, to a greater or less degree, apart from the community was to prove a highly significant development in the history of child welfare in the province. Although organized with the apparent purpose, in most

[36]*Ibid.*, 1852–53, c. 67.
[37]*Ibid.*, 1861, c. 114; 1864, c. 145. [38]*Ibid.*, 1863 (1st sess.), c. 63.
[39]*Ibid.* [40]*Ibid.*, 1861, c. 114; 1864, c. 145.
[41]*Ibid.*, 1863 (1st sess.), c. 63; 1864, c. 145.

instances, of caring for children only until such time as they could be apprenticed, these institutions tended to develop programmes for the long-term care of children. Their initial establishment reflected the limitations of apprenticeship to operate effectively, even in respect to the children most eligible for apprenticeship, and indicated its failure to meet the needs of young or handicapped children for whom placements as apprentices were not available. The continued growth of the institutions, which was to be characteristic of the post-Confederation period as well as of the latter part of the Union period, indicated the increase in the numbers of children for whom non-institutional placement could not be found. It also reflected a tendency for institutional care to become an accepted form of long-term care for the parentless and neglected child.

The eleven institutions for children and unmarried mothers that were given recognition by the province in the Union period, either through being incorporated or through receiving provincial grants, displayed a number of differences in their auspices, purposes, and programmes. Two were Roman Catholic institutions, while the remainder either were representative of all groups in the community or were formed through co-operative action by members of various Protestant denominations. In general, the homes provided care for both boys and girls, although two homes wholly for boys and one for girls were established in Toronto. Four of the institutions indicated that their work extended to women as well as children,[42] two referring particularly to widows and one of these also mentioning that it would offer "temporary refuge to female servants out of place."[43]

The acts establishing the institutions often referred to the children and women to whom they were offering help as friendless, homeless, and vagrant. Neglect by parents and orphanhood were mentioned in the act incorporating the Boys' Industrial School of the Gore of Toronto.[44] This act also referred to the evil habits which boys were acquiring and which often led to the commission of crime, and it stated the object of the institution to be the protection and reclamation of youth. Reclamation from vice was also referred to as the central purpose of the Magdalen Asylum and Industrial House of Refuge[45] of Toronto, and religious and moral instruction was mentioned by a number of others. Only one, the Industrial School of Hamilton, included education among its objects,[46] while the Boys' Home of

42Ibid., 1851, c. 34; 1862, c. 97; 1864, c. 150; 1865 (1st sess.), c. 62.
43Ibid., 1865 (1st sess.), c. 62.   44Ibid., 1862, c. 82.
45Ibid., 1858, c. 73.   46Ibid., 1864, c. 145.

Toronto stated that its purposes were "to provide for the destitute, homeless, and vagrant boys and children of drunken or dissolute parents and to promote and encourage habits of honest industry in these poor out-casts."[47]

Most of the incorporated children's institutions received grants from the provincial government, though the fact of incorporation was in itself neither a pre-requisite for nor a guarantee of provincial aid. Seven institutions for children and unmarried mothers were receiving grants in 1866 and had been for a number of years. Five of the institutions were in receipt of annual amounts of $640, one of $480, and one of $320. The amounts granted are more suggestive of a predilection on the part of the provincial treasurer for multiples of 160 than they are a reflection of the extent or quality of the service provided by the institutions in question. Furthermore, no provision of any kind was made for provincial inspection of institutions receiving provincial grants until 1857, and, although the Prison and Asylum Inspection Act of that year authorized the Board of Inspectors to inspect institutions on the direction of the governor, the necessary order was never given and the only record of an inspector's visit to a children's institution was that of Meredith in 1861 to the Boys' Home in Toronto, on the invitation of its board and in an unofficial capacity.[48]

Although not involved in the inspection of children's institutions, the inspectors did, none the less, begin to express concern about the welfare of children and to formulate definite views about the extension of existing measures. They began to feel that the problem of juvenile delinquency, about which the public became concerned in the late 1850's, was not susceptible of solution simply or primarily through the work of the prisons for young offenders, but required other and more basic approaches. This view became evident in their first report. In reviewing the work of the boys' reformatory and reflecting on the previous condition and habits of the children in its custody, they identified the use of children for begging as an important cause of crime and as an indication that some form of action to deal with the matter was needed.

As it belongs to the functions of the Inspectors to indicate the *causes* of crime and misery, when they obtain clear views of them, this is no unfit occasion to remark on the terrible effects of the mendicity carried on in cities by young children. The poor, whether they be young or old, are no doubt privileged to ask for bread; but it is the duty of the charitable part of

[47]*Ibid.*, 1861, c. 114.
[48]Canada, *Sessional Papers*, 1861, no. 24, n.p.

society who care for the salvation of souls to provide that young children shall not, by the practice of mendicity, contract habits of idleness and vagrancy, which, becoming inveterate, may lead them to vice and crime. Most of the children sent to our Reformatories, and great numbers of prostitutes, have made shipwreck of their moral character while engaged in the practice of begging, whether in all honesty, or for the purpose of fraud; for if there are, among the class of beggars, some poor outcasts commissioned by their parents to obtain relief of their real distress in the houses of the rich, there are also of the number, youthful vagrants who prey upon public charity for the purpose either of procuring indulgence of their own growing passions or of feeding the deeply rooted vices of their unhappy parents.

Benevolent societies and houses of refuge constitute the appropriate remedy for these evils.[49]

In the following year, Meredith made a more thorough analysis of the question and presented his findings and recommendations to the government early in 1862.[50] In his annual report, he referred to the work of the Boys' Home in Toronto and similar institutions in caring for children who might otherwise become involved in criminal activities, and expressed the view that

no class of institutions, penal or reformatory, is calculated to produce so large results in this way, and at so small a cost to the community, as those institutions (whether styled "Ragged Schools", "Homes", or "Industrial Farms") which, seeking out the neglected and perishing children, who otherwise would grow up in our midst in ignorance and vice, afford these unfortunate outcasts the necessary education and training to earn an honest living for themselves.[51]

Meredith indicated that the children he thought should be cared for in such homes were those "destitute and neglected pauper children" who could be further classified as:

1. Vicious and incorrigible children
2. Vagrants
3. Children without parents or protectors, or children whose parents or natural protectors, from poverty or other causes, are unable or unwilling to afford them that education which they require, and to which they are entitled.[52]

Although thus expressing the view that such children were "entitled" to education and, by implication, to the forms of care necessary to the acquisition of an education, Meredith did not regard the provision of the measures necessary to realize this entitlement as wholly or even primarily a public responsibility. He did believe, however, that the

49*Ibid.*   50*Ibid.*, 1862, no. 19, n.p.
51*Ibid.*   52*Ibid.*

province had a certain legislative rôle to play and that the municipalities might have a financial responsibility. In his proposal to the government, he recommended

that the Circuit or County Judges, and the Recorders of cities, should, under certain restrictions and conditions, have authority to commit such children to "Homes" regularly established, for certain limited periods. That the managers of the "Homes" should give the children a suitable training and education, and afterwards apprentice them to some farmer or tradesman, or otherwise put them in the way of earning an honest living. It was recommended that the homes should be supported, mainly at least, by voluntary contributions, or by payments from the municipalities sending children to them, and that the aid of the Legislature should be invoked for the purposes, principally, of legalizing the establishments, and of conferring the necessary power upon the magistrates to send the children to the "Homes", and on the managers to retain the children for the periods prescribed by law, and afterwards to apprentice them out.[53]

In their last report before Confederation, the inspectors referred to their many endeavours over the years "to arouse public attention and to enlist public sympathy on behalf of the destitute and neglected children, 'City Arabs' as they have been termed, who are found in such large numbers in all our principal cities."[54] The inspectors repeated Meredith's observation that "for this large class of children, our admirable and costly Common Schools are perfectly useless."[55] These children were not attending the common schools but were too often finding their way into the common gaols and from there to the juvenile reformatory. What was needed, in the view of the inspectors, was the missing link "between the Free School and the Reformatory; an Institution recognized by law, where these destitute and neglected outcast children may receive such a training and education as will induce and enable them to earn an honest living for themselves."[56]

In support of this proposal, the inspectors quoted a number of the resolutions that were adopted by a select committee of the British House of Commons in 1851.[57] This committee had recommended the establishment of industrial schools similar to what Meredith called "Homes." However, in contrast to Meredith's view that the homes should be under voluntary auspices and largely financed from voluntary sources, the select committee had recommended that they "should be founded and supported partially by local rates, and partially by contributions from the State, and that power should be given for raising

[53]*Ibid.*
[54]*Ibid.*, 1866, no. 6, p. 38.
[55]*Ibid.*
[56]*Ibid.*
[57]Great Britain, *Sessional Papers*, 1861, vol. VII (*Report of the Select Committee on the Education of Destitute Children*).

the necessary amount of local rates."[58] Thus, the select committee viewed the problem of neglected children as one in which the expression of public responsibility for their care and education could not be made dependent on voluntary initiative and support. Although Meredith's proposal fell short of the British committee's advocacy of full public responsibility for neglected and dependent children, it went well beyond existing practice. It would have given the courts the power of decision as to whether a child was in need of protection and care and the right to place him in an institution established to provide either intra-mural care or placement as an apprentice.

In view of the inspectors' concern with the condition of children and their interest in institutional and other measures on their behalf, it might appear surprising that they did not urge upon the government the implementation of section 28 of the Inspection Act[59] under which they could have been instructed by the governor to visit and report upon the voluntary institutions. There is no record that they sought this power, however, perhaps because of the special issues that the inspection of institutions might have raised in Lower Canada, or perhaps because they could not undertake this further work without adversely affecting responsibilities clearly assigned to them under the act. As a result of this failure of the government to extend inspection to the voluntary institutions for children and its further and more significant failure to act on Meredith's recommendation for legislation extending the power of the state in respect to the uncared-for-child, public responsibility for children in the Union period did not progress beyond the point reached in the Apprentice and Minors Act of 1851.

POST-CONFEDERATION PERIOD, 1867–1893

Apprenticeship Legislation

The earliest measures for children taken by the province of Ontario were those which, as described in the preceding chapter, established the residential schools for the education of deaf and blind children and young adults. When the Legislature turned its attention to children other than those with special handicaps, it followed pre-Confederation practice in placing the emphasis on apprenticeship. An act passed in 1872[60] amended the statutes enacted in the Union period[61] to reaffirm

[58]*Ibid.*, p. 39.
[59]Canada, *Consolidated Statutes*, 1859, c. 110.
[60]Ontario, *Statutes*, 1871–72, c. 17.
[61]Canada, *Statutes*, 1851, c. 11, and *Consolidated Statutes of Upper Canada*, 1859, c. 76.

the powers of mayors, magistrates, and judges to bind as an apprentice any minor who was an orphan or who was dependent upon public charity for support. The real purpose of the amendment, however, was to fortify the apprenticeship arrangement against action that might be taken by a parent to withdraw the child from it. This prohibition, which had been requested by some of the institutions,[62] applied not only to situations where formal apprenticeship proceedings had been instituted and where the child was being maintained in a charitable institution, but also to cases where the child was with a private person who was "charitably . . . taking care of such minor."[63] Where a parent sought to remove a child from any of these situations, he was obliged to obtain permission from a mayor, judge, or magistrate. This official could, in his judicial capacity, refuse to grant the required permission "notwithstanding the strict legal right of the applicant to the custody and control of such minor"[64] if the official was not satisfied that the permission would "tend to the benefit and advantage of such minor."[65]

In 1874 a new act[66] was passed respecting apprentices and minors, incorporating the main provisions of the pre-Confederation statute, the amendment of 1872, and a number of new provisions. The terms of the act were arranged and designated to indicate more clearly than in previous legislation the rights and responsibilities of minors who became apprentices, the guardianship rôle of persons accepting a child as an apprentice, the powers of parents, charitable societies, and designated officials to bind children as apprentices, the procedures for the transference of an apprentice on the death of his master, the procedures for dealing with complaints by an apprentice against his master and by a master against his apprentice, and the procedures for appeals against decisions made in respect to such complaints. The new provisions relating to complaints went further than had the act of 1872 in strengthening the means of protecting an apprentice against exploitation or abuse. The 1874 act provided that the complaint of an apprentice against his master could be brought by someone on his behalf, as well as directly by the apprentice himself. It also gave any judge or police magistrate the right to annul the indenture, a power previously reserved to courts of quarter sessions.[67] The new act also dropped the provision in the Union statute freeing a master from the

---

[62]For example, the Girls' Home in Toronto, *Annual Report*, 1865, p. 3, referred to in Bain, "The Role of J. J. Kelso," p. 95.
[63]Ontario, *Statutes*, 1871–72, c. 17.
[64]*Ibid.*
[65]*Ibid.*
[66]Ontario, *Statutes*, 1874 (2nd sess.), c. 19.
[67]Canada, *Consolidated Statutes of Upper Canada*, 1859, c. 76, s. 18.

obligations of the indenture where an apprentice became insane or was convicted of a felony.

In two other important respects the act went beyond the earlier statutes respecting apprenticeship. One was the recognition it gave to the rôle that charitable societies were playing in apprenticeship,[68] and the second was the control it gave the provincial government over the societies undertaking this work. Under the act, the lieutenant-governor-in-council could confer on a society the right to bind children as apprentices and, by inference, to exercise a protective interest in them after their placement. The order-in-council could confer the right for an indefinite or a limited period of time, and if the order-in-council was revoked the society lost its powers to take apprenticeship action until it was again authorized to do so by a new order-in-council.

TABLE XIII

RESIDENTS OF CHILDREN'S INSTITUTIONS RECEIVING GRANTS
UNDER SCHEDULE C OF THE CHARITY AID ACT, 1874–1893

Year	Residents on September 30	Residents during the year	Aggregate days care
1874	896	1,490	208,346
1875	970	1,727	342,570
1876	1,190	2,295	436,861
1877	1,305	2,504	478,890
1878	1,408	2,696	521,697
1879	1,405	2,725	506,372
1880	1,404	2,865	527,086
1881	1,415	3,032	531,956
1882	1,426	2,967	530,863
1883	1,591	3,137	553,330
1884	1,683	3,407	600,813
1885	1,639	3,296	614,590
1886	1,717	3,239	623,801
1887	1,732	3,527	657,709
1888	1,747	3,452	653,157
1889	1,855	3,706	652,164
1890	1,805	4,090	650,904
1891	1,859	3,907	682,225
1892	1,814	3,742	671,985
1893	1,747	3,992	667,880

SOURCE: Ontario, *Reports of the Inspector of Prisons, Asylums and Public Charities*, 1875–94.

The Charity Aid Act

Earlier in the year that had witnessed the passage of the Apprentices and Minors Act, another statute of importance in the development of services for children also became law. The Charity Aid Act to regulate

[68]Ontario, *Statutes*, 1874 (2nd sess.), c. 19.

TABLE XIV

INSTITUTIONS RECEIVING A PROVINCIAL GRANT UNDER SCHEDULE C OF THE
CHARITY AID ACT IN 1893

Institution	Location	Expenditures (in dollars)	Provincial grant	
			Total (in dollars)	Percentage of expenditure
Roman Catholic Orphan Asylum	Toronto	11,463	2,204	19.2
Protestant Orphan's Home	Toronto	11,074	1,416	12.8
Girls' Home	Toronto	7,271	708	9.7
Boys' Home	Toronto	6,239	607	9.7
Newsboys' Lodgings	Toronto	3,000	139	4.6
Infants' Home and Infirmary	Toronto	8,938	1,272*	14.2
St. Nicholas Home	Toronto	4,928	343	7.0
The Haven	Toronto	4,273	387	9.1
St. Mary's Orphan Asylum	Hamilton	5,404	865	16.0
Protestant Orphan Asylum	Hamilton	3,951	109	2.8
Boys' Home	Hamilton	3,265	468	14.3
Girls' Home	Hamilton	3,535	366	10.4
Home for the Friendless	Hamilton	3,312	378†	11.4
Orphans' Home	Kingston	3,889	440	11.3
House of Providence Orphan Asylum	Kingston	— †	436	—
Hotel Dieu Orphan Asylum	Kingston	1,296	258	19.9
Orphans' Home	Ottawa	4,968	340	6.8
St. Patrick's Orphan Asylum	Ottawa	— ‡	562	—
St. Joseph's Orphan Asylum	Ottawa	6,024	895	14.9
Roman Catholic Orphans' Home	London	— ‡	646	—
Protestant Orphans' Home	London	2,240	343	15.3
Women's Refuge and Infants' Home	London	1,185	239†	20.2
Protestant Home, Orphanage Branch	St. Catharines	1,367	79	5.8
Orphans' Asylum	St. Agatha	1,956	373	19.1
Orphans' Asylum	Fort William	3,485	503	14.4
Hotel Dieu Orphanage	Windsor	302	12	4.0

SOURCE: Ontario, *Sessional Papers*, 1894, no. 28, pp. 69–70.
*Includes 10¢ per day for mother nurses and 7¢ for other nurses, also $200 for the infirmary.
†Includes 10¢ per day for mother nurses and 7¢ for other nurses.
‡Separate orphanage expenditures not available.

public aid to charitable institutions was to have immediate impact on these services. Provincial grants to the children's institutions and to the institutions for unmarried mothers grouped with them under schedule C of the act increased from approximately $7,350 in 1874 to nearly $15,000 in 1893, and the number of persons thereby assisted increased from some 1,850 to 4,125 during that period.[69] The trend in the numbers of persons assisted annually in the children's institutions is

[69]For more details of the act, see above pages 56–64.

shown in Table XIII. The figures on aggregate days care show a rapid increase in 1875 and 1876, followed by a steady growth in nearly all subsequent years to 1893, although the last two years of the period were to witness a modest decline in the amount of care provided.

The significance of the Charity Aid Act in providing financial assistance to the children's institutions is indicated in Table XIV. These figures show that the provincial grant as a percentage of expenditures ranged from 2.8 for the Protestant Orphan Asylum, Hamilton, to as much as 20.2 for the Women's Refuge and Infants' Home, London; the median percentage was 11.4 and the mean was 13.2. For most of the institutions, the extent of provincial support under the Charity Aid Act was thus quite limited, and its inadequacy was strongly criticized by Langmuir in his reports for 1877 and 1878. In the latter he recommended "for the favorable consideration of the Government and the Legislature, that the Provincial aid to orphanages be increased to *five* cents per diem for each inmate, and to Magdalen Asylums *seven* cents per diem."[70] The case he made for the increases in these rates, though forcibly and indeed eloquently stated, suffered from the same defect as the considerations on which the rates were initially established. It was not based on any examination of what it cost to maintain a child or an unmarried mother in an institution, nor did it consider what the province ought to pay, as a proportion of the total cost, to ensure adequate standards. Perhaps because of this limitation, Langmuir's recommendation went unheeded, and the rates paid to orphanages and magdalen institutions remained unchanged throughout the period.

Although no change was made in the rate structure as set out in the statute, the government contrived, in apparent disregard of the terms of the act, to provide additional aid where a strong case was made out for it. Thus, without any alteration in the legislation, three institutions which cared for very young children were assisted at the rate of ten cents a day for those serving only as nurses. In addition, one of these institutions, the Infants' Home, Toronto, was on Langmuir's recommendation[71] given a special grant of $200 a year to assist in the operation of its infirmary.

There is no conclusive evidence, however, that the limited amount of financial aid from the province restricted the development of the institutions. There were a number of references by the inspectors to institutions lacking sufficient funds, and at various times they exhorted the public to be more generous to the institutions as a group[72] or to

[70]Ontario, *Sessional Papers*, 1879, no. 8., p. 8.
[71]*Ibid.*, 1878, no. 4, p. 224.
[72]*Ibid.*, 1882–83, no. 8, p. 64 (refuge and orphanage report).

individual institutions[73] experiencing financial problems. In general, however, the boards of the orphanages seemed able without undue difficulty to find the means to carry on their work on the lines of contemporary practice. Most of them expanded their operations more than once during the period, and extensive building programmes and periodic renovations were the rule rather than the exception. A number of institutions were the beneficiaries of substantial legacies and others enjoyed the support of wealthy patrons. Thus, for example, the Orphans' Home, Kingston, enjoyed the patronage of John Watkins, the Convalescent Home of the Hospital for Sick Children, Toronto, that of John Ross Robertson, and the Orphans' Home, Toronto, that of William Gooderham.

Children's Institutions

The supervision required under the Charity Aid Act was carried out by the various inspectors who served during the period in a manner that was beneficial in raising the standards of the institutions. Langmuir began his inspections of the children's institutions with a strong conviction about their value, though he felt obliged to justify their work in terms of their preventing children from becoming criminals. In considering, in 1872, whether children's institutions should be included under the proposed reorganization of provincial grants to charitable institutions, he argued that the province, as well as private benevolence and the municipal corporations, had a responsibility for their support.

If . . . we consider for a moment the character and necessities of the youths who find a home within their walls, abundant proof will be furnished in favour of Government aid being extended to them, and perhaps more liberally than has been the case in the past. If the good accomplished by the operation of these Institutions is measured even by the low standard of public economy, who can tell the saving that has been effected to the Province in its criminal administration and maintenance, by the sheltering, reclaiming and deterring hand that was extended to the 1,200 orphans, and neglected and abandoned children, who found a home in these ten Institutions during the year 1871? How many of the children thus provided for would, if left to themselves, in a very few years have become inmates of our gaols, reformatories, and penitentiary, and a constant charge upon the public? It is, therefore, very clear that even in the interests of public economy, to say nothing of humanity, it is expedient to assist with Provincial funds these Institutions.[74]

[73]*Ibid.*, 1875, no. 4, p. 181; 1879, no. 8, p. 239; 1889, no. 11, p. 83; 1893, no. 10, p. 57.
[74]*Ibid.*, 1872–73, no. 2, p. 72.

Langmuir and his successors approached their rôle of supervising the children's institutions in the same straightforward manner that characterized their inspection of the other types of institutions. They were required to give particular attention to the securing of accurate data on which to base the provincial grant, and, having satisfied themselves in that regard, they directed their attention to the organization, operation, and programme of the institutions. They did not hesitate to commend or criticize any aspect of the work of the institutions. Langmuir, in an endeavour which anticipated by several decades the work of social planning councils, felt no constraint in attempting to bring about the merger of two institutions with similar programmes and a common constituency, and which he felt "might be joined . . . with great advantage, both of a moral and financial kind."[75]

STATISTICS

The children's institutions appeared to present more than their quota of problems in the matter of statistics. In 1878 Langmuir remarked that it seemed "to be almost impossible to get the lady managers of this class of institution to comply with the regulations made with a view to obtaining a correct and complete statistical record of the operation of the charities under their care."[76] The solution advocated by the Inspector was for the board of an institution to assign the responsibility to a member of the staff rather than to have the work performed by the honorary secretary.[77] Eventually, this course appears to have been adopted, with good effect, by most of the institutions.

PLANT AND FACILITIES

As they did in the case of the other types of institutions under the Charity Aid Act, the inspectors took the view that the orphanages ought to occupy buildings constructed on a high standard, with up-to-date conveniences and good facilities. Where the institutions fell short of these criteria, the inspectors employed various means to register their disapproval, one of the more extreme being that of exposing the matter to the public in their published reports. This usually produced the hoped-for results. Thus it was not difficult to predict remedial action following Langmuir's report in 1873 respecting the Orphans' Home of Ottawa that "the dormitories for the children are in the attic and are not well ventilated, while the best rooms are

[75]*Ibid.*, 1875, no. 4, p. 4 (supplement); 1877, no. 2, pp. 198–99.
[76]*Ibid.*, 1879, no. 8, p. 242.
[77]*Ibid.*, 1882, no. 8, pp. 295, 304.

used by the officers."[78] The following year he was able to report that great improvements had been made and that the "garret which I complained of in my last report as being used for the boys' dormitories ... is no longer used for that purpose, and the boys now occupy a cheerful room on the first flat."[79] The institution, moreover, was planning to build a new home.

It was this course—the erection of new and specially designed buildings—that the inspectors advocated whenever an institution was facing the question of expansion or extensive renovation. Langmuir, on learning that the Protestant Orphans' Home, London, was considering the purchase of "a building which was very ill-adapted in its internal arrangement to the wants of the Home ... strongly urged them against the purchase and recommended the erection of an entirely new building."[80] He also opposed the practice of renting or leasing either buildings or land, holding that "it is most desirable . . . that all charitable institutions in receipt of Government aid should own the property they occupy, in order that permanency and stability may characterize their operations, and that structural alterations may take place when required."[81] In 1883, Christie was able to remark with satisfaction that "the managers of the various Orphanages are alive to the importance of housing their young charges in properly constructed and arranged buildings"[82] and to conclude that "if such activity as has prevailed during the past few years be continued, there will in a very short time be a specially constructed building for every Orphanage in the Province."[83]

The inspectors showed no less interest in the interior arrangements and equipment of the homes. Year after year, they drew attention to such situations as overcrowding[84] and poor sanitation,[85] and such hazards as unprotected window-ledges and stair-wells[86] and conditions which could result in fires.[87] In general, the situations they complained of were remedied, and no children's institution resisted action recommended by an inspector to the degree displayed by two or three of the refuges. The only comparable issue involved the securing of proper seats for children in the orphanage school rooms. Dr. O'Reilly found that a number of the homes had seats of a grossly defective design which he was convinced could be permanently damaging to the children's health. Accordingly, he strongly advised their removal, but

[78]*Ibid.*, 1874 (vol. VII), no. 2, p. 148. [79]*Ibid.*, 1875, no. 4, p. 183.
[80]*Ibid.*, 1877, no. 2, p. 198. [81]*Ibid.*, p. 201.
[82]*Ibid.*, 1884, no. 32, p. 32. [83]*Ibid.*
[84]*Ibid.*, 1879, no 8., p. 233. [85]*Ibid.*, 1886, no. 14, p. 40.
[86]*Ibid.*, p. 51. [87]*Ibid.*, 1888, no. 40, p. 68.

encountered considerable resistance in securing concurrence, particularly by two of the institutions in Hamilton. After getting no response to his first call for the replacement of the desks, O'Reilly attempted in 1883 to appeal, in the case of the Protestant Orphan Asylum, to "the well-known solicitude of the lady managers for the well-being of the children under their care."[88] In the case of the Girls' Home, which he knew to be well endowed, he employed the opposite tactic of attempting to shame the board of management into action, remarking that the "only excuse" which could be accepted for the delay would be "extreme paucity of funds."[89] When the latter institution took no action by the following year, he warned that he would recommend that "the Government withhold its grant to this Orphanage if an improvement be not made in this respect."[90]

In addition to his concern that poor desks might cause physical impairment, Dr. O'Reilly saw this issue as an indication of discriminatory attitudes that appeared at various times and in various forms in the operation of the orphanages. Thus, he remarked in 1881 that because improper seats had been replaced in the public schools, "the same protection should . . . be extended to orphans."[91] When he found a further manifestation of the same attitude in the failure of two orphanages to provide proper heat for their buildings in mid-October 1887, he commented scathingly on those who "think it necessary to freeze the inmates of these institutions a few days before they will light the furnaces."[92] In the case of one of the institutions, he took it upon himself to order the closing of the schoolroom until the furnace was repaired and the institution properly heated.[93] In their attack on this view that second-rate provisions were good enough for orphans, the inspectors were critical of institutions which lacked adequate recreational areas and facilities[94] for the children, and they also condemned institutions which provided adequate buildings, but did little to make them attractive. Thus Dr. O'Reilly once again referred unfavourably to the Girls' Home, Hamilton, remarking that "with the fine building owned by this charity, it seems a pity it should be allowed to remain in the dingy, cheerless condition it is always found in."[95]

More often, however, the inspectors offered encouragement and emulation rather than criticism and the threat of sanctions. They

88*Ibid.*, 1884, no. 32, p. 53.　　　　89*Ibid.*, p. 56.
90*Ibid.*, 1885, no. 40, p. 53.　　　　91*Ibid.*, 1882, no. 8, p. 310.
92*Ibid.*, 1888, no. 40, p. 55.　　　　93*Ibid.*, p. 54.
94*Ibid.*, 1879, no. 8, p. 248; 1882, no. 8, p. 294.
95*Ibid.*, 1889, no. 11, p. 72.

repeatedly praised institutions which erected new, well-designed, and well-equipped buildings,[96] and complimented those homes that modernized their facilities through introducing new types of heating and sanitation and new conveniences like the telephone.[97]

MANAGEMENT, OPERATION, AND STAFFING

In general, the inspectors applied to the management, operation, and staffing of the children's institution the same criteria they applied to other types of institution. They praised uniformity, order, and cleanliness, and equated the lack of any of those qualities with bad management. They appear to have given little leadership in a thoughtful consideration of the objects to be sought in the administration of the children's homes or in the means by which such objects might be attained. With the exception of Chamberlain, they reported sparsely on staffing, only occasionally referring to the work of a particularly able matron. Chamberlain alone felt it important to mention the matrons by name, and he was the only inspector who discussed staff establishments, indicating in his reports the extent to which work was performed by the residents, and where necessary, as in the case of an institution in which there were "only two paid employees to look after the welfare of seventeen infants and nine women,"[98] expressing criticism of the size of the staffs expected to perform the work of the homes.

PROGRAMME

Although the lack of discussion by the inspectors of concepts of institutional care for children contrasts with the thought they gave, in such areas as corrections, to basic aims and the means of achieving them through administration, the inspectors' record in encouraging specific measures for the improvement of the programmes of the children's institutions was good, and in a piecemeal way they contributed significantly thereby to the advancement of institutional care.

This was particularly true of the rôle of education in the programme of the institutions. When he began his inspections, Langmuir found that most of the homes were providing schooling for their children within their own walls and out of their own resources, using such staff as they could employ or spare for this purpose. In 1876 he recommended that the schools in the institutions be conducted according to the school laws, and that teaching staff and other forms of aid be

[96]*Ibid.*, 1888, no. 40, p. 61; 1892, no. 6, p. 75.
[97]*Ibid.*, 1890, no. 15, p. 85.   [98]*Ibid.*, 1893, no. 10, p. 86.

provided by the local school boards in conformity with their responsibility for all the children in the community.[99] This recommendation was acted upon,[100] therefore helping to ensure that the children in the institutions received an education comparable to that of other children. Some institutions added what was referred to as industrial or mechanical employment as part of their educational programme,[101] and this was regarded favourably by the inspectors. They also expressed approval of activities such as gardening, shoe-making,[102] and carpet-weaving,[103] and endorsed the policy of the Boys' Home in Toronto of having all the painting, whitewashing, and woodcutting for the home done by the boys, as well as having them mend their own clothes. This practice was described as "a very good one as it teaches the boys to be useful and forms in them habits of industry."[104]

By the mid-1880's, however, the inspectors were distinguishing between the work-content and the educational value of such activities. Accordingly, when Dr. O'Reilly found, during an inspection of the Protestant Orphans' Home, London, that "children who ought to have been at school were employed during school hours at work about the building and grounds," he made it clear that "this, of course, should not be."[105] He pointed out to the lady managers not only that they should be making full use "of the liberality of the Government and the School Board,"[106] but that they had "the same obligation to see that the education of these children is not neglected as . . . to provide shelter and food for them."[107]

The inspectors also encouraged types of education which were not purely utilitarian in aim. Thus Dr. O'Reilly, in describing his inspection of the Orphans' Home and Female Aid Society in Toronto, reported being "charmed by the proficiency attained by the pupils in singing," and praised the teacher and the institution for appreciating "at its full value the importance of this branch of a child's education."[108]

Dr. O'Reilly, more than the other inspectors, also stressed the importance to children of recreation. When he found "a marked absence of toys and playthings" in the Orphans' Home, Kingston, he remarked that "little things to afford amusement are a great necessity"[109] and could be provided at a small cost. A similar situation in

[99]Ibid., 1877, no. 2, p. 195.
[100]Ibid., 1878, no. 4, p. 222; 1879, no. 8, p. 234.
[101]Ibid., p. 243.
[102]Ibid., p. 245.   [103]Ibid., 1888, no. 40, p. 47.
[104]Ibid., 1881, no. 8, p. 258.   [105]Ibid., 1886, no. 14, p. 61.
[106]Ibid., p. 62.   [107]Ibid., pp. 61, 62.
[108]Ibid., 1882, no. 8, p. 292.   [109]Ibid., p. 307.

the Protestant Orphan Asylum, Hamilton, caused him to remark that "these little ones, being without domestic associations and family ties, have all the more need for such amusements as can be supplied to them,"[110] and to express the view that the people of Hamilton would gladly fill the need if attention were drawn to it.

It was also important, in the opinion of Dr. O'Reilly, that the children in institutions should be helped to create and enjoy attractive surroundings. He praised the decorations which the children had been encouraged to put up in the Boys' Home, Toronto,[111] and criticized the lack of similar activities in the Girls' Home. He remarked that "this feature is especially important in an institution of this kind, in view of the fact that most of these children are to be domestic servants or poor men's wives and should be taught not only habits of cleanliness and industry, but also what can be done in the way of cheaply embellishing a home where taste and skill are present."[112]

In those institutions caring for children beyond the infant age group, the inspectors gave strong support and encouragement to various measures to ensure the promotion and preservation of good health. They were alert to any conditions which seemed likely to constitute a threat to health and safety. They consistently impressed on the institutions the necessity of proper ventilation[113] and sanitation.[114] When Dr. O'Reilly, for example, came upon pungent evidence of defective sanitary facilities in the Boys' Home, Hamilton, he "called the attention of the Assistant Matron to this matter and requested her to at once report it to the Board of Managers."[115] The health record of most of these institutions for older children was thus remarkably good, and the inspectors, in their concern to keep it so, looked upon any significant indication of ill-health as the signal for action. They repeatedly suggested that the institutions have their own infirmaries, preferably quite separate from the remainder of the home,[116] and they encouraged the policy of isolation or separation to deal with specific problems, such as that of the persistent skin disease which plagued the residents of the Girls' Home, Toronto, for a number of years.[117] In the case of the Protestant Home, London, where there were recurrent outbreaks of ringworm, Dr. O'Reilly reached the conclusion that the "care . . . is not all that it ought to be" and recommended the appointment of "a competent nurse who can give her undivided attention to the children."[118]

[110]*Ibid.*, 1886, no. 14, p. 50.　　　　[111]*Ibid.*, 1882, no. 8, p. 295.
[112]*Ibid.*, p. 293.　　　　　　　　　　[113]*Ibid.*, 1878, no. 4, p. 222.
[114]*Ibid.*, 1886, no. 14, pp. 40, 51.　　[115]*Ibid.*, p. 52.
[116]*Ibid.*, 1887, no. 21, p. 48.　　　　[117]*Ibid.*, 1888, no. 40, p. 45.
[118]*Ibid.*, 1882–83, no. 8, p. 54 (refuge and orphanage report).

In respect to the three or four institutions which cared for infants, however, the actions of the inspectors were somewhat less vigorous and reflected the contemporary attitude of fatalism towards appalling levels of infant mortality. The one notable exception was Langmuir's reaction to the high death rates in the Infants' Home, Toronto.

As 151 infants were in the home during the twelve months, and 60 died, it would appear that the rate of mortality was equal to forty per cent of the whole number under care. Making every allowance for the unusually low physical condition of the class of infants admitted to this Home, it must still be admitted that the death-rate is very great. It is suggested by the managers that an infirmary for sick infants should be attached to the Institution, where they may receive such special medical care and nursing as their ailments demand. I would strongly recommend that the suggestion be acted upon and that additional Provincial aid to a small extent be granted to assist in defraying the increased expenses that would have to be incurred in this laudable effort of the lady managers to save infant life.[119]

The province acted on Langmuir's recommendation: the Infants' Home was given an annual grant of $200 for its infirmary[120] and later the provincial grant respecting unmarried mothers who remained in the institution to act as "mother nurses" was raised to ten cents per day. The establishment of the infirmary and the extended use of the policy of having all children breast fed seemed to have the desired effect, and the mortality rate dropped from 40 per cent in 1877 to 33 per cent in 1878[121] and to 14 per cent in 1882,[122] before beginning to rise again to higher figures by the mid-eighties.[123]

Meanwhile, an institution, the Bethlehem Home for the Friendless, had opened in Ottawa, also to care for infants, but employing "artificial" feeding. The home appeared to be working under various handicaps, and these combined to produce almost total failure of the institution to save the lives of the infants admitted.[124] Christie, after commenting on the high death rate in 1882 and attributing its cause to artificial feeding, seemed to regard the matter as closed. The following year, he reported without comment the sombre record of 199 deaths in a year in which there had been 224 admissions.[125] Similarly, as the death rate climbed in the infirmary section of the Infants Home, Toronto, exceeding 50 per cent in 1889,[126] Christie was prepared to

---

[119]*Ibid.*, 1878, no. 4, p. 224.   [120]*Ibid.*, 1880, no. 8, p. 276.
[121]*Ibid.*, 1879, no. 8, p. 237.   [122]*Ibid.*, 1882, no. 8, p. 298.
[123]Further information on this institution is provided in: Elspeth A. Latimer, "Methods of Child Care as Reflected in the Infants Home of Toronto" (University of Toronto, unpublished M.S.W. thesis, 1953), pp. 11–37.
[124]Ontario, *Sessional Papers*, 1882, no. 8, p. 313.
[125]*Ibid.*, 1884, no. 32, p. 63.   [126]*Ibid.*, 1889, no. 11, p. 65.

accept the explanation that "this largely increased death-rate . . . has been due to disease of an hereditary character"[127] and to consider that the province had no further responsibility in the matter. Therefore, Langmuir's initial attempt to meet the situation in the Infants' Home represents the only significant effort made by the inspectors to deal with perhaps the most serious situation coming within the scope of their office.

As the inspectors' experience in working with the children's institutions lengthened, they showed a growing appreciation that children's needs were not being fully met merely by adequate food, clothing, shelter, education, and health. Dr. O'Reilly was the most vigorous and consistent of the inspectors in expressing this point of view. Christie showed some awareness of the limitations of large institutions in the nurture and development of children:

. . . the congregating of large numbers of children renders it impossible to treat or deal with them in any other way than as a mass, instead of as individuals. This individual treatment is one of the most important factors in the proper management of an Orphanage. A child brought up, looked upon and treated as one out of so many children who have to be washed, dressed, fed, taught, and put to bed at certain stated times, loses all individuality, becomes part of a machine, and when sent out in the world is almost helpless.[128]

Christie's views on this matter were probably useful in combating "the tendency . . . to enlarge the scope of institutions already extensive enough, instead of to found new ones to meet increased wants."[129] However, the fact that he was warning against "erecting huge buildings capable of holding five or six hundred" suggests that many of the institutions in the province had already become too large.[130] It also raises doubts about the extent of individual treatment in the existing institutions, even the best of which seem to have been sparsely staffed.

In contrast to his understanding of the need for individual treatment was Christie's attitude, and that of the other inspectors, to evidences of behaviour problems presented by the children. In 1884, Christie

[127]*Ibid.*
[128]*Ibid.*, 1884, no. 32, p. 32.
[129]*Ibid.*
[130]At the end of the previous fiscal year, one institution had some 250 residents, another had just over 150, and three others had a few over 100 (Ontario, *Sessional Papers*, 1884, no. 32, p. 33). By 1893, the number of institutions with over 100 children had dropped from five to four, two with between 120 and 130 children, one with over 190 and one with 276.

gave the following account of a situation he had come upon during his examination of the House of Providence Orphan Asylum, Kingston:

The Sisters in charge called my attention to a boy, about six years of age, who had manifested an alarming amount of youthful depravity. Although prepossessing in appearance, he seemed to be possessed with destructive propensities of no ordinary character. Amongst his latest efforts was an attempt to blow up the Institution by putting gunpowder in the kitchen stove, and upon being detected, he repeated the attempt by pouring a quantity of powder in an interstice of the floor, but fortunately was caught in the act of trying to fire it with a match.[131]

The inability of the inspectors to offer the institutions help in dealing with serious behaviour problems of this kind reflected the limitations of contemporary knowledge about children, particularly about children deprived of normal care. In contrast to the situation in the fields of corrections and of special education for the deaf or the blind, the inspectors would have found little by way of either authoritative literature or authenticated experience in other forms upon which to draw. Thus, in approaching their implied responsibility to give consultative help and leadership to the children's institutions, the inspectors were handicapped by the state of the behavioural sciences and of the field of child welfare.

The inspectors might, none the less, have been expected to discuss the broader issues respecting dependent and neglected children more fully than they did. It is curious to find that the inspectors in the pre-Confederation period, though having little contact with child welfare except through their work in the field of corrections, interested themselves more deeply in the subject than did their counterparts in the post-Confederation period. Perhaps by this later period the development of children's institutions in all the major centres seemed to be meeting the more obvious manifestations of the problem to a degree that had not been true prior to Confederation. Yet, one might still have expected the inspectors to give some attention to four important questions: the adequacy with which the institutions were performing their self-appointed task of caring for children without families; the extent to which they were finding homes for children in the younger age group; the extent to which children who remained in the institutions to the normal age of discharge were prepared for meeting life in the outer world; and the extent to which the work of the institutions was meeting the total problem of neglected and dependent children in the community. There is little evidence to indicate that the

[131]Ontario, *Sessional Papers*, 1885, no. 40, p. 55.

inspectors addressed themselves seriously to any of these problems. Although critical of many aspects of the plant, operation, and programmes of the homes, they did not question the major purposes of the institutions or their success in achieving them. On the few occasions that they did discuss these matters, the inspectors were unstintingly and uncritically laudatory.

The inspectors were also remarkably silent on the degree to which the institutions were performing the function of placement, which many of their acts of incorporation had identified as one of their major purposes. There are only a few references to young children being placed for adoption.[132] Towards the end of the period, the inspectors did show an interest in the methods being used for placing, as apprentices or in less formal work situations, children who had reached the discharge age,[133] but their references to such matters were random and descriptive. They did not seem to feel called upon to express any critical judgments on the placement programmes or to give any leadership respecting them, and they accepted at face value the claims of one or two institutions which had organized placement programmes for older children that these were wholly successful.[134]

The records and reports of the inspectors, especially after the resignation of Langmuir, were particularly deficient relative to the fundamental question of the extent to which the voluntary institutions were substantially meeting the problem of neglected children. When new institutions opened or closed, one finds in their reports no assessment of the effect of these events on the needs of the children in the community. In 1885, for example, the Bethlehem Home for the Friendless was dropped from the list of institutions assisted under the Charity Aid Act. Although it had been notably unsuccessful in saving the lives of infants, the question of alternative provisions for them inevitably arises; yet, it was neither asked nor answered in the inspectors' reports. The advanced and constructive thinking with which the inspectors must be credited in many areas of social welfare has little parallel in the field of child welfare.

Magdalen Institutions

Magdalen institutions, as we have seen, were grouped with children's institutions under schedule C of the Charity Aid Act, and in the first

---

132*Ibid.*, 1888, no. 40, p. 47.
133*Ibid.*, 1892, no. 6, pp. 76, 92; 1894, no. 28, p. 75.
134*Ibid.*, 1888, no. 40, p. 47; 1894, no. 28, p. 75.

few years after the passage of the act data on these institutions and on the children's homes were presented in the same tables in the inspector's reports. Separate reporting was initiated in 1878[135] and continued throughout the remainder of the period. In 1873, the two magdalen institutions covered by the act were located in Toronto and Ottawa; the former had cared for 69 residents during the preceding year and the latter 96. Together they had provided 33,580 days of care and had a total of 100 residents when the fiscal year ended.[136] Within the next ten years the number of magdalen institutions rose to five, with the number of persons cared for in them reaching its highest point in the mid-1880's. In 1884, some 68,026 days of care were provided to a total of 474 inmates, the number in residence at the end of the year standing at 176.[137] By 1893 two of the institutions, the Home for the Friendless, Hamilton, and the Women's Refuge and Infants' Home, London, had been reclassified as orphan asylums,[138] and in 1893 the Good Shepherd Magdalen Asylum, Ottawa, ceased to appear in schedule C, while an institution called the Refuge of our Lady of Charity, with a similar programme, appeared for the first time among the refuges under schedule B.[139] Thus, as the period closed, there were only two magdalen asylums listed under the act, both located in Toronto. In 1893 they provided 26,209 days of care to a total of 133 residents.[140]

The change in the status of three out of five of the homes is indicative of some lack of definition as to what constituted a magdalen asylum. In fact, all of the institutions referred to by this name appeared to have had varied admission policies and programmes. In his report on the Magdalen Asylum, Ottawa, in 1875, Langmuir reported, for example, that the institution combined "various aims for the reclamation of fallen women," of whom there were 22 in the home, with the care of 29 "young girls who give evidence of being inclined to vicious courses" and 30 "young children (girls) whose parents have either abandoned them or utterly neglected them, and who, if not cared for, would, in all likelihood, fall into crime and vice."[141] At the time, Langmuir expressed no objection to this association of various types of residents, and he concurred in similar arrangements in the Magdalen Asylum in Hamilton where he noted that "not more than two inmates are allowed to occupy a sleeping room," and where "some attempt is

[135]*Ibid.*, 1878, no. 4, p. 179.
[136]*Ibid.*, 1874 (vol. VI), no. 2, pp. 135, 137.
[137]*Ibid.*, 1885, no. 40, pp. 64–66.
[138]*Ibid.*, 1888, no. 40, pp. 56–57, 66–67.   [139]*Ibid.*, 1893, no. 10, pp. 40–41.
[140]*Ibid.*, 1894, no. 28, pp. 103–4.   [141]*Ibid.*, 1875, no. 4, p. 184.

made to classify them according to antecedents and general conduct."[142] He was highly critical of the Magdalen Asylum, Toronto,
however, where "confirmed prostitutes . . . and others who, although
fallen from virtue, had not yet entered upon a life of prostitution . . .
were associated together in the same dormitories and work-rooms."[143]
Langmuir was convinced that such association would render the work
of the institution fruitless, remarking on one occasion that "separation
and classification . . . are above all things the great desiderata in
institutions of this class."[144] He came, in particular, to object to magdalen asylums' combining their care of "fallen women" with the care
of "respectable girls . . . even if the two branches were entirely
separated,"[145] and on these grounds he recommended against provincial
grants to the Refuge for Fallen Women in Ottawa.

The attempt by the inspectors to have the institutions limit their
work to "fallen women" alone, however, did not meet with success.
By the end of the period, while the term magdalen asylum
appeared to be going out of fashion and the remaining institutions
were referring to themselves as female or industrial refuges,[146] their
programmes and admission policies appeared to be the same as in
the 1870's. The residents of the Good Shepherd Female Refuge,
Toronto, were composed of three classes—old ladies, destitute girls,
and fallen women—and the sister institution in Ottawa was described
as having "a branch department in which are domiciled children from
two to fourteen years of age."[147]

Although having relatively little to say about the operation and
programmes of the magdalen institutions, the inspectors indicated their
belief that the work the homes were undertaking for the reclamation
of fallen women was necessary and that it deserved public support.[148]
In 1883 Dr. O'Reilly expressed his satisfaction "that charitable people
were waking up to the importance of this much-neglected branch of
Christian work,"[149] and that the prospects for the institutions which had
been "struggling in the throes of poverty"[150] were thereby improved.

[142]Ibid., 1878, no. 4, p. 233.
[143]Ibid., 1877, no. 2, p. 201.   [144]Ibid., 1879, no. 8, p. 251.
[145]Ibid., p. 252.   [146]Ibid., 1894, no. 28, pp. 105–7.
[147]Ibid., 1892, no. 6, p. 97.   [148]Ibid., 1879, no. 8, p. 7.
[149]Ibid., 1882–83, no. 8, p. 64 (refuge and orphanage report).
[150]Ibid. Unlike other types of institutions under the Charity Aid Act, the
magdalen asylums derived a significant income from the work of their residents—
usually laundry work but also sewing and knitting. Like other enterprises, this
work was affected by business conditions, and the asylum in Ottawa saw its
monthly income fall in 1879 to around $80 from $400 a few years earlier (Ontario,
Sessional Papers, 1880, no. 8, p. 293).

From time to time, nevertheless, the inspectors expressed some concern about the success of the magdalen institutions in achieving their avowed objectives. Noting the rate of turnover of the residents and the number of re-admissions, the inspectors came to the view that the homes would achieve better results if compulsion could be used to extend the stay of their residents.[151] They appeared to feel that there was little likelihood of achieving, through a voluntary programme, the reclamation of women who in many cases "might have been classed as habitual offenders against public morals"[152] and who might more appropriately, in the inspectors' view, have been sentenced to the women's reformatory. This approach to the matter was no doubt prompted by the fact that the magdalen institutions and the local gaols often provided alternative types of temporary shelter for luckless prostitutes. When, for example, the Good Shepherd Magdalen Asylum in Ottawa was unable, through lack of funds, to receive as many applicants as usual, the result was an "abnormally large number of prostitutes . . . in the Ottawa Gaol."[153]

Although mentioning at various times that not all the "fallen women" cared for in the magdalen asylums were prostitutes, the inspectors failed to indicate the extent to which the institutions were caring for unmarried mothers who found it necessary to leave their homes and communities in search of care during their pregnancy, and who needed help in planning for themselves and their children following their confinement. While the magdalen asylum is to be regarded as a predecessor of the home for unmarried mothers of later periods, the inspectors did not identify the care and protection of the unmarried mother as a significant rôle of these institutions; nor did they contribute in any way that is visible in their reports to the development of this necessary type of programme for the unmarried mother and her child.

The Industrial Schools Act

The Industrial Schools Act of 1874[154] ranks with the Charity Aid Act in its importance to institutional care for children during the post-Confederation period. The act may be regarded as a response to the need, described by the inspectors during the Union period, for the creation of a type of institution coming between the public school,

---

[151]Ontario, *Sessional Papers*, 1879, no. 8, p. 249.
[152]*Ibid.*, 1881, no. 8, p. 275.   [153]*Ibid.*
[154]Ontario, *Statutes*, 1874 (1st sess.), c. 29.

which large numbers of neglected children were failing to attend, and the reformatory, which was needed only for children with established records of delinquent behaviour.[155]

The new statute defined industrial schools as schools "in which industrial training is provided and in which children are lodged, clothed and fed, as well as taught." The right to establish such schools was conferred on the boards of public or separate school trustees in the cities. The founding of the schools was not mandatory, but, once established, any such school was initially to be certified by the chief superintendent of education[156] as "fit and proper . . . for the reception of children to be sent there," and henceforth was to "be under the same inspection, and subject to the same laws in all respects, as other schools established by the school corporation," except where such laws were inconsistent with the terms of the act. The act further provided that all rules drafted by the school board for the management and discipline of the school had to be approved by the province before they could be put into effect. The imposition of provincial control in these various ways was not accompanied by any specific assurance of provincial financial support, although the act provided that "in case any money is granted or provided by the Legislature for the support of industrial schools, it shall be the duty of the Chief Superintendent . . . to apportion the money . . . to the several industrial schools in the province."

Admission to a school was limited by the act (as passed in 1874), to children under the age of fourteen committed to the school by police magistrates. The latter were authorized to commit any child coming within any of the following descriptions:

1. Who is found begging or receiving alms or being in any street or public place for the purpose of begging or receiving alms;

[155]The same arguments, favouring residential schools for neglected children, were, of course, frequently repeated in the early post-Confederation period. One formal discussion, which advocated the establishment of industrial schools in Toronto, Ottawa, Hamilton, Kingston, and London, was W. B. McMurrich, "Industrial Schools," *Canadian Monthly*, Nov. 1872, pp. 424–28. See also J. George Hodgins, *The Establishment of Schools and Colleges in Ontario, 1792–1910*, vol. III (Toronto, 1910), pp. 372–75. Hodgins refers to a public meeting in 1868 in Toronto which advocated the establishment of industrial schools by the school board. The board felt it had no power to act, but in 1871, after the new School Act, it sent a committee to the United States to study schools there. It reported in favour of Toronto's establishing such schools, though this would require an amendment to the School Act and provincial financial aid "to cover expenses over and above that which would be incurred for purely educational purposes."

[156]With the establishment of a ministry of education in 1876, the responsibility of certification was assigned to the minister of education.

2. Who is found wandering and not having any home or settled place of abode or proper guardianship, or not having any lawful occupation or business or visible means of subsistence;

3. Who is found destitute, either being an orphan or having a surviving parent who is undergoing penal servitude or imprisonment;

4. Whose parent, step-parent or guardian represents to the police magistrate that he is unable to control the child and that he desires the child to be sent to an industrial school under this act;

5. Who, by reason of the neglect, drunkenness or other vices of parents, is suffered to be growing up without salutary parental control and education, or in circumstances exposing him to lead an idle and dissolute life.

A child could then be detained in an industrial school for any period of time thought necessary by the magistrate for his training, but not beyond his sixteenth birthday. Although residence within the school was regarded as the normal practice, the act made provision for a child "to live at the dwelling of any trustworthy and respectable person," providing that the chief superintendent was informed of the arrangement.

The legislation gave the chief superintendent the right at any time to discharge a child from an industrial school either absolutely or on any conditions he thought appropriate. The school boards were not given as complete rights of discharge, but in the case of a child who had conducted himself well in the school the board could "bind him, with his own consent, apprentice to any trade, calling or service." The board, moreover, could discharge a child to his parents if it was proved "that the parents . . . have reformed and are leading orderly and industrious lives and are in a condition to exercise salutary parental control over their children, and to provide them with proper education and employment."[157]

Parents and guardians could be required under the act to pay the corporation a weekly amount not exceeding one dollar for the maintenance of the child, and when the child, for a year prior to his commital, had not been a resident in the city where the school was established the city could recover the expense of the child's maintenance from the municipality where the child had last resided for a period of one year.

The central purpose of the act was to have the children who were sent to the schools instructed in various "branches of useful knowledge." However, the responsibilities that would have faced any municipal school board attempting to operate an industrial school would

[157]Where the parents were dead, the board could transfer the child to any other suitable person able to assume the same responsibilities.

have gone well beyond educational matters and would have been very different from those attached to the operation of the ordinary public schools. Similarly, the officials of the provincial Department of Education, in carrying out their responsibilities, would have found themselves confronted with a wide range of unfamiliar and complex problems.

Perhaps it was a reluctance to move beyond their normal spheres of responsibility into unfamiliar areas, as much as unwillingness to assume new financial burdens, that deterred the school boards of the cities from undertaking to establish industrial schools. To meet this situation, the Legislature amended the Industrial Schools Act in 1884[158] to provide that a board of school trustees could delegate its "powers, rights and privileges" respecting industrial schools to any incorporated philanthropic society. But, to ensure liaison and a measure of control over the activities of the society by the school board, the new act provided that the chairman and secretary of the board should be members of the board of management of the philanthropic society. The school boards were also to supply the necessary teachers, and, as an emphasis on the educational purpose of the schools, "when practicable" the general superintendent of the institution should be selected from the teachers so appointed. Some control by the province was furnished through the requirement that the by-laws of the society "be subject to the approval of the Lieutenant-Governor in Council."

Although most of the changes made in the act related to the delegation of powers to philanthropic societies, a further provision of importance was the addition of the delinquent to the types of children who could be committed to the schools. The delinquent child was described in the act as one "who has been found guilty of petty crime, and who, in the opinion of the . . . Magistrate . . . should be sent to an industrial school instead of to a gaol or reformatory."[159]

The changes permitting voluntary groups to take the initiative in the establishment of a school succeeded at last in bringing the act to life, although by 1893 only two schools, the Victoria Industrial School for Boys and the Alexandra Industrial School for Girls, had been established, both in the Toronto area. These schools and the movement that brought about their establishment, however, had an influence on child welfare that extended well beyond the work of the institutions themselves.

[158]Ontario, Statutes, 1884, c. 46.
[159]Ibid., s. 7, ss. 6. The new act provided for cases to be heard before county court judges and justices of the peace.

The first of the schools, established at Mimico in 1887,[160] was one result of the growing concern for social welfare problems felt by some of the prominent citizens of Toronto, many of whom had taken part in other endeavours in the fields of charities and corrections. The group forming the Industrial School Association of Toronto included, for example, E. A. Meredith and John Langton who had both retired to Toronto after outstanding careers in the Dominion civil service and were able to help in bringing to fruition one of the ideas they had first advocated some twenty-seven years earlier as members of the board of inspectors during the Union period. W. H. Howland's concern about the social problems affecting youth that were brought to his attention as mayor of the city was such that he undertook the chairmanship of the board of management of the association. The association's vice-presidents included Goldwin Smith and John Macdonald, both of whom had played important rôles in a variety of other social welfare endeavours in the city. Its honorary solicitor was W. B. McMurrich who had been a vigorous advocate of industrial schools long before the adoption of the act in 1874. The board of governors of the association, representing Toronto's élite[161] from the bench, the university, the professions, and business, included Samuel Blake, William and Henry Gooderham, and John Ross Robertson of the Toronto *Telegram*. The press was also represented by John Cameron, editor of the *Globe*. Thus, the composition of the board of governors at once expressed and ensured broad and generous support for the erection of the first buildings. The planning of the school, its opening by the Governor-General, and its first annual meeting aroused wide interest and marked the readiness of the public to move forward in corrections and child welfare through supporting projects that gave promise of dealing constructively with child delinquency and neglect.

The first fifty boys admitted to the new school gave some indication of the rôle it would play in child welfare and corrections. Twenty-five of the group were sent "on the application of a parent or guardian who charged them with being uncontrollable and drifting into criminal habits."[162] The remainder "were sent as vagrants, waifs, or charged with petty thefts; one was charged with drunkenness." Although the number admitted at the request of parents seems unduly large, the

[160]Ontario, *Sessional Papers*, 1888, no. 7, pp. 253–62.

[161]The president was William Proudfoot who held the judicial position of vice-chancellor. Daniel Wilson, president of the University of Toronto, was a vice-president, and William Mulock, vice-chancellor of the university, was a member of the board of governors.

[162]Ontario, *Sessional Papers*, 1888, no. 7, p. 253.

initial group and later admissions indicated that the school was receiving children of all of the "descriptions" set out in the act.

The school operated on what was described as the "family plan" or "cottage system." The boys lived in a cottage home under the care of a matron and guard who, in the words of the annual report, "act as 'mother' and 'father' of the 'family' and who endeavour to have the home feeling restored and implanted in the breast of each boy."[163] The "cottages," however, were designed to accommodate fifty boys, and thus the expectation that a family atmosphere could be achieved appeared to be somewhat unrealistic.

The programme of the school placed more emphasis on training through work than on academic education. Four hours a day were devoted to the former, and three hours in the late afternoon to the latter.[164] Some emphasis was given to recreation, and discipline appears to have been maintained with little recourse to negative measures.[165]

At the end of a year and a half of operations, the board of management was planning to double the accommodation of the school, and it felt sufficiently convinced of the success of the undertaking to urge the establishment of a similar institution for girls as "a place of education and training for the waifs of the city and Province."[166] By 1892, this goal had been achieved, and Ontario had thereby acquired for both boys and girls a new type of institutional resource. Two years earlier, one of the purposes that the industrial schools were expected to serve had been outlined in "An Act respecting the Commitment of Persons of Tender Years."[167] This statute prevented the confinement in the boys' reformatory of boys who had been convicted of offences and who were under the age of thirteen years,[168] while authorizing the commitment of such offenders in industrial schools.

Although the programme of the industrial schools was not basically different from that of the boys' reformatory or the girls' refuge or from that of a number of the voluntary children's institutions, admissions to the industrial schools, unlike those to the voluntary institutions, were defined by legislation and made only on the authority of the courts.

163Ibid.

164Ibid., 1889, no. 6, p. 225.

165Ibid., p. 224. Much was made in the school's second report of the absence of attempts at escape, even when the boys were given a day on their own at the Toronto Exhibition.

166Ibid.

167Ontario, Statutes, 1890, c. 76.

168This provision was somewhat modified by another statute passed at the same time, entitled "An Act respecting the custody of Juvenile Offenders" (ibid., c. 75).

And although the schools were built through voluntary initiative and with more private than public money,[169] there was a much greater degree of public responsibility than in the case of the incorporated and grant-aided children's institutions. What emerged from the development of the two industrial schools in Toronto was the application of a significant type of organization and shared public and private responsibility of which the main elements were the following: provincial legislation and supervision, together with some financial support by way of annual grants; municipal financial responsibility for maintenance payments for children committed to the schools and for the provision of teaching staff, the right of the municipality to make further grants, and the right to representation on the board of the philanthropic society formed to develop and operate the schools; and private participation in initiating, developing, operating, and financing the institutions within the framework of provincial law.

Reports of the Industrial School Association were included as appendices in two successive annual reports of the Department of Education. Thereafter, to the end of the period, there were no further references to the schools, indicating that the departmental administrators[170] regarded them as peripheral, if not foreign, to the main work of the department and suggesting that the initiative for the development of industrial schools in other centres would not come from the Department of Education.

Non-institutional Measures for the Protection of Women and Children

Although the period from the mid-1870's to the late 1880's was one in which concern for the welfare of children was expressed primarily through the development of institutional programmes, it also witnessed significant advances in other areas of importance to children. Through statutes passed in 1877, 1881, and 1887[171] the position of the child requiring a guardian because of the loss of one or both of his parents was significantly improved over that set out in the act of 1855 when, among other limitations, the mother could be made the legal guardian

169The province made a grant of $6,000 in 1887 and $1,000 in 1888; the city made a grant of $3,000 in the latter year. The extent of private giving exceeded $8,000 in 1888 and $5,000 in 1889.

170The deputy minister of education from 1876 to 1889 was Dr. J. G. Hodgins who gave outstanding leadership in social welfare endeavours in Toronto and who was interested in the development of industrial schools. The decline in the department's interest in industrial schools appears to have coincided with his retirement from the post of deputy minister.

171Ontario, *Statutes*, 1877, c. 8; 1881, c. 16; 1887, c. 21.

of her child only to his twelfth year. The newer legislation not only removed the existing limitations on the mother's right to be appointed her child's guardian, but provided, as well, that the court could appoint the mother of a minor to be his guardian even when this was contrary to provisions made by the father in his will.[172] In addition, the mother acquired equal rights with the father to appoint guardians for their children in the event of both their deaths.[173] In instances where the mother named a guardian to act jointly with the child's father following her death, the court was empowered to confirm this arrangement if it was convinced that the father was unfit to be the child's sole guardian.[174]

These changes thus reflected an advance in the legal status of women and a better appreciation of the importance to a child of his mother's care, and indicated that the traditional legal position of the father, which had emphasized his prerogatives rather than his responsibilities, was giving way to an emphasis on the protection of wives and children. A further and more direct affirmation of this emphasis was embodied in an act, passed in 1888, "respecting the Maintenance of Wives deserted by their Husbands,"[175] which provided that a husband who had deserted or was failing to provide for his wife and family could be required by the court to pay a weekly amount for their support.

During the 1880's, the province also began to take measures for the protection of children in the industrial plants that were rapidly multiplying in number and growing in size with the bourgeoning industrialization of southern Ontario. Public attention was drawn to working conditions in factories by a commission appointed by the Dominion government in 1881 "to enquire into the working of Mills and Factories of the Dominion, and the labor employed therein."[176] The immediate impetus for the inquiry was the request for action by the member of Parliament for Cornwall, Dr. Darby Bergin, who was deeply concerned about working conditions in factories and particularly about the employment of children as factory hands, with no provision being made for their education.[177] As a remedy for this situation, Dr. Bergin advocated the "half-time system" which had been developed in England and under which children employed in factories attended school during half of the working day.

[172]*Ibid.*, 1877, c. 8.   [173]*Ibid.*, 1887, c. 21.
[174]*Ibid.*   [175]*Ibid.*, 1888, c. 23.
[176]Canada, *Sessional Papers*, 1882, no. 42, p. 1.
[177]*Ibid.*, no. 83, pp. 1–3.

The two commissioners made a six months' tour through five provinces, finding many conditions in the plants that required remedial action, none more urgently than the unrestricted employment of children. When they attempted to determine the number of children employed, they found that many children did not know their own ages.[178] It was also apparent that some employers were representing children as older than they were. Thus, the figure of 2,295 children under fourteen years of age, of whom about one-tenth were under ten, out of a total of 43,511 workers in all the plants covered, was recognized as conservative. The commissioners discovered that the employment of children was increasing, with the supply in some localities unequal to the demand. Some of the children were working to help support their families where the father was dead or missing. There were also cases of children preferring to work rather than attend school, and of others being required to work by idle parents "who live on the earnings of children" or who, though having "good positions as mechanics," made their children work from "cupidity."

The long hours which the children worked were described by the commissioners in the following terms:

It must be borne in mind that the children invariably work as many hours as adults, and if not compelled, are requested to work overtime when circumstances so demand, which has not been unusual of late in most lines of manufactures. The appearance and condition of the children in the after part of the day, such as may be witnessed in the months of July and August, was anything but inviting or desirable. They have to be up at the mills or factories at 6:30 A.M., necessitating their being up from 5:30 to 6 o'clock for their morning meal, some having to walk a distance of half a mile or more to their work. This undeniably is too heavy a strain on children of tender years and is utterly condemned by all except those who are being directly benefited by such labour.

The conditions in many plants in which the children worked (along with their elders) were equally undesirable, and poor ventilation, overcrowding, dampness, bad sanitary provisions, and accident hazards were reported by the commissioners to be common in a large number of the factories they visited.

The commissioners found little interest in the proposal for combining work and education. They noted that it would violate Ontario's existing school attendance law which, though ineffective through lack of machinery for enforcement, required children from seven to twelve years to attend school for at least four months each year. Although

[178]This and the following references to the commission's report are from *ibid.*, no. 42, pp. 1–16.

the commissioners were not explicit on the question, they seemed to feel that the problem of child labour could best be handled through the strict enforcement of school attendance, at least until the age of twelve. This was the course recommended to them by the Trades' Council of Toronto, and the commissioners felt that most employers would not oppose school attendance laws as long as the supply of child labour was thereby also cut off from their competitors. The commissioners noted that "a demand is gaining for intelligent and educated labor in our mills and factories."

Because the conditions censured in the Dominion government's inquiry existed to at least as great a degree in Ontario as in the other provinces surveyed, action by the province was called for, and in 1884 the government responded by introducing "an Act for the Protection of Persons employed in Factories."[179] This was a strong and comprehensive measure covering all the matters which the commissioners had reported as constituting a threat to health and safety. It provided for the appointment of provincial inspectors to enforce the act, and imposed severe penalties for breaches of its terms. The act prohibited the employment of boys under twelve and girls under fourteen years of age. Boys between twelve and fourteen and girls between fourteen and eighteen, as well as women, were not to be employed for more than ten hours a day or more than sixty hours a week. To deal with those parents who encouraged or forced their children to work in factories, the act provided that they, like the employer, could be fined or imprisoned if their children worked in factories in contravention of the legislation.

In 1888, similar legislation, the Shops' Act,[180] was passed to limit the number of hours that boys under fourteen and girls under sixteen years of age could work in wholesale and retail establishments. Although the act permitted as many as seventy-four hours' work, including rest periods, during the week, this represented an improvement over what actually prevailed in some shops at the time. Unlike the Factories' Act, however, the new statute did not provide for the appointment of provincial inspectors and enforcement was left to the municipalities or to individuals who might be prepared to charge employers and parents with violation of the legislation.

Associated with the conviction that children should not be overworked in shops and factories was the concern for other aspects of their moral, physical, and educational well-being. In 1886, legislation

179Ontario, *Statutes*, 1884, c. 39.
180*Ibid.*, 1888, c. 33.

was passed by which the keeper of a billiard or pool room could be fined for admitting any minor under the age of sixteen years,[181] and in 1892 an act[182] was adopted providing a minimum fine of ten dollars against any person "who either directly or indirectly" supplied tobacco in any form to a minor under eighteen years of age. A year earlier, the Legislature had greatly strengthened school attendance provisions with "an Act respecting Truancy and Compulsory School Attendance."[183] Although previous legislation had accepted one hundred days of attendance in a school year as sufficient,[184] the new act required all children between eight and fourteen years of age to attend school for the full term in which it was open. The provision was to be enforced through truant officers appointed, according to the type of local government, by police commissioners, municipal councils, or school trustees. By way of removing any inducement for the employment of children during the school term, the act also imposed penalties on any person who employed a child under the school-leaving age.[185]

These measures to promote the education of children and to provide them with various forms of protection, supplemented by the advancements taking place in the field of public health, offered the average child growing up towards the end of the period improved prospects of survival and the possibility of wider opportunities as he reached maturity. But these advantages, available to the child living within a strong family unit, were out of reach of many other children. Children who suffered the loss of their parents or who were born out of wedlock, or whose parents were unable to deal with the problems of life in the industrial towns and cities, faced numerous hazards. For many, the orphanages provided maintenance and care, but through the 1870's and '80's increasing numbers of children were reported to be growing up virtually uncared for and with little prospect of becoming useful members of the community. The situation would no doubt have been substantially improved if industrial schools had been established in all the cities of the province, and if there had been a further development of other types of children's institutions. There was a growing public concern, however, about the effectiveness of prolonged institutional care as a preparation for adulthood. Increasing interest was being expressed in alternatives to institutional care, although there could be no return to the exclusive reliance on apprenticeship that

[181]*Ibid.*, 1886, c. 41. Half the fine so imposed was to be paid to the informer.
[182]*Ibid.*, 1892, c. 52.   [183]*Ibid.*, 1891, c. 56.
[184]*Ibid.*, 1885, c. 49, s. 210.   [185]*Ibid.*, 1891, c. 56.

had been characteristic of much of Upper Canada's early history. Thus, by the latter part of the 1880's attention turned to the possibility of developing or extending other types of arrangements that would give children the opportunity of growing up within a family setting.

Placement of Children

This awakening interest in placement was stimulated by a number of developments. One was the experience in extra-mural placement that had been built up over the years by the children's institutions themselves. With some of these, as we have observed, the placement of children with families had been a principal object at the time of their founding, and although, in general, they eventually came to regard intra-mural care as their chief function, all were obliged to interest themselves in the placement of children who had reached the ages of twelve or fourteen or, at the most, sixteen. A further stimulus was provided by the reports of the success of non-institutional care in other jurisdictions. For many years, the press and magazines had carried reports of the programmes of Charles Loring Brace in the United States,[186] and Mrs. Nassau Senior and Miss Florence Hill in England.[187]

More direct testimony was provided by a number of the American authorities attending the meetings in Toronto of the National Prison Association in 1887. Gardiner Tufts, for example, referred to the work of the state board of charities in Massachusetts whose agents had placed many hundreds of children in foster homes.[188] Warren Spalding, in referring to the work of child placement by a society for the prevention of cruelty to children in the same state, expressed the view "that the last thing that should be done for any person, young or old, is to put him into an institution."[189] Francis Wayland referred to Connecticut's laws on neglected and abused children which included a strict prohibition upon maintaining children under three years of age in alms-houses and encouraged their placement in families.

Similar reports of non-institutional programmes for children were presented at the annual conference of the American Humane Society held in Toronto in October 1888, and the *Globe* drew particular attention to the work of the Children's Aid Society of Pennsylvania in placing children in private families.[190] By the early 1890's, as well,

[186]*Globe*, April 18, 1874.
[187]*Canadian Monthly*, Sept. 1877, p. 294.
[188]National Prison Association of the United States, *Proceedings of the Annual Congress, Toronto, 1887* (Chicago, 1889), p. 257.
[189]*Ibid.*, p. 216.   [190]*Globe*, Oct. 19, 1888.

reports of the success of foster-home placements in Australia had gained some currency[191] and were to influence J. M. Gibson, the provincial secretary, in the formulation of the child protection legislation of 1893.[192]

IMMIGRANT CHILDREN

Within the province itself, however, a massive demonstration of the placement of children within families was provided by the sponsors and managers of projects for the immigration to Canada of children from the British Isles. Under these projects, homes were found in Ontario for nearly 23,000 children during the period from 1868 to 1893.[193] This extensive movement of British children to Canada and its effect on public attitudes towards child welfare are among the unexplored areas in the Canadian history of child welfare.[194] Nevertheless, the placing of immigrant children on this scale must have helped materially in preparing the public in Ontario for the rôle it would be called upon to play after 1893 in meeting the need for good homes for local children who were growing up without proper parental care.

The immigration of British children to Ontario was initiated in 1868 by Miss M. Rye who established at Niagara a centre for the reception, placement, and supervision of children and who, except for two years in the mid-seventies when her activities were impeded by British officials, brought out groups of children annually throughout the period. She was followed two years later by Miss A. McPherson who developed a somewhat larger programme, and by a number of other sponsoring individuals or groups, including Cardinal Manning, Dr. Barnardo, and the directors of the Shaftesbury's Boys' Home. The total number of children brought out under these various auspices is shown in Table XV. The number arriving annually in Ontario under these projects rose to over 500 early in the 1870's and, after falling below this figure for five years, beginning in 1875 rapidly increased to over 1,000 in the early 1880's, and during the last decade of the period averaged more than 1,500.

The work of the sponsoring individuals and groups reflected the

[191]The work in Victoria, for example, was reviewed by the Royal Commission on the Prison and Reformatory System of Ontario in 1890 (Ontario, *Sessional Papers*, 1891, no. 18, pp. 86–87).

[192]Bain, "The Role of J. J. Kelso," p. 99.

[193]Ontario, *Sessional Papers*, 1894, no. 15, p. 15.

[194]Various proposals for bringing immigrant children from the British Isles to Upper Canada began to be made at least as early as the 1820's. See Upper Canada Sundries, Otway to Maitland, Sept. 10, 1827; Radcliffe to Hillier, July 13, 1829.

TABLE XV

BRITISH IMMIGRANT CHILDREN BROUGHT TO ONTARIO, 1868–1893

Name of sponsor	Location of home	Number of children
Miss M. Rye	Niagara	3,402
Miss A. McPherson	Stratford	4,893
Mrs. Billborough Wallace	Belleville	3,532
Mrs. J. T. Middlemore	London	1,778
Rev. Dr. Stephenson	Hamilton	1,140
Dr. T. J. Barnardo	Toronto*	4,866
Shaftesbury's Boys' Home	Hamilton	849
Cardinal Manning and others	Ottawa	1,402
Mr. W. Quarrier	Belleville†	1,001
TOTAL		22,863

SOURCE: Ontario, *Sessional Papers*, 1894, no. 15, p. 15.
*Dr. Barnardo also had a receiving centre at Peterborough.
†Mrs. Wallace's centre was used for children sent out by Quarrier (Ontario, *Sessional Papers*, 1880, no. 6, p. 23).

interest of philanthropic groups in Great Britain, not only in "rescuing" children from poor surroundings, including the English work-houses, but also in seeking to secure for them the best future possible. A set-back in the work was experienced in the mid-1870's as a result of the report of an official inquiry undertaken for the British government into the operations of the two initial projects, but it was only temporary because the conclusions of the report were challenged by the findings of an inspection ordered by the Dominion government. These findings were reviewed, along with additional evidence, by a select committee of the Canadian House of Commons which concluded that the "children have been carefully placed, and are, with very trifling exceptions, doing well."[195]

The Dominion government expressed further interest in the projects through financial aid[196] and through continued visits of inspection by its immigration agents to the homes in which the children were placed. Although these visits were made mainly with a view to ascertaining whether a satisfactory type of child was being sent out by the sponsors, the agents also reported on the type of treatment the children were receiving. In general, their reports were favourable. The Dominion

[195]Canada, *Journals*, 1876, Appendix 8, p. 2.
[196]This took more than one form. In 1875, the Dominion government made a special grant of $1,000 to Miss Rye "to assist in keeping open the home at Niagara" (*Canadian Monthly*, Sept. 1877, p. 297). Later assistance took the form of a bonus of $2 for each immigrant child brought into the country. See, for example, Canada, *Public Accounts*, 1875, p. 125; 1879, p. 119; 1881, p. 129; 1883, p. 137; 1885, pp. 137–45.

immigration agent at Kingston, for example, reported as follows in 1888:

I have inspected a large number of children brought to Canada from England this year, and am still of opinion that this branch of immigration is of great service to the Province and to the children placed with farmers in my district. . . . During my several annual inspections I have been agreeably surprised at the very few unsuitable children, and at the general satisfaction given by them to the persons with whom they are placed, as well as the good homes that have been secured and the kind treatment generally shown to the children. Of course, there are exceptions, but these are rare indeed.[197]

In other reports, the federal agents described and discussed the work of the juvenile immigration agencies in the reception of the children and in the securing, approving, and supervising of the homes in which they were placed. The children were normally brought to the reception centres and rapidly sent forward to pre-selected farm families chosen by the staff of the centres on the basis of written applications that were supplemented by references from a minister or public official. The superintendent or other staff members[198] usually visited the children at least once a year,[199] and if they found that a placement was unsatisfactory they arranged for the child to move to another home or to return for a time to the centre. The children could communicate with the centre by mail if they had any need for assistance.[200]

The basis on which the children were placed by the various sponsors is not entirely clear, but it appears to have involved, in all cases, some formal contract or indenture indicating the terms on which the placement was made and setting out the respective obligations of the head of the family and the child. It was normal to include a requirement that the child attend school for at least part of the year, and this obligation appears to have been honoured—the Dominion agent for Hamilton reporting that "most of the children attend day school during the winter and the majority attend all the year round, whilst all attend Sunday School and church with very few exceptions."[201] The agents occasionally referred to the adoption of the children, but the contem-

[197]Ontario, *Sessional Papers*, 1889, no. 18, p. 6.

[198]Dr. Barnardo stated that his agency had "a staff of skilled and experienced visitors whose whole time is occupied in making surprise visits all over the country. Ladies only visit the girls and men visit the boys" (*ibid.*, 1891, no. 18, p. 440).

[199]The Dominion agent based in Hamilton was critical of Miss Rye's failure to have a policy of regular visiting, in contrast to Miss McPherson, Mr. Stephenson, and the Earl of Shaftesbury's Home (*ibid.*, 1889, no. 18, p. 15).

[200]*Ibid.*, 1891, no. 18, p. 441. Dr. Barnardo provided his children with stamped and addressed cards or envelopes.

[201]*Ibid.*, 1887, no. 19, p. 18.

porary use of the term is not clear. A writer in the *Canadian Monthly* referred to adoption as the condition in which the child was "treated in all respects as one of the master's and mistresses own children,"[202] but he threw some doubt on the application of his definition when he indicated that a girl could be said to be adopted when she took her meals with the family and otherwise joined in its activities.

Although the province of Ontario in the early years after Confederation took advantage of its concurrent power with the Dominion government in the field of immigration to develop a vigorous immigration programme, it played a relatively minor rôle in respect to the various projects for the immigration of British children. Its agents who met the ships arriving in Quebec and travelled with the immigrants to Ontario provided various forms of help to the juvenile groups, on some occasions offering free meals during the journey.[203] For a few years in the mid-1870's as well, the province provided a bonus of six dollars for each immigrant child, but this was discontinued after 1878.[204] From then on and generally throughout the period, the province seemed prepared to have the Dominion government assume the major responsibility for this type of immigration. There is, moreover, no evidence that the Provincial government saw any need to integrate the work of the receiving centres with that of the other children's institutions already engaged in the placement of older children.

The government's failure to play a more significant rôle in so important a development within the province may be regarded largely as a reflection of its general lack of comprehensive measures for children. Its approach may also have been affected by the public criticism to which the projects of juvenile immigration were exposed; for although they were, in general, well accepted they were also, from time to time, under attack. One type of allegation made against the projects was that they were knowingly bringing worthless and dangerous delinquents into the province and thereby increasing pauperism and crime.[205] A further criticism was that the youths brought in were taking jobs from native Canadians.[206] Although these and related

---

[202]*Canadian Monthly*, Sept. 1877, p. 296.

[203]Ontario, *Sessional Papers*, 1878, no. 35, pp. 6–7.

[204]*Ibid.*, p. viii; 1880, no. 6, p. viii.

[205]*Queen's College Journal*, June 1888, for example, while not wholly critical of juvenile immigration, referred to the trouble caused by some immigrant children, as well as adults, who had "turned out to be veritable plague spots in the physical and moral life of the community."

[206]This charge was made by D. J. O'Donoghue before the Royal Commission of 1890. In comparing the placement policies of some of the juvenile immigration agencies with that of St. Patrick's Orphan Asylum, Ottawa, he stated that

charges did not assume proportions that necessitated a public inquiry, they may have been sufficient to cause the provincial government to avoid any unnecessary identification with the projects.

INFANTS

Despite the growing use and success of placements for older children, the experience in Ontario of the employment of foster homes for infants was less reassuring. The mortality rates in these homes and in the baby farms which had made their appearance in the larger urban centres were even higher than the rates in the few institutions established especially for infants. The Infants' Home of Toronto was established because of concern over the conditions known to exist in the private boarding homes,[207] and for many years after its founding it continued to receive children who, often at the point of death, were brought from these homes.

Although the deplorable conditions in the infant boarding homes were frequently brought to the attention of government and public alike by the directors of the Infants' Home and had been the subject of editorial criticism for many years,[208] no action had been taken on the matter by the mid-1880's. In 1886, a special committee of the board of the Infants' Home was formed to discuss the matter with the Premier[209] who agreed that the province should take remedial measures along the lines of the Infant Life Protection Act which had been passed in England in 1872.[210] The following year, the Legislature adopted a measure[211] which, closely modelled on the British act, seemed to promise strict control of infant boarding homes. It provided for the municipal registration of all homes in which children under the age of one year were boarded, prescribing the method to be followed in the registration of the homes, the kinds of records the homes were to maintain, and the penalties to be imposed for any violation of the act's provisions. Though not specific concerning the standards to which a home or its operator should conform, it required that a person to whom registration was granted be of good character and able to maintain infants in the age group covered by the legislation.

"farmers got imported children in preference to the children out of homes here. The reason is that we take good care to look after our own children. We see how they are treated and insist upon their being cared for properly and not abused; but as regards children brought from the old country, they can do with them as they please" (Ontario, *Sessional Papers*, 1891, no. 18, p. 744).

[207]Latimer, "Methods of Child Care," p. 9.
[208]For example, the *Globe*, June 8, 1875.
[209]Latimer, "Methods of Child Care," p. 47.
[210]Great Britain, *Statutes*, 1872, c. 38.   [211]Ontario, *Statutes*, 1887, c. 36.

The statute appeared to be mandatory, stating that "the municipal council of every local municipality shall keep a register of the names of persons applying to register for the purposes of this Act." It also required, or appeared to require, the municipality to inspect all registered homes, although it did not indicate the nature of the inspection to be performed. Presumably, the inspector was to report any registrant who "has been guilty of serious neglect or is incapable of providing the infants entrusted to his care with proper food and attention." These were sufficient grounds for a council to "strike his name and house off the register." However, the act did not provide for provincial supervision, nor did it assign responsibility for the administration of the legislation to any existing provincial department or office. Thus, although it seemed to be mandatory legislation, the lack of effective provincial machinery to see that it was acted upon left to the municipality the actual responsibility for initiating and carrying out the act.

There appears to have been little municipal action, and even in Toronto, where a group of citizens was concerned that the legislation be enforced, seriously inadequate boarding homes for infants continued to exist during and beyond the period covered in this study.[212] Thus the lack of strong provincial leadership in improving the institutions for infants, to which attention was drawn earlier, had a parallel in the ineffective measure adopted by the province respecting infant boarding homes.

The Humane Movement

In addition to the experience gained during the 1880's in developing and improving both institutional and non-institutional measures for children, the welfare of children was materially advanced towards the end of the decade through the work of the Humane Society of Toronto.[213] The society was established in 1887 as an expression of public concern about cruel and neglectful treatment of both children and animals. The initiative for its formation came from J. J. Kelso[214] and was one of Kelso's early endeavours in the field of social welfare.

[212]Latimer, "Methods of Child Care," pp. 48–49.

[213]The humane movement in the province was of long standing, an act of the Union Legislature having been passed in 1864 to incorporate the Humane Society of Canada (Canada, Statutes, 1864, c. 146). In 1873 the Ontario Society for the Prevention of Cruelty to Animals was formed in Toronto, but it appears to have become inactive within a few years of its founding.

[214]For an account of the formation and development of the Humane Society and the rôle of Kelso in its work, see Bain, "The Rôle of J. J. Kelso," pp. 40–57, from which the following references on the society are taken.

He found ready support from many of the leaders in the community who were active in various other social welfare programmes. Thus John Macdonald agreed to serve as chairman of the public organization meeting; Mayor Howland was among the supporting speakers; and the slate of officers, which included Kelso as secretary, had among its vice-presidents, Samuel Blake, Goldwin Smith, and George Hodgins.

In 1888, the society identified seven objectives for the protection of children and proceeded to promote these through public education and by representations to civic and provincial officials. Among its more general aims were "the protection of children of drunken, cruel and dissolute parents or guardians" and "the punishment of child-beaters and of heartless parents and guardians." It urged the "licensing and police oversight of bootblacks, and of vendors of newspapers and smallwares on the streets" and called for total prohibition from these activities of young girls. By way of resources to aid in the achievement of these objectives, the society advocated the establishment of a girls' industrial school similar to the school recently opened for boys at Mimico, and "a temporary refuge for destitute and neglected children until they are disposed of or provided for." It also suggested "the desirability of having some officer specially entrusted with the duty of looking after the waifs and strays of the city."

Among the society's accomplishments were its success in securing improved treatment for children in the police courts and in having controls placed on street trading. It also succeeded in bringing to Toronto the annual conference of the American Humane Association which helped to enlarge Canadian knowledge of child welfare developments in the United States. In addition, the society influenced, directly or indirectly, three highly important developments of the late 1880's and early 1890's: the child protection legislation in 1888, the appointment of the Royal Commission on the Prison and Reformatory System in 1890, and the establishment of the Children's Aid Society of Toronto in 1891.

The Children's Protection Act of 1888

Within a few months of its establishment, the Humane Society realized that it was handicapped in its attempts to deal with neglected children because of the lack of legal authority. The principal legislation dealing with children was the Apprentices and Minors Act which gave the courts the right to bind as apprentices children who had been deserted, who were dependent upon public charity for support, or whose parents were in gaol.[215] It also prevented parents from withdrawing from institutions and from the homes of private persons children whom they had abandoned earlier. However, the only legislation which gave the courts the power to set aside the normal rights of parents who were neglecting their children or to act on behalf of children lacking parents was the Industrial Schools Act and the Refuge for Girls Act. But because these acts were regarded as being intended to deal primarily with delinquent rather than neglected children, and because they provided only a limited disposition of the children brought to court under their provisions, they failed to meet the need of many children for some effective intervention to remove them from damaging surroundings and to provide them with adequate maintenance and care thereafter.

By way of bringing about a solution to this problem, Kelso and other members of the Humane Society drafted a bill which was submitted to the Premier early in 1888.[216] The proposal was adopted by the government and passed by the Legislature in March 1888, under the title "An Act for the Protection and Reformation of Neglected Children."[217] Essentially, the act reaffirmed the authority of the courts to commit neglected children to the industrial schools and to the refuge for girls, and extended the authority to other types of institutions and "to any suitable charitable society authorized under 'The Act respecting apprentices and Minors'." The child could be kept by the society or institution until he attained the age of eighteen years, with the cost of his care, up to a maximum of two dollars a week, being borne by the municipality where he was resident at the time of his committal.

The wording of the act suggested that it envisaged only institutional care for the children committed,[218] and because it did not deal specifically with the question of apprehending or taking children into care from damaging surroundings it would not seem to have advanced the protection of children very far, or to have greatly extended the effectiveness of a protective agency, such as the Humane Society. Its importance in the evolution of child welfare legislation in the province is that it established public responsibility for the maintenance of neglected children in all of the types of children's institutions which had previously received provincial recognition. And although the act

---

[215]Ontario, Revised Statutes, 1887, c. 142, s. 8.

[216]Bain, "The Role of J. J. Kelso," pp. 53–54.

[217]Ontario, Statutes, 1888, c. 40.

[218]In referring to the charitable society, the act referred to its willingness "to receive such child to be there kept, cared for and educated."

accepted the rôle of charitable societies in child protection only on the assumption that they had institutional programmes, it indicated the course later legislation would inevitably take when the rôle of non-institutional methods of providing protection and care for children became better understood and was more widely accepted.

The Royal Commission of 1890

Perhaps the most important single event in advancing public knowledge and official action respecting child welfare was the Royal Commission on the Prison and Reformatory System of 1890. The terms of reference[219] of the commission, though designed primarily to elicit information on correctional problems and to suggest solutions to them, were broad enough to cover much of the contemporary field of social welfare and had particular relevance to child welfare. Child welfare was, in fact, directly involved in each of the first three of the seven matters referred to the commission for investigation: those relating to the causes of crime, the improvement of the industrial schools, and the rescue of destitute children from criminal careers.

On the basis of their review of the literature on correctional subjects and their numerous interviews in Canada and the United States, the commissioners attempted to identify the principal causes of crime in the community.[220] They listed them as including hereditary tendencies towards crime, intemperance, idleness, ignorance, poverty, the eagerness to acquire wealth, and the failure by society and governments to take positive action to "save those who are in danger and to raise those who have fallen." In addition to these seven causes of crime, a number of which had implications for child welfare, the commissioners gave prior attention and importance to an eighth which they described as "the want of proper parental control; the lack of good home training and the baneful influence of bad homes, largely due to culpable neglect and indifference of parents and the evil effects of drunkenness."

In the combined consideration which the commissioners gave to improving industrial schools and rescuing destitute children from criminal careers, they carefully reviewed British, European, American, and Australian experience before turning to Ontario's methods of dealing with juvenile offenders and destitute children. On reviewing the work of the boys' reformatory and the girls' refuge, they found

219Ontario, *Sessional Papers*, 1891, no. 18, p. 5.
220This and the following references to the commission's report are from *ibid.*, pp. 40–47, 100, 214–18.

some serious grounds for criticism, but they were not strongly critical of the province's legislation on industrial schools. They felt, indeed, that it bore comparison with similar enactments elsewhere and referred to the Industrial Schools Act as representing "great progress . . . towards a thorough system of dealing with destitute and neglected children and those who have committed petty offences." They noted, too, that the act granted extensive powers to the boards and the minister of education to "place children out on license or probation and recall them when such action seems necessary." Nevertheless, the commissioners felt that the system created by the act was defective in one or two important respects. In particular, they pointed out that there was no provision "for the reformation or preservation of children in their own homes as is done under the probation system of Massachusetts," or "for placing in any other home, unless through the industrial school, the children of vicious parents or those who are destitute."

The commissioners regarded with approval the work being done by the boys' industrial school at Mimico, and recommended that the establishment of industrial day schools should "be made compulsory" in every large city and town:

Provision [should] be made in these schools for the control and instruction during the day of disorderly or neglected children belonging to what is generally described as the "Arab class"; of habitual truants; of those who cannot be controlled by parents or guardians or who otherwise require special supervision, and of destitute and foresaken children who may not be proper subjects for constant residence in charitable institutions, but require partial assistance in obtaining proper food and clothing; and for carrying on work of a simple kind for the industrial training of these classes.

In the view of the commissioners, the counties should undertake the erection and maintenance of residential industrial schools "unless within a reasonable time a corporate association under the terms of the existing Act, and with the assistance of a legislative grant and private aid, shall establish such an industrial school to the satisfaction of the government." Such schools should have land attached for farm training, but should also have "the means of giving a good technological training to such boys as will not adopt farm life." Whenever possible, however, the schools should place the children committed to their care "in a private family, either as apprentices or boarders." All children "not thoroughly vicious" should, indeed, "be so placed out even before they have received their literary instruction." Provision would be made in such cases for them to attend a local school from their new homes, where they would continue to be under "the vigilant and kindly supervision" of officers of the industrial school. These officers would be authorized, with provincial approval, "to recall any child so placed out, or remove him or her from one family to another."

This apparent assignment to the industrial schools of responsibility for the placement and subsequent supervision of their students was perhaps not quite consistent with a further recommendation of the commissioners respecting children leaving both the industrial schools as well as the boys' reformatory and the girls' refuge. The commissioners referred to the vital importance "that none should be allowed to leave these institutions unless to return to a good home or until such employment has been provided on a farm or elsewhere as will afford the boy or girl a fair opportunity of earning a respectable living and leading a moral life." To this end and to ensure "that supervision and care may be judiciously exercised over discharged, paroled or apprenticed children," they recommended that "an association . . . be formed having local boards in every important centre of the Province who shall take upon themselves the important but delicate duty of looking after and caring for these children." If the commissioners had been asked to suggest a descriptive name for their proposed association, they might well have suggested a term such as "children's aid association." They did not, however, develop the idea further, though two of their other suggestions were complementary to it. One was that municipal and provincial authorities should extend "the most cordial encouragement and assistance" to the charitable and philanthropic bodies engaged in practical measures for the saving of children. A second was that the province defray "the actual expenses incurred" by the proposed voluntary association which would place and supervise children. The commissioners also recommended provincial financial aid to the counties for establishing and maintaining industrial schools. This should take the form of grants for the acquisition of land and the erection of buildings, together with the application to the schools of the provisions of the Charity Aid Act—the schools to have the status of refuges, thus qualifying for between five and seven cents a day per resident.

Although the proposals of the commissioners relating to industrial schools and a chain of voluntary associations represented their major positions on the development of child welfare resources and programmes in the province, they made a number of other important recommendations. They attached particular importance to school attendance and urged the adoption of measures for its "vigorous enforcement." They also suggested municipal curfew laws, the development of supervised municipal playgrounds and gymnasia, the inspection of pawn-shops and other places which might encourage children to engage in petty thieving, and the restriction and control of juvenile immigration. In the area of corrections, as we have seen, they recommended the separate trial and separate detention of children and the use, where possible, of suspended sentences, the development of a system of probation, and the wider use of the indeterminate sentence.

Progress in carrying out the recommendations of the Royal Commission was more impressive in the field of child welfare than in most other areas with which the commissioners had dealt. For example, the suggestion respecting the enforcement of school attendance laws was legislated upon almost immediately.[221] The recommendations respecting industrial schools, on the other hand, were destined not to be acted upon, though a number of the principles incorporated in the Industrial Schools Act and endorsed by the commissioners were to form the foundation of the child welfare legislation adopted in 1893.

The Children's Aid Society of Toronto

An essential prior step to the formulation of that legislation was the development of the prototype of the kind of association which would form the administrative core of the new measure. This was the Children's Aid Society of Toronto which was organized in 1891 and which represented at once the culmination of trends long apparent in the community and the beginning of a new era in child welfare in Ontario.

Although the society was not exactly the kind of voluntary association recommended by the commissioners, it was in essential harmony with it, differing mainly in the greater range of activities on behalf of children that its organization and purposes would permit it to undertake. The commission, moreover, contributed to the founding of the new society through the amount of public interest it had aroused in child welfare questions. This response was fully appreciated by Kelso, who, as we have observed, presented evidence before the commission and who, as a journalist, reported and commented on its work, for he had already developed the capacity that was to be characteristic of his later career for promoting social welfare causes at propitious moments in terms of aroused public interest. Thus, the actions he took in the months of April to August 1891 in organizing the Children's Aid

[221]See above, page 258.

Society were undoubtedly timed in relation to the presentation of the commission's report to the government on April 8 and the public discussion that followed.

But the new society, though thus aided by the recommendations of the commission, was actually an outgrowth of three community activities that had been developed on behalf of children, and in which Kelso had been the prime mover: the humane movement which has been referred to earlier, the Children's Fresh Air Fund which provided outings for poor children in the summer, and the Santa Claus Fund which provided parties for them at Christmas. The experience gained in these early endeavours by Kelso and the group of prominent and devoted citizens who were associated with him was of significance both in the formation of the Children's Aid Society and in its initial activities. The work of the society during Kelso's brief period as its president and thereafter has been described by Kelso[222] and other writers[223] and does not require elaboration here. What is to be emphasized is that the society offered, at least potentially, a flexible instrument for protecting neglected children in their own homes, for arranging the care of those lacking proper homes, and for bringing to the attention of the general public and of public officials situations affecting the welfare of children which required remedial action.

Partly because of its roots in the humane movement, the Children's Aid Society believed that much could be accomplished by warnings and, where necessary, by legal action against persons who were abusing or exploiting children. The new society also carried forward and managed to implement the earlier proposals of the Humane Society for the appointment of a paid agent to provide direct protective service to neglected children and for the establishment of a temporary shelter in which children who were homeless or who needed to be removed from a damaging situation could be kept until the cause of their neglect could be remedied and a plan for their future care developed. It was soon evident, however, that the society lacked authority to protect children in situations where its action was resisted by the children's parents or guardians. Stronger legislation than the Protection Act of 1888 was required both for that purpose and for the incorporation, into a single statute, of provisions which had appeared in various earlier enactments. Above all, there was need for a measure

---

[222]J. J. Kelso, *Early History of the Humane and Children's Aid Movement in Ontario, 1886–1893,* (Toronto, 1911).

[223]Notably, Bain, "The Role of J. J. Kelso," pp. 58–70.

that would recognize the necessity for a type of child welfare agency that had adequate authority to take action for both the protection and the care of children who were being deprived of a normal and healthy upbringing.

Fortunately, the government favoured a strong measure in the field of child welfare, particularly one which could be justifiably represented as deriving from some of the basic proposals of the Royal Commission. Having encountered difficulty in acting on the major recommendations dealing directly with corrections, the government was bound to look with interest at any proposed legislation which might improve the position of those groups of children from whom the criminal population of the province was largely recruited and which would incorporate the essentials of the sixteen recommendations on juvenile criminality. A major problem, however, was whether the industrial school should be made the administrative core of the new child welfare programme or whether confidence and responsibility could be placed upon the newer type of organization, the children's aid society. Selection of the former would have been more in harmony with the commission's report; selection of the latter involved an act of faith that the new type of organization could meet the child welfare needs of the province and thereby contribute to the reduction of crime. Nevertheless, the times favoured the children's aid society over the industrial school. The movement for industrial schools, which had been largely limited to Toronto, had achieved its major purpose in the establishment of the Victoria and Alexandra schools; it was a spent force there, and its work was not being emulated in other centres. Further development of industrial schools would depend primarily upon action by the municipal governments. This would not be obtained easily, as the government would have known from long experience with municipal reluctance to carry out social welfare measures. The children's aid society movement, on the other hand, was arousing wide interest and beginning to enlist active voluntary support. Its leaders were confident that, if given adequate legislative authority and a measure of public financial aid, children's aid societies could provide a comprehensive, effective, and inexpensive way of meeting the needs of the province's children. The passage in the spring of 1893 of "An Act for the Prevention of Cruelty to, and better Protection of Children"[224] represented the adoption by the government and by the legislature of this point of view.

[224]Ontario, *Statutes*, 1893, c. 45.

The content and significance of this act have been dealt with in other studies,[225] and it is necessary to refer here only to its main provisions. One of its main emphases was upon the protection of children through the punishment of those found guilty of neglecting or exploiting them. Fines of up to $100 and imprisonment for as long as three months could be imposed.[226] These sections were taken quite directly, and perhaps somewhat uncritically, from the British statute of 1889 for the protection of children.[227] Ontario's act also borrowed the British provisions on the removal of neglected children to places of safety and on the "disposal of children," but went significantly further than its British counterpart in adding to those under whose charge a neglected child might be placed "any duly authorized children's aid society."[228] By thus allowing for the founding of children's aid societies, and by providing, in addition, for the appointment of children's committees and for the establishment of the office of superintendent of neglected and dependent children, Ontario's legislation moved well beyond the British statute and created the framework for a broad child welfare programme throughout the province.

The act defined a children's aid society as "any duly incorporated and organized society having among its objects the protection of children from cruelty and the care and control of neglected and dependent children, such society having been approved by the Lieutenant-Governor-in-Council for the purpose of this Act." The act, in various of its sections, proceeded to give to the societies or their officers wide powers, including the apprehending of children, their "supervision and management" in municipal shelters, and the status and prerogatives of legal guardians respecting children committed to them by a court. Notwithstanding the breadth of the powers and responsibilities assigned to the societies by the legislation, the act did not contain any provisions concerning the societies' organization, membership, or management.

In marked contrast, the act set out in considerable detail the composition of the children's visiting committees which, both in their

[225]Bain, "The Role of J. J. Kelso," pp. 93–94; Russell Jolliffe, "The History of the Children's Aid Society of Toronto, 1891–1947" (University of Toronto, unpublished M.S.W. thesis, 1950), pp. 7–19; Dean Ramsey, "Development of Child Welfare Legislation in Ontario" (University of Toronto, unpublished M.S.W. thesis, 1949).

[226]Ontario, Statutes, 1893, c. 45. If the ill-treatment of the child caused his death and the person charged had a financial interest in the death, the fine was up to $250 and imprisonment for nine months.

[227]Great Britain, Statutes, 1889, c. 44, s. 1, 2, 3.

[228]Ontario, Statutes, 1893, c. 45, s. 6.

initial concept and in their actual functioning, were a much less significant part of the new child welfare structure than the children's aid societies. In each electoral district of the province, the act required the appointment of a committee of six persons, one of whom was to be the member of the Legislative Assembly. Of the remainder who were to be appointed by specified local officials, three were to be women. As a committee, they were expected to perform a number of functions including the promotion of a "philanthropic sentiment on behalf of neglected, abandoned and destitute children"; the adoption of such methods as they may think best for securing voluntary subscriptions "for carrying out the objects of the Act"; the selection of foster homes; the visitation of children in foster homes in their area at least once every three months; and the removal of children from one foster home to another when this appeared necessary. They were to co-operate with the children's aid societies in respect to children placed in their district by the societies and report periodically to the societies and to the superintendent of neglected and dependent children. That this range of functions was too much to expect of a voluntary body serving without compensation, and that the visiting committees and children's aid societies would have difficulty distinguishing their respective rôles might perhaps have been predicted, but in default of organized children's aid societies the aim of the act—of providing child welfare services throughout the province without delay—could be achieved only through the creation of some type of body such as the visiting committees.

The act provided for the appointment by the lieutenant-governor-in-council of a superintendent of neglected and dependent children who was to have broad powers and duties in respect to the new act and existing child welfare legislation. Thus, he was to encourage the development of children's aid societies "for the protection of children from cruelty, and for the due care of neglected and dependent children in temporary homes or shelters and the placing of such children in properly selected foster homes." He was also "to advise children's visiting committees and to instruct them as to the manner in which their duties were to be performed." In addition, he was required "to inspect houses registered for the reception of children under the *Act for the Protection of Infant Children,* and to instruct local children's aid societies and visiting committees as to the proper supervision of such houses." Since the act referred to[229] had given to the municipal councils the duty of inspecting infant boarding homes, the assignment

[229]*Ibid.,* 1887, c. 36.

of this duty to the superintendent under the new legislation was at once an admission that the provision in the earlier act was inoperative and that the government preferred to deal with the resulting problem in a round-about and irregular way. A somewhat similar comment could be made about a further duty of the superintendent: "to visit and inspect industrial schools."[230]

Although the act thus lacked clarity in respect to certain of the superintendent's duties and left a number of other questions about its operation unresolved, its administrative and other provisions constituted a vigorous and thorough attempt to deal with matters affecting the welfare of children and to create machinery through which all neglected and dependent children could receive protection and care. Whether it would become an effective measure achieving its full potential would depend on the person appointed to the superintendency. What was required was a person with a thorough knowledge of the hazards to which children were exposed and of the best contemporary methods of protecting and helping them. What was even more necessary was that the superintendent should have a capacity for creating throughout the province a concern for the welfare of children and the ability to channel such concern into community action towards the formation and support of children's aid societies. To a remarkable degree, J. J. Kelso possessed the qualities needed to fill the post. He was the obvious choice to administer an act that owed much to his advocacy, that bore the imprint of his ideas, and that would depend for its success on the type of voluntary associations which he had been so successful in promoting. Although not without his detractors, he was generally well regarded by his contemporaries and was acceptable to J. M. Gibson, the provincial secretary, who had secured the acceptance of the act by the government and the Legislature and with whom the superintendent would need to work in close accord. With the warm

---

[230]Ibid., 1893, c. 45, s. 9(b). The question here was that of multiplicity of inspections. Under the Industrial Schools Act as originally passed, inspection of new industrial schools to determine their fitness to receive children was to be carried out by an inspector of the city schools, and the industrial schools were thereafter to be subject to the same educational inspection as other schools. In an amendment to the Industrial Schools Act in 1893 which made the schools eligible for grants on the same basis as refuges under the Charity Aid Act, the inspector of prisons and public charities was required "from time to time" to "visit and inspect every industrial school and make all proper inquiries as to the maintenance, management and affairs thereof" (Ontario, Statutes, 1893, c. 50, s. 8). Thus, three types of supervision of the industrial schools were required, without any clear indication of their respective limits.

approval "of the various philanthropic organizations of the Province,"[231] Kelso was appointed Ontario's first superintendent of neglected and dependent children and assumed his duties on July 1, 1893.

Kelso probably realized, in accepting the post, that he would face formidable difficulties in gaining acceptance of the new approach to child welfare throughout the province and in fitting the work of the superintendency into the existing structure for the administration of social welfare programmes within the provincial government. These obstacles, notwithstanding, Kelso welcomed the appointment as an unsurpassed opportunity to lead in rectifying the provincial negligence "in the matter of children" which had been the text of his presentation, three years earlier before the Royal Commission.

[231]Henry James Morgan, *The Canadian Men and Women of the Time* (Toronto, 1898), p. 525.

Review: The Rôle of Public Welfare
in a Century of Social Welfare Development

THE MAIN LINES of social welfare advance through the century from the establishment of Upper Canada to the final decade of the nineteenth century can now be traced against the foregoing examination of particular aspects of that development, by way of bringing these into better perspective and as a means of delineating the rôle of public welfare and especially the part played by the province.

The Development of the Services

By their nature the pioneer conditions of Upper Canada involved hardship and privation. At best, the development of social welfare services would have been slow, and the period in which many human needs would have been even partially met, if at all, would necessarily have been lengthy. This period, however, was much prolonged by weaknesses in the structure of the provincial and local governments of Upper Canada, the former developing into an oligarchy at frequent odds with the popular branch of the Legislature; the latter lacking a popular base, limited in its powers, and having grossly inadequate revenues relative to its responsibilities for physical and social development.

In addition to the burden of a defective constitution, Upper Canadians had to bear the consequences of bad policies introduced by the colonial administration. Such, in the realm of social welfare, was the decision to reject the English poor law, a decision which can only in the most formal sense be regarded as made by the Legislature of Upper Canada. The decision was unfortunate both for the situation it created and for the myth it engendered. It created a vacuum in policy destined to be filled by slow stages and by the piecemeal assumption of the responsibility initially denied.

The same session of the Upper Canadian Legislature which concurred in the rejection of the poor law took steps to establish gaols for the better provision of law and order in the colony. The gaols were destined to serve as poor houses and asylums, as well as places of detention and correction. They performed none of these tasks well, and by the 1820's they were, in particular, being regarded by the more perceptive as cradles of criminality. In the 1830's, through the establishment of a penitentiary, action was taken to divest the gaols of part of their basic function, but moves to relieve them of their ancillary rôles of housing the poor and the insane had little more than promising beginnings. An act passed to establish institutions for the poor lay dormant on the statute books. Legislation was passed to establish a provincial asylum for the insane, but as the decade closed no action was being taken to remove the afflicted from the cells of the district gaols.

From the sick poor of the 1830's, however, public aid could not wholly be withheld. With the appearance of cholera, the very safety of the colony demanded their treatment and the supplying of their elemental needs. But direct aid through combined action by the province and the districts was limited to the dire emergencies of the two epidemics. A historic beginning was made, nevertheless, in the provision of indirect aid by way of public grants to private charities: to the relief societies dealing with immigrants and the victims of fire, to the first permanent hospitals, and to the first house of refuge.

By the end of the 1830's, and simultaneously of the pre-Union period, some of the enduring lines of social welfare development in the province were strongly in evidence. Responsibility for social welfare programmes was either assigned specifically to the municipalities or assumed to reside there until the incapacity or unwillingness of the municipalities to perform certain functions satisfactorily, if at all, forced the province to develop programmes at the provincial level. Thus the inability of the districts to operate their gaols in an effective manner caused the province to withdraw the more serious offenders from local responsibility. Similarly, the province had agreed before 1840 to provide for the mentally ill. As a second consequence of the failure of local government to provide social welfare services, action was taken by private citizens in voluntary associations who, finding that their resources for meeting community needs were inadequate, began to turn to the province for additional support. Out of the small beginnings in the pre-Union period, various types of voluntary social welfare institutions were to develop, sometimes to be wholly supported by private giving, but increasingly in the two later periods to receive public grants and to accept with them public supervision.

The Union period witnessed an impressive growth of these voluntary institutions, including the development of the first institutions for children and the establishment of hospitals in the large centres. No less notable was the strengthening of the municipal governments which enabled them to aid the poor in their own homes, to make grants to the voluntary institutions, and to build houses of refuge. The latter was a right which they had been granted in the pre-Union period and which they refused to act upon in both periods, notwithstanding an attempt, as the Union period closed, to make such action mandatory.

Even greater progress during the Union period was made at the provincial level where the responsibilities in the fields of health, welfare, and corrections increased to the point that special machinery was required to deal with them. Thus in 1859 the Board of Inspectors of Prisons, Asylums and Public Charities was created and given responsibility for the provincial quarantine and marine hospitals on the lower St. Lawrence, the provincial penitentiary and the newly established reformatories for boys, the provincial asylum in Upper Canada, and the local gaols. The board, which had among its members some of the ablest public servants in the province, including E. A. Meredith, the assistant secretary for Upper Canada, was able to bring about important extensions and improvements in social welfare programmes and services.

The terms of the British North America Act respecting social welfare reflected the Upper Canadian approach to this field, and Confederation was looked upon by provincial leaders as offering Ontario the opportunity for unimpeded advance in this as in other areas regarded as being of special provincial interest. Rapid progress in social welfare was thus predictable in the post-Confederation era. The remarkable extent of the development, particularly during the first fourteen years after Confederation, is very largely attributable to the outstanding administrative capabilities of J. W. Langmuir, the first inspector. Langmuir continuously examined the social welfare needs of the province and made frequent recommendations for new or expanded programmes which he presented to the government with well-worked-out proposals for their implementation. The government, which was in possession of more revenue than it required for its basic functions and for the developmental projects to which it gave the next priority, accepted many of the recommendations. Measures incorporating them were placed before the Legislature and enacted, and were well received throughout the province.

Thus by 1882 the mental hospitals of the province had been greatly expanded and improved, and a special institution had been established for the mentally retarded. Significant improvements had been made in local gaols, and the establishment of intermediate prisons for both men and women and a refuge for girls had removed from the gaols further types of persons with which they were unfitted to deal. Legislation had been passed for the establishment of industrial schools by the municipalities, but this had not been implemented. Schools for the deaf and the blind, however, had been built by the province and were meeting a need that had been long neglected. The passage in 1874 of the Charity Aid Act had placed grants to private institutions on a systematic basis. The assurance of significant public support and recognition, together with the effect of provincial supervision, promoted a broad expansion and outstanding improvements in the voluntary institutions.

Following Langmuir's resignation in 1882, and a division of the duties within the office of inspector, there was a loss of integrated administrative leadership and a slackened pace in meeting social welfare problems, although these were becoming more pressing with the advance of industrialization. The need for an examination of the adequacy of existing programmes led to the appointment of a royal commission in 1890 which, although concerned particularly with corrections, reviewed many other areas of social welfare and made extensive recommendations. Some of these were being carried into effect as the period closed, particularly those relating to child welfare —a field which, except for its corrections aspect, had been largely neglected by the province.

Expenditures on Social Welfare

Throughout the period, the development of social welfare depended, as always, on the willingness of governments, voluntary bodies, and individuals to express their interest and concern in meeting social welfare needs through the provision of the funds required to support the necessary programmes and services. In the primitive economy of the early decades in Upper Canada, the paucity of social welfare services was a reflection of the poverty in the province—poverty at least in terms of the lack of capital which could be spared from the vital tasks of developing the basic economy. The limitation of taxable resources, combined with the scale of priorities of the early communities, was such that even the gaols, often the sole social welfare resource, were financed with difficulty. The plight of the gaols and of other welfare programmes bore early testimony to the flaws in provincial-municipal relationships and the resulting problem of determining what social welfare functions should be delegated by the province to the municipality and how such functions, if delegated, should be financed. As a result, from the 1830's to the end of the Union period, although municipal expenditures on social welfare expanded sporadically and unevenly, voluntary giving in the development of hospitals, houses of refuge, and orphanages increased, probably in rough proportion to the growth of private wealth, and there was a manifold expansion of provincial expenditures on correctional institutions, mental hospitals, and other charities. By 1867, the social welfare costs borne by the province were close to a quarter of provincial expenditures.

After Confederation, notwithstanding federal assumption of the penitentiary and of the welfare services for immigrants, provincial expenditures on social welfare continued to expand and to do so at an accelerated rate. Table XVI details this increase and shows that it applied both to existing services as well as to new programmes initiated during the period. Although the years shown are fairly typical, they

TABLE XVI

PROVINCIAL EXPENDITURES ON SOCIAL WELFARE, 1868, 1878, 1888, 1893
(in dollars)

Item	1868	1878	1888	1893
Office of the inspector	1,181	8,068	10,739	15,641
Mental institutions	177,585	457,045	679,940	743,020
Gaols,* prisons, and reformatories	66,992	174,499	224,793	218,109
Grants to private institutions	39,000	70,673	113,686	164,896
Deaf and blind institutions	—	103,073	86,130	99,901
Assistance to indigents	—	8,791	660	190
Grant to the industrial school	—	—	1,000	6,500
Grant to the Prisoners' Aid Association	—	—	1,000	1,000
Measures for public health	—	—	7,252	10,700
Inspection of factories	—	—	4,245	4,275
Protection of children	—	—	—	960
TOTAL	284,758	822,149	1,129,445	1,265,192

SOURCE: Ontario, *Public Accounts*, 1869, 1879, 1889, 1894.
*Provincial expenditure in support of the county gaols is submerged in the public accounts in the item "Administration of Justice in the Counties." On the basis of figures given by Langmuir in the statements of expenditures with which he concluded the introductory pages of most of his reports, a conservative estimate of $40,000 has been made, and included in this item for each of the years shown.

do not fully indicate the extent of capital construction of provincial institutions in the post-Confederation period. In 1880, Langmuir stated that 2.5 million dollars had been expended on the erection of social welfare institutions in the previous decade. Despite the slackened pace after 1880, the figure for the quarter century from Confederation to 1893 undoubtedly exceeded 3 million dollars.

The amounts expended on social welfare by the province assume more significance when presented, as in Table XVII, in relation to

TABLE XVII

TOTAL PROVINCIAL EXPENDITURES COMPARED WITH PROVINCIAL EXPENDITURES ON SOCIAL WELFARE, 1868, 1878, 1888, 1893

| | | Social welfare expenditures | |
Year	Total provincial expenditures (in dollars)	Total (in dollars)	Percentage of total provincial expenditures
1868	1,182,388	284,758	24.1
1878	2,784,321	822,149	29.5
1888	3,536,248	1,129,445	31.9
1893	3,907,145	1,265,192	32.4

SOURCE: Ontario, *Public Accounts*, 1869, 1879, 1889, 1894.

total provincial expenditures. The latter increased as the province found it necessary to take on many new or expanded functions arising from the burgeoning of new types of economic development. None the less, provincial expenditures on social welfare grew more rapidly than total expenditures: the increase in the latter during the period was roughly threefold, while the increase in social welfare expenditures was nearly fivefold.

In Table XVI, the principal items of expenditure shown for the year 1868 were for mental institutions, for gaols, prisons, and reformatories, and for assistance to private institutions. Although reclamation and restoration were among the stated objectives of the programmes of various institutions within each of these categories, the bulk of the expenditure was for custodial care. The newer items of expenditure shown for the later years indicate the emergence of a philosophy of prevention. The institutions for the training of the deaf and the blind, for example, were established to prevent the hardship, wastage, and dependency resulting from the failure to develop the remaining potentialities of persons who were deprived of their hearing or their sight. The prevention of illness, disability, and dependency was also at the core both of the new provincial public health programme and of the measures for the inspection of factories. Grants to the Prisoners'

Aid Association and to the industrial school were motivated by the hope that recidivism could be prevented by programmes which emphasized, in one case, rehabilitative assistance to the ex-prisoner and, in the other, a non-punitive system of youth training. Finally, the expenditure for a child welfare programme which appeared for the first time in the public accounts in 1893 represented the willingness of the province to launch a new non-institutional type of programme aimed at preventing crime and dependency through timely assistance to the neglected and dependent child.

Types of Provincial Action

The province, in its progressive assumption of social welfare responsibilities, found it necessary to employ a wide variety of means. These often reflected the current level of its development. Among the most basic was the enactment of legislation clarifying rights and responsibilities: for example, the right of a parent to place his child as an apprentice or the right of the child to maintenance and training from the master to whom he was apprenticed. Legislation of this kind might constitute the full extent of necessary action by the province or, as in the case of the Apprentices and Minors Act, might represent a stage in the assumption of greater public responsibility over the course of time. Throughout the whole period, this type of legislation continued to be a significant aspect of the province's rôle in social welfare.

Of greater importance, however, was the type of legislation which identified an area of need and assigned responsibility for some type of service or programme to deal with it. During the period, responsibility for different social welfare matters was assigned to the municipalities, to voluntary social agencies or institutions, to boards or commissions serving at the pleasure of the provincial government, and to officials or departments within the government.

THE MUNICIPALITIES

Much of Ontario's progress, at least from 1850, is attributable to the willingness of the people of the province to govern and tax themselves at the local level and to undertake to carry out a wide variety of functions delegated by the province. Limited in their resources, however, the municipalities have never been able to give equal attention to all of the functions assigned to them. In the scale of municipal priorities, social welfare programmes have been apt to rank low. Thus, the history of municipal action in social welfare during the period provides scant support for the view that the level of government in closest proximity to human need is the one most disposed to meet it. Dr. Workman felt justified in describing "the philanthropy of municipal bodies" as "close akin to the 'tender mercies of the wicked,' "[1] and Langmuir, in commenting on the refusal of many municipalities to contribute to the education of their blind and deaf children, remarked on municipal failure to implement "*permissive* legislative enactments . . . of a moral and social character, no matter how high the aim, or urgent the need may be."[2] He could have illustrated his remark in reference to houses of refuge, industrial schools, boards of health, and many other matters, and his successors might have referred to the failure of the municipalities to provide the necessary machinery for the implementation of the provincial statute concerning the inspection of infant boarding homes. They could have commented, as well, on the reluctance of the cities to provide relief and their failure to appoint welfare or relieving officers, a condition rectified in Toronto only as the period was ending and then only because of a generous private subsidy to establish the office. Even where the legislation was mandatory, municipal action was by no means assured. In respect to the gaols, where the legislation was unequivocal and the tradition of municipal responsibility as old as the province itself, the greatest difficulty was encountered in securing municipal action. The inspectors often despaired of developing a satisfactory correctional system as long as the local gaols were subject to the neglect and mismanagement of the counties.

Yet the record of municipal action in the field of social welfare was not wholly bad. The extent to which the municipalities were found to be granting relief in 1874 and 1888 was surprisingly high; a number of municipalities did take seriously their responsibilities to maintain adequate gaols; and in the post-Confederation period nine municipalities built houses of refuge entirely without provincial support.

Whatever their record, the municipalities must not ultimately to be blamed for their failure to assume responsibilities assigned to them by the province. As we have seen, the province was obliged in various ways to adjust itself to municipal inadequacies. At no point during the period, however, is there evidence that the province explored the question of the basis on which social welfare functions were or should be apportioned as between the provincial and local levels of government. Throughout the period, it continued to assign responsibilities

[1]Quoted in James Bovell, A *Plea for Inebriate Asylums* (Toronto, 1862), p. 24.
[2]Ontario, *Sessional Papers*, 1872–73, no. 2, p. 47.

to all municipalities of a given type as though they were equally able to assume them. And although there was a gradual reduction of the extent of municipal responsibility through the development of provincial programmes for particular categories of need, this very process, being based on no clearly defined division of rôles between the two levels of government, encouraged the municipalities to default on a particular function which they did not want to carry, in the expectation that the province would assume the entire responsibility for, or at least increase the amount of its financial contribution towards, this function. Thus, the municipalities that refused to send indigent children to the schools for the deaf and the blind as long as municipal sharing in the cost of the maintenance of the children was involved succeeded in having the requirement withdrawn. Similarly, the refusal of a majority of the counties, towns, and cities to establish houses of refuge won the better terms represented by the provincial grant for the construction of these institutions. It would thus appear that, to a very considerable degree, the failure of the municipalities to carry the social welfare functions assigned to them is to be attributed to defects in the policies of the province.

VOLUNTARY INSTITUTIONS AND AGENCIES

Communities which elected municipal governments committed to restricting the range of municipal action in social welfare paradoxically often gave generous support to voluntary institutions that were created because of the lack of public programmes. Thus, while municipal programmes of social welfare remained relatively meagre and ill-developed, private welfare flourished. From the 1850's on, the establishment of orphanages, hospitals, and houses of refuge in the urban centres offers a fair index of their growth in wealth and population.

No barriers, of course, stood in the way of the formation of private institutions; their boards, usually made up of the most influential citizens in the community, encountered no difficulty in having the institutions incorporated by governments happy thereby to be relieved of becoming directly involved with problems for which they had an ultimate, if unavowed, responsibility. When the boards of the institutions returned later, requesting financial grants to support their undertakings, the province was unable to deny the public stake in the work they were performing. The problems of the province lay in deciding how much and on what basis the grants should be given. No answers to these problems were found throughout the pre-Union or Union periods or, indeed, until 1874 when the Charity Aid Act stipulated that grants were to be based both on the service performed by the institutions and on the amount of funds they received from sources other than the province, and that payment was to be contingent upon provincial supervision. These principles, although sound in concept and constructive in practice, were, however, formulated within too narrow a frame of reference. They envisioned an extension of public supervision over the operations of the institutions that brought themselves within the terms of the act, but the resultant control was by no means complete. Langmuir, for example, could not effect the amalgamation of the two agencies he found providing the same services to the same constituency, and conversely the province could not require a private institution to extend its services or its coverage beyond the margins of its own interest and concern.[3] Moreover, the act embodying these principles became so sacrosanct that despite some manipulation and violation of terms the legislation was at no time throughout the remainder of the period subjected to reappraisal or basic amendment.

There is no doubt that the voluntary agencies performed work of the highest value to the province, work which it is hard to conceive public agencies performing on a comparable scale during the nineteenth century, but these private institutions could not meet all the needs of a growing industrial society. In such a society, the implementation of the principle of public responsibility for social welfare services becomes imperative. Thus, the province was faced with the problem of how best to utilize existing voluntary agencies and those which would be formed in the future, while continuing to develop a basic structure of public programmes. As the period closed, it was making slow but discernible progress in this direction. It was, in particular, attempting to have public houses of refuge formed in all parts of the province to complement the work of the voluntary institutions. And in the field of child welfare, it was embarking on an attempt to utilize private agencies to undertake the protection and care of neglected and dependent children under provincial legislation. In the years ahead, the province, in developing an adequate social welfare structure, would find the existence of the voluntary agencies at once an asset beyond value and a complex impediment to the development of comprehensive public services.

APPOINTED BOARDS AND COMMISSIONS

In the pre-Union period, for lack of other administrative machinery, the province was obliged to make extensive use of appointed boards or commissions to perform various functions such as the building

[3]Though Langmuir appears to have caused the hospitals to broaden their admission policies.

and later the operation of the penitentiary and asylum, as well as the establishment of standards in the building and the operation of gaols, and in the licensing of medical practitioners. The members of the boards served with little or no remuneration, and in all cases carried out with some measure of success the functions assigned to them. Except for the short-lived board on gaol standards, however, they all became involved in public controversy and were prone to internal dissension. The weaknesses of the board of inspectors of the penitentiary as they were identified by the Royal Commission of 1848 applied in some degree to the other boards: all were defective in the vital matter of carrying into effect the designs and purposes of the executive branch of government.

As the provincial executive and civil service developed, the need for appointed boards declined, and they played only a minor rôle after 1850. Certain of their values continued to be recognized, however, particularly in the field of public health where they were appointed to serve advisory and interpretive as well as policy-making functions.

DIRECT PROVINCIAL ADMINISTRATION

The province moved in two stages to direct provincial administration of social welfare programmes following the Royal Commission of 1848. The first stage was the appointment of two paid inspectors responsible only for the penitentiary, and the second was the appointment of the permanent Board of Inspectors in 1859. The board operated with a high degree of harmony and efficiency, and on the basis of its record appeared to constitute a successful experiment in social welfare administration. After Confederation, the replacement of the board by a single inspector was, at least throughout the period of Langmuir's inspectorship, also abundantly successful. But the golden age of social welfare expansion and improvement under the administrative direction and leadership of Langmuir was perhaps more a stroke of good fortune than of good planning. Because of his extraordinary capacities, Langmuir was able to guide and integrate the whole range of social welfare programmes coming within the scope of his office.

The expansion of social welfare activities eventually necessitated the division of administrative functions within the office of the inspector. Thus, in 1881 the duties of the office were divided into two roughly equivalent halves and in 1891 a third inspector was added. These decisions represented the obvious but wrong answer to the problem of covering the statutory functions of the office, and they inevitably failed to meet the crucial requirement for a continuation of strong and integrated administration able to plan, co-ordinate, and direct the social welfare programmes that were necessary to meet the existing and emerging needs of the province.

The Royal Commission of 1890, though aware that there had been failure in the 1880's to sustain the pace of progress achieved in the '70's, did not fully identify its causes, attributing them almost wholly to the gaps or deficiencies in the social welfare programmes and hardly at all to their central administration.[4] Perhaps Langmuir, as chairman of the commission, was unfitted for the task of analyzing the decline in the effectiveness of the office which he had filled with such singular success. The Royal Commission did, nevertheless, make many worthwhile recommendations; indeed, it placed before Ontario a social welfare assignment comparable in magnitude to that facing the province immediately after Confederation. To be carried out, it would need broad public support, the adoption of firm policies by the government, and their translation into effective legislation, and, not least, it would require administration of a quality equal to that provided by Langmuir in the early post-Confederation period.

As the period closed, however, only meagre progress was being made in acting on the commission's recommendations. One new initiative—that in the field of child welfare—was expressed from the new office of superintendent of neglected and dependent children, but the over-all lack of administrative vigour and direction from the office of the inspector meant that the programmes would continue to pursue their separate courses. This condition was destined to endure for nearly forty years when, as the product of another royal commission, a provincial department of public welfare would be formed.

[4]Other than to discuss the relative merits of independent welfare boards and direct provincial administration.

Appendix A

A Chronological Summary of Social Welfare Developments in Ontario during the Period When J. W. Langmuir Was Inspector of Prisons, Asylums and Public Charities*

1868

Legislation was passed for building a new asylum at London and an institution for the education of the deaf at Belleville. New gaols were completed in three centres.

The use of mandamus was recommended against counties refusing to improve their gaols. Improved facilities were suggested for the boys' reformatory. The need for one or more industrial prisons was stressed. A policy on admissions and fee charging was proposed for the school for the deaf. An institution for the blind similar to that for the deaf was advocated.

1870

The new asylum at London was opened, as were two new wings of the provincial asylum at Toronto. The site was selected and plans drawn for an institution for the education of the blind at Brantford. Workshops were completed and new dormitories were under construction at the boys' reformatory. Through the use of mandamus two counties were forced to improve their gaols.

A central prison was again recommended as part of a prison system "having for its aim not only the punishment of criminals but, as far as possible, the introduction of sound, wholesome reformatory and restraining influences, combined with a well-defined plan of utilizing the labour of criminals."

1871

The Legislature voted $150,000 for a central prison. The institution for the blind was under construction. The London asylum and the school for the deaf each had completed a successful year of operation.

Many specific recommendations were made on the construction and

*Data in the chronology are summarized from Langmuir's reports: Ontario, *Sessional Papers*, 1868–82.

operation of the central prison. The removal of the boys' reformatory from Penetanguishene was recommended. An institution for mentally defective children was suggested in connection with the asylum at London.

1872

The institution for the blind was opened at Brantford. Arrangements for the industrial employment of inmates of the central prison were completed successfully. A study was ordered on the establishment of a better basis for distributing grants to charitable institutions.

An inebriate hospital was recommended for the treatment of alcoholics. Langmuir submitted a plan for increasing asylum accommodation and urged action to provide accommodation for the mentally defective.

1873

The Legislature appropriated $100,000 to build a hospital for inebriates. Specific suggestions were made for reforming the method of making grants to private institutions.

1874

The central prison was completed and industrial work for prisoners fully organized. The Legislature passed the Charity Aid Act.

Langmuir recommended the conversion of buildings at Orillia for use as an institution for idiots. He again urged that an industrial prison for women be established.

1875

Langmuir reported that the Charity Aid Act was successfully in operation.

The Inspector drew up extensive plans for the increase of accommodation for the mentally ill and mental defectives. Attention was directed to the need for public houses of refuge or industry. The establishment of a prison for women was again urged.

1876

A broad plan for increased asylum accommodation was adopted involving conversion of the inebriate hospital to this purpose.

Langmuir recommended extension of the cottage system for the chronic insane, a separate training school for retarded children at Orillia, and enlargement of the schools for the deaf and blind.

1877

Legislative appropriations were made for the increase of asylum accommodation by 600 beds. A marked improvement was reported in the structural conditions as well as the management and discipline of the county gaols.

Additions were recommended to the newly acquired Rockwood Asylum at Kingston, and to the schools for the deaf and the blind. The Inspector suggested a labour programme for able-bodied vagrants in county gaols. He also recommended changes in the discipline and internal economy of the boys' reformatory.

1878

Plans were adopted to build a reformatory for women and a refuge for girls. Asylum cottages were completed at London and extensions were in progress at Hamilton. Extensions were completed to the schools for the deaf and the blind. Commitments to gaols were down from the previous year for the first time since Confederation.

Additions were recommended to the institution for mental defectives at Orillia. A further wing was requested for the institution for the blind. Langmuir suggested an increase of the per diem grant to orphanages.

1879

Construction began on the women's reformatory and girls' refuge. Objectionable penal features of the boys' reformatory were being progressively removed. Specific proposals were made for added accommodation for 150 inmates at Orillia. A similar increase was recommended for the Kingston asylum.

1880

The Mercer reformatory for women and the associated refuge for girls were opened. The gaol population remained static for the third year.

Langmuir suggested the formation of voluntary prisoners' aid societies to help prisoners after discharge and to assist their families while they were incarcerated. Specific improvements to the programme of the boys' reformatory were outlined.

1881

Recoveries in the asylum during the year increased to 33 per cent of the year's admissions. Langmuir was able to report improvements in the discipline and management of the common gaols and of the boys' reformatory. The central prison and the Mercer reformatory and refuge were operating to the Inspector's satisfaction. A prisoners' aid association had been formed in Toronto.

Langmuir urged the attainment of even higher standards in the asylums, holding that it was "of paramount importance that their standard as Hospitals for cure should continue to be raised." He recommended extensions to four asylums to add 420 beds.

Appendix B

An Excerpt from the Annual Report of the Inspector of Prisons, Asylums and Public Charities for 1878 Outlining the Duties of the Inspector*

The official duties devolving upon me, as Inspector, . . . comprise the general supervision and control, as well as the statutory inspection, of the following institutions exclusively owned and managed by the Government of the Province, namely: Four Asylums for the Insane, the Asylum for Idiots, the Institution for the Education of the Deaf and Dumb, the Institution for the Education of the Blind, the Central Prison in Toronto, the Provincial Reformatory in Penetanguishene, and the Reformatory Prison for Females, now being erected in Toronto,—ten institutions in all. The supervisory direction of the affairs and the inspection of thirty-seven County Gaols and five District Lock-ups; the inspection, including the annual examination of the books and general operations of twelve hospitals, thirteen Houses of Refuge, five Magdalen Asylums, and nineteen Orphan Asylums, receiving aid from the Province under the provisions of the Charity Aid Act.

The purely inspectorial work performed in connection with these 101 Asylums, Prisons and Public Charities during the past year, was represented by eighteen statutory inspections of the Asylums for the Insane; seven of the Institutions for the Deaf and Dumb, and the Blind; six of the Central Prisons and the Provincial Reformatory; seventy-six of the County Gaols and Lock-ups, and fifty-six of the Public Charities—in all, one hundred and sixty-three statutory inspections, besides other visits made during the twelve months for the transaction of special business.

Besides the general supervision and control of the maintenance routine of the Institutions owned by the Government, the Inspector is charged with the preparation of sketch plans of all new structures and structural changes in existing buildings, upon which, and the recommendations connected therewith, the Departmental plans and specifications are founded by the Architect of Public Works. He has also to give the initiatory instructions and suggestions for all new gaol structures and for alterations and additions to old ones, and must finally approve of the plans and specifications thereof, before they can be acted upon. In addition, he is charged with the preparation of all specifications for the furnishings for new buildings, the renewals

*Ontario, *Sessional Papers*, 1879, no. 8, pp. 1–3.

of furniture generally, as well as the originating of all extraordinary repairs to the Government buildings under his control.

He is further charged with the letting of all contracts for supplies and the general supervision of the purchase of goods required for the ten public institutions directly controlled by the Government, as well as with the monthly audit of all the amounts incurred for the maintenance and of the statements of revenue derived from all sources. He has also to make an annual audit of the receipts and expenditures of all public charities aided by Legislative grants, for the purpose of determining the amount each institution is entitled to receive under the provisions of the Charity Aid Act. The Government expenditures, incurred in the maintenance of these institutions, of which an audit has to be made, aggregated, during the past official year, the sum of $520,009.70.

The Inspector has to make enquiry into the cases of all lunatics committed to the County Gaols and to allocate their distribution among the various asylums. He has also to select from the prisoners committed to the gaols throughout the Province, such as are mentally and physically fit to perform hard labour, and effect their removal to the Central Prison, and has to arrange for and supervise the transfer from the gaols of those prisoners sentenced direct to the Institution just named.

The Inspector has, under the provisions of law, the charge of the estates of all lunatics committed to the asylums of the Province, who have no Committees appointed by the Court of Chancery, and is empowered to deal with such estates subject to the revision and approval of the Attorney-General, in the same manner as a Committee duly nominated by the said Court. Since the passing of this law, the estates of seventy-four lunatics have been administered to, and upwards of $30,000 have been collected for the maintenance of such lunatics, and paid into the Treasury of the Province.

He has to frame the by-laws and regulations for governing the discipline, management and general economy of all the Public Institutions directly controlled by the Government and for defining the duties of all officers and employés in the Institutions service, and he has to examine into and approve of all by-laws framed for the good government of Public Charities. He has, in addition, to perform judicial duty as a Commissioner, under the provisions of Section 8 of Chapter 229 of the Revised Statutes of Ontario, which empowers him to take evidence under oath and to generally enquire into all charges preferred against officers and employés of the Institutions placed under his supervision and inspection, including County Gaols, or into alleged irregularities in the conduct of their affairs, and report the same for the action of the Government. Since these powers were conferred, close upon one hundred investigations have been conducted by the Inspector, some of which were protracted for weeks.

The clerical work of the Department for the past year was represented by the reception of 7341 letters, and the transmission of 7689 letters, reports, recommendations, etc., exclusive of inspection minutes and instructions recorded in the books of the various institutions at the time of the inspection thereof. In addition, the work of preparing the Inspector's Annual Report, which has increased from a volume of 48 pages to one of nearly 400, is a task requiring a great deal of care and time.

The whole of the official duty, thus briefly summarized, is performed by a staff, comprising an inspector, a secretary, who is also a short-hand writer, a chief clerk, who acts as accountant, an ordinary clerk and a messenger, and at an annual cost to the Province for salaries, travelling expenses, office contingencies, and all other charges, of $7,350.

Selected Bibliography

PRIVATE PAPERS

MEREDITH, E. A., Diary and Papers (Public Archives of Canada).
—— Letters and Miscellaneous Documents (held by Colonel C. P. Meredith, Ottawa).

PUBLIC DOCUMENTS: UNPUBLISHED

CANADA

Executive Council Minute Books, 1841–59 (Public Archives of Canada).

ONTARIO

Correspondence Record Books and Correspondence and Memoranda Relating to the Work of the Office of the Inspector of Prisons, Asylums and Charitable Institutions, 1868–93 (Department of the Provincial Secretary).

UPPER CANADA

Executive Council Minute Books, 1791–1841 (Public Archives of Canada).
Upper Canada Sundries, 1792–1840 (Public Archives of Canada).

PUBLIC DOCUMENTS: PUBLISHED

CANADA

Census, 1851–52, 1871, 1881, 1891, 1931.
Censuses of Canada, 1665–1871, vol. IV (Ottawa, 1876).
Journals of the Legislative Assembly, 1841–67.
Journals of the House of Commons, 1876.

Parliamentary Debates on Confederation, 1865.
Public Accounts, 1866–67, 1875, 1879, 1881, 1883, 1885.
Sessional Papers, 1860–67, 1868, 1876.

GREAT BRITAIN

Sessional Papers, 1851–52.
Statutes, 1791, 1835, 1865, 1867, 1872, 1875, 1889.

ONTARIO

Gazette, 1867–93.
Journals, 1868–94.
Sessional Papers, 1868–94.
Statutes, 1868–93.

UPPER CANADA

Gazette, 1793–1840.
Journals, 1792–1840.
Statutes, 1792–1840.

NEWSPAPERS

Globe (Toronto), 1859, 1868, 1873, 1874, 1882, 1889.
Recorder (Brockville), 1830–39.
Upper Canada Herald (Kingston), 1819–21.

BOOKS AND PAMPHLETS

BIGGAR, C. R. W., *Sir Oliver Mowat* (2 vols., Toronto, 1905).
BOVELL, JAMES, *A Plea for Inebriate Asylums; Commended to the Considera-
tion of the Legislators of the Province of Canada* (Toronto, 1862).
BRUNO, FRANK J., *Trends in Social Work as Reflected in the Proceedings
of the National Conference of Social Work 1874–1946* (New York,
1948).
BULL, WILLIAM PERKINS, *From Medicine Man to Medical Man* (Toronto,
1934).
CANNIFF, WILLIAM, *History of the Province of Ontario* (Toronto, 1872).
—— *The Medical Profession in Upper Canada, 1783–1850* (Toronto,
1894).
CARELESS, J. M. S., *Brown of the Globe*, vol. I (Toronto, 1959).
CARTWRIGHT, C. E., *Life and Letters of the Late Hon. Richard Cartwright*
(Toronto, 1826).
CLARK, S. D., *The Social Development of Canada* (Toronto, 1942).
CLARKE, CHARLES K., *A History of the Toronto General Hospital* (Toronto,
1913).
CLARKE, CHARLES, *Sixty Years in Upper Canada* (Toronto, 1908).

CONANT, THOMAS, *Upper Canada Sketches* (Toronto, 1898).

COTE, J. O., *Political Appointments and Elections in the Province of Canada from 1841 to 1865* (Ottawa, 1866).

COTE, N. OMER, *Political Appointments, Dominion of Canada, 1867 to 1895* (Ottawa, 1896).

CREIGHTON, DONALD GRANT, *Dominion of the North* (Boston, 1944).

—— John A. Macdonald: *The Young Politician* (Toronto, 1952).

CROOKS, ADAM, *Reform Government in Ontario* (Toronto, 1879).

CRUIKSHANK, E. A., *The Correspondence of Lieutenant-Governor John Graves Simcoe, with Allied Documents Relating to His Administration of the Government of Upper Canada*, vols. I, IV (Toronto, 1929).

DADE, C., *Notes on the Cholera Seasons of 1832–4* (Pamphlet #1428, Public Archives of Canada, Catalogue of Pamphlets, vol. I).

DEFRIES, R. D. (ed.), *The Development of Public Health in Canada* (Toronto, 1940).

DENT, J. C., *The Last Forty Years: Canada Since the Union of 1841* (2 vols., Toronto, 1881).

FRASER, ALEXANDER, *A History of Ontario* (Toronto, 1907).

GOURLAY, ROBERT, *General Introduction to Statistical Account of Upper Canada, Compiled with a View to a Grand System of Emigration in Connection with a Reform of the Poor Laws* (London, 1822).

—— *Statistical Account of Upper Canada, Compiled with a View to a Grand System of Emigration in Connection with a Reform of the Poor Laws* (London, 1822).

HARKNESS, J. G., *Stormont, Dundas and Glengarry: A History, 1784–1945* (Oshawa, 1946).

HEAGERTY, J. W., *Four Centuries of Medical History in Canada* (2 vols., Toronto, 1928).

HODGETTS, J. E., *Pioneer Public Service: An Administrative History of the United Canadas, 1841–1867* (Toronto, 1955).

HODGINS, J. GEORGE, *The Establishment of Schools and Colleges in Ontario, 1792–1910*, vol. III (Toronto, 1910).

KELSO, J. J., *Early History of the Humane and Children's Aid Movement in Ontario, 1886–1893* (Toronto, 1911).

—— *Protection of Children: Early History of the Humane and Children's Aid Movement in Ontario* (Toronto, 1911).

KENNEDY, W. P. M., *Statutes, Treaties and Documents of the Canadian Constitution, 1713–1929* (London, 1930).

KIDMAN, JOHN, *The Canadian Prison: The Story of a Tragedy* (Toronto, 1947).

KILBOURN, WILLIAM, *William Mackenzie and the Rebellion in Upper Canada* (Toronto, 1956).

LOGAN, H. A., *Trade Unions in Canada: Their Development and Functioning* (Toronto, 1948).

LUCAS, C. P. (ed.), *Lord Durham's Report on the Affairs of British North America*, vol. I (3 vols., London, 1912).

MASTERS, D. C., *The Rise of Toronto, 1850–1890* (Toronto, 1947).

MIDDLETON, JESSE EDGAR, and FRED LANDON, *The Province of Ontario: A History 1615–1927*, vol. I (Toronto, 1927).

MORGAN, HENRY JAMES, *The Canadian Men and Women of the Time* (Toronto, 1898).

MOWAT, HON. OLIVER, *Speeches on Reform Government in Ontario* (Toronto, 1879).

National Prison Association of the United States, *Proceedings of the Annual Congress, Toronto, 1887* (Chicago, 1889).

Ontario Liberal Association, *Liberal Government 1872–1896* (Toronto, 1898).

POPE, JOSEPH, *Confederation Documents Bearing on the British North America Act* (Toronto, 1895).

RICH, MARGARET E., *A Belief in People: A History of Family Social Work* (New York, 1956).

RIDDELL, W. R., *The Life of John Graves Simcoe, 1792–96* (Toronto, 1926).

ROBB, DR. JOHN M., *The Hospitals of Ontario: A Short History* (Toronto, 1934).

SHORTT, ADAM, and ARTHUR G. DOUGHTY (eds.), *Documents Relating to the Constitutional History of Canada, 1759–1791* (Ottawa, 1918).

—— *Canada and Its Provinces: A History of the Canadian People and Their Institutions*, vol. XVIII (Toronto, 1914).

SMITH, GOLDWIN, *Social Problems: An Address Delivered to the Conference of Combined City Charities of Toronto* (Toronto, 1889).

SPETTIGUE, C. OWEN, *An Historical Review of Ontario Legislation on Child Welfare* (Toronto, 1957).

STRONG, MARGARET KIRKPATRICK, *Public Welfare Administration in Canada* (Chicago, 1930).

THOMSON, DALE C., *Alexander Mackenzie, Clear Grit* (Toronto, 1960).

WALLACE, ELISABETH, *Goldwin Smith: Victorian Liberal* (Toronto, 1957).

WEISMAN, IRVING, *Social Welfare Policy and Services in Social Work Education* (New York, 1959).

WINES, E. C., *Report on the Prisons and Reformatories of the United States and Canada* (New York, 1867).

WORKMAN, JOSEPH, *On Crime and Insanity* (Montreal, 1877).

ARTICLES

THE BYSTANDER, "Pauperism and Its Remedies," *Bystander*, May 1881.

—— "Relief of the Poor," *Bystander*, July 1883.

A CANADIAN, "Juvenile Pauper Immigrants," *Canadian Monthly*, Sept. 1877.

HART, GEORGE E., "The Halifax Poor Man's Friend Society, 1820–27: An Early Social Experiment," *Canadian Historical Review*, June 1953.

"The Immigration of Child and Adult Paupers," *Queen's College Journal*, June 1888.

McMURRICH, W. B., "Industrial Schools," *Canadian Monthly*, Nov. 1872.

MEALING, S. R., "The Enthusiasms of John Graves Simcoe," *Canadian Historical Association, Annual Report, 1958* (Ottawa, 1959).

MOREHOUSE, FRANCES, "Canadian Migration in the Forties," *Canadian Historical Review*, Dec. 1928.

"Philanthropy," *Queen's College Journal*, April 1887.

REES, T. P., "Back to Moral Treatment and Community Care," *Journal of Mental Science*, April 1957.

SPLANE, RICHARD B., "The Inebriate Hospital Act of 1873," *Alcoholism Research*, April 1955.

—— "Recommendations on Alcoholism by the Royal Commission of 1891," *Alcoholism Research*, July 1956.

WALLACE, ELISABETH, "The Origin of the Social Welfare State in Canada, 1867–1900," *Canadian Journal of Economics and Political Science*, Aug. 1950.

"Work of Dr. Barnardo," *Queen's College Journal*, May 1889.

THESES

AITCHISON, J. H., "The Development of Local Government in Upper Canada, 1783–1850" (Ph.D. dissertation, Department of Political Economy, University of Toronto, 1954).

BAIN, IAN, "The Role of J. J. Kelso in the Launching of the Child Welfare Movement in Ontario" (M.S.W. thesis, School of Social Work, University of Toronto, 1955).

JOLLIFFE, RUSSELL, "The History of the Children's Aid Society of Toronto, 1891–1947" (M.S.W. thesis, School of Social Work, University of Toronto, 1950).

LATIMER, ELSPETH, A., "Methods of Child Care as Reflected in the Infants Home of Toronto" (M.S.W. thesis, School of Social Work, University of Toronto, 1953).

PRICE, GIFFORD A., "A History of the Ontario Hospital, Toronto" (M.S.W. thesis, School of Social Work, University of Toronto, 1950).

RAMSEY, DEAN, "Development of Child Welfare Legislation in Ontario" (M.S.W. thesis, School of Social Work, University of Toronto, 1949).

ROYCE, MARION J., "The Contribution of the Methodist Church to Social Welfare in Canada" (M.A. thesis, Department of History, University of Toronto, 1940).

Index